BRINGING EQUITY BACK

Research for a New Era in
American Educational Policy

BRINGING EQUITY BACK

Research for a New Era in
American Educational Policy

Edited by

JANICE PETROVICH
AMY STUART WELLS

Foreword by Alison Bernstein
Afterword by Wendy Puriefoy

Teachers College, Columbia University
New York and London

27.00

Published by Teachers College Press, 1234 Amsterdam Avenue, New York, NY 10027

Library of Congress Cataloging-in-Publication Data

Bringing equity back : research for a new era in American educational
   policy / edited by Janice Petrovich and Amy Stuart Wells.
      p. cm.
   Includes bibliographical references and index.
   ISBN 0-8077-4576-6 (cloth : alk. paper)
   1. Educational equalization—United States.   2. Minorities—
Education—Political aspects—United States.   3. Minorities—
Education—Government policy—United States.   I. Petrovich, Janice.
II. Wells, Amy Stuart, 1961–
LC213.2.B75   2005
379.2'6'0973—dc22   2004063670

ISBN 0-8077-4576-6 (cloth)

Printed on acid-free paper
Manufactured in the United States of America

12 11   10   09   08   07   06   05   8   7   6   5   4   3   2   1

Contents

PART III:
Education Reform Since the 1980s: Excellence Trumps Equity

Foreword

In May 2004, people across the country gathered to commemorate the 50th anniversary of one of the most important civil rights victories of the 20th century: the U.S. Supreme Court's ruling in *Brown* v. *Board of Education.* Arguing once and for all that this ideology no longer had a place in American society, this decision overturned the doctrine of "separate but equal." As Harvard legal scholar, Charles Ogletree, Jr., has recently written, "The *Brown* decision marked a critical effort by the Supreme Court to send the country a strong message: that legalized racial inequality in America would no longer be tolerated" (2004, p. xiii). I would argue that, philosophically, if not legally, the *Brown* decision had a profound effect on how people thought about other forms of inequality—not only racial, but those based on gender, or ethnic, immigrant, or other minority group status. Before *Brown*, most Americans seemed rather comfortable with separating people according to perceived differences of race, ethnicity, and gender. After the decision, many more people came to question legal separations and exclusions in new ways: "Separate might be unequal" with regard to a range of conditions both legally mandated and existing on the ground in a de facto or extra-legal way. This led directly, I believe, to later challenges in higher education with the complex set of concerns around the historically black public college and university sector, as well as "gender exclusive" public higher education institutions, like all-male military academies or women-only universities.

Especially relevant to the subject of this volume, however, was the Court's finding in *Brown* that race-based disparities in public education had to end. Thus, it is hard to *over*estimate the influence of *Brown* in the framing of public education debates around equity over the past half-century. Brown set an "equity agenda in motion fifty years ago which moved from Kansas and the South eventually into the North and the challenges to the de facto segregation of public education in cities like Boston." Charles

Ogletree and other distinguished legal scholars are now debating the legacy of *Brown* because of the famous, and somewhat oxymoronic words, "all deliberate speed," (how, one asks, can speed be deliberate?) in a second decision which served to undermine the urgency of dismantling racial inequities in public education.

While the legal assessments of the impact of *Brown* are crucial, there are other "communities of concern"—researchers, policy analysts, educational leaders, community activists, parents, and teachers—who are also deeply engaged in struggles to make public schools reflect the "equity" premise underlying the *Brown* decision. Fifty years of post-*Brown* litigation and policymaking suggests that no one would now push to establish race- or gender-exclusive public schools. Or would they? How does the *Brown* legacy relate to the newer reform movements focused on the establishment of charter schools? Or school vouchers? What does research and practice have to tell us about other related equity issues and struggles that have emerged, building upon *Brown* and taking us to other complex legal and policy-making terrains where reformers are working daily. For example, what are the issues embedded in the fiscal-equity challenges in several states? This is not an argument about racial exclusion per se, though its fairly obvious that inner-city and isolated rural districts with high numbers of poor and minority residents do not have the same tax base upon which to build an adequate education as mandated by state constitutions. Another quite important variation on the "separate is inherently unequal theme," as articulated in *Brown*, concerns what happens after the district desegregates its schools but leaves academic "tracking" in place? And, if we switch gears to the subject of college readiness, what does it mean if public high schools that enroll large numbers of Black and Latino kids do not offer the same set of advanced courses that exist in schools serving upper-middle-class kids? Is this just a more subtle form of race-exclusive public education which should be struck down if we are to follow the line of argument as first enunciated in *Brown?*

The essays in this important volume begin to flesh-out many of the most important post-*Brown* equity issues facing American public education. While few would say that all of these issues were contemplated at the time when the U.S. Supreme Court heard this landmark case 50 years ago, I do not doubt that the arguments of Thurgood Marshall and Charles Hamilton Houston presaged the continuing, and ever more urgent, challenge we face in providing the best possible education for the greatest number of students in ways that respect difference but do not reinforce disadvantage.

REFERENCE

Ogletree, C. J. (2004). *All deliberate speed: Reflections on the first half century of* Brown *v.* Board of Education. New York: Norton.

Alison R. Bernstein
Vice President
The Program on Knowledge, Creativity, and Freedom
December 2004

PART I

Setting the Context

The first part of this book describes the context in which current education reform is taking place. In the introductory Chapter 1, Janice Petrovich traces the historical shifts from educational policy favoring inclusiveness to a concern with promoting educational "excellence." Equity and excellence have been discussed historically as opposite poles of a spectrum. Shifts from one extreme to another have reflected swings in the political and economic environment from policies promoting distributive justice to those emphasizing economic growth. But educational excellence for all and a well-functioning democracy require policies that address both. Petrovich explains how this book is intended to advance that goal, and she introduces the pertinent themes that connect the chapters.

In Chapter 2, Marilyn Gittell summarizes a 9-state study of the politics of education reform. Study findings demonstrate the key role that state governors have played in setting the agenda for reform. In addition, her research shows that the suburban population has grown in importance and influence in terms of defining and determining governors' educational reform agendas. Suburban growth has resegregated this country's neighborhoods and schools and has created growing disparities in funding for public schools between suburban and urban schools. Gittell concludes with a call for the federal government to provide leadership to promote equity in education and for equity-minded people and organizations to bridge the urban/suburban divide.

book suggests that even as older, equity-focused reforms are being dismantled and subverted, the reforms of the past 2 decades, which largely have attempted to improve education through competition between schools or by requiring students to meet certain "standards," are doing little to improve either educational excellence or student achievement. This is a disturbing picture. In the current reform climate, we stand a good chance of failing to improve the quality of schools even as we fail to achieve equity.

Policies pursuing equity in education traditionally have favored a more fair distribution of educational access, opportunities, and resources such as public funds, qualified teachers, and educational facilities. Such redistributive policies have been less important to those arguing for greater "excellence" in education. Instead they advocate a free-market approach to education that allows parents to choose schools for their children and forces schools to improve so they can effectively compete for students. Faith in the private sphere rather than government and the confidence in market mechanisms to improve efficiency and quality are replacing values of social solidarity, trust in public institutions, and "the conception of a national community with duties and obligations to one's fellow citizens" (Schulman, 2001, p. iv).

The interest of those in power continues to drift away from policies favoring a more equitable distribution of society's resources and toward policies favoring the creation of more wealth. And wealth indeed has been created in the past few decades, but it has been done unevenly. Indeed, the concentration of wealth at the top of the socioeconomic ladder is now greater than at any time since the Depression (see Greenstein & Shapiro, 2003). As social policies targeting equity decrease, the wall between the rich and the poor grows higher, and this country risks eroding the civic life that holds democracy together.

Education reform typically has mirrored the contemporary beliefs and values of the country's political leaders. The shift in the educational policy focus from equity to quality, therefore, reflects national ideological and political changes. These new efforts to improve school quality in the United States have not been based on research evidence, but on the interests of the politically powerful. Policymakers have put in place new policies and programs, such as charter schools, voucher programs, and high-stakes assessments, that are largely untested. Meanwhile, as noted earlier, research now is showing that the reforms of the 1960s and early 1970s, while not perfect, did indeed advance equity goals such as closing the achievement gap between White and minority students and a rapid increase in the high school completion and college-going rates of all students between the 1960s and early 1980s (Johnson & Viadero, 2000). In addition to examining these broad trends, this book provides more detail on the accomplishments of the older, equity-minded reforms and the potential of the newer policies that seek to promote "excellence."

SOCIAL JUSTICE, ECONOMIC GROWTH, AND SCHOOL REFORM

The U.S. education system is caught up in the historical tension between the expectations of equality that are part of the democratic political system and the need for free markets and competition that is part of the capitalist economic system. Democracy strives to create community and a strong civic life and retains an interest in addressing social disparities through a more equal distribution of society's resources. On the other hand, our capitalist economy strives for continuous economic growth and capital accumulation, with the expectation that a rising tide will lift all boats. Michael J. Sandel observes in his book *Democracy's Discontent* (1998) that "in contemporary American politics, most of our economic arguments revolve around two considerations: prosperity and fairness" (p. 124). History shows that the predominance of these ideals has shifted back and forth in the midst of often-intense political struggle between forces favoring distributive justice and those favoring economic growth as the mechanism to help the poor and solve all social ills. Proponents of such economic growth argue that it will do more for the poor than distributing existing resources more equally. Public schools have been a battleground of these two oppositional perspectives.

The U.S. public education system has a relatively brief history of a little over 100 years. It was only at the turn of the 20th century that formal elementary schooling was made available to the majority of school-aged children. The expansion of schooling responded to the interests of the elites in "civilizing" immigrants and the poor and to the needs of a growing industrial economy for skilled and appropriately socialized workers. But the expansion of schooling also responded to egalitarian interests of workers and of leaders like Horace Mann who sought to develop "common schools" that would mix the classes and create opportunities for advancement for the "lower classes" (Carnoy & Levin, 1985). Thus, the growth of the education system provided new opportunities for White immigrant children and those from social classes previously excluded. Black children, however, were not part of this desired "mix" and were largely excluded from education.

Yet in the process of expanding the public system, reformers created a stratified education system that moved away from the concept of a uniform curriculum by initiating an alternative vocational curriculum for the children of the working class. Thus, from its early days, the U.S. public education system was differentiated by class and by race, reflecting the social hierarchies of the country. Public education prepared the children of workers and recent immigrants for lower-status occupations in the work force, and the children of professionals for higher-status management positions (Carnoy & Levin, 1985). Public schools for Blacks led nowhere in terms of jobs (Ravitch, 1983).

Early in the 20th century, the growing education system was financed primarily by local property taxes. Thus, the disparity in tax revenues between wealthy and impoverished communities exacerbated the difference between schools for the rich and those for the poor (Carnoy & Levin, 1985). The principle of schooling for all was undercut by the "social geography of American cities," which created residential patterns segregated by race and class that remain to this day (Katzelson & Weir, 1985, p. 208). The additive nature of inequity—that poor kids live in poor neighborhoods with poor schools that produce poor academic outcomes that lead to poor job prospects—was evident even then.

The 1930s witnessed another period of public investment and expansion in education and attention to equalization. World War I had created a sense of greater social equality and the Great Depression witnessed the emergence of social movements that succeeded in winning social reform. By the 1940s most teenagers attended high schools.

Economic growth in the 1950s was accompanied by a growing demand for attention to inequities in school finance, curriculum differentiation, and the needs of students of color and other disadvantaged and special needs students. Desegregation of public schools followed, after many delays, the Supreme Court's 1954 decision in *Brown* v. *Board of Education*. New compensatory education programs were created in the next 20 years, abetted by this decision and by the Civil Rights Movement. Title I of the Elementary and Secondary Education Act, the largest federal education program to date, was created in 1965 to decrease educational disparities, particularly within large-city districts. In the late 1960s and the 1970s, a slew of federal legislation and court cases created many reforms—affirmative action, bilingual education, desegregated schools, special education, and minority scholarships—designed to promote greater equity in K–12 and higher education by expanding opportunities for access and success for children previously excluded from the education system (Tyack, 1990).

By the late 1970s, the growth in population, jobs, and political power had shifted from the northeast to the south and west. Voters of this "Sunbelt" region have played a critical role in electing all the U.S. presidents since 1964. Growing numbers of southern conservatives gained political power and brought with them a belief in smaller government and the power of the free market. Schulman (2001) argues that "the ideal of social solidarity, the conception of a national community with duties and obligations to one's fellow citizens elicited greater skepticism during the 1970s, while the private sphere commanded uncommon, and sometimes undeserved, respect" (p. xiv). Thus, the activism of the 1960s in favor of the rights of disenfranchised groups began to shift in the late 1970s to a focus on the rights of individuals. In education, for example, public policies in the 1960s established programs such as bilingual education, which attempted to promote educational success of groups of students. In the 1990s, public policy favored programs such as charter schools, which are designed to allow individual families to choose the school for their child. Individual choice and success were substituted for group access and achievement in the policy discourse.

By the late 1970s, the oil crisis led the country into economic inflation and increasing federal deficits. In the 1980s the federal government decreased funding for education of the disadvantaged, bilingual, special needs, and female populations. This reflected the increasing reluctance of conservative political leaders to invest more public dollars in education and to have the federal government play a larger leadership role in education. Private alternatives to public schools became important components of educational debate and practice. By the 1980s, excellence became the rallying cry of the country's political leadership, leaving equity in the dust.

National policies of the 1960s and 1970s grew out of fundamentally different assumptions than those that followed. Earlier strategies favored distributive justice, but since the early 1980s, strategies have favored economic growth. Equity-minded policies of the 1960s and 1970s argued for a stronger government role, for laws protecting civil rights, for publicly funded efforts to repair and compensate for historical forms of discrimination. The "excellence"-oriented policies of today argue for lower taxes and less government regulation, for more choices and competition to improve quality, for rewards to those who succeed and clear consequences for those who don't. In the public discourse, the balance has shifted from concerns for group access to individual merit; from equity to quality; from entitlement to choice.

Today's transnational economy has led some to argue that the imperatives of global competition and technological change require greater public spending on education and job training. And indeed, education remains a top priority at the state and federal levels, even though budgets have tightened since September 11, 2001. The most prominent of the current policy alternatives—vouchers, charter schools, standards, and high-stakes testing—focus on market models of increasing competition between public schools to drive schools to improve. The majority of states have instituted curriculum standards accompanied by tests for students to measure whether the standards are being met. In contrast, the programs created to promote access of excluded groups to education—affirmative action, bilingual education, desegregated schools, minority scholarships, and so forth—are being challenged in court, defunded, or dismantled. Moreover, over half of the states are battling in court over inequities in school finance formulas that largely favor suburban White children. In places such as New Jersey, and more recently New York (see Chapter 12), where the courts have ordered more public resources for impoverished public schools, political leaders counter the court orders, and the implementation of remedies can drag on for years.

This disregard for equal educational resources for underserved students is occurring at a time when the demographic profile of students in the United States has changed dramatically, with Latinos, African Americans, and Asians growing precipitously in number relative to Whites. The U.S. Census projects that by 2050, ethnic/racial minorities will account for 50% of the nation's population (U.S. Census Bureau, 2004). As of 2001, students of color made up 40% of the total public elementary and secondary school students (U.S. Department of Education, 2003). In 22 of the 25 largest urban school districts, White students are the minority (Cross City Campaign for School Reform, 2001).

In light of their growing numbers, recent data on minority and poor students present a truly disturbing picture, suggesting that the "excellence" reforms of the 1980s and 1990s have not helped to raise all boats.

- Although they make up one-third of high school seniors, African Americans, Latinos, and American Indians accounted for only one in ten 12th graders scoring "advanced" on the National Assessment of Educational Progress (NAEP) (Johnson & Viadero, 2000).
- NAEP scores showed White 4th graders maintaining a lead of 30 points or more over their minority classmates throughout the past decade (Manzo, 2001).
- Current trends indicate that White children now in first grade are twice as likely as African American children and three times as likely as Latino children to complete a college degree (Johnson & Viadero, 2000).
- Minority children are concentrated in large, outdated, overcrowded schools that need repair and have large proportions of teachers who are not certified to teach in their subject areas (Johnston, 1999; Richard, 2000).
- Nearly one in five students lives in poverty (Cross City Campaign, 2001).
- The nation's schools became increasingly more separated by race in the 1990s (Orfield, 2001).

The centerpiece of President George W. Bush's educational policy, the No Child Left Behind Act (NCLB), highlights the importance of addressing these achievement gaps. It requires states to implement a system of annual student testing. Schools where students fail to improve over time are to be closed down. In keeping with the free-market approach to school improvement, students would then be able to choose better schools. While the strict provisions of NCLB may seem at odds with conservatives' beliefs in less government regulation, these provisions devolve its implementation to the states. Furthermore, by eliminating underperforming schools, NCLB promotes the "survival of the fittest" schools, a concept that is at the core of the free-market approach to education reform.

Critics of NCLB point out that the Act does not provide the additional funds needed to achieve its goals of school improvement. Moreover, with the cuts in federal taxes approved by Congress in 2003, the capacity of the federal government to increase funding for education will be severely limited by a smaller revenue base and increasing demands for funds devoted to defense and anti-terrorism. In many states and localities citizens have mobilized in light of tight state and local budgets, voting to increase their taxes so that local public schools have the resources they need. Also, many education advocates fear that closing underperforming schools will be used to justify vouchers for private schools.

The cumulative effects of economic and political decisions at the local, state, and federal levels have constrained the ability of schools to sustain high achievement. Poverty, racial isolation, and class segregation remain important impediments to education reform (Anyon, 1997).

In addition, the relationship between wealth and educational attainment and between educational attainment and income appears to be stronger than ever. Public education in the United States historically has provided opportunities to generations of poor and immigrant people to move up the social and economic ladder. However, upward mobility via education may be becoming more difficult. Indeed, while children from wealthier families have always been more likely to obtain a college degree and attain significantly higher incomes throughout their lifetimes, today, as the wealthy continue to provide advantages for their children, the poor increasingly are trapped in lower income brackets. Availability of scholarship funds for poor students has not kept pace with the increase in college costs, making postsecondary education more and more out of reach for the poor (National Center for Public Policy and Higher Education, 2002).

While socioeconomic progress has never been easy, recent data demonstrate the continued difficulties the poor face in obtaining higher levels of education and the benefits to those who do so. For instance, the likelihood of students from the richest quarter of the population earning college degrees by age 24 jumped from 39.5% in 1970 to 57.1% in 1994. Conversely, the likelihood of students from the poorest quarter earning college degrees decreased from 6.5% to 4.6%. That is, students from wealthier families used to be six times more likely to finish college than poor students. Now they are 14 times more likely (Mortenson, 2000).

Furthermore, while proportionately few poor and minority students finish college, the payoff for those who do so is great. The U.S. Census Bureau reports that the mean annual earnings of a high school graduate in 1999 were about $24,000 compared with approximately $44,000 for a college graduate. That translates to a projected lifetime value of at least $700,000 for a college degree compared with a high school diploma.

Such data speak to the growing income inequality in the United States where wealth has grown at unprecedented levels, but the gap between the rich and the poor has continued to widen. The Center on Budget and Policy Priorities predicted that by 2000, the top 1% of the population would receive a larger share of income than in any year since 1929 (Greenstein & Shapiro, 2003). Most other income groups, including the middle class, were expected to receive at most as small a share of the national after-tax income as at any point during this period. Moreover, the tax plan adopted by Congress in June 2003 provides huge and disproportionate benefits for the wealthy.

The Center on Budget and Policy Priorities also reports that wealth is more concentrated at the top than at any time since the Depression. In fact, wealth is more concentrated than income, with the wealthiest 1% of households owning nearly 40% of the nation's wealth in 1995. Meanwhile, the bottom 80% of households owned just 16% of the nation's wealth (Shapiro & Greenstein, 1999; also see Krugman, 2002).

These data show that this country's equity agenda is far from done and that most of the current, high-profile education reforms are doing little to decrease educational inequalities. This book presents evidence that persisting disparities are unlikely to be eliminated through the increasingly popular high-stakes testing and market models of school reform.

BRINGING EQUITY BACK: AN OVERVIEW

Michael J. Sandel observes in *Democracy's Discontent* (1998) that as the rich and the poor grow further apart, "their sense of shared fate [is] diminished, and with it the willingness of the rich to invest, through higher taxes, in the skills of their fellow citizens" (p. 331). Sandel also notes, "As affluent Americans increasingly buy their way out of reliance on public services, the formative, civic resources of American life diminish. The deterioration of urban public schools is perhaps the most conspicuous and damaging instance of this trend" (p. 332). If unchecked, current inequalities will continue to give rise to increasingly separate ways of life, where children of the prosperous enroll in private schools or relatively homogeneous suburban schools, leaving urban public schools to the poor.

In 1995, the Ford Foundation launched an initiative to increase civic capacity and engagement to promote a high-quality education for all students. The initiative was premised on the understanding that education systems can and should seek to achieve both excellence and equity. Further, the initiative was grounded in a research-based conclusion: For school reform to happen and be sustained over time, an informed and mobilized public is required. The premise was that for educational policy to be effective in promoting equity and excellence, the public needs solid data on what works (research); effective dissemination of that information (communications); and organizations that can connect people, establish consensus, and mobilize them to act (constituency building). Grants from the Ford Foundation initiative supported all three kinds of activities and sought ways to network participants to promote greater impact.

As part of this initiative, the authors of this book were supported by the Ford Foundation to undertake the research summarized in the following chapters. However, the opinions of the authors are their own and do not necessarily represent those of the Ford Foundation. Each author elected to study a different issue, but they share the Foundation's interest in helping to build knowledge on the impact of educational policies and practices on all students, but particularly those who are less likely to receive an adequate education because of family income, race, ethnicity, dominant language, geographic location, and/or gender.

Each chapter presents new analyses either of the current status of equity-oriented reforms enacted in the 1960s and 1970s, such as desegregation, ending ability tracking, and affirmative action, or of more recent reforms, including high-stakes testing, vouchers, and charter schools. The authors turn empirical attention to historical, economic, and political conditions that generate inequalities in the distribution of wealth and educational opportunity, and they analyze both the equity *and* quality educational dimensions of particular reforms—be they old or new. Class, gender, and race are central to this inquiry as mechanisms for according status and privilege (O'Connor, 2001).

This book, therefore, is intended to inform policymakers and the general public about the research evidence regarding recent efforts to improve public education. It is the goal of this book to stimulate more public dialogue and debate on school reform options.

It follows then that the chapters of this book are connected by a number of themes. The first theme that derives from this body of research suggests that *achieving an excellent education for all children requires policies and practices that address both quality and equity*. Recent policy efforts have focused largely on accountability for outcomes. The research here addresses equity dimensions of reform that include a concern for the fair distribution of educational inputs—qualified teachers, per-pupil expenditures, school facilities, and materials—as well as educational outputs such as high academic achievement, high school graduation, college admissions, and college graduation. The authors analyze the connection between the reform that is the focus of their research and these dimensions of fairness. Furthermore, all agree that equity strategies are context-specific. In other words, a strategy that promotes equal opportunity for high-quality education in one place, can curtail opportunities in another place. For example, a charter school might create opportunities for some Black children if it places them in a better-resourced school environment. On the other hand, parents who do not know how to choose a good school or who cannot transport their child to it, might end up with their child in a low-achieving school. It is important to emphasize that the authors of this book do not see equity as either static or ever completely achievable. Rather, equity has to be pursued consistently in the attempt to create a more just society. And as indicated before, equity and excellence are not oppositional goals; both are integral to a well-functioning democracy.

The second theme that ties these chapters together is that *education reform is inherently political*. At its best, education reform rejects the kind of politics that is characterized by the "opportunistic pursuit of personal gain or partisan advantage," and embraces the common well-being by pursuing collective goals (Stone & Henig, 2001, p. 8). Research can help communities recognize, understand, and define issues to coalesce various sectors in sustained support for reform. Research optimally can provide the evidence that citizens need to mobilize around educational policies and practices that are effective in promoting excellent and equitable education. Recognizing the vital role of politics—the activity of reconciling a diverse citizenry toward a common purpose—in promoting educational change, researchers promoting equity do not rely exclusively on an elite policy audience. They agree that equity reform requires linking research to social movements.

The third theme that cuts across several chapters is that *a student's race, class, and newcomer status largely predefine his or her educational opportunities*. Residential segregation leads to educational segregation. Schools servicing poor and minority students have fewer financial and educational resources than those serving middle-class White students. As various chapters in this book demonstrate, this creates a situation of "additive inequality" where one disadvantage layers onto another, creating few opportunities for students from poor families to succeed.

The fourth theme on which the authors agree is that *mandates matter but coalitions are vital to their successful implementation.* Court orders and laws can only create a context for change. A community has to come together to address its problems. School finance reform provides a vivid example. States that have restructured effectively to create a more equitable system are those where an active citizenry defined the needed policy reform, mobilized to ensure its passing, and, once policy change was achieved, monitored its effective implementation and outcomes. Stone and Henig (2001) posit the importance of civic capacity in reforming schools: "Civic capacity is a broad (that is, cross-sector) base of involvement along with a shared and durable understanding of public education as a major area of community concern and a high priority for action" (p. 27). To be effective, reform is neither top-down nor bottom-up. It is both.

Fifth, *the conflicting demands between policies promoting centralization and those promoting decentralization in school reform hamstring educators.* For example, charter schools allow communities to take control of what their children learn. At the same time, uniform testing requirements centralize the power to determine the content of the curriculum. Teachers are forced to teach what tests measure instead of what they may understand is appropriate. Decentralizing the authority to develop curriculum is meaningless if centralized tests determine what needs to be taught.

Finally, *education reform is never finished.* It takes public commitment to generate reform and to sustain it over time. Sustainable reform requires the active involvement of various segments of the community and a change in its power relationships. "If change is to occur and reform is to 'stick,' then sub-system relations need to be altered in a lasting way; an 'institutional legacy' has to be established" (Stone & Henig, 2001, p. 7). In addition, there is a historical tendency for people knowingly or unwittingly to subvert a reform. For example, teachers may sort children into different "ability groups" and end up producing racially segregated classrooms within desegregated schools; or college admissions officers may use a variety of criteria to ensure institutional diversity, even though race legally cannot be a criterion for admissions.

Schools are embedded in a structure of inequality that they cannot single-handedly overcome. Nevertheless, as one of the few public spaces with the potential of mixing the classes, forming the habits of citizenship, and providing civic glue for a diverse country, schools remain a vital link to a strong democracy. As such, schools need to fulfill their potential of providing opportunities for all young people to become productive, fulfilled, and civically engaged adults.

The authors of the chapters in this book and I hope that these studies will inspire more research, policy, and practice that focus less narrowly on individual student achievement and turn attention to addressing social impediments to a more equitable distribution of opportunities. We further hope that the stories and data presented in this book will help to reinvigorate the public debate on these issues as they relate to the future of American educational policy. Will our education reform agenda contribute to increasing the gap between the rich and the poor in this country? Or, conversely, will policymakers, educators, parents, and concerned citizens reinfuse our public education system with a heavy dose of democratic vision—a vision that was so salient only 30 years ago? If this nation is ready to bring equity back into the conversation about the future direction of school reform, then this book offers some answers to point us in the appropriate direction.

REFERENCES

The achievement gap. (2000, March 15, 22, 29; April 5). A four-part special report in *Education Week.*

Anyon, J. (1997). *Ghetto schooling.* New York: Teachers College Press.

Carnoy, M., & Levin, H. (1985). *Schooling in the democratic state.* Palo Alto, CA: Stanford University Press.

Cross City Campaign for School Reform. (2001, August). *The changing face of public schools.* Chicago: Author. Available: http://www.crosscity.org/pubs/flashfacts.htm

Greenstein, R., & Shapiro, I. (2003, September 23). *The new definitive CBO data on income and tax trends.* Washington, DC: Center on Budget and Policy Priorities.

Johnson, R. C., & Viadero, D. (2000, March 15). Unmet promise: Raising minority achievement. *Education Week.* Available: http://www.edweek.org/sreports/gap.htm

Johnston, R. (1999, May 12). Governors vie with chiefs on policy, politics . . . *Education Week,* p. 22.

Katzelson, I., & Weir, M. (1985). *Schooling for all: Class, race and the decline of the democratic ideal.* New York: Basic Books.

Krugman, P. (2002, October 20). For richer. *New York Times Magazine,* Section 6, p. 62.

Manzo, K. K. (2001, August 8). Math NAEP delivers some good news. *Education Week,* p. 24.

Mortenson, T. (2000). *Postsecondary participation of students from low income families.* Washington, DC: Postsecondary OPPORTUNITY. Available http://www.postsecondary.org

National Center for Public Policy and Higher Education. (2002). *Losing ground: A national status report on the affordability of American higher education.* Washington, DC: Author.

O'Connor, A. (2001). *Poverty knowledge.* Princeton, NJ: Princeton University Press.

Orfield, G. (2001). *Schools more separate: Consequences of a decade of resegregation.* Cambridge, MA: The Harvard Civil Rights Project. Available: http://www. law.harvard.edu/civilrights

Ravitch, D. (1983). *The troubled crusade.* New York: Basic Books.

Richard, A. (2000, July 12). NCES pegs school repair costs at $127 billion. *Education Week*, p. 10.

Sandel, M. J. (1998). *Democracy's discontent.* Cambridge, MA: Belknap Press.

Schulman, B. J. (2001). *The seventies.* New York: Free Press.

Shapiro, I., & Greenstein, R. (1999, September 4). *The widening income gulf.* Washington, DC: Center on Budget and Policy Priorities. Available: http://www. cbpp.org

Stone, C., & Henig, J. (2001). *Building civic capacity.* Lawrence: University Press of Kansas.

Tyack, D. (1990). "Restructuring" in historical perspective: Tinkering toward utopia. *Teachers College Record, 92*(2), 170–191.

U.S. Census Bureau. (2004). *U.S. interim projections by age, sex, race, and Hispanic origin.* Available: http://www.census.gov/ipc/www/usinterimproj/

U.S. Department of Education. (2003). *Mini-digest of education statistics 2003.* Washington, DC: National Center for Education Statistics.

The Politics of Equity
in Urban School Reform

MARILYN GITTELL

America has become a suburban nation. Between 1960 and 1995, the pro-portion of people living outside central cities increased 15% (Oliver, 1997). In fact, by the mid-1990s, 60% of the people who lived in 320 major metro-politan areas lived in the suburbs, and the majority of jobs in these metro areas were in the suburbs as well (Rusk, 1995). Indeed, most of the eco-nomic growth of the 1980s and 1990s occurred in the suburbs (Orfield, 1997). Suburbs have become so large that many suburban officials and residents believe they are autonomous entities that are unconnected to their central cities. Garreau (1991) calls such places "edge cities." In their denial of a social or economic connection to the central city, edge-city residents are typically unwilling to pay for city services such as schools and public housing. The economic and political dominance of suburbs has created sharp divisions in the interests and policy priorities of cities and suburbs and contributed significantly to inequities in the allocation of resources within states.

By creating a physical separation between Black urban and White suburban populations, suburbanization has propelled White, middle-class, suburban populations to electoral domination in state politics. This has fueled the national shift to conservatism. This chapter is based on research on state political "regimes" and their impact on urban school reform from 1997–2000 in nine states—Maryland, Georgia, Texas, Pennsylvania, New

Jersey, Michigan, Illinois, California, and Minnesota. By the term "regime" I mean those who hold power and establish the vision of policy and control its direction. The study, which was conducted by researchers at the Howard Samuels State Management and Policy Center, included extensive field interviews and focus groups in each state with state and city elected officials, school officials, activist leaders, union offices, and legislators. Using school financial policy as an important and salient example, I illustrate the political shifts related to suburbanization in these nine states. I also offer an explanation of these changes by examining the ways in which the suburban political regimes controlled the state policy-making process.

For instance, demographics proved to be an overwhelming factor in our analysis. These states experienced dramatic population shifts in the past 4 decades that created soaring suburban growth and population decline in center cities. The suburban demographic shift in many of the states we studied is reflected in the party shifts in state legislatures and governors' offices and is having a profound impact on state educational policies. In three of our case study states—Illinois, Michigan, and Minnesota—more conservative governors were elected in the past decade by large suburban votes.

Thus, by the end of the twentieth century, the election of conservative governors in states with large city populations intensified these conflicts by promoting education agendas that were insensitive to equity issues. The new state education regimes, led by these governors, rejected court-ordered redistributive school finance policies that should have been used to equalize resources throughout the state, particularly between suburbs and cities. Indeed, either court actions to redress fiscal inequities have been halted or court decisions to improve the balance of funding have not been implemented by state policymakers. The declining state commitment to equity issues reinforces the disparities of schooling by race and class that were created by segregated residential patterns and racism in earlier eras (Katzelson & Weir, 1985).

THE IMPACT OF SUBURBANIZATION
ON THE POLITICS OF EQUITY

The increasing disparity between suburban and city interests is magnified by class and race issues. Rusk (1995) has labeled cities that have experienced major population loss in the past several decades, have a high percentage of minorities, and have average per capita incomes of less than 70% of suburban income levels, "point of no return cities." The urban core of poverty and racial segregation is intensifying. For example, a HUD study found that Philadelphia lost 68,125 jobs between 1990 and 1995, and Baltimore lost 60,991 jobs in the same period (U.S. Department of Housing and Urban Development, 1997).

According to Rusk (1995), suburban growth is especially damaging to inelastic cities that cannot expand their boundaries because of geographic or political obstacles. Income inequality between cities and their suburbs is especially significant in inelastic cities where residents have much lower incomes than their suburban counterparts. In Detroit and Cleveland, for example, urban incomes are 53% of suburban incomes (Rusk, 1995). Inelastic cities are more prevalent in the northeast and midwest, and they have higher rates of poverty and segregation. Table 2.1 shows the decline in middle- and upper-income families in the central cities.

As a result of these demographic shifts, suburbs have gained significant political power at the state level, while cities have lost influence (Orfield, 1997). An historical anti-city bias among suburban elites has made it difficult for state policymakers to garner support for educational policies that benefit urban schools. According to Cliff Zukin, a Rutgers University political scientist and pollster, not only do many suburbs not need the cities anymore, but suburban residents actually resent the high cost of providing

Table 2.1. Distribution of Central-City and Suburban Families by Income, 1969–1999 (in percents)

Year	Low income		Middle income		High income	
------	Central Cities	Suburbs	Central Cities	Suburbs	Central Cities	Suburbs
1969	20.2	14.5	59.9	60.6	19.9	24.9
1979	23.6	14.7	58.0	60.4	18.4	24.9
1989	24.5	14.0	57.6	60.4	17.8	25.7
1999	25.8	14.5	57.0	60.2	17.3	25.3

Source: Census of Population and Housing.

Note: Low-income families have incomes below the national 20th percentile family income. Middle-income families have incomes between the national 20th and 80th family income percentiles. High-income families have incomes above the national 80th percentile family income. Suburb data are defined as the total for the All MSAs/PMSAs (Metropolitan Statistical Areas/Primary Metropolitan Statistical Areas) less the sum of data for these cities: All Central Cities, U.S.

Data for years 1969–89 were reprinted from *State of the Cities*, p. 38, 1997, U.S. Department of Housing and Urban Development. The 1999 data are taken from the State of the Cities Data System.

services to them. He was quoted in the *New York Times* as saying that many suburban legislators are enraged at how much money is going to city schools. "They don't want to take any more out of the suburban taxpayers' pockets to pay for urban revitalization" (Herszenhorn, 2001, p. 39).

Clearly, both racism and classism have strengthened urban/suburban cleavages. Jon J. Sure, president of New Jersey Policy Perspective, a liberal policy group, pointed out that "poor minorities live in cities but poor whites are as likely to live outside the city as inside the city" (Herszenhorn, 2001, p. 39). Indeed, claims about the need for local control and frustration with big-city bureaucracies notwithstanding, many of the anti-city sentiments are tied to racism. These differences are reflected strongly in political and voting behavior. Central cities tend to vote Democratic, while the suburbs vote Republican (Orfield, 1997). In the 2000 presidential election, 90% of Blacks voted Democratic, exhibiting the sharp differences in racial voting patterns.

Despite claims that Blacks and Latinos also have migrated to the suburbs, census data show that the increase in minority populations in the suburbs is relatively insignificant. Between 1980 and 1990, the minority population increased in both urban and suburban areas by only 3%. In 2000, Whites continued to be the most important suburban population; nationally, nearly 71% of Whites live in the suburbs. Meanwhile, in 2000, only 49% of Hispanics (up from 46% in 1990) and 39% of African Americans (up from 34% in 1990) lived in the suburbs. Importantly, African American suburban populations have increased largely in the south in metropolitan areas with Black central cities like Atlanta or Washington, DC. In a recent Brookings study, quoted by the Lewis Mumford Center (2001b) at SUNY–Albany, it is noted that in the largest 102 metropolitan regions (those areas, including a central city and its suburbs, with more than 500,000 population) the population is 9% Black, 12% Hispanic, and 5% Asian. The Lewis Mumford Center (2001a) further reports, "On the whole, black residential enclaves have been maintained at about the same level as in 1990."

Furthermore, we know that although there has been some Black suburbanization, the Black suburbs tend to be "simply poor, declining cities that happen to be located outside the city limits," such as Camden, New Jersey, which is considered a suburb of Philadelphia (Massey & Denton, 1993, p. 69). Significantly, Black suburbs do not eliminate the spatial isolation of Blacks, nor do they solve the political inequalities that grow out of that spatial isolation. Indeed, whether they are called suburbs or cities, predominantly Black and poor municipalities lack the political clout they need at the state level.

Herbert Simmens, director of the New Jersey Office of State Planning, says that big cities in New Jersey simply do not have political muscle any longer. "Their influence and prominence is relatively minimal in the state, and that is part of the historic pattern in New Jersey." According to Jon Sure, because the cities have such a small percentage of New Jersey's population, they don't have much clout in the legislature. He also noted that many suburbs that once looked to New Jersey cities as centers of employment and commerce, no longer do. For instance, he said, "Cherry Hill, which is next to Camden, doesn't look to Camden for anything anymore" (Herszenhorn, 2001, p. 39). The 2000 census data suggest that segregation by class and race continues to dominate American communities.

Table 2.2 shows that urban and suburban Black populations remained relatively stable through 1990, although suburban Black populations declined in Illinois and New Jersey. In five of the nine states included in our study, the percentages of urban populations that were Black increased slightly during the 1980s. Hispanics, on the other hand, increased in both locations, as they migrated to the suburbs. Thus, the new suburban population growth was predominantly among White and Hispanic populations.

Placing these data in a larger context, we see that, nationally, residential segregation declined from 1970 to 1990, but that many older northeastern and midwestern cities remained highly segregated (Farley & Frey, 1994). For instance, Jargowsky (1993) found that Black ghettos (urban census tracts with at least a 40% poor, Black population) increased 36% between 1980 and 1990, and the physical size of ghettos expanded as well. Ghetto expansion is caused by metropolitan labor markets that have moved jobs to the suburbs and by residential settlement patterns that have encouraged the middle class to move to the suburbs. Blacks remain the most segregated racial group in the United States (Frey & Farley, 1996).

Meanwhile, many of the socioeconomic problems facing inner-city Blacks have been closely linked to their segregation and spatial isolation (Immergluck, 1998). According to Massey and Denton (1993), Black ghettos are responsible for the perpetuation of Black poverty. They and others suggest that racism operates throughout the economic and political system in ways that isolate and segregate Blacks. Ghettos, they argue, are the result of "well-defined institutional practices, private behaviors, and public policies by which Whites sought to contain growing urban Black populations" (p. 10). For the most part, Whites are unwilling to tolerate a high percentage of Blacks in their neighborhoods.

At the same time that Blacks are isolated in urban ghettos, many scholars argue that suburbs are politically apathetic places where private life dominates and civic life is nearly nonexistent (Duany & Plater-Zyberk, 1991). Wood (1959) termed this the "vacuum model of suburban politics," which is caused by the economic and racial homogeneity of suburban populations, the lack of political conflict, and the dearth of social problems. J. Eric Oliver (2001) in his book, *Democracy in Suburbia*, notes

Table 2.2. Percentages of Residents in Urban and Suburban Areas Who Are
Black and Hispanic for Each State, in 1980 and 1990

State/National Data by Race/Ethnicity	Urban Areas		Suburban Areas	
	1980	1990	1980	1990
California—Black	12.27%	10.44%	5.08%	5.10%
California—Hispanic	20.99%	28.89%	18.43%	24.29%
Georgia—Black	52.16%	51.93%	14.99%	19.32%
Georgia—Hispanic	1.37%	1.80%	1.18%	1.88%
Illinois—Black	33.99%	31.51%	6.05%	5.66%
Illinois—Hispanic	11.55%	15.29%	3.20%	4.51%
Maryland—Black	50.91%	52.15%	15.23%	18.48%
Maryland—Hispanic	0.95%	1.07%	1.83%	3.15%
Michigan—Black	43.07%	45.94%	3.89%	4.38%
Michigan—Hispanic	2.87%	3.81%	1.47%	1.67%
Minnesota—Black	4.93%	7.28%	0.49%	1.03%
Minnesota—Hispanic	1.60%	2.35%	0.63%	0.93%
New Jersey—Black	33.87%	35.49%	8.75%	8.62%
New Jersey—Hispanic	17.29%	27.98%	4.91%	6.24%
Pennsylvania—Black	26.68%	27.83%	3.19%	3.40%
Pennsylvania—Hispanic	3.32%	5.38%	0.67%	0.93%
Texas—Black	17.67%	16.52%	5.39%	6.78%
Texas—Hispanic	26.83%	32.44%	13.78%	18.07%
USA—Black	22.19%	21.35%	6.00%	6.76%
USA—Hispanic	10.83%	14.79%	5.36%	7.56%

Source: United States Census 1980 and 1990.

The high degree of racial segregation, particularly between cities and suburbs, calls into question whether American democracy has achieved race
neutrality. Discrimination against citizens according to race or ethnicity may
no longer be legally sanctioned, but most local American political institutions,
including cities, counties, and school districts, are highly bifurcated along
racial lines. The civic consequences of this racial separation are unclear. In a

polity committed to principles of racial equality yet divided into racially distinct political entities, do its democratic institutions provide an equal voice in politics for all citizens? In other words, is racial segregation distorting the process of self-governance in the United States? (p. 108)

A major consequence of suburbanization is segregation by race and income. Previously rich and poor lived in separate neighborhoods, but today they are separated by municipal boundaries (Massey & Eggars, 1990). Public schools are perhaps the institutions that are most reflective of this separate and unequal condition.

In other words, the racial prejudice that has shaped geographic patterns of housing growth and development has resulted in segregated neighborhoods and school districts. Hochschild (1985) points out that the most progress toward school desegregation was made between 1968 and 1972, with no progress since 1976. Orfield's (1997) data show that schools became less segregated from 1968 to 1980 and then became segregated again, supporting the analysis of the racial implications of suburban politics on school politics. Schools in large central cities remain segregated and poor. Northeastern and midwestern cities are characterized by shrinking urban school systems that are bordered by multiple suburban districts. Racial isolation is more pronounced in the north where half of all Black students attend schools whose populations are made up mostly of minorities, compared with one-quarter of Black students in the south (Hochschild, 1985). Residential segregation of Blacks and Whites has perpetuated a system of separate public schools in the north and midwest. Public schools are generally more integrated in the south, where large urban systems have been integrated by court-ordered desegregation plans and districts are countywide, linking cities and suburbs (Rusk, 1995). Still, even in the south, school desegregation policies are being dismantled, leaving large, racially diverse countywide districts with very segregated schools (Orfield & Eaton, 1996).

In this way, the same regime politics that benefits suburbs at the expense of cities also negatively affects urban public school districts as state policymakers—most of whom are elected by suburban voters—fail to vote in favor of urban schools and their students.

EXCELLENCE VERSUS EQUITY

As pointed out in Chapter 1, since the turn of the twentieth century, advocates for various education reform movements have used the rhetoric of either equity or excellence in defining their priorities for public education, suggesting that the concepts are in conflict. The school reform movements prior to the 1960s created a two-tiered model of public education, promoting excellence but only for a small elite segment of the population. The Civil Rights Movement of the 1960s and 1970s, driven by issues of equity, challenged the two-tiered system, which discriminated particularly against the poor, immigrants, and Blacks. During this era, school reform was redefined to give priority to racial desegregation and the improvement of inner-city schools. It also promoted more-universal access to higher-quality public education, and reformed systems of school governance (Bastian, Fruchter, Gittell, Greer, & Haskins, 1986). The decentralized school systems throughout the United States, which were up until this time shaped almost entirely by state and local school district policies, had produced gross inequities in standards, financial support, and services. These systems were challenged by the equity-based reform efforts of this era and by the Civil Rights Movement's accusations that they had violated basic rights of poor students and students of color. The argument was that these wrongs could be corrected only by federal legislation and court orders. The movement's efforts produced landmark federal legislation such as the Vocational Education Act of 1963, the Economic Opportunities Act of 1964, the Civil Rights Act of 1964, and the Elementary and Secondary Education Act of 1965, as well as bilingual education and special education acts. These major federal laws, which completely changed the degree of control state and local school systems had enjoyed over who had access to what educational opportunities, were justified because they were compensatory and categorical, and thus redressed inequities in American school systems by targeting resources to those students who had not been well served historically. But while these reforms extended inclusion, they failed to transform education (Gittell, 1980). Even as the role of the federal government in education was expanding, the states and localities remained the primary policymakers on a number of critical school issues, including finance, standards, curriculum, and personnel.

In the 1980s and 1990s the rhetoric of "excellence" again emerged. Equity goals fell out of favor, reflecting the changes in state priorities and the profound shifts in population and politics. The Reagan administration shifted the emphasis away from federal compensatory action in the 1980s and strongly favored and supported state control of education regardless of the inequities legislated in certain states. The inequities in funding, facilities, and standards related to race and income were ignored. In 1994, the creators of the federal Goals 2000 legislation failed in their effort to include Opportunity to Learn Standards—designed to measure schools' capacity to teach to high standards—to retain some emphasis on equity. By the late 1990s, high-stakes testing and state-imposed standards were offered as the panacea for all school failure. New state policies—carrot and

stick responses to the federal Goals 2000 legislation—centered their attention on new goals that had nothing to do with achieving equity. By
2001, 20 states had high-stakes graduation tests (Heubert, Trent, Beatty,
& Neisser, 2001), and many others had policies that created some sort of
stake or consequence for either schools or students based on test scores.

The effect of these reforms, which were characterized as pursuing
excellence, was to punish the most vulnerable students in the cities, those
in the lowest-performing schools with the least qualified teachers—the
students who had no real opportunity to learn these standards. Table 2.3
illustrates the various levels and targets of the stakes or consequences of
testing among the 50 states.

Also during this era, social science researchers tended to ignore issues
of equity. O'Connor (2000) argues that this movement of social scientists
away from studying inequality and its causes to studying the behavior of
the victims of such inequality in the 1980s was a shift in emphasis that
paralleled policymakers' efforts to develop "blame the victim" policy solutions that ignored major institutional forces such as racial stratification
and racial politics.

For instance, the multitude of policymakers who advocate higher
standards and greater accountability via high-stakes standardized tests
often blame poor schools and/or poor students and their parents for low
achievement. Meanwhile, there is a strong correlation between low test
scores and racial minority status, which is related to a whole host of factors, including the concentration of poverty, discrimination, and language
barriers that are beyond the control of educators or students. A presidential panel, the President's Advisory Commission on Educational Excellence for Hispanic Americans, found in 1999 after a 5-year study that
high-stakes tests were unfair to Hispanics (Zehr, 1999). Indeed, there is a
growing number of examples of ways in which "excellence" reforms via
standards and testing are very punitive to low-income students and students of color. For instance, reports from New Jersey and California tell
of minority students being prevented from taking advanced placement
classes and being disadvantaged as a result of performance on state tests
("Huge Drop," 1998).

Although advocates for excellence and equity declare their support
for both goals, when translated into public policy the two concepts are often
competitive. The reason has much to do with financial constraints and the
politics of resource allocation. The way policymakers often see it, educational "excellence" can be satisfied by the investment of limited new resources and assurance that the most endowed receive the rewards of the
system. Equity goals are far more costly because they require that larger
numbers of students receive the same benefits. The conflict occurs when

Table 2.3. Testing Consequences Among the 50 States

		Consequences for Students		
		High	*Moderate*	*Low*
Consequences for Teachers, Schools, and Districts	*High*	Alabama Alaska* California* Delaware* Florida Georgia * Indiana * Louisiana Maryland* Massachusetts* Mississippi* Nevada New Jersey New Mexico New York North Carolina Ohio South Carolina Tennessee Texas Virginia* Wisconsin *	Arkansas Colorado* Connecticut Illinois Michigan Pennsylvania West Virginia	Kansas Kentucky Missouri Nebraska Oklahoma* Rhode Island Vermont*
	Moderate	Arizona * Minnesota Utah* Washington*	Oregon	Hawaii Maine Montana New Hampshire North Dakota South Dakota Wyoming
	Low	Idaho*		Iowa

Source: Shore, Pedulla, and Clarke (2001).

High stakes—regulated or legislated sanctions (e.g., accreditation, money, receivership) linked directly to test scores

Moderate stakes—by default, all states that do not fall within high or low

Low stakes—no consequences attached to test scores

* policy has not taken effect yet

resources are limited and choices have to be made. When American society has been willing to make a major investment in education—such as in the Head Start program or the G.I. Bill of the post-World War II period—it has successfully combined its commitment to equity and high-quality education. Yet, as the data from our project show, this is not happening in the states we studied. And, given the suburban political regimes that dominate the policy-making process in these states, it is unlikely that many equity-minded reforms will occur soon

FUNDING INEQUITIES IN THE STATES

In this section of the chapter we use school finance policies and reform efforts as one of the most pervasive examples of the way in which suburban regime politics has shifted the policy focus away from equity. Indeed, we argue that the disparity in school finance capacity across different districts *within* states is the most fundamental equity issue in education today. School systems funded largely by local property taxes are structurally unequal since inequities are directly tied to community wealth. State aid and equalization of funding are the only source of redistributive policies within states. These state policies are controlled by suburban-dominated legislatures and governors who see their support for suburban interests as essential to their reelection. Wealthy suburban school districts eschew redistributive state school aid formulas, which would help cities. Anti-city state legislators respond to their major supporters in suburban districts by promoting and passing policies that underfund city schools. Huge gaps between urban and suburban school spending exist in many states, and the segregation resulting from suburbanization supports these discrepancies.

The problem of financial inequities in state school aid is fundamental to the issue of reform of education in the United States. The ability to pay for schools, teachers' salaries, facilities, and equipment is a major determinant of the adequacy of education, according to recent court decisions in Alabama and New Jersey as well as other states. The discriminatory aid policies of the states, according to these court decisions, are what produce inadequate or inferior education. It could be suggested that the change in the use of terms in court decisions to include "adequacy" as a concept replacing "equity" is yet another sign of the declining interest in equity as a societal goal. The language change represents an appeal to suburbanites who otherwise would reject equity as a value and purpose of court actions. In fact, the failure of the courts to act, or when they act to have legislatures and governors ignore their mandates, suggests that neither the new language nor definition has appealed to those who hold power in the states. Tests and rhetoric about high standards do not address the reasons for inadequate education.

Table 2.4, based on a special report published in *Education Week*, provides data indicating the ways in which states have institutionalized inequities in distributing aid for education. Since the mid-1990s, *Education Week* (Quality counts, 1997, 1998, 1999, 2000, 2001) has graded each state based on the degree of equity in its school spending system. Based on a "coefficient of variation," the grade focuses on spending differences across the districts within a state. Those with the higher grades have the least variation. When tallying the 1999 grades, *Education Week* introduced a score for each state evaluating its effort to equalize disparities in district funding by their financial aid. The more recent data, presented in Table 2.5, show that, for the most part, these trends have not changed. Indeed, Tables 2.4 and 2.5 indicate the continued inequities in the large majority of the states between poor and wealthy districts and the failure of states to address these disparities in their funding formulas.

State constitutions promote a common vision and goal for education when they contain provisions that require that all children must be provided with an equal and adequate education, and typically require education to be provided in a "free," "uniform," "efficient," "thorough," "ample," or "basic" way (Augenblick, 1998). Although most state equity funding challenges brought to the courts in the 1970s sought to address only financial inequities under states' equal protection clauses, more recent cases have used these same constitutional requirements to challenge other inequities, such as facilities, equipment, and teaching, as a part of the "adequacy" concept—that students have the right to an adequate education, as stipulated in most state constitutions. The adequacy arguments also allow reformers to include governance and restructuring as areas for court review and reform. Thus, the differential between rich and poor districts and the relationship of funding to performance has been the basis of wide-ranging "adequacy" court cases in nearly half the states in the past decade.

Pursuing litigation as a means to reform may prove advantageous in forcing a recalcitrant legislature to action and in providing an impetus for necessary tax increases or reformulations. However, if the court disregards political realities, legislative action and implementation are not likely to occur (Gittell, 1998).

In nearly half of these cases, state court judges have ruled in favor of the plaintiffs, declaring existing funding systems unequal and unconstitutional.[1] For instance, Chief Justice Stephens in the Kentucky case declared that "the premise for the existence of common schools is that all children in Kentucky have a constitutional right to an adequate education" (Gittell,

Table 2.4. *Education Week's State by State Evaluation of Financial Equity (1996–1999)*

| | 1996 Grades | | 1997 Grades | | 1998 Grades | | Overall grade for equity using next year's system | | 1999 Grades Overall grade for equity using current system | |
| | Relative equity in per-pupil spending among all districts | | | | | | | | | |
	Grade		Grade	Coefficient of variation	Grade	Coefficient of variation	Grade		Grade	Coefficient of variation
Hawaii*	A	100	A	0.0%	A	0.0%	A	100	A	0.0%
New Mexico	C-	71	?	?	C	12.9%****	A-	90	C	11.9%
Idaho	C+	77	C-	14.7%	C-	14.3%	B+	89	C-	14.6%
Arkansas	B	83	?	?	C	11.8%****	B	86	C	11.0%
Utah	B+	89	C+	10.6%	C+	10.8%	B	86	C	11.7%
Nevada	B	86	B-	9.2%	B-	9.8%	B	84	C	11.4%
Washington	C+	78	B-	9.6%	B-	9.9%	B	83	B-	9.4%**
Florida	C+	79	B	7.4%	B	7.6%	B-	82	B	7.0%
Oklahoma	B-	81	?	?	C-	14.9%****	B-	82	C	13.9%
Minnesota	B-	82	C+	10.9%	C	11.3%	B-	81	C	11.1%**
Texas	D	65	C	12.1%	C	12.5%	C+	78	C	13.0%
West Virginia	A	93	A-	4.8%	B+	5.8%	C+	78	B+	5.2%
Kansas	C	75	D	16.6%	D	16.0%	C+	77	D	16.1%
Wyoming	B-	82	D+	15.1%	C	13.6%	C+	77	C-	14.7%
Georgia	B	86	C	12.2%	C	11.2%	C	76	B-	9.6%
Alaska	D+	69	F	30.1%	F	31.9%	C	75	F	32.4%
California	D	65	?	?	C	13.1%****	C	75	C	11.4%***
Colorado	B-	82	?	?	C+	10.2%****	C	74	B-	9.9%
Kentucky	B+	88	?	?	C	13.0%****	C	74	B-	9.8%**
Mississippi	B+	87	C+	10.9%	C+	10.2%	C	74	B-	9.7%
Oregon	C+	79	C+	10.9%	C+	10.5%	C	74	C+	10.2%
South Carolina	B+	89	B	8.9%	B	8.7%	C	74	B-	9.0%
Alabama	B+	89	C+	10.8%	C+	10.4%	C	73	B-	9.8%
Michigan	B	84	D+	15.5%	C-	14.0%	C	73	C	13.6%
North Carolina	A-	90	B	7.8%	B	8.2%	C	73	B	7.4%

28

State										
Iowa	B	85	B	8.4%	B	7.9%	C-	71	B	8.6%
Wisconsin	B	83	B-	9.4%	B-	9.2%	C-	71	B-	9.4%
Indiana	B	85	C+	10.5%	C	11.4%****	C-	70	B-	9.6%
Louisiana	C	74	B-	9.8%	B-	9.9%	C-	70	B-	9.4%
Nebraska	C+	79	D+	15.2%	D	16.0%	C-	70	D+	15.8%
Maine	B	84	C	13.5%	C-	14.8%	D+	69	C	13.5%
Delaware	A-	92	B	6.5%	B	6.7%	D+	67	B	7.4%
Rhode Island	D	65	C	12.6%	C	12.1%	D+	67	C	11.9%
Tennessee	B	86	C	13.4%	C	12.3%	D	66	C	12.1%
Virginia	B+	87	C	12.5%	C	12.8%	D	66	C	13.0%
Maryland	A-	90	C	12.3%	C	11.2%	D	64	C+	10.7%
Arizona	C	74	C-	14.9%	C-	14.6%	D	63	C	13.6%
Connecticut	C-	72	C	11.6%	C	11.1%	D	63	C	11.4%
North Dakota	B-	81	B	7.8%	D	17.4%	D	63	D	16.5%
South Dakota	B-	82	?	?	C	12.7%****	D	63	C	11.6%
Massachusetts	D+	67	D	16.2%	D	16.8%	D-	60	D+	15.6%
Missouri	C-	72	F	25.9%	F	24.9%	D-	60	F	20.3%
New Jersey	D+	67	?	?	C	12.8%****	D-	60	C	11.8%
Pennsylvania	C+	79	C-	14.5%	C-	14.6%	D-	60	C-	14.5%
New York	C	75	D	17.7%	D	17.7%	F	56	D-	19.6%
New Hampshire	B-	80	D	17.1%	D	16.8%	F	55	D	17.5%
Illinois	C-	70	D	16.7%	D	17.6%	F	54	D	16.9%
Montana	B-	80	D	17.2%	D	16.5%	F	54	D+	15.4%
Ohio	C+	79	D	17.0%	D+	15.4%	F	53	D+	15.6%
Vermont	B-	80	D-	19.0%	D	16.1%	F	50	D	16.2%

Note: State Equalization Effort = (1 - Targeting Score) × State Share of Funding

*Hawaii has a single statewide district.

**These states did not report IEP student data, so enrollment could not be adjusted to reflect such data.

***Only 81% of California's school districts could be analyzed because of a lack of data on property wealth.

****Data on disadvantaged students, used to adjust spending figures, were missing or not reported for 46% to 90% of districts.

? State did not participate in national assessment, survey, or data collection.

Table 2.5. *Education Week's* State by State Evaluation of Financial Equity (2000–2001)

State	2000 Grades		2001 Grades		State	2000 Grades		2001 Grades	
Hawaii*	A	100	A	100	Iowa	C+	77	C+	77
New Mexico	B	84	B+	88	Wisconsin	C	75	C+	78
Idaho	C+	78	C	76	Indiana	D+	69	C-	71
Arkansas	B-	80	C+	79	Louisiana	C	73	C+	79
Utah	B+	89	B+	88	Nebraska	D+	67	D+	68
Nevada	B	86	B	83	Maine	D+	68	C-	71
Washington	C+	79	C+	78	Delaware	B-	80	C-	72
Florida	C+	78	B	83	Rhode Island	D+	69	D+	67
Oklahoma	B	83	B-	82	Tennessee	D+	68	D+	67
Minnesota	C	76	B-	82	Virginia	D	66	D+	68
Texas	B-	81	C+	78	Maryland	F	55	D-	62
West Virginia	C+	79	C+	77	Arizona	D+	68	D	65
Kansas	B-	80	B-	80	Connecticut	D	63	D	64
Wyoming	C	74	C	75	North Dakota	D	63	F	58
Georgia	C	75	C-	72	South Dakota	C-	70	C	76
Alaska	C	75	C	75	Massachusetts	C	73	D	66
California	C+	78	C+	78	Missouri	D-	60	D+	67
Colorado	C+	77	C-	72	New Jersey	D-**	62**	D	64
Kentucky	C+**	78**	C+	79	Pennsylvania	D-	60	D-	61
Mississippi	C-	71	C	73	New York	F	55	D+	67
Oregon	C-	72	C+	79	New Hampshire	F	52	F	56
South Carolina	C	75	C	76	Illinois	F	55	F	57
Alabama	C	74	C+	77	Montana	F	57	D-	61
Michigan	C-	72	C-	72	Ohio	F	58	D-	61
North Carolina	C	74	C	76	Vermont	F	56	C-	71

*Hawaii has a single statewide district.
**Data on special education student enrollment, used to adjust spending figures, are missing for these states.

30

1998). The Kentucky court ruled not only that the financing was inequitable but also that the state system of governance that perpetuated both inequitable financing and the resulting gross disparities of opportunity among districts was unconstitutional. Similarly, the Alabama court ruled not only that children in that state have a right to due process in the determination of state aid, but also that they have a substantive right to both equitable and adequate educational opportunity provided by the state. The court admitted evidence as widely varying as textbook availability, a survey of the physical condition of the schools, classroom overcrowding, teacher salary comparisons, and the testimony of school finance experts. In effect, the judges argued that quality and equality are inseparable. However, in a more recent decision, although the Alabama State Supreme Court ruled that the system of funding public schools was a constitutional violation, it refused to order the state legislature to devise a remedy ("Quality Counts," June 2002).

These state court decisions were exceptional in their joining the issues of equity and quality, but some scholars argue that court orders alone are not enough. For instance, in a recent analysis of the issue comparing the efforts in West Virginia and Kentucky, Werner (2002) concluded that dependence solely on the judicial arena, "without laying the groundwork for change," results in failure (p. 63). He describes the process in West Virginia as "a handful of plaintiffs representing their own particular interests in a single county" (p. 60). In contrast, Kentucky's case stemmed from the combined concerns of 66 counties and was fueled by the support of groups from all over the state representing diverse points of view. Kentucky, singular among the state fiscal equity efforts, tied the legal battle to a well-organized political campaign and a structure, the Pritchard Committee (Hunter, 1999; Werner, 2002). Werner concludes from his comparative analysis, "Kentucky got it right. It sowed the seeds for reform in a grassroots movement" (p. 80). There is no moral imperative to the equity issue, which will negate the need for strong organizing of diverse constituencies within states to achieve policy changes in funding formulas. In New York, The Campaign for Fiscal Equity has adopted the Kentucky approach and organized a statewide effort to support its legal action and the implementation of the court decision. Moreover, Kentucky is the only state that has followed a strong court decision with strong public organization and active political pressure to produce decisive state policies to change aid and redistribute resources within the state. Too often, court orders in the favor of equity reforms are squelched by a suburban political regime that controls state policymaking, thus thwarting attempts to implement redistributive school finance laws, despite what the courts have mandated. The process by which this has occurred is discussed in the next section.

THE POLITICS OF EQUITY IN STATE SCHOOL REFORM

In four states studied—Pennsylvania, New Jersey, Maryland, and Minnesota—city activists and poor school districts challenged the system of funding schools in the courts but achieved limited success. The stories of these states reflect the national picture of declining interest in equity. Plaintiffs from underfunded school districts in rural and urban areas brought their cases before the state supreme courts and claimed that the lack of financial equity in their states was a violation of the state constitution. In Pennsylvania, three cases on behalf of the city of Philadelphia and one case brought by the rural schools have been considered. By 1999 all of these cases had been deemed nonjusticiable by the state supreme court. In *Powell* v. *Ridge*, (189 F.3d 387 [3rd Cir. 1999] and 247 F.3rd 520 [2001]), reformers turned to the federal courts, seeking relief from the racially discriminatory effects of Philadelphia's school finance system under the regulations implementing Title VI of the Civil Rights Act. In New Jersey, the state supreme court has ruled positively on the need for financial equity since 1970, repeatedly ordering the state to provide adequate education funding and facilities to students in New Jersey's 30 high-needs school districts. On February 19, 2002, Governor McGreevey finally signed an executive order creating the Abbott Implementation and Compliance Coordinating Council, a cooperative board that is, in theory, held accountable for implementing the court-ordered reforms. In Minnesota, there were two financial equity court cases—one on behalf of Minneapolis and the other on behalf of St. Paul. In 2000 an NAACP suit against the state was resolved, with both parties agreeing to create a new accountability system for the Minneapolis schools and expand the access of low-income families to magnet and suburban schools. In Maryland, Baltimore and the ACLU filed a case against the state in 1995, but the case was dropped as a result of a compromise agreement worked out between the state and the city. When plaintiffs returned to court in 2000, the circuit court declared that the state was still failing to live up to its constitutional duty to provide an adequate education. The state government had failed to comply with the compromise agreement and was ordered to provide additional funds, over $2,000 per student. The state refused to comply with that order, but in April 2002 a new financing system, based on a state commission's findings, was enacted. Among its provisions was more state funding for high-needs districts. The new system was to be phased in over 6 years (Access, 2002).

Urban school districts were often the plaintiffs in the court cases, including the school districts in St. Paul and Philadelphia. In Philadelphia, the district's high-profile superintendent, David Hornbeck, was actively involved in the city's need for additional school funding. He brought a case against the state in 1997 and worked politically at the state level to achieve additional funds for the city. Several times, he appealed to the governor to provide more money for Philadelphia schools. In early 1998, despite the threat of bankruptcy, the state continued to refuse to help the city school system. The governor and state legislatures commented negatively about the failure of Philadelphia to use its funds more efficiently. The continued poor performance of Philadelphia schools led to the takeover by the state of the city school system in December 2001 and the creation of the Philadelphia School Reform Commission to oversee the system. In April 2002 the Philadelphia School Reform Commission voted to hand over 42 of the city's worst-performing schools to private organizations, including Temple University and the for-profit company, Edison Inc. This move can be seen as an initiative of the state government, since, of the five-member commission, the three members appointed by the governor voted for the move, while the two members appointed by the mayor of Philadelphia voted against. However, some privatization was perhaps inevitable, as Mayor John Street and the commission members appointed by him had put forward a more modest plan to privatize 25 of the city's 265 public schools. By fall of 2004, Philadelphia had 45 schools managed by Educational Management Organizations (EMOs)—20 of which were still run by Edison. According to state testing data, half of those schools and about 40% of the regular public schools have increased student achievement since the late 1990s (Gewertz, 2004). The results of this ambitious plan (the largest-ever public school privatization effort) are yet to be seen, but school privatization has an ambiguous record and is fiercely opposed by labor unions and activist groups.

Philadelphia is not unique in terms of the attitudes that state policymakers have toward urban public schools. The effects of suburbanization on state school politics are evident in the reflection of several governors and legislators regarding "the futility of funding failing urban school systems" (Gittell & McKenna, 1998, p. 6). When the court rules that the state has to decrease fiscal inequities, the governor and the legislature are responsible for putting together a reform policy. Reformers committed to fiscal equity, therefore, cannot focus only on the courts. Influencing state politicians is equally, if not more, important because the state's response to the court can vary greatly. State policymakers can put forward a progressive, ambitious reform, as they did in Kentucky; they can put together a substitute reform that is again challenged by the courts, as was done in New Jersey; or they can entirely disregard the court order, as appears to be the case in Pennsylvania. Because the legislature and the governor are so important in fiscal equity policy, creating the political atmosphere for reform is just as important as putting together a successful legal case.

Taxpayer organizations and representatives from wealthier suburban districts are very influential in pressuring state politicians to preserve the status quo. We concluded, from the study of educational policymaking in nine states, that city reformers were far less effective at the state level, often lacking an appreciation of how state politics shaped school policies in cities. Furthermore, policymakers elected to statewide offices such as governor generally are not beholden to city voters. For example, former New Jersey Governor Florio's defeat in the 1993 election was certainly due to successful efforts by suburban groups who disliked his proposals for tax increases and redistribution of state aid from wealthy to poor communities. Governor Whitman's successful 1997 re-election bid was strongly supported by those same wealthy suburban districts. In our study, we found that all nine governors faced resistance to any redistributive tax increase or finance restructuring proposals, reflecting the strong position of suburban interests in state financial policies.

Teachers and other school professionals are important actors in the politics of state school reform, but they have their own agenda, which may or may not promote more equity in the system, depending on their organizational interests in a particular context. In our research we found that the unions also reflected and were influenced by the effects of suburbanization and race politics. Thus, the teachers' unions in the states we studied tended to be supportive of only equity reforms that proposed to infuse more money into the system, but these professionals also believe strongly that no spending caps should be placed on wealthier school districts and that teachers' salaries should not be affected by reforms. Because over three-quarters of school costs can consist of salaries and fringe benefits for teachers and school staff (New York State Education Department, 2000), a shift in funds is likely to affect salaries, making many school professionals wary of equity reforms.[2] Teachers' unions are not united on these issues. The National Education Association (NEA) and the American Federation of Teachers (AFT) sometimes choose to support different types of equity cases. This was the case in Pennsylvania. The Pennsylvania State Education Association, an affiliate of the NEA, was supportive of the rural court case, while the Philadelphia Federation of Teachers, Philadelphia's branch of the AFT, supported Philadelphia's cases.

In three states that we studied—Illinois, Texas, and Michigan—governors proposed restructuring the system of financing schools. These reforms came without the pressure of a court decision. Michigan's 1994 finance reform plan ended school funding's reliance on property taxes. Instead, the state pays for about 80% of K–12 education in each district. In 2001 major reductions in state spending for schools required drastic reductions in district budgets.

In 1996, Governor Edgar of Illinois similarly proposed a more equitable distribution of school fiscal support. The plan held all districts harmless and combined an increase in the state income tax, property tax relief, and modest increases in overall spending on education through an increase in the foundation formula, replacing the local property tax with a state tax. This original plan was not successful due to concerns that it would raise taxes in wealthy districts, and a more modest law was passed in late 1997.

In Texas, then-Governor Bush's Property Tax Cut Act of 1997 was designed to restructure the state's taxation system and would have affected the system of educational finance. The Governor's proposal would have lowered property taxes by $2.8 billion a year and paid for the cut with a half-cent increase in the state sales and motor vehicle taxes, and with a business activity tax. It would have abolished the corporate franchise tax and the school property tax on business investment and replaced them with a 1.25% levy on all forms of business that brought in more than $500,000 after certain expenses and capital investments were subtracted. This proposal, like Governor Edgar's, failed because nobody could agree on what tax should be raised. Businesses bitterly opposed any plan that would have increased taxation. The plan also failed to get the support of the state GOP's Christian Right wing, which feared that the reform would centralize taxation and give more power to the Texas Education Association (Beinart, 1998).

The Texas reform, while it would have interfered with the financing of education, was not a plan to achieve further equity. In fact, many interviewees believed that it would worsen the situation. They also said that then-Governor Bush believed that this reform was a means for him to gain national recognition that would help with his 2000 Presidential race, and the plan did become a major talking point in his national campaign.

Anti-tax sentiment in suburban communities in Illinois and Texas contributed to watering down of the finance reform plans. Furthermore, in some states, opposition to changing the system of taxation came from the business community. For example, in Texas, the business community was very opposed to Bush's tax reform, although in other states the business community has supported change in the property tax because rising school costs increase corporations' tax burden as property owners.

In Maryland, finance reform not only was a court issue but also was addressed in a meaningful way by the governor in response to the lawsuits. In a unique arrangement, the city of Baltimore, in exchange for a state takeover of the schools, received additional funding despite suburban complaints. Thus, Maryland is unique among the states in our study because additional funding eventually was provided to Baltimore. The Maryland policy also uniquely links finance reform to governance reform. This state was the only one in our study that focused its education reform efforts on the city. This can be attributed in part to the mayor's importance in state-wide politics and his activist role in shaping state education policy and in part to the activism of parent groups at the state level. (See also Orr, 1999, for a different interpretation of Baltimore school funding.)

In December 1994, the Baltimore ACLU chapter filed a lawsuit for more education dollars for the city district. The suit focused on the high cost of educating at-risk students and claimed a denial of the right to an adequate education guaranteed by the state constitution. The ACLU also argued that Baltimore was prevented by the lack of funds from adhering to the Maryland School Performance Program (MSPP) (Bowler, 1994). The city faced sanctions from the state for not meeting the program's performance requirements, as measured by standardized tests. In February 1995, the state school board ordered Baltimore to reform three more schools that did not meet MSPP requirements and offered $1.5 million in assistance (Thompson, 1995). Perhaps it was the ACLU's lawsuit that got the state's attention.

Governor Glendening took office in January 1995 with a more urban electoral base than that of most recent governors. His base included Baltimore City, Prince George's County, and the Maryland State Teachers Association. After being in office for a while and studying school reform, he took public positions favoring the state takeover efforts and reappointed Nancy Grasmick, the Baltimore superintendent that former Governor Schaefer had appointed (Bowler, 1995). Grasmick had feuded with the unions and Baltimore over school reform. Glendening attempted to find middle ground between the legislature, the bureaucracy, and the interests of Baltimore. In September 1995, Baltimore itself filed a lawsuit against the state demanding more school funding. This case also focused on adequacy and would later join the ACLU case. Parties representing Baltimore included the mayor, the city council, and the city school board. The state filed a countersuit claiming that any problems were the result of local mismanagement (Portner, 1996).

In 1992, the Baltimore Board of Education had put some of its schools in the hands of a private, for-profit management company, Education Alternatives, Inc. (EAI), and Mayor Schmoke ordered an independent evaluation of this program in July 1995. This evaluation failed to show any sign of improvement in the privately managed schools, and when in December 1995 EAI demanded more money, Mayor Schmoke canceled the contract. At that time, 35 of the 37 Maryland schools that the Maryland State Department of Education identified as needing "reconstitution" for having fallen below performance standards were in Baltimore. Under the MSPP, reconstituted schools may be taken over by the state for other managing arrangements.

The Maryland legislature created a Baltimore School Funding Bill in May 1996. Because the bill did not call for adequate funding and provided for state takeovers with no local control, Mayor Schmoke convinced Governor Glendening to veto the legislation (Zorzi, 1996). Schmoke had endorsed Glendening in the 1994 election, and this may have been Glendening's way of repaying that favor. Finally the state and city worked out a more generous deal for school finance and governance. Baltimore would receive $254 million in extra state aid over 5 years, and the reconstituted schools would be managed under joint powers, with the mayor and the governor cooperating in the appointment of a new board of directors. The CEO of this new board must produce annual reports and may be fired if the schools do not perform. In exchange for these concessions the mayor agreed to end both lawsuits (Brown, 1998). Almost all of Baltimore's schools are in the reconstitution plan and are governed by the new board. When new schools are identified for reconstitution, based on declining standardized test scores, they are given 2 years to improve. Nine schools in Prince George's County have been identified for reconstitution if they do not improve (Brown, 1998). There are also two rural schools on the list.

Interviewees in Baltimore perceived this reform as a positive effort of the state government to respond to city school needs. Yet, as I noted above, Maryland is exceptional in this study because of its unique political culture and party competition. It is one of the few of the nine states to have a Democratic legislature and governor. The state has many government employees, and the African American community is highly organized, both of which contribute to its solid Democratic and pro-government culture (Orr, 1999). The wealthier suburbs and some rural areas, which are Republican, are in the minority. Because of Democratic control, Baltimore is often important in statewide elections, and Baltimore mayors are often prominent in state politics. Thus, the strong Baltimore mayor, strong statewide government, and weak teachers' unions in Maryland contribute to its particular approach to finance reform.

GOVERNANCE: DECENTRALIZATION AND CENTRALIZATION

The conflict between excellence and equity is devised by people who see the allocation of resources as the major issue in school reform. Suburban districts benefit from a more localized tax system that keeps the dollars where the wealthy people live and can control them. In the past several decades these suburban interests have asserted their control over state school finance policy decisions to protect their resources in state aid formulas. Anti-city attitudes reinforce their inclination to eschew equity as a goal compatible with excellence, ignoring the fact that the excellence of education is dependent on the ability to broaden its impact to all populations within the state and the society as a whole.

Directly tied to these issues is the question of school governance and the process of decision making. Historically in the United States, we have depended on more centralized and larger units of government to pursue equity in redistributive politics. The federal government is accordingly responsible for guaranteeing basic rights and equity for all citizens. Following this theory, state policymakers should be better positioned to see the concerns of all their citizens, while school district officials are more likely to favor only the needs of their most powerful constituents. Often, however, politics at all three levels may significantly change roles and confuse the process. Conservative forces at the national and state levels have resisted equity goals and set a tone for the entire country. Occasionally, some local districts demonstrate unusual concern and broader vision of social equity needs.

Devolution of power and responsibility from the federal government to the states by the past several administrations was a response to what was described as over-centralization of policy at the national level. The states, it was assumed, would be more responsive to local needs. Our research identifies the political impact of that decision as more complex. State governments are more and more dominated by suburban interests, which define their needs as control over resources that otherwise would be shared with cities and rural areas. Racial segregation not only minimizes equity as a primary value; it also ensures that politically it is almost impossible to accomplish. The continuing failure of states to address fiscal equity, even in the face of court action asserting its fundamental value, is a reflection of the negative effect of state politics on achieving a system of social justice.

Our research on state policies and urban school reform found that finance reform was not even an issue in the courts or in the legislature from 1995–1997 in many states. Even when forced by the courts to address education inequities, officials in some states dodged the issue. In at least two states, Pennsylvania and New Jersey, improved standards were proposed by the governor as a substitute for equity.

State inattention to fiscal equity has several explanations. Most significant is the shift in control of state legislatures and governors' offices to suburban voters. The current state regimes—those that control educational policy—have little interest in improving educational funding for cities; in general they lack interest in city schools. Although some governors have shown interest in providing more money to their constituencies in rural and working-class suburbs, raising or restructuring taxes also has become even more politically unpopular as more and more people with wealth and political clout flee to separate municipalities and even gated communities— separated and segregated from those with less.

ACHIEVING EXCELLENCE WITH EQUALITY

American education can achieve its full potential—excellence with equity—only under a dynamic federal system that encourages all levels of government to work together with a more common vision. Equity is the essential goal in a democratic society. Emphasis on equity to produce high standards for a larger segment of the population is an achievable goal. The results of the education reforms of the 1960s are evidence of that fact. Those reforms asserted equity as the major priority; however, significant quali- tative improvement—or greater "excellence"—was achieved as a part of these policies. Assessments of compensatory education and SAT scores conducted by the National Assessment of Educational Progress prior to the cutbacks in the early 1980s reported a narrowing of the gap between mi- nority and White student performance that can be attributed in part to the success of Title I. (See Education Commission of the States, 1981; Stonehill & Anderson, 1982.)

In contrast, state school reform in the 1980s and 1990s, which stressed testing, assessment, accountability, devolution, and competition, did not reduce educational inequities. Rather, it improved quality for those who were already advantaged (Gittell & McKenna, 1998).

The federal government may well be the only potential source of na- tional policies to meaningfully redistribute resources and opportunities, thereby creating greater equity. Federal policies can promote improved governance, broader participation, higher standards, more equitable fund- ing, and encouragement of public debate. An essential part of the federal role is its assertion of national leadership in confirming social values and priorities.

The continuing debate about how best to formulate and administer educational policies—for example, whether centralized or decentralized systems are more efficient and more responsive to larger segments of the population—is complicated by the constraints of political culture and eco- nomics, history, and race, class, and gender prejudice. Educational policy throughout much of the world is promulgated by central governments. In federal systems, intermediary subnational governments (i.e., states and provinces) have varying degrees of power and input into the allocation of resources and the accessibility of adequate education. Implementation of those policies at the local and school levels also results in wide disparities in service and outcomes. Accordingly, decentralized schools and school districts reflect local politics and social conditions.

The United States is unique in its major reliance on the states to fund nearly half the cost of education, with a limited federal government contribution that peaked at less than 10% in the 1970s. Thus, ours is a highly decentralized system with local districts providing, on average, almost the other half of the costs of educating children.[3] Thus, we have an unusually heavy reliance on state and local funding for education (U.S. Department of Education, National Center for Education Statistics, 2001). Although states vary in their practices, generally marginal populations have not fared well in heavily decentralized school systems. State power structures respond to economic elites to maintain low levels of tax and school funding. Competition for funds has resulted in state aid formulas that reward those with resources and power. Minority groups in cities have looked to federal support for guarantees of equity and funding for compensatory education.

Our research on state education politics gave us valuable insights into why certain local groups have not been successful in influencing state educational policies. Activist organizations representing the interests of marginal groups, particularly new minorities in cities, see the national government as most accessible and responsive to their needs. Cities and city groups in most states have little positive experience in securing policies responsive to their particular needs. State governments early on were responsive to rural and propertied elites and in more recent years have catered to suburban propertied interests, which have an historical anti-city, anti-immigrant, anti-minority bias. Traditions die hard, and our research found that city school activists are not well represented among state educational policymakers. They lack access often because they are not organized at the state level. They have not taken advantage of possible coalition building with poor rural communities that share most of their needs. State legislators from cities often do not work with a common purpose, mayors avoid leadership roles that create coalitions with activists, and activists lack familiarity with and are alienated by state politics. In many states, race politics dominate all decisions, and structural mechanisms have been created to restrict representation and access of marginal groups. State governments also are significantly influenced by teachers' and professional educators' unions and associations, which spend more money to elect legislators and lobby policymakers than most other lobbyists. As I noted above, these organizations cannot be relied on to advocate for greater equity in public education, especially when their members' interests are at stake.

Furthermore, our research found that the isolation of marginal groups from state politics has been intensified by the emergence of conservative governors in the 1990s who were uninterested in or opposed to urban school reform and issues of school equity. Devolution of power to the states therefore has not served cities or city schools well. Still, the blame must rest at least in part with the organized city interests that eschew state politics and have failed to create working coalitions around the issues of greatest import to them. In light of the Bush administration's educational policies and strategies, the question of the most appropriate division of power in education becomes ever more complex. President Bush has promoted federally mandated testing and assessments as a centerpiece of his educational policies, most notably the No Child Left Behind Act, which he signed into law in early 2002. Even though states can use their own assessments, which they established under the 1994 Goals 2000 legislation, the traditional role of local districts, schools, and even states is challenged by these mandates, because they require states to test students in certain subjects in certain years, thereby eroding the notion of "local control" in U.S. education.

CONCLUSION

Equitable funding of schools and school districts is fundamental to our national vision for school systems that promote social justice and equity. The long-term success of school reform agendas is, in part, dependent on whether they have a comprehensive view of change that emphasizes these goals. Guaranteeing broader participation of a wider cross-section of stakeholders in education confirms our commitment to improved governance and to the democratic political process. Parents and communities are clearly stakeholders whose increased involvement moves us toward ensuring that commitment. School reform in America should be an ongoing and dynamic process, as is the democratic system itself.

The ultimate success of strong coalition organization in campaigns for school reform, whether fiscal equity, governance, or equality, depends on building a base of engaged citizens and participation for broader goals of social justice. Guinier and Torres (2002), both experienced and highly regarded civil rights attorneys, describe the vital role to be played by long-term, cross-race coalition building as a part of the "street-level democracy" essential to the framing of issues, informing elites, and winning battles for social equity inside and outside the courts.

Centralizing to the federal level at least some aspects of the implementation of court-ordered equity remedies might provide one way to get around state-level regimes that generally deny poor urban or rural constituents a place at the table. Unfortunately, under the current administration, the only education reform effort that is being centralized and led by the federal government is more standardized testing and high-stakes accountability systems. This suggests a rather dismal outlook for poor schools and districts in the near future. Without adequate resources and support, these districts and the students they serve will only continue a downward trend, further legitimizing the distance suburban dwellers wish to maintain from their darker and poorer neighbors.

NOTES

Acknowledgments. I want to thank Mitchell Glodek, Elisabeth Jacobs, Kimberly Jones, and Laura McKenna, research staff at the Howard Samuels State Management and Policy Center, for their contributions.

1. Decisions early in the 1980s upheld existing formulas in AZ, MI, ID, OR, PA, OH, GA, CO, NY, and MD, and struck down those in CA, NJ, KS, WI, CT, WA, WV, WY, and AK. Second-wave decisions (in the late 1980s) include court support for systems in OK, NC, LA, and SC, and decisions striking down systems in MT, KY, TX, NJ, and TN (*The State of Inequality*, 1991).
2. In New York City public schools, salaries and fringe benefits for teachers and support staff make up 78% of the budget, with administrative staff's salaries and benefits taking up an additional 2% of the budget. Public school budgets in other parts of the state are similar: for example, Nassau County—teachers 77%, administrators 2%; Westchester—teachers 76%, administrators 2%; Yonkers—teachers 80%, administrators 1%.
3. Table 157 of the *Digest of Education Statistics 2000* shows that on average in the 1998–99 school year, the federal government provided 7.1% of funds, the state governments 48.7% of funds, and local governments the remaining 44.2%. See http://www.nces.ed.gov/pubs2002/digest2001/tables/dt157.asp.

REFERENCES

Access [Website]. (2002). *Finance litigation: Maryland.* Retrieved March 10, 2004 from http://www.accessednetwork.org/litigation/lit_md.html.
Augenblick, J. (1998). The role of the state legislatures in school finance reform: Looking backward and looking ahead. In M. Gittell (Ed.), *Strategies for school equity: Creating productive schools in a just society* (pp. 89–100). New Haven, CT: Yale University Press.
Bastian, A., Fruchter, N., Gittell, M., Greer, C., & Haskins, K. (1986). *Choosing equality: The case for democratic schooling.* Philadelphia: Temple University Press.
Beinart, P. (1998, March 16). The big debate. *New Republic*, pp. 21–25.
Bowler, M. (1994, December 7). ACLU suing Maryland. *Baltimore Sun*, p. 1B.
Bowler, M. (1995, August 30). Maryland school chief given extension by state board. *Baltimore Sun*, p. 1B.

Brown, D. L. (1998, January 29). Nine Prince George's schools under threat of take-over; Md. demands fast action to improve schools. *Washington Post*, p. A1.

Duany, A., & Plater-Zyberk, E. (1991). *Towns and town-making principles*. Cambridge, MA: Harvard University Graduate School of Design.

Education Commission of the States. (1981, April). *Has Title I improved education for disadvantaged students? Evidence from three national assessments of reading* (Rep. No. S4-D5-50 of the National Assessment of Educational Progress). Denver: Author.

Farley, R., & Frey, W. (1994). Changes in the segregation of whites from blacks during the 1980s: Small steps toward a more integrated society. *American Sociological Review, 59*, 23–45.

Frey, W., & Farley, R. (1996). Latino, Asian and black segregation in US metropolitan areas: Are multiethnic metros different? *Demography, 33*, 35–50.

Garreau, J. (1991). *Edge city: Life on the new frontier*. New York: Doubleday.

Gewertz, C. (2004, September 1). Philadelphia cheers better test scores. *Education Week, 24*(1), 6.

Gittell, M. (1980). *Limits to citizen participation: The decline of community organizations*. Beverly Hills, CA: Sage.

Gittell, M. (Ed.). (1998). *Strategies for school equity: Creating productive schools in a just society*. New Haven, CT: Yale University Press.

Gittell, M., & McKenna, L. (1998). The ends and the means of education. In M. Gittell (Ed.), *Strategies for school equity: Creating productive schools in a just society* (pp. 1–7). New Haven, CT: Yale University Press.

Guinier, L., & Torres, G. (2002). *The miner's canary*. Cambridge, MA: Harvard University Press.

Herszenhorn, D. (2001, August 19). Rich states, poor cities and mighty suburbs. *New York Times*, p. 39.

Heubert, J., Trent, W., Beatty, A., & Neisser, U. (2001). *Understanding dropouts: Statistics, strategies, and high-stakes testing*. Washington, DC: National Academy Press.

Hochschild, J. (1985). *Thirty years after Brown*. Washington, DC: Joint Center for Policy Studies.

Huge drop in Blacks, Latinos, admitted to U. Cal. (1998, June 5). *Examiner*. Retrieved from www.fairtest.org.

Hunter, M. A. (1999). All eyes forward: Public engagement and educational reform in Kentucky. *Journal of Education Finance, 28*, 485.

Immergluck, D. (1998). Progress confined: Increases in black home buying and the persistence of residential segregation. *Journal of Urban Affairs, 20*(4), 443–458.

Jargowsky, P. A. (1993). *Ghetto poverty among blacks in the 1980s*. Unpublished paper. Reported in *U.S. News and World Report* January 18, 1993.

Katzelson, I., & Weir, M. (1985). *Schooling for all: Class, race, and the decline of the democratic ideal*. New York: Basic Books.

Lewis Mumford Center. (2001a). *The new ethnic enclaves in America's suburbs*. Retrieved February 12, 2001 from http://mumford1.dyndns.org/cen2000/suburban/SuburbanReport/page1.html.

Lewis Mumford Center. (2001b). *The new ethnic enclaves in America's suburbs.* Retrieved February 12, 2001 from http://mumford1.dyndns.org/cen2000/suburban/ SuburbanReport/page2.html

Massey, D., & Denton, N. (1993). *American apartheid: Segregation and the making of the underclass.* Cambridge, MA: Harvard University Press.

Massey, D. S., & Eggers, M. L. (1990). The ecology of inequality: Minorities and the concentration of poverty, 1970–1980. *American Journal of Sociology, 95*(5), 1153–1188.

New York State Education Department. (2000, July). *Statistical profiles of public school districts.* Albany, NY: Author.

O'Connor, A. (2000). Poverty research and policy for the post welfare era. *Annual Review of Sociology, 26,* 547–562.

Oliver, J. E. (1997, August). *Civic involvement in suburbia: The effects of metropolitan economic segregation on participation in local civic affairs.* Paper prepared for delivery at the annual meeting of the American Political Science Association, Washington, DC.

Oliver, J. E. (2001). *Democracy in suburbia.* Princeton, NJ: Princeton University Press.

Orfield, G., & Eaton, S. E. (1996). *Dismantling desegregation: The quiet reversal of Brown v. Board of Education.* New York: New Press.

Orfield, M. (1997). *Metropolitics: A regional agenda for community and stability.* Washington, DC: Brookings Institution Press.

Orr, M. (1999). *Black social capital: The politics of school reform in Baltimore, 1986— 1998.* Lawrence: University Press of Kansas.

Portner, J. (1996, November 20). Deal gives state new role in Baltimore schools, boosts aid. *Education Week.*

Quality counts: A supplement to *Education Week.* (1997).

Quality counts '98: A supplement to *Education Week.* (1998).

Quality counts '99: A supplement to *Education Week.* (1999).

Quality counts 2000: A supplement to *Education Week.* (2000).

Quality counts 2001: A supplement to *Education Week.* (2001).

Quality counts 2002: A supplement to *Education Week.* (2002).

Rusk, D. (1995). *Cities without suburbs* (2nd ed.). Baltimore, MD: Johns Hopkins University Press.

Shore, A., Pedulla, J., & Clarke, M. (2001). *The building blocks of state testing programs.* Boston, MA: National board of Education Testing and Public Policy. Available: http://www.bc.edu/research/nbetpp/statements/V2NY.pdf.

The State of Inequality. (1991). Princeton, NJ: ETS Policy Information Center.

Stonehill, R., & Anderson, J. I. (1982). *An evaluation of ESEA Title I—Program Operation and Educational Effects: A report to Congress.* Washington, DC: U.S. Department of Education.

Thompson, J. (1995, February 2). Reform ordered at three schools in Baltimore. *Baltimore Sun,* p. 1A.

U.S. Department of Education, National Center for Education Statistics. (2001). *Statistics of state school systems; revenues and expenditures for public elementary and secondary education; and common core of data surveys.* Retrieved from http://www.nces.ed.gov/pubs2002/digest2001/tables/dt157.asp.

U.S. Department of Housing and Urban Development. (1997). *State of the cities*. Washington, DC: Author.

Werner, J. R. (2002, Winter). No knight in shining armor: Why courts alone, absent public engagement, could not achieve successful public school finance reform in West Virginia. *Columbia Journal of Law and Social Problems, 35*(2), 61–82.

Wood, R. H. (1959). *Suburbia: Its people and their politics*. Boston: Houghton Mifflin.

Zehr, M. A. (1999, September 29). Texas exit exam under challenge in federal court. *Education Week*, p. 5.

Zorzi, W. F., Jr. (1996, May 31). Special session sought by GOP. *Baltimore Sun*, p. 1B.

How Equity-Minded Policies Have Fared in the Era of "Excellence"

The authors of the chapters included in Part II have studied current aspects of educational policies that were put in place following the 1954 Supreme Court decision that mandated the desegregation of public schools and greater access to higher education. These analyses are particularly pertinent as the nation celebrates the 50th anniversary of *Brown*. In Chapter 3, Roslyn Mickelson presents data from her study of public schools in Charlotte, North Carolina, and analyzes the persistent barriers to achieving truly desegregated schools in that city. Her data show that even though school buildings may have achieved desegregation goals, school classrooms are still segregated through curriculum tracking that separates children by some measure of "ability." She found that White and middle-class families were more success-ful in ensuring that their children were placed in upper tracks that typically had the most experienced, credentialed teachers. However, data show that Black pupils benefit from being in desegregated classrooms. They are shown to have higher achievement levels than Black children in segregated class-room settings. Mickelson concludes that the intentions of educational policy need to be explicit not only in their design, but also in their implementation. School-based practices, such as tracking, can subvert the best-crafted policies.

Chapter 4 continues the theme of ability grouping in the classroom as a form of "second-generation" discrimination. In their study of three communities that turned to litigation within the federal court system, Kevin Welner and Jeannie Oakes found that legal decisions can provide the supportive context for "de-tracking." However, these top-down mandates need to occur in conjunction with bottom-up reforms in order for educa-tional improvement to occur and be sustained. Their conclusions, like Marilyn Gittell's in Chapter 2, point to the need for informed citizens and change agents to help frame and implement policy mandates.

In terms of the access of students of color to higher education, Marguerite Clarke, George Madaus, and Arnold Shore summarize in Chapter 5 two of their studies on the impact of testing on equity in college admissions. In their first study, a mathematical simulation using a database of students in California, they conclude that the large score differences on college admissions tests between students of different racial and ethnic backgrounds greatly reduce the probability that African American and Latino students will be admitted to college. The conclusions of that simulation hold when compared with actual admissions data for the University of California system, showing dramatic consequences for the racial composition of the student body in the aftermath of the repeal of affirmative action in California. Clarke, Madaus, and Shore's second study explores the factors that those responsible for making admissions decisions weigh in selecting new students for their universities. The information presents an intriguing look at the ways admissions officers use the tools at their disposal to encourage minority students to apply and to balance their sometimes lower test scores with other kinds of information. The authors find that many admissions officers consider a diverse student body to be a goal for their institutions and attempt to pursue that goal even with the constraints of policies opposing affirmative action. The Supreme Court's 2003 decision on the University of Michigan law school reiterated the importance of this type of holistic analysis of student qualifications in the admissions process.

Still, Clarke, Madaus, and Shore note that disparities in education in terms of resources, teacher qualifications, and levels of student academic achievement build on themselves over time and add up to large consequential effects over the course of a student's educational career. One such resource difference is the availability of advanced placement courses in high school. The existence of AP courses reflects the presence of a college-bound track within high schools.

In Chapter 6, Maya Federman and Harry Pachón analyze the distribution of AP courses in all California high schools. They find that the number of AP courses offered relates to the economic status of the student body in the high school, with proportionately fewer courses in the poorer, high-minority schools. Since California's Proposition 209 outlawed affirmative action in college admissions, successfully completing AP courses was seen to enhance the college admissions prospects of minority students. This is why the American Civil Liberties Union brought a class-action lawsuit charging a California school district with denying Black and Latino high school students an adequate education and an opportunity to compete for college admissions.

3

How Tracking Undermines Race Equity in Desegregated Schools

ROSLYN ARLIN MICKELSON

Beginning with the Supreme Court's declaration in *Brown* v. *Board of Education* (1954) that public schools separated by race are inherently unequal, school desegregation has played a central role in efforts to provide the equality of educational opportunity that is essential to the American dream. The rationale for school desegregation rests largely on claims that it improves minority students' access to the higher-quality education more often provided to Whites. For this reason, desegregation has been expected to improve both minorities' educational outcomes as well as their longer-term life chances. Consequently, since 1954, desegregation has been considered an essential tool in the struggle for race equity in education.

This chapter advances our understanding of the persistent barriers to equality of educational opportunity by presenting findings from a detailed case study of the relationship of school segregation and tracking to race equity in the Charlotte–Mecklenburg Schools (CMS)—a district that, prior to the end of its federal court order in 2002, was considered to be one of the nation's most successfully desegregated school systems. In this chapter I raise questions about the extent to which CMS actually deserved that reputation. I demonstrate that curriculum tracking resegregated students within the district's high school classrooms, thereby subverting much of the potential academic gains from school desegregation at the school level. At the same time, this chapter compares achievement outcomes of students who attended segregated and desegregated schools, and demonstrates that racially diverse learning environments are clearly better than segregated ones. In other words, this chapter offers empirical support for the use of desegregation at both the school and classroom levels to close the racial gap and provide more equal educational opportunities.

Too few studies have actually examined the impact of second-generation resegregation issues (namely, tracking) on the remedies designed to address first-generation segregation between schools (the kind of segregation outlawed by *Brown*). At the same time, this chapter shows that simply "balancing" school-level enrollments by race will not accomplish true integration or provide equal access to the quality education we, as a nation, have pledged to provide to every child.

For the past decade or so, critics of school desegregation have defined it, for the most part, as a "failed social experiment." Other observers consider desegregation an underrated success. The study presented here pushes us to consider both evaluations of desegregation. The chapter, using CMS as a case study, raises the issue of the extent to which racial integration ever was genuinely implemented, even in school systems considered to be desegregated. At the same time, it shows that those CMS students who experienced desegregated schooling benefited from this equity-minded reform. This chapter, then, speaks to several issues central to the history of school desegregation and how it should be understood and interpreted.

WHY RACE EQUITY IN EDUCATION REQUIRES DESEGREGATED SCHOOLS *AND* CLASSROOMS

The relationship between school desegregation and classroom tracking often is discussed in terms of first- and second-generation segregation. First-generation segregation generally refers to the racial segregation among schools in the same district, and it has been the focus of national desegregation efforts since *Brown*. Second-generation segregation refers to the relationship between race and the allocation of educational opportunities within schools, typically brought about through curricular tracking of core academic classes in English, math, social studies, and science. Black and Latino students are far more likely to be in the low-track classes where their opportunities to learn are limited relative to high-track classes.

Any serious discussion of desegregation must include the topic of tracking. In theory, tracking is designed to enhance teaching and learning through targeting instruction and course content to the student's ability and prior knowledge. However, there is no consistent evidence that, as implemented, tracking is the best form of classroom organization for maximizing opportunities to learn for the majority of students. On the contrary, ample evidence suggests that tracking hinders mid- and low-ability students' opportunities to learn, while there is a growing body of evidence that diverse learning environments maximize opportunities to learn for all students (see Chapter 4, this volume). Moreover, as I noted above, track placements are strongly correlated with students' race/ethnicity and social class. In racially diverse schools White students typically are disproportionately found in the top tracks, while children of color are disproportionately found in the lower ones. In this way, tracking limits Blacks' access to higher-quality education. The federal courts recognized that tracking has the ability to undermine the potential benefits of policies, such as busing, designed to eliminate racial segregation among schools (*Hobson* v. *Hansen*, 1967).

The fact that tracking can subvert potential gains from desegregation is very important for understanding the relationship between school desegregation policy and racial equity in education. There is considerable unambiguous evidence that desegregation positively affects minority students' long-term outcomes such as educational and occupational attainment (see Wells & Crain, 1994, for a review). Yet the evidence with respect to desegregation's effects on short-term educational outcomes like achievement is more ambiguous and contested (see Crain & Mahard, 1972). Design flaws in desegregation programs, their implementation, and many of the studies that evaluate them contribute to this ambiguity (see Crain & Mahard, 1983). Another reason for the ambiguity is that much prior school desegregation research did not examine the ways in which segregated academic programs or tracks *within* desegregated schools affect race equity in academic outcomes.

The complicated relationships among race equity in education, desegregation, and tracking lie at the heart of this chapter in which I investigate their effects on the academic outcomes of students in the Charlotte–Mecklenburg Schools. CMS is an especially interesting district in which to study the effects of desegregation on the academic outcomes of students because of its pivotal role in school desegregation history. CMS's historical significance rests on its use of mandatory busing to desegregate its schools. This practice was upheld by the U.S. Supreme Court in its 1971 decision, *Swann* v. *Charlotte–Mecklenburg Schools*. Since the mid-1970s, CMS has been considered one of the nation's premier desegregated school systems. For many years, CMS served as a model for other school systems of how to provide seemingly equitable, high-quality, desegregated public education using busing and other tools (Douglas, 1995).

As of Spring 2002, however, the Charlotte–Mecklenberg Schools were no longer under federal court orders to desegregate. In 2001, the 4th Circuit Court of Appeals declared the district "unitary," or legally desegregated, and in 2002 the U.S. Supreme Court refused to hear the case, thereby leaving the Appeals Court's ruling in place. In Fall 2002, CMS began a student assignment policy based on neighborhood schools and parental choice. As a consequence of the new student assignment plan, levels of desegregation have decreased markedly since I collected the data for this study (see Mickelson, 2003; Walsh, 2002).

The return to a neighborhood school-based assignment plan makes this chapter highly relevant because it provides an assessment of the significance of the district's 3-decade-old effort to desegregate its schools. Indeed, what this chapter reveals is that despite CMS's laudable attempts to racially balance enrollment in its schools, the race gap in achievement persisted (Smith & Mickelson, 2000). A central component of that gap is racially correlated curricular tracking. In 1997, when the survey data used in this study were collected, anyone familiar with the historical relationship between tracking and race who observed a math, science, social studies, or English classroom in any of CMS's regular high schools or middle schools could accurately guess the academic level of the course simply by observing the racial composition of the students in it. Other key findings are:

- On a positive note, those Black (and White) students who experience desegregated education achieve more, have higher test scores, and hold higher future aspirations than their counterparts who experience segregated schooling.
- Yet 30 years after *Swann*, even though CMS was under a court order to eliminate all segregation from 1971 through 2002, both first- and second-generation segregation continued in the Charlotte–Mecklenburg Schools.
- Both forms of segregation harm academic achievement.
- The more time Black (and White) students spend in segregated Black elementary schools (first-generation segregation), the lower their high school track placements, grades, test scores, and future aspirations are compared with their comparably able peers who are educated in desegregated learning environments.
- Track placement (second-generation segregation) is influenced by a student's race as well as by degree of exposure to segregated Black elementary education. Black students are more likely to be in lower tracks than White students with comparable prior achievement, family background, and other individual characteristics, including self-reported effort.
- Track placement, in turn, has an extremely powerful effect on high school grades and scores on standardized tests, including the SAT.
- Resource differences between racially segregated and desegregated learning environments suggest some reasons why separate is not equal.

- The pattern of continuous segregation in spite of the 1971 Supreme Court *Swann* decision ordering the district to desegregate is important because CMS is considered by many to be one of the nation's most successfully integrated school systems. Thus, Charlotte's failure to *implement* desegregation and to provide equitable education for all children is reflective of our nation's inability to seriously address the roots of the race gap in academic achievement.

Using the Charlotte–Mecklenburg Schools as a case study, this chapter shows why racially segregated schooling is inimical to race equity in education. It demonstrates how the full desegregation mandated by the *Swann* decision was subverted by the continued existence of school segregation and the pervasive resegregation of secondary students into racially identifiable tracked math, science, English, and social studies classes.

Because of the persistence of the race gap in academic achievement, and the many questions raised about the efficacy of desegregation to improve the academic outcomes of Black students, the findings from Charlotte offer important insights for understanding why so many desegregation programs seem to offer minority students such limited redress from the inequality in educational opportunities mandated by *Brown*. At the same time, the chapter also demonstrates why desegregation is an essential element of educational equity: The more that CMS students—both Black and White—were exposed to truly desegregated education, the better were their academic outcomes. Before turning to the presentation of the study's design, research questions, and findings, readers may find some historical background a useful context for the rest of the chapter.

A BRIEF HISTORY OF DESEGREGATION IN CMS

Charlotte, North Carolina, is the second largest financial center in the nation. Its burgeoning financial sector has driven Mecklenburg County's rapid growth and development since the mid-1980s. The countywide Charlotte–Mecklenburg School District, with 110,000 students in 140 schools, is the 27th largest in the nation. As is true of many other southern school systems, CMS is struggling to transform itself in order to meet the needs of students destined for an economy built on the high-tech, information-age jobs that are replacing the area's traditional textile manufacturing, poultry processing, and agricultural jobs.

In 2004, the CMS population was 43% Black, 43% White, and about 14% Latino, Asian, and American Indian (www.cms.k12.nc.us/inside/general/index.htm). At the time of the original *Swann* order in the late

1960s, only a handful of CMS students were neither White nor Black. For this reason, the federal district court orders in *Swann* categorized children as either Black or White/other (collapsing Whites, Asians, Latinos, American Indians, and students from other ethnic backgrounds into a single category of White/other). Currently, CMS categorizes students as White, Black, Latino, Asian, American Indian, mixed race, and other.

From roughly 1974 to 1992, CMS used mandatory busing to racially balance its schools. CMS aimed to have all schools approximate the racial composition of the school system. The plan relied heavily on a system of paired elementary schools. Desegregation of secondary schools was accomplished by designing attendance zones that drew from Black and White neighborhoods. Under this system, almost all students were bused to schools outside their neighborhoods for at least some portion of their educational careers. Blacks typically rode the buses for more years and for greater distances than did Whites. Importantly, though, as a result of the mandatory busing, the majority of students in CMS attended a racially desegregated school during some portion of their academic careers.

In the early 1990s, much of the mandatory plan was replaced by other desegregation strategies, most notably a program of controlled choice among magnet schools. This policy shift came about largely as a result of pressure both from business elites, which complained that the existence of the desegregation plan hindered the recruitment of new families to the city and thus economic development, and from newly relocated middle-class White parents who were dissatisfied with the race and class integration of the schools in Mecklenburg County (Mickelson & Ray, 1994; Mickelson & Smith, 1999).

Ironically, however, the use of racial guidelines for magnet school admissions eventually was challenged by White parents who brought the suit to declare the district unitary—meaning it no longer operated a dual system with officially sanctioned separate schools for Blacks and Whites—and to end the use of race-conscious policies of any kind. This lawsuit led to a reactivation of the entire *Swann* case.[1] In September 1999, the federal judge hearing the case declared the district unitary. He enjoined the school system from using race in any of its official actions, and awarded to the White plaintiffs monetary compensation for damages to their constitutional rights suffered under the school system's use of a race-conscious magnet lottery. The damage award to the White plaintiffs was remarkable for several reasons, not the least of which was that no Black plaintiff had ever been awarded compensatory damages in any previous desegregation victory in the United States.

In November 2000, a three-judge panel of the 4th Circuit Court of Appeals overturned the lower court's decision declaring Charlotte–

Mecklenburg Schools as unitary. The White plaintiffs appealed, and almost a year later, the full 4th Circuit Court of Appeals, sitting *en banc*, reversed the three-judge panel, reinstating the lower court's unitary decision. In December 2001, the Black plaintiffs appealed the reinstatement to the U.S. Supreme Court, which denied certiorari, meaning it refused to hear the case, in April 2002. This left the district little choice but to dismantle many components of its school desegregation policy.[2] In fact, even before the U.S. Supreme Court decision, CMS had approved a neighborhood school-based pupil assignment plan for the 2002–03 school year.

PREVIOUS RESEARCH ON DESEGREGATION AND TRACKING

This chapter's findings illuminate an important set of relationships in educational policy research and practice: how tracking and desegregation contribute to racial differences in academic achievement.

Does Desegregation Have a Positive Effect on School Outcomes?

Since the 1966 Coleman report described how Blacks who attended desegregated schools had better academic outcomes than those who attended segregated ones, social scientists, civil rights advocates, and ordinary citizens have studied and debated the social and academic consequences of school desegregation. These findings can be summarized as follows:

1. Desegregation has a positive effect on minority students' long-term outcomes such as educational and occupational attainment and racial attitudes (Wells & Crain, 1994, 1997).
2. Overall, the short-term effects of desegregation are positive (Bankston & Caldas, 1996; Hallinan, 1998; Hochschild, 1984; National Association for the Advancement of Colored People, 1991; Orfield & Eaton, 1996; Wells & Crain, 1994, 1997). Researchers conclude that when schools employ practices to enhance equality of opportunity (including the elimination of tracking and ability grouping), desegregation has clear, albeit modest, academic benefits for Black students and does no harm to Whites. But attending a desegregated school that does little to equalize educational opportunity in the classroom brings few benefits to minority students.
3. Recent empirical research offers further evidence that there are positive academic outcomes from desegregated schooling. Using large, nationally representative samples, Brown (1999) found that

average levels of academic achievement for minorities and Whites are higher in integrated schools. She reported the ideal racial mix is between 61% and 90% White or Asian American and between 10% and 39% Black and Hispanic. Schools with this racial mix have the highest average academic achievement for all race groups and the smallest gap between the races in test scores.

4. Similarly, Schiff, Firestone, and Young (1999) found that after controlling for family background, both Black and White students who attended racially desegregated schools with majority White enrollment had higher NAEP reading and math scores than students who attended either segregated Wwhite or segregated Black schools.

5. Using the entire state of Louisiana as a sample, Bankston and Caldas (1996) examined the influence of the racial composition of a school on individual achievement. They found that minority concentration in a school has a powerful negative effect on achievement of Blacks and Whites, even after they controlled for family, individual, and school-level factors that influence educational outcomes.

Research on Tracking

Because most secondary students learn in tracked classrooms, it is also important to consider the effects of tracking on academic outcomes when assessing the effects of desegregation on race equity in educational outcomes. The weight of scholarly evidence suggests that the practice of tracking assigns minority students disproportionately to lower tracks and excludes them from accelerated ones; it offers them inferior opportunities to learn.

Tracking affects both academic and social dimensions of students' lives. Assignment to different tracks results in students receiving quite different content and instruction, and exposure to academically successful peers. Summarizing the empirical literature from several decades, Oakes, Muir, and Joseph (2000) report that students in high-track classes generally have more challenging instruction than do those in low-ability classes. They conclude that the rudimentary curriculum content in low-track classes frequently locks students into low-track levels because they are not exposed to the prerequisite knowledge required for transfer to higher levels. Other studies show that less effective teachers typically are assigned to lower-track classes (Finley, 1984; Ingersoll, 1999). In this way, tracking tends to reinforce the learning problems of socially and educationally disadvantaged students by providing them with less effective instructors who teach the least rigorous curricula using the methods least likely to challenge them to learn.

Moreover, tracks socialize students to accept their position in the school's status hierarchy where the top tracks are the most valued, and they convey to students a designated path for their future occupations given the school's identification of their ostensible potential. Because tracks tend to be rather homogeneous with respect to race, ethnicity, and social class, students have limited exposure to individuals who differ from themselves on these important characteristics. For these reasons, academic achievement, as well as future occupational and educational aspirations, are shaped by track placement.

Given the differences in opportunities to learn described above, educational advantages cumulate for those in the top tracks relative to those in the bottom tracks. In this way, racially stratified tracks create a discriminatory cycle of restricted educational opportunities for minorities that leads to diminished school achievement, which, in turn, exacerbates racial and social class differences in school outcomes (Lucas, 1999; Mickelson, 1998; Oakes, 1990, 1994; Oakes et al., 2000).

Because of tracking's record of resegregating students even in a school district operating under court-mandated desegregation plans, a federal district court held in *Hobson* v. *Hansen* (1967) that the use of tracking to intentionally separate Black and White students is unconstitutional.

Questions for This Study

Given the nature of the problem outlined in the preceding paragraphs, the following questions guided this investigation of the effects of segregation on the academic outcomes and educational equity of CMS students:

- Did first-generation segregation exist in CMS in 1997?
- If it did, what are the effects of first-generation segregated education on academic outcomes?
- Does second-generation segregation exist in CMS?
- If it does, what are the effects of second-generation segregated education on academic outcomes?
- What are the effects of both types of segregation on educational equity?

A SURVEY OF HIGH SCHOOL STUDENTS

The research reported in this chapter is part of a 14-year-long case study of school reform in the Charlotte–Mecklenburg Schools. The results come from a survey of high school seniors I conducted in 1997. A random sample of about 50% of the 1997 graduating class answered questions about their family background, school experiences, attitudes toward education, and plans for the future. Their answers were combined with information provided by CMS on their grades, test scores, and educational histories. The Methodological Appendix offers a more detailed discussion of the methods I used to collect and analyze the survey data.

This study's design offers a number of advantages over previous research on the effects of desegregation. Most important, my measure of the effects of segregation is unique in the history of desegregation research. It is an individualized longitudinal measure of the effects of segregation (from kindergarten through grade 6) on each student's academic outcomes. In contrast, cross-sectional studies of the effects of segregation examine the relationship of attending a segregated school to student achievement at the time when the student's achievement was measured. Also, the study utilizes an entire school system rather than a selection of schools isolated from the context of their larger societal and educational environments. Finally, the fact that CMS was under a mandatory desegregation order means there is minimal selection bias in either schools or students.

LESSONS LEARNED

The findings can be grouped conveniently into five categories: (1) trends in first-generation segregation; (2) direct effects of first-generation segregation on academic outcomes; (3) indirect effects of first-generation segregation on outcomes; (4) effects of second-generation segregation on academic outcomes; and (5) why segregated schooling negatively affects academic outcomes and undermines educational equity and why desegregated education has positive effects.

First-Generation Segregation

Although first-generation segregation in CMS was never fully eliminated, during the early 1980s, the district came very close to fulfilling the court's order to eliminate the dual system. By the late 1980s, however, the number of racially identifiable schools began to grow so that by the 1998–99 school year, about one-fourth of schools were racially imbalanced, Black or White, at the building level (Armor, 1998; CMS, 1970–1999; Mickelson, 1998; Peterkin, 1998; Smith, 1998; Trent, 1998).

In the early1980s when CMS was approximately 38% Black, fewer than 5% of Black students attended schools whose Black enrollment exceeded court-mandated ceilings; in the mid- and late 1990s when CMS was ap-

proximately 40% Black, the corresponding figure attending racially imbalanced Black schools was approximately 27% (Smith, 1998). Ironically,
this increase in school segregation at the building level occurred while
Mecklenburg County became less residentially segregated than it was in
1971 (Lord, 1999).

Until 2001, CMS was a majority-White school district. Court desegregation guidelines defined a school as racially imbalanced if it had fewer
than 44% White students. Of the 1997 CMS seniors who participated in this
study, 15% of Whites and 37% of Blacks had had some experience in segregated or racially imbalanced elementary schools that had Black student
enrollments higher than the balanced schools. (See the Methodological
Appendix for a discussion of how I calculated these students' experiences
in segregated and desegregated elementary schools.)

Direct Effects of School-Level Segregation. Attending a segregated Black
elementary school has direct negative effects on achievement and track
placement. Even after I hold constant a number of individual and family
background characteristics, the statistical analyses (multilevel regression)
indicate that the more time students—both Blacks and Whites—spend in
segregated Black elementary schools, the lower are their 6th-grade California Achievement Test (CAT) and 12th-grade End of Course (EOC)
scores. Segregated elementary school experiences also lower their high
school track placement. Given that CAT scores, the measure of prior
achievement I used, and high school track placement are the most powerful predictors of grades and high school test scores, elementary school
segregation's negative impact on students' academic trajectories is note-
worthy. These findings are summarized in Figure 3.1. The arrows from each
factor in the model to the next indicate the causal paths, and the positive
or negative signs above the path indicate the direction of the relationship.
For example, the arrow with a negative sign from segregated elementary
schooling to CAT scores indicates that the greater the proportion of a
person's elementary education that took place in segregated schools, the
lower were his or her CAT scores, controlling for the student's race, gender, family background, peer groups, attitudes toward education, effort,
and so on.[3] Similarly, the arrows with negative signs from segregated elementary education to high-track placement and grades, EOC, and SAT
scores indicate that as time in the former increases, values of the latter
decrease.

To be sure, the magnitude of the direct effects of elementary segregation on achievement is relatively small in comparison with the effects of
track placement and prior achievement, the two most powerful influences
on academic outcomes. What is relevant to our understanding of the effects

Figure 3.1. Schematic Model of the Effects of Segregation on Academic
          Outcomes

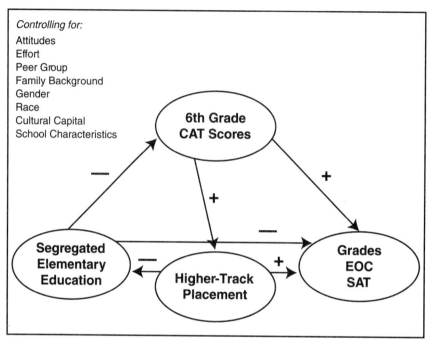

of segregation, though, is that even after controlling for student and family background factors, elementary segregation still has a significant direct negative effect on both Black and White students' North Carolina EOC scores, the influential high-stakes standardized measure of what they have learned in high school.

Indirect Effects of School-Level Segregation. In addition to the direct effects of segregated elementary education on test scores and track placement, it also has an indirect effect on academic outcomes. As noted earlier, CAT scores and track placement are the most powerful forces underlying EOC scores, high school grade point averages, and SAT scores. If one traces the pathways in Figure 3.1 from segregated elementary education to achievement outcomes, one must pass through track placement and CAT scores. This is the reason school-level segregation has an indirect negative effect on high school seniors' academic outcomes.

Taken together, the results presented in Figure 3.1 indicate the consistent pattern of direct and indirect negative effects of segregated Black elementary education on student achievement and track placement. Whether the measure of achievement is local (grade point average), state-wide (North Carolina EOC), or national (CAT and SAT scores), the greater the proportion of a 12th grader's elementary education that took place in a segregated Black school, the lower are his or her grades, test scores, and high school track placement compared with otherwise similar students whose elementary education took place in desegregated environments. These findings are true for both Black and White students alike, but because Blacks are more likely to have learned in a segregated environment, the results have a particular salience for Black students' opportunities for educational equity.

Tracking, or Second-Generation Segregation

Tracking, or grouping that resegregates students within desegregated schools, is known as second-generation segregation. My analysis of the racial composition of all math, science, English, and social studies courses taken by the entire 1997 student high school population reveals that, within CMS high schools, courses were tracked.[4] In all CMS high schools, not only are core academic classes tracked, but irrespective of the racial composition of the schools—even within schools considered to be racially balanced—tracking resegregates students such that the lowest tracks (special education) are largely Black and the highest tracks (advanced placement and international baccalaureate) are overwhelmingly White. Thus, a majority of CMS high school students learned social studies, math, science, and English in racially imbalanced classrooms. Figures 3.2–3.5 demonstrate the magnitude of second-generation segregation through tracking in all CMS high school core academic subjects. For example, controlling for each high school's racial composition, the analysis shows that in none of the core academic areas (math, science, social studies, and English) was a majority of classes racially balanced. The most racially balanced discipline was English, with 46% of classes racially balanced, and the least was social studies, with only 37% racially balanced.[5] Given that track placement is a powerful influence on high school grades, EOC scores, and SAT scores, the presence of racially imbalanced tracks is relevant to questions regarding the efficacy of school desegregation policies to enhance students' equality of educational opportunities.

One might argue that track assignments merely reflect technical decisions to allocate opportunities to learn commensurate with student merit, and that any correlations with student race are coincidental. But students' track assignments *are* related to their race. As the previously discussed regression analyses of track placement indicate, even after I held constant

Figure 3.2. Racial Balance, CMS High School Math Courses, 1996–97

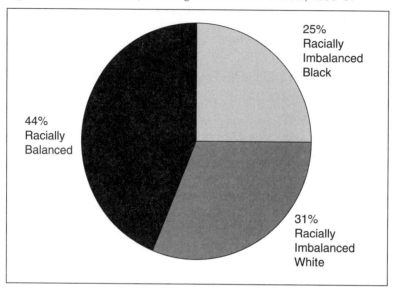

Figure 3.3. Racial Balance, CMS High School English Courses, 1996–97

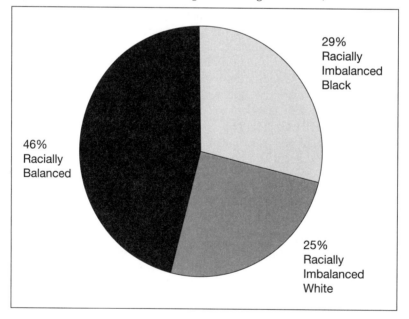

Figure 3.4. Racial Balance, CMS High School Science Courses, 1996–97

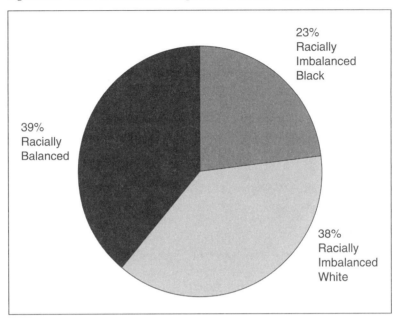

prior achievement, effort, and family background, among students with comparable 6th-grade California Achievement Test scores, Black students are disproportionately found in lower tracks while Whites are disproportionately found in higher tracks.

The relationship of a student's race to his or her likely track placement is also clear when I conducted a decile analysis comparing the 12th-grade English track placements of Blacks with those of academically similar Whites. For this comparison, I used CAT scores as a measure of prior achievement. I first divided students' 6th-grade CAT English battery scores into deciles. Next, I compared 12th-grade English track placements of Blacks and Whites whose 6th-grade CAT scores fell within the same decile range. If race does not affect track placement, Blacks and Whites within a given 6th-grade CAT score decile should have similar 12th-grade track placements. Yet I found that among students whose 6th-grade CAT English scores ranged from the 40th to 49th percentile, 56% of Whites compared with 74% of Blacks were placed in regular English. Among the best students—those with 6th-grade CAT scores between the 90th and 99th percentiles—52% of Whites but only 20% of Blacks were in advanced placement or international baccalaureate English.

Figure 3.5. Racial Balance, CMS High School Social Studies Courses, 1996–97

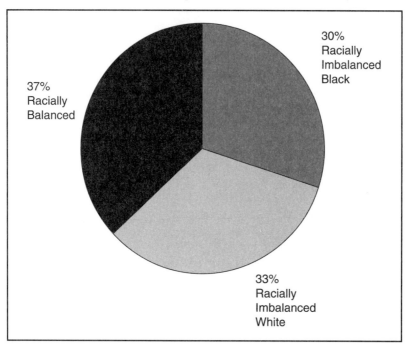

37%
Racially
Balanced

30%
Racially
Imbalanced
Black

33%
Racially
Imbalanced
White

The findings from the decile analysis, taken together with the regression analyses I described earlier, indicate that achievement or merit alone cannot explain track placement. They suggest that subjective judgments—influenced by students' ascribed characteristics of race, gender, and family background—affect track placements.[6]

Why Segregation Undermines Educational Equity

There are specific reasons why segregated Black elementary schools and racially correlated lower tracks offer students fewer opportunities to learn. In Charlotte, as is true across the nation, segregated Black learning environments offer fewer material and teacher resources compared with desegregated ones. Both racially identifiable tracks and segregated Black schools suffer from similar teacher resource inequities. For example, Table 3.1 presents the correlations between percentage of Black students and various characteristics associated with teacher quality. Table 3.1 shows that the higher the percentage of Blacks in a school, the lower the percentage of the

Table 3.1. Correlation Between Selected High School Characteristics and Percent African American in Student Population, Charlotte-Mecklenburg Schools, 1996–1998

Selected Characteristics of High Schools (N = 11)	*Correlation with % African American in Student Population*
% Gifted in Student Population	–.60
% Teachers with Full Licensure	–.72
% Teachers with MA Degree	–.43
% Students on Free/Reduced Lunch	.95
% ESL Students	.64

Source: Charlotte-Mecklenburg Schools, electronic data files, 1996–1998.

school's teachers who are fully credentialed, are experienced, and possess master's degrees (Mickelson, 1998; Peterkin, 1998; Smith, 1998; Trent, 1998).

Qualified, certified teachers are the most important resource available to children. Starkly different levels of material resources (up-to-date media centers, ample access to current technology, and newer buildings) are also related to the racial composition of a school, with fewer resources associated with higher percentages of Black students (Gardner, 1998; Peterkin, 1998). In 1997, segregated Black high schools also had fewer advanced placement offerings, and racially identifiable Black elementary schools at all levels had proportionately fewer services for gifted and talented students (Mickelson, 1998, Exhibit 1A-1H; Peterkin, 1998). As late as 1999, racially identifiable Black high schools had far fewer formal classes and informal SAT preparation opportunities (after school, weekend, or at a Stanley Kaplan review course) than did either desegregated or racially identifiable White high schools. The fewer the Blacks in a high school, the more opportunities, both formal and informal, there are for SAT preparation (Mickelson, 2003).

In addition to this, students in the highest tracks (academically gifted, advanced placement, international baccalaureate)—which are disproportionately White—are the most likely to have teachers who are credentialed and teaching in their field. Conversely, students in the lowest non-special education track (regular)—who are disproportionately Black—are much more likely to be taught by unlicensed, inexperienced instructors who are teaching out of their field. The consensus among the CMS high school principals who were interviewed about tracking, race, and opportunities to learn is that while students in the lower tracks may have fully licensed and experienced teachers with advanced degrees, those in the highest tracks always do (Mickelson, 1998–1999).

In CMS, then, access to the greatest number of opportunities to learn is strongly related to the racial composition of the elementary school a child attends and the level of the secondary track in which the student learns. For these reasons, and others I do not discuss here because of space considerations, it is not surprising that segregated Black educational settings offer fewer opportunities to learn, and that those who learn in these environments are less likely to succeed academically compared with peers educated in desegregated settings. The findings also suggest the importance of heeding Gittell's (Chapter 2, this volume) call for equity in resource allocation in public education.[7]

FURTHER CONSIDERATIONS

In this chapter, I report on the positive effects of school-level and classroom-level desegregation, and the negative effects of both forms of segregation on the academic achievement of students in the Charlotte–Mecklenburg Schools. Although CMS had been operating under a court-ordered desegregation plan since the early 1970s, both racially segregated schools (first-generation segregation) and racially segregated tracks (second-generation segregation) continued. Results of my survey of the graduating class of 1997 indicate that both forms of segregation have significant negative effects on Black and White students' academic outcomes. In this way, the district's practices and policies subverted *Swann*'s mandate to provide equitable opportunities to learn for all students.

The findings discussed in this chapter most likely underestimate the magnitude of the effects of segregation on academic outcomes because of the students not included in the sample and because of the conservative measure of desegregation employed in this study. There are three reasons for this underestimation. First, many of the students most likely to have experienced segregated Black elementary education are missing from the sample. They either never made it to 12th grade or were relegated to special education classes or special programs where they were not surveyed.

The second reason for the likely underestimation involves the conservative measure of segregated Black elementary education that I used in this study. Until very recently, the Charlotte–Mecklenburg Schools had very, very few Hispanic, Asian, and American Indian students. Consequently, in almost every CMS elementary school during the years the 1997 seniors attended them (1984–85 through 1990–91), the percentage of minority students was also the percentage of Black students. During this period, in only 12 elementary schools (of approximately 80), was the non-Black minority population greater (by 3–5%) than the Black student population. The proportion of time spent in a segregated *minority* school could have served as an indicator of segregated elementary education, but instead I employed the more conservative segregated *Black* school as my measure.[8]

The third reason my analysis underestimates the effects of segregation on achievement concerns those students who did not attend CMS elementary schools or who had high levels of mobility in and out of the schools. I dropped them from the sample, further biasing it in a conservative direction. The most mobile students are poor Blacks, and they are also the students most likely to attend segregated Black elementary schools.

CONCLUSION

For more than 50 years, communities across the United States have grappled with *Brown*'s mandate to provide equality of educational opportunities to Black children—to all children—by ending segregated schooling. Yet despite significant narrowing in the past quarter-century, the Black–White gap in achievement that existed in 1954 continues today. And today, even thoughtful observers question the efficacy of school desegregation for closing that gap. Other critics lament the social, educational, and political fallout from it. They point to a host of adverse consequences to the Black community, including job losses, removal of cultural integrity in the curriculum, and destruction of extended caring communities that were integral to the well-being of Black children and their education during Jim Crow (Anderson, 1988; Walker, 2000). Although it is important to acknowledge these losses, it is also important to avoid romanticizing segregated Black schools. To do otherwise is to substitute an idealized conception of segregated education for the brutal realities of grossly inferior opportunities to learn that characterized segregated Black schools in Charlotte and elsewhere (Anderson, 1988; Douglas, 1995; Gaillard, 1988; Kluger, 1977; Walker, 2000).

As I pointed out earlier, while there is considerable unambiguous evidence that desegregation positively affects students' long-term outcomes, such as enhancing educational and occupational attainment, the situation with respect to short-term educational outcomes has been more ambiguous and contested. Contributing to the ambiguity are design flaws in many desegregation programs, in their implementation, and in the studies that evaluate them. Based on my findings, I suggest that one reason for previous studies' ambiguous conclusions regarding the academic benefits of desegregated schooling is that the studies typically did not examine whether second-generation segregation undermines the benefits of first-generation desegregation. My research does precisely this, and I find that second-generation segregation, in the form of tracking, undermines or subverts much of the potential of first-generation desegregation to close the racial gap in equity in educational opportunities and outcomes.

This study's distinctive design addresses many of the shortcomings found in previous research on the effects of desegregation. The unique design includes a longitudinal measure of exposure to segregated Black elementary education, multiple indicators of educational outcomes, measures of track location, numerous control variables, and a large representative sample of 12th graders from an entire school system. The fact that even with this conservative methodology the study demonstrates both direct and indirect effects from segregated education, indicates, to paraphrase Cornel West, that with respect to educational equity—race matters. This chapter, then, moves us toward a greater understanding of the contributions of segregated schooling to maintaining the racial gap in academic achievement, by demonstrating how first- and second-generation segregation jointly affect academic outcomes for all students, and how—even in an ostensibly desegregated school system—Whites retain privileged access to greater opportunities to learn.

At the same time, the findings offer hope. The results of the analyses also show clearly that for all those students who experienced it, desegregated education had a positive effect on their academic outcomes. Effectively implemented desegregation, then, is a prime example of a successful equity-minded reform. This is an especially important finding with regard to Black students. Both the scholarly and popular literature is replete with claims that desegregation fails to improve the academic achievement of Black students. The findings presented in this chapter demonstrate otherwise. They show that Black students educated in desegregated learning environments do better than their comparable peers schooled in segregated ones. This is true even when holding constant school- and individual-level factors such as family background, individual effort, peer group influence, attitudes toward education and the future, and prior achievement—social forces that typically confound the effects of desegregation.

The findings also suggest the importance, once again, of attending to educational policy implementation issues. The policy of desegregation—no matter how well crafted and designed—is of little value if it is unevenly implemented and if it coexists with other initiatives, policies, and practices—like tracking—that counteract or subvert desegregation's intent.

analytic dilemmas. In the past, researchers had to choose between the individual, the classroom, or the school as a unit of analysis. Whichever was chosen meant a sacrifice in precision. I used multilevel modeling to estimate individual student outcomes as a function of school-level factors and student characteristics within the schools (Kreft & de Leeuw, 1998). For example, in the case of this study, individual students are nested within high schools. Multilevel analysis permits me to analyze the contribution the specific schools *and* the individual students' characteristics make to the outcome variables.

In order to model the between-school (school level) and within-school (individual level) components of the explained variance of the response variables, multilevel regressions with random intercepts were performed, using STATA, on all dependent variables. However, multilevel modeling allows for simultaneous analysis of multiple units of analysis.

The low value of rho, the intraclass correlation (ICC) that measures the proportion of the total variance in outcomes that is between schools, indicates negligible between-school effects on the outcomes. All six multilevel regressions reveal that less than 3% of the variance lies between schools (the ICCs range from .000 to .027). The results reported in this chapter are from the multilevel regressions. The analysis of students' track placement was a multilevel ordered multinomial logistic regression. I am grateful to Jan de Leeuw for his assistance with the multilevel analyses reported in this chapter.

The results of the OLS regressions for the same equations are almost identical to the multilevel regressions. The Adjusted R^2s for the equations are: 70.2%, GPA; 30.1%, EOC; 24.1%, CAT; 41.4%, college track; 58.7%, SAT Math; 65.8%, SAT Verbal; and 71.6%, Total SAT. Unstandardized coefficients and their standard errors for the multilevel regressions and the OLS results are available upon request.

Third, to explore whether Black and White students with comparable prior achievement in elementary school were enrolled in similar tracks in secondary school, I conducted a contingency table analysis of high school English track placement. To do this, I converted students' 6th-grade CAT Total Language Battery Achievement into normal curve equivalent deciles. Within each decile range, I compared the 12th-grade English track placements of Black and White students. This allowed me to see where academically comparable Black and White 6th graders ended up as high school seniors.

And fourth, in order to examine whether there is a relationship between the racial composition of schools and the quality of the teaching staff at given schools, I correlated the percentage of Black students with a variety of teacher indicators of experience, professionalism, and training.

NOTES

Acknowledgments. A more detailed version of this chapter's argument appears in a 2001 article of mine, which is adapted here with permission of the American Educational Research Association: "Subverting Swann: First- and Second-Generation Segregation in the Charlotte-Mecklenburg Schools," *American Educational Research Journal, 38*(2), 215–252 (Copyright © 2001 by the American Educational Research Association). In that article, readers will find a more complete description of the methods, data, analyses, and results, including tables presenting results of the statistical analyses. The research reported in this chapter is supported by grants from the National Science Foundation (RED-9550763) and the Ford Foundation (985–1336). I wish to thank George Farkas, Willis Hawley, Chandra Muller, Meredith Philips, Kathryn Schiller, Stephen S. Smith, Elizabeth Stearns, Richard Valencia, and Anne Velasco for their helpful comments on earlier drafts. Debbie Agata and Ita Kreft provided valuable technical assistance.

1. In 1999, CMS returned to court to defend against a new legal challenge to its desegregation plan. I served as an expert witness for the defendant, the Charlotte–Mecklenburg Schools. In 1997, White plaintiffs (*Capacchione et al.*) sued the Charlotte–Mecklenburg Schools seeking a declaration of unitary status, an end to mandatory desegregation, and an end to any race-conscious policies. Shortly thereafter, the original *Swann* plaintiffs, perceiving the lawsuit as a threat to the *Swann* ruling, intervened by reactivating their original case against CMS. Two young Black families with students in CMS joined the *Swann* plaintiffs as plaintiff-interveners. For this reason, the case also is known as *Belk et al.* The two lawsuits mirrored each other—the Whites requesting a declaration of unitary status and the Blacks requesting a thorough implementation of the original *Swann* order to desegregate; therefore, the judge consolidated the two cases (*Swann/Belk* and *Capacchione*) into one. Several months after filing the lawsuit, the Capacchione family moved from Charlotte, NC, to Torrance, CA. In order to sustain the lawsuit's viability, several other White families joined the lawsuit as plaintiff-interveners. The judge hearing the case, Robert Potter, was an activist against mandatory busing before President Reagan appointed him to the federal bench. He did not recuse himself from the case.

2. The three-judge panel of the Court of Appeals remanded the case back to Judge Potter, along with clear criteria for him to weigh the evidence and to apply relevant case law in his new deliberations. In a blistering opinion, the panel's majority carefully listed the multiple legal errors committed by Potter in reaching his decision. The opinion of the panel's majority held that Potter failed, among other errors, to correctly conduct a *Green* analysis necessary to determine whether a dual school system is unitary (*Belk et al.* v. *Charlotte–Mecklenburg Schools*, 1999). The White plaintiffs appealed the panel's decision to the full 4th Circuit Court (all 11 judges sitting *en banc*), known to be one of the nation's most conservative. In a split decision, a majority of the court ruled in September 2001 that CMS was, in fact, unitary, thereby ending the district's legal mandate to desegregate its schools. However, the full court upheld the three-judge panel's decision to overturn both

Potter's injunction against the use of race in any school policies and his award of damages to the White plaintiffs and of fees to their attorneys.

3. The effects of segregated Black elementary education on CAT scores are still important even though their level of significance is only slightly larger than that of conventional standards (p < .06). It is worth noting that the sample does not include a sizable portion of the CMS student population that is most likely to have had extended exposure to segregated Black elementary education—those who dropped out of school before reaching 12th grade and those who, as 12th graders, were enrolled in special education classes, special programs, and special high schools. Consequently, this regression model likely underestimates the effects of elementary segregation on CAT scores.

4. A CMS document showing the course name, track level, student count by race, period, and teacher name for every course offered in each of the 11 high schools provides the data for this analysis (CMS, 1996–1999).

5. I considered a high school classroom to be racially balanced if its percentage of Black students lay within plus or minus 15% of the specific school's percentage of Black enrollment. This standard reflects an extrapolation to the classroom of the standard used to determine whether a school was racially balanced. The 38-page table that presents this analysis is available from the author upon request. It appeared as Exhibit A1-H1 in my expert report in the *Capacchione* case (Mickelson, 1998).

6. Four years after I collected the survey data discussed in this chapter, CMS was still engaging in course selection and placement processes that resulted in comparably able Blacks and Whites being assigned to different tracks, with Blacks more likely than Whites to be in the lower ones. For example, in early Fall 2001, about 8,000 CMS middle school students, a majority of whom are Black, were found to be tracked into lower-level math classes even though many had passed or excelled on their previous year's End-of-Grade (EOG) math tests. In response to this pattern, during the early part of the fall semester the superintendent ordered the misplaced students to be moved into higher-level, reconstituted math classes. The superintendent said a number of decisions led to the misplacement of Blacks into lower-level math courses, including racial stereotyping. "I think people need to face that there are issues of bias and prejudice that play into this," he told the *Charlotte Observer* (Cenzipur, 2001, p. A7).

7. When the CMS school board adopted its 2002–03 neighborhood school-based Family Choice Pupil Assignment plan, thereby ending all efforts to racially balance CMS schools, board members were keenly aware of the likely resegregation of the schools and the concomitant problems that accompany concentrating poor, low-performing students in certain schools. To ensure that students attending newly segregated Black schools did not unduly suffer from educational inequities, the school board pledged to fund efforts to make all schools and programs equitable. This goal was abandoned less than 2 years after the launch of the Family Choice plan when the new Republican-dominated County Commission failed to carry out its promise of funding equity, and when the severe overcrowding of suburban schools resulted in the governing body revisiting its promise to use bond money to renovate Black schools in order to build White ones in the seriously understaffed distant suburbs.

8. Arguably from educational and sociological perspectives, the injurious effects stemming from segregated schooling operate similarly in schools where the minority population is entirely Black and where it is a combination of Blacks and a small percentage of other children of color. In fact, the results from regression analyses using the percentage of minority students (counting all Blacks, Latinos, and Asians) and the analyses using the percentage of Black students (as reported herein) are almost identical.

REFERENCES

Anderson, J. D. (1988). *The education of blacks in the south, 1860–1935*. Chapel Hill: University of North Carolina Press.

Armor, D. (1998). Expert report to the court in the case of *Capacchione et al.* v. *Charlotte–Mecklenburg Schools*.

Bankston, C., & Caldas C. (1996). Majority African American schools and social injustice: The influence of de facto segregation on academic achievement. *Social Forces, 75*, 535–552.

Belk et al. v. *Charlotte–Mecklenburg Schools 99–2389*. (1999).

Brown v. *Board of Education I, 347 U.S. 483* (1954).

Brown, S. (1999, August). *High school racial composition: Balancing excellence and equity*. Paper presented at the annual meeting of the American Sociological Association, Chicago.

Capacchione et al. v. *Charlotte–Mecklenburg Schools*. (1997).

Cenzipur, D. (2001, December 17). New standards hit minorities hard. *Charlotte Observer*, pp. A1, A7.

Charlotte–Mecklenburg Schools. (1970–1999). *Monthly reports*. Author.

Charlotte–Mecklenburg Schools. (1996–1999). *Class counts*. Author.

Coleman, J., et al. (1966). *Equality of educational opportunity*. Washington, DC: U.S. Government Printing Office.

Crain, R., & Mahard, R. E. (1972). *Desegregation plans that raise black achievement: A review of the research*. Santa Monica, CA: RAND.

Crain, R., & Mahard, R. E. (1983). The effects of research methodology in desegregation achievement studies: A meta-analysis. *American Journal of Sociology, 88*(5), 839–854.

Douglas, D. M. (1995). *Reading, writing, and race. The desegregation of the Charlotte schools*. Chapel Hill: University of North Carolina Press.

Finley, M. (1984). Teachers and tracking in a comprehensive high school. *Sociology of Education, 57*, 233–243.

Gaillard, F. (1988) *The dream long deferred*. Chapel Hill: University of North Carolina Press.

Gardner, D. (1998). Expert report to the court in the case of *Capacchione et al.* v. *Charlotte–Mecklenburg Schools*.

Hallinan, M. T. (1998). Diversity effects on student outcomes: Social science evidence. *Ohio State Law Journal, 59*, 733–754.

Hobson v. Hansen, 269 F. Supp. 401 (DC Cir. 1967).

Hochschild, J. L. (1984). *The new American dilemma: Liberal democracy and school desegregation*. New Haven, CT: Yale University Press.

Ingersoll, R. (1999). The problem of underqualified teachers in American secondary schools. *Educational Researcher, 28*, 26–37.

Kluger, R. (1977). *Simple justice*. New York: Random House.

Kreft, I., & de Leeuw, J. (1998). *Introducing multilevel modeling*. London: Sage.

Lord, D. (1999). Expert report to the court in the case of *Capacchione et al. v. Charlotte–Mecklenburg Schools*.

Lucas, S. R. (1999). *Tracking inequality*. New York: Teachers College Press.

Mickelson, R. (1989). Why does Jane read and write so well? The anomaly of women's achievement. *Sociology of Education, 62*, 43–67.

Mickelson, R. A. (1990). The attitude–achievement paradox among black adolescents. *Sociology of Education 63*(1), 44–61.

Mickelson, R. A. (1998). Expert report to the court in the case of *Capacchione et al. v. Charlotte–Mecklenburg Schools*.

Mickelson, R. A. (1998–1999). Interviews with CMS Principals. Palo Alto, CA.

Mickelson, R. A. (2001). Subverting *Swann*: First- and second-generation segregation in the Charlotte–Mecklenburg schools. *American Educational Research Journal, 38*, 215–252.

Mickelson, R. A. (2003). Achieving equality of educational opportunity in the wake of judicial retreat from race sensitive remedies: Lessons from North Carolina. *American University Law Review, 52*(6), 152–184.

Mickelson, R. A., & Ray, C. A. (1994). Fear of falling from grace: The middle class, downward mobility, and school desegregation. *Research in Sociology of Education and Socialization, 10*, 207–238.

Mickelson, R. & Smith, S. S. (1999, November). *Race, tracking, and achievement among African-Americans in a desegregated school system: Evidence from the Charlotte–Mecklenburg schools*. Paper prepared for the Stanford University Conference on Race, Stanford.

National Association for the Advancement of Colored People. (1991, June 21). School desegregation: A social science statement. In Amicus Curiae Brief of the NAACP et al., *Freeman v. Pitts*, U.S. Supreme Court on Writ of Certiorari to U.S. Court of Appeals for the Eleventh Circuit.

Oakes, J. (1990). *Multiplying inequalities: The effects of race, social class, and tracking on opportunities to learn mathematics and science*. Santa Monica, CA: Rand.

Oakes, J. (1994). More than misapplied technology: A normative and political response to Hallinan on tracking. *Sociology of Education, 67*, 84–88.

Oakes, J., Muir, K. & Joseph, R. (2000, May). *Course taking and achievement in math and science: Inequalities that endure and change*. Paper presented at the NISE Conference, Detroit.

Orfield, G., & Eaton, S. E. (1996). *Dismantling desegregation. The quiet reversal of Brown v. Board of Education*. New York: New Press.

Peterkin, R. (1998). Expert report to the court in the case of *Capacchione et al. v. Charlotte–Mecklenburg Schools*.

Schiff, J., Firestone, W., & Young, J. (1999, April). *Organizational context for student achievement: The case of student racial composition.* Paper presented at the annual meeting of the American Educational Research Association, Montreal.

Smith, S. S. (1998). Expert report to the court in the case of *Capacchione et al.* v. *Charlotte–Mecklenburg Schools.*

Smith, S. S. & Mickelson, R. A. (2000). All that glitters is not gold: The outcomes of educational restructuring in Charlotte, North Carolina. *Education Evaluation and Policy Analysis, 22,* 101–127.

Swann v. *Charlotte–Mecklenburg,* 402 U.S. 1,15 (1971).

Trent, W. (1998). Expert report to the court in the case of *Capacchione et al.* v. *Charlotte–Mecklenburg Schools.*

Walker, V. S. (2000). Valued segregated schools for African American children, 1935–1969. *Review of Educational Research, 70,* 253–286.

Walsh, M. (2002, April 24). High court closes historic desegregation case. *Education Week.* Available: http://www.edweek.com/

Wells, A. S., & Crain, R. L. (1994). Perpetuation theory and the long-term effects of school desegregation. *Review of Educational Research, 64*(4), 531–556.

Wells, A. S., & Crain, R. L. (1997). *Stepping over the color line.* New Haven, CT: Yale University Press.

4

Mandates Still Matter

Examining a Key Policy Tool for Promoting Successful Equity-Minded Reform

KEVIN G. WELNER
JEANNIE OAKES

Education reform is difficult. Huge challenges face those who attempt to change the practices, structure, or goals of America's schools. And, for those who attempt reforms designed to benefit low-income students of color, the obstacles multiply. We studied three American communities struggling with just such a reform—a difficult but meaningful equity-minded school reform. These communities are spread throughout the United States: San Jose, California; Rockford, Illinois; and East Pittsburgh, Pennsylvania. Notwithstanding their geographic differences, they shared similar histories and embarked on a common struggle to make the equitable treatment of students a reality within their schools. In particular, members of each of these communities turned to litigation within the federal court system to prompt the reduction or elimination of ability grouping in classrooms. They believed that the districts' tracking practices, intended to target curriculum and instruction to students of different designated levels of ability, had been used discriminatorily against African American and Latino students.

In this chapter, we use the term *tracking* rather than the term *ability grouping*. Most literature uses these two terms interchangeably, although some researchers and educators have drawn distinctions between the two terms, usually labeling as "tracked" those systems that place students at a given level across subject areas, and labeling as "ability grouped" those systems that group students class-by-class (see discussion in Slavin, 1993). In reality, both terms are misnomers, since some students "jump the tracks" of almost every tracking system and since placements in these systems are, at best, based on *perceived* ability (Welner, 2001a). More important, the day-to-day reality is virtually the same for the vast majority of students in schools approximating either definition. (For a more comprehensive definition of tracking, see Oakes, 1991.)

In each of the communities we studied, the plaintiffs alleged that the school districts used tracking as a form of second-generation discrimination in response to court-ordered school desegregation. That is, they contended that tracking subverted between-school desegregation by separating students within the school site.

Before turning to litigation as a policy tool, the change agents in these communities first considered and attempted other, more grassroots reform strategies. But these bottom-up attempts to bring about change starting at the local, grassroots level came up empty. The political and normative (meaning relating to values and beliefs) environment in and around these school districts was fundamentally inhospitable to the initiation of a de-tracking reform. Politically, detracking efforts generally must overcome local opposition and build supportive communities both within and outside the school. Normatively, tracking is grounded in widespread negative beliefs about human capacity and ethnic and class-based discrimination. In addition, tracking is supported by technical (or organizational) forces that interconnect it to schools' other practices (Oakes, 1992). In most places, such local barriers would draw the story to a close; however, the change agents in these three districts continued to fight for reform. They did so by moving their efforts to a forum where their political disadvantage would be a lesser impediment: the federal courts.

The resulting legal cases from these three communities carry with them lessons of great importance, and this chapter uses these lessons to support the contention that conventional, bottom-up or top-down approaches to school reform fall short when equity is the desired result. As the actors in these three communities have learned, enormous obstacles block the path to success for reforms aimed at benefiting those students who hold less powerful positions in schools and communities (generally speaking, African Americans, Latinos, and the poor). The courts do not really smooth this path, but they do provide a boost to educators committed to working on the local level to overcome obstacles to equity-minded changes in public schools. For those change agents with a strong commitment to equity-minded reforms such as detracking, these cases and their effect on local change agents hold great promise in otherwise bleak situations.

For the past 2 decades and into the present, top-down mandates, especially those emanating from the federal government, have been criticized for minimizing local control and working against grassroots, bottom-up initiatives for change. For example, federal Title I funding now is provided to states, and ultimately to schools, in block grants with the expectation that people at the school level know better how to use the federal money for poor students. No Child Left Behind, the latest reauthorization of the federal law that provides Title I funding, did not change this, although state and local decisions now must be made in a highly proscriptive context tied to outcome measurements—and the backlash against this centralized role clearly is growing (Hoff, 2004; Hooper, 2004).

Federal- and state-level education reformers also have placed great faith in charter schools, which, in theory at least, are envisioned, designed, and governed by community members. Overall, the call for greater decentralization and local control has, at least since the early 1980s, been louder and more powerful than calls for centralized measures to ensure more equal educational opportunities between districts, schools, and students.

We agree that reforms initiated from the bottom-up, with substantial local buy-in, are generally preferable to top-down initiated reforms, and some research shows the need for an involved constituency for reforms to commence and prosper. Meanwhile, our research also shows that some school and community contexts are overwhelmingly inhospitable to locally initiated change. In those settings, top-down mandates may be necessary to help change that context in order to open a policy window for equity-minded reform. But this is not an argument for top-down mandates *as opposed to* bottom-up change. In fact, we reject such a dichotomy. Instead, we contend, based on the three communities we studied, that top-down mandates alone are unlikely to bring about equity-minded reforms. Rather, such mandates must be accompanied by bottom-up reforms grounded in the logic and strategies employed in social and political movements. This combined effort is more likely to expose, challenge, and, if successful, disrupt the prevailing norms of schooling inequality that frustrate equity-focused reforms that are exclusively bottom-up or top-down, but not both. Therefore, we conclude, as detailed below, that successful equity-minded reform generally must combine top-down and bottom-up reform strategies.[1]

In what follows, we argue that equity-minded change requires a fundamental reworking of the theory and practice of both top-down and bottom-up reform, and we offer some concrete suggestions toward this end. In particular, we urge those embarking on such controversial reforms to be aware of, and to respond to, the powerful normative and political obstacles that they will likely encounter as they move forward with the initiation and implementation of their change ideas. As discussed below, we view equity-minded, top-down pressure as an important ally in this struggle. We also encourage practices that develop, among teachers in particular, normative beliefs consistent with the reform's principles. And we emphasize the need for political mobilization.

THE THREE CASES: WHERE COURT ORDERS
MEET LOCAL INITIATIVE AND RESISTANCE

San Jose, Rockford, and East Pittsburgh are all mid-sized urban/suburban communities with fairly stable school district populations and court-ordered school desegregation plans. Unlike bigger cities, where White and middle-class flight has made school desegregation so difficult, these communities have racially mixed schools with sizable middle-class enrollments. Our access to these communities, schools, and data collected for the courts allowed us to conduct in-depth, cross-case analyses of the districts as they struggled with issues of racial equity and school reform. The East Pittsburgh community of Woodland Hills, in particular, provided an opportunity to collect extensive data in the form of interviews, observations, and school district statistics concerning the detracking reform that followed from the court order.[2]

We learned of each of these communities when Oakes was asked (depending on the case, by either the plaintiffs or a combination of interested parties) to analyze tracking and detracking issues regarding racial segregation. The school district in each community was placed under a court order requiring "detracking" and the creation of racially balanced classrooms.[3]

The schools in Woodland Hills, Rockford, and San Jose all changed as a result of their court orders. And they changed to the general advantage of the districts' African American and Latino students. Undoubtedly, they could have changed more, and the changes could have resulted in greater benefits for these minority students. But the federal court orders and other supportive forces, such as reform-minded teachers, administrators, and community members, did not exist in isolation. Instead, these pro-reform forces existed along with a wide variety of additional forces, many of which pushed against the reform. These combined forces—bottom-up and top-down—resulted in a reform environment far more favorable to the detracking effort than it would have been in the absence of the court order. Still, the environment was far from ideal and changes were hard-won.

This nuanced conclusion should not obscure the fact that dedicated people in these districts spent years struggling to improve and as a result of their efforts, aided by the court mandates, schools became better places for low-income students and students of color. Furthermore, as we will demonstrate, the effects of these changes for White and more-affluent students in these three districts largely depended on how their teachers reacted to the equity-minded mandates. Below, we discuss how these themes evolved in each of the three districts we studied.

Woodland Hills

Prior to the detracking court order in Woodland Hills, this district's classes were extensively tracked, and these tracks racially segregated children within schools. But the court order prompted important changes. The district hired a new, reform-minded superintendent who was charged by the school board to implement the equity-minded changes that the court demanded. This superintendent and other school leaders instituted considerable detracking, particularly in the district's English courses, thereby enhancing the educational opportunities of students who for years had been disadvantaged by district policies.

For Woodland Hills's more advantaged students, those formerly enrolled in the higher-tracked classes, detracking brought mixed blessings. On the one hand, some teachers responded to the challenge presented by heterogeneous grouping and reformed their instructional methods. All students in these classrooms saw greater use of authentic instruction and assessment and more lessons designed to develop higher-order thinking. On the other hand, some teachers made insufficient changes, or none at all, to adapt to the new classes. Notwithstanding quantitative analyses indicating that detracking did not present an overall disadvantage to the formerly high-track students (Welner, 2001a), those students placed in detracked classrooms with less-skilled or resistant teachers probably experienced some of the poor teaching previously confined to the low-track environment. Interestingly, only one opponent of detracking acknowledged that these unsuccessful teachers also had no success under the former, tracked system.[4] This opponent, a White parent, described these teachers as "set in a rut, back in whatever year they started; they use the same dittos that they used then."

Detracking, however, exposed these weaknesses in two ways. First, while such teachers had never taught much in the way of higher-order thinking skills, they did pace their drill and memorization lessons at a rate they believed to be suitable for the tracked student body. The switch to heterogeneous classes pulled that comfortable rug out from under them, leaving them pondering whether to "teach to the top" or water down the lessons to the "middle" or the "bottom."

Second, and more important, detracking exposed more privileged students to these weaker teachers. Before detracking, such teachers taught primarily the low tracks—a system that was effectively enforced by powerful parents. A secondary school principal noted that wealthy White parents knew the identity of the good teachers and "scream[ed]" if the school placed their children with the weaker teachers. This principal noted that the most knowledgeable parents, who are also the wealthiest, "will get the better teachers." Yet the district will "allow those [weaker] teachers to stay there and let the kids [with parents who are less politically savvy] fall where they may. It is unfair."

Another principal contended that this disparity arises because the "general kids" and their parents demand much less of their teachers.

> They don't go home and tell their parents, "Yeah, all we did today was a worksheet. Yep. All we did today, again, was a worksheet." They're thrilled to do that. Their parents are thrilled that they're not in trouble. Their parents are thrilled that someone's keeping them there for 40 minutes. I don't mean to be smart. I'm just telling you that's the way it is. If your child was in the college prep or academic, you would say to the child, "What did you do today?" Child might say, "I did a worksheet." That's okay. That'd be okay. If you came home the second day, "What did you do?" "I did a worksheet." Third day, "I did a worksheet." Now you're going to start to be concerned. "Do you read?" You will start asking him to tell things like that.

A high school teacher agreed. The less successful teachers in the detracked classes also accomplished little before detracking, he said, but "in the regular English classes, they were dealing with kids whose parents wouldn't complain that there were no standards. Now they are dealing with kids whose parents will complain when there are no standards."

Yet the situation was equally untenable from the perspective of the teachers who had been assigned to those low-track English classes prior to the detracking effort. One called them "nightmare classes." Another recalled, "You could hardly get through anything because [the students] just wanted to come and fool around." Students in these low-tracked classes were clearly bored with what educators described as poor academic instruction. A top district administrator characterized the old regular English course as "mindless synonyms, antonyms, drill, [and] sentence structure." A principal admitted that teachers generally made "no attempt to teach the lower group." A teacher acknowledged, "We weren't doing what was right by [the low-tracked students]. I don't think we met their needs." And a school board member declared that she "could point out any number of pitfalls with the old system: The old system labeled children. The old system did not challenge."

Similarly, an African American parent recalled that teachers had miserably low expectations for students in the low-track English class. When these students misbehaved or ignored their work, the teachers did nothing, since the students "act[ed] just the way they [were expected to act], anyway." Detracking, she said, "put [these teachers] to the challenge." And some teachers began to meet that challenge; according to one, "I see some real benefits occurring for the regular student because he's expected to do more. I think . . . in many ways they're progressing."

Under either a tracked or a detracked system, Woodland Hills, like most districts, would contain some inferior teachers. But the poor teaching became much more apparent to powerful constituencies when highlighted by detracking. Those involved in school change often find the limitations of a traditional system (tracked classes, in this case) to be less noticeable than the limitations of the revised system. Researchers who have made the best attempts to measure the effects of tracking conclude that tracked students gain no achievement advantage over comparable nontracked students—even without accounting for changed instructional methods or curriculum. This holds true whether the students test in the high, medium, or low range (Slavin, 1990). And the quantitative data from Woodland Hills support these conclusions (Welner, 2001a).

The fact remains, however, that even though overall conditions in detracked classes were superior to those of the old tracked classes, some students who formerly were in high-track English classes likely did receive poorer instruction and more disruptions in their new detracked classes. To the extent that the parents of these students were upset about the decrease in the quality of their children's school experience, one might argue that their complaints were justified. However, the district's most vocal reform opponents campaigned for nothing more than a return to tracking. They did not aim to improve instructional methods throughout the school; rather, they sought a return to the previously flawed system. As their only concession, they called on the district to ensure nondiscriminatory class placements. While these parents complained loudly about the poor instruction their own children purportedly received in detracked classes, they remained willing to foist that same (or worse) instruction on other children.

Detracking opponents took a similar approach to classroom disruptions. Although most teachers contended that these disruptions decreased overall following detracking, resistant White parents focused exclusively on the purported disruption increase in their children's classes as compared with the old advanced classes.

In addition, this resistance appeared to be prompted by other, less legitimate issues. Some parents objected to the withdrawal of status, for example, when the district removed the symbolic gold stars of high-track ranking from their children's foreheads. It is natural and reasonable for parents to view their own children as special; but these parents also felt entitled to demand something extra. Other resistant parents did not hide their simple preference for the advanced courses' racial and class demographics.

Similar positions surfaced in all three districts we studied, and we believe, based on our research and review of school change research literature, that most, if not all, American school districts house parents with comparable perspectives and attitudes. In many such districts, these powerful parents hold political sway, as they did for a long time in Woodland Hills, making it unlikely that the district would initiate equity-minded detracking reform. Even in the face of the court mandate, these parents maintained considerable influence and in some ways succeeded in watering down the reform efforts. Nevertheless, because of the power of the court order, real change ensued within Woodland Hills. This mandate, in concert with the support of some community members, teachers, and administrators newly empowered by the court order, pushed the district in a positive direction—a direction the district otherwise would not have taken. Such changes did not resolve all the district's problems, such as uneven teaching quality. Yet, from a perspective recognizing the district's former inequities, the change clearly did result in greater opportunities for African Americans, the group of students who had most suffered in the past.

This highlights two important themes of this chapter and of this book. The first was mentioned earlier: Equity-minded reform efforts benefit from a combination of top-down and bottom-up pressures. The second focuses on the nature of successful equity-minded policies. The detracking mandates that we studied were intended and designed specifically to make the school districts more equitable. While the policies also may have had unintended beneficiaries among the broader student body—for example, they may have led to improved instruction and better qualified teachers across all classrooms—they were targeted at minority students identified by the courts as having suffered discrimination. In this way, these mandates differ tremendously from the popular excellence- and choice-oriented policies that dominate today's landscape (e.g., standards, charter schools, and vouchers). Instead of targeting specific groups of students who have been disadvantaged in the past, these more recent reforms are supposed to change the entire educational system by infusing greater accountability and competition and, theoretically, freeing all parents and students to vote with their feet by leaving failing schools and choosing good schools instead. Some advocates of these contemporary reforms may have equity-minded goals, and these goals sometimes are affixed to the broader policy, but the theory underlying these goals is generally that a rising tide will lift all boats (Hoxby, 2003).

As discussed in other chapters in this book, such nontargeted policies are not likely to further an equity agenda. In contrast, we found substantial progress toward equity goals in these districts, which were subjected to detracking mandates. Accordingly, our findings highlight this second theme: Equitable educational practices are unlikely to come about as an artifact of policies specifically promoting only excellence or choice; policies instead must be targeted directly at achieving equity goals.[5]

San Jose

With these themes in mind, and also keeping in mind a perspective recognizing these districts' former inequities, we now consider the reform process that we observed in the San Jose Unified School District. There the district leadership began with great enthusiasm for the consent decree containing the detracking mandate, enthusiasm described by one observer as a "love fest." Over time, however, as the change process proved to be politically complicated, the leadership shifted its focus away from a commitment to the reforms' success and toward the goal of obtaining a unitary status ruling and thus a release from the detracking mandate.

Nonetheless, since the time of the initial court order in 1985, the district participated in a variety of innovative reforms, including Henry Levin's Accelerated Schools and the College Board's Equity 2000. Thus, despite the district leadership's waning interest in detracking, San Jose's schools and classrooms did become more integrated, and remedial classes were eliminated. As a result of the lawsuit and the court order, empowered community groups with equity-minded missions formed and helped to raise the consciousness of many in the community concerning issues of educational equity and racial justice.

One of the many San Jose teachers we interviewed indicated, at the beginning of the interview, that her impression of the court order was that it had failed. As we talked, she mentioned a variety of programs and advances that she had witnessed over the years. Near the end of the interview, we asked her whether she thought those changes would have occurred without the lawsuit, and—seemingly surprised at her own answer—she said, "no." Most educators in the district, she explained, otherwise would not have embarked on these types of equity-minded activities. Other educators and community members in the districts we studied shared similar sentiments. These court orders, it turns out, did not fail. They merely failed to accomplish all that they theoretically could have were it not for the districts' many other forces—including parents and advocates of high-track students—resisting these changes. Still, the court orders clearly brought about much more equity-minded change than would have occurred had these policies not been targeted specifically toward such goals.

Rockford

Meanwhile, reformers in Rockford began their efforts facing even greater hurdles than those in either San Jose or Woodland Hills. The within-school segregation was more overt, the racial divisions more pronounced, and the district leadership extraordinarily resistant.[6] From this perspective, in particular, Rockford also accomplished a great deal. While the district retains tracking, the lowest tracks have been eliminated, and the highest tracks are no longer reserved for White children. The tracks are also less rigid, allowing some upward movement. Even given the hostility of high-level policymakers toward these reforms, the court forced real change.

UNDERSTANDING THE NORMATIVE AND POLITICAL HURDLES FOR EQUITY-MINDED REFORM

The key lesson from these three communities (and from other de-tracking schools we've studied[7]) is that districts and schools that initiate detracking reforms without preparing to overcome normative and political obstacles are likely to see their change efforts substantially undermined. The initiation, implementation, and sustainability of equity-minded reforms all depend on the creation of a policy context favorable to the reform's goals. Creating such a favorable environment requires bottom-up efforts, including grassroots constituency building and mobilization, but often it also requires top-down efforts such as federal court orders and legislation.

Because many education reform movments approach the change process from a technical perspective, rarely do reformers focus on the political and normative issues that hold inevitable sway over any efforts to affect equity-minded change. Detracking depends on the commitment and re-sourcefulness of teachers, administrators, counselors, parents, students, lawyers, and others in attending to these normative and political needs from both a top-down and bottom-up perspective. In fact, the success of almost all equity-minded reform depends on what people believe about learning and students, about who can and must learn, and about whether some students must receive less in school in order for other students to receive "the best" (see Oakes, Wells, Datnow, & Jones, 1997).

We observed in all three of the districts we studied that tracking's strongest supporters, whether teachers, students, or parents, invariably focused their attention on preserving the quality of high-track classes; they could not defend, and thus rarely addressed, the poor-quality education routinely offered in low-track classes. In fact, most parents who denounce their local schools' efforts to detrack, no doubt would fight ferociously to keep their own children out of those schools' lower tracks. Tracking's benefits, if they exist, adhere to those outside the lowest tracks.

These perceived benefits, moreover, are extremely visible. High-track classes are the most coveted in any given school. They produce the National Merit Scholars, the science fair winners, the "good kids." Teachers enjoy these classes because the students appear more motivated and better behaved. Students form cliques of friends within these classes, and they can be very reluctant to let go of that security and camaraderie. Parents of high-track students value the higher-quality instruction as well as the symbolic status tied to their children's achievement as recognized in the track placement. All are aware of the college admissions criteria that place a premium on honors, advanced placement (AP), and international baccalaureate (IB) courses. For all these reasons and many more, many teachers, students, and parents see detracking as redistributive. Far from a neutral organizational change, detracking becomes a perceived threat to some of the most highly valued aspects of a high-track child's education.

In important ways, many would-be detrackers acknowledge these concerns held by supporters of tracking. For instance, most detracking reforms are designed around retaining the challenging instruction often found in high-track classes and extending these benefits to all students (e.g., Henry Levin's Accelerated Schools). Schools engaged in this reform are exceedingly wary of the potential for "watering down." Most senior high schools retain (and even extend) the availability of AP and IB courses. Many schools also make a concerted effort to inform parents and teachers of the research noting tracking's educational harms and detracking's educational benefits.

However, these same detrackers usually do little if anything to respond to the considerable opposition brought on by their efforts, even when such opposition is not tied to rational, straightforward educational concerns. For example, consider the teachers of high-track classes in the districts we studied who perceived detracking as requiring them to lower their academic expectations and resort to watering down their curriculum. Even some teachers of low-track classes were apprehensive about detracking, particularly those who would be required to move away from teaching rudimentary skills and thus adopt a more rigorous curriculum; they felt unprepared to engage their new heterogeneous classes in more-challenging instructional methods and curriculum. Teachers also must overcome normative biases, most notably their long-held values and beliefs about student ability and potential. For detracking to be most successful, teachers must buy in to the belief that each of their students can learn at a high level.

In addition, for equity-minded reforms to succeed, parental opposition must be addressed. Some parental concerns, as stated above, are decidedly legitimate. Parents should not be criticized for seeking the best educational opportunities for their children or for doing their best to prepare their children for the college admissions game. But we have found that, particularly in communities with socioeconomically and racially diverse student bodies, many parents' and educators' concerns go far beyond these legitimate, educational issues. Detracking reforms confront a familiar conflation of race and intellectual ability. That is, many people inside and outside American schools continue to believe that students of color are less intelligent. These concerns mirror those of some teachers: belief in the noneducability of low-track students.

A detracking reform also can be counted on to bring to the fore the related cultural anxieties carried by many White parents and educators about disruptions and even violence, especially from low-income and African American males. A related parental fear—one that we see even in racially and socioeconomically homogeneous schools—is that the low-track students will expose their high-track children to an undesirable "culture" in various forms—for example, drugs or a de-emphasis on academics. Often, these objections are honest expressions of deeply held cultural prejudices.

We have painted this picture of normative and political opposition to detracking because the success of attempts to move beyond tracking, or to pursue any equity-minded reform, usually depends on overcoming that opposition. These normative and political forces create contexts that are inhospitable to equity-minded reform efforts. Only the combination of top-down mandates plus new approaches to bottom-up support for reform is likely to counter their powerful resistance.

BUILDING A NEW ATTITUDE TOWARD TOP-DOWN MANDATES

The three cases discussed above demonstrate that complex forces come into play when reform threatens to redistribute precious resources and to renegotiate the meaning of high-status culture. As important, these cases demonstrate the need for a reframing of conventional thinking, as set forth in most scholarly research and practitioner-oriented publications, about

educational change. Few axioms are as well accepted in the change literature as Milbrey McLaughlin's (1990) "We cannot mandate what matters"
(p. 15). Moreover, the relative lack of success experienced by many attempts
at top-down, mandated change would seem to provide strong support for
this axiom. However, the communities we studied show that equity-driven,
top-down mandates should not be viewed as new attempts to mandate
what matters. Instead, these are attempts to *change* pre-existing mandates—
mandates including both articulated and unarticulated cultural imperatives
to do things in particular ways.

We define a top-down mandate as a force external to a local school or
community that shapes policy in that school or community. Such mandates
carry with them a legal, economic, or administrative power-based obligation to comply or face consequences in the form of some type of sanction
or setback. In our multilayered democratic system, top-down mandates are
perpetually and inevitably being issued and include the pressures derived
from college admissions practices and the real estate market. New mandates simply add to the mix. Thus, a single, top-down mandate, unless it
is an extremely powerful one, is unlikely to be effective in tremendously
influencing the overall impact of a myriad of external influences on a school
or community.

We also question the assertion within much of the so-called "school
change" literature that successful policymakers set the conditions for effective administration but refrain from predetermining how those decisions
will be made, instead charging local practitioners with the development
of solutions (Elmore & McLaughlin, 1988; Firestone & Corbett, 1989). The
bottom-up focus of the change literature looks to local educators and community members as the foremost generators of school change. However,
at the local level, equity issues rarely emerge as primary concerns of the
political majority. As a result, decentralization of policy-making authority
to these local communities may lead to a severe neglect of the equity concerns of the politically less powerful (Elmore, 1993). In normal circumstances, "local elites" can (and often do) block reforms that they perceive
as grounded in values different from their own (Wells & Serna, 1996).

On the other hand, more-central authorities sometimes are able to
advance equity policy goals to a much greater extent than local authorities
(Peterson, 1981). Even Arthur Wise (1982), a strong critic of centrally mandated reform, acknowledges that some local schools are unwilling or unable to solve some equity-minded problems, and, in such cases, central
authorities are more likely to be successful. Further, bottom-up strategies
diminish the opportunity and responsibility of leaders with status and
power to inspire and educate on behalf of their least politically powerful
constituents.

Accordingly, community resistance to practices perceived by politically powerful local residents as harmful to their personal interests (i.e., those perceived as substantively equity-minded and redistributive policies) usually prompts the need for top-down mandates and monitoring (Peterson, 1981). Discussing tracking specifically, Wells and Oakes (1998) point out the importance of recognition by policymakers that local political resistance to reforms aimed at giving low-income and non-White students access to high-status knowledge will be difficult to counteract in a highly decentralized system.

These researchers seem to be describing what can be termed as an "equity exception" to the general recommendations against top-down mandates requiring specific changes. This exception arises because equity-minded reforms differ from other reforms in kind, not merely in magnitude. A central policy-making body desiring to promote an equity-minded reform would, for example, be ill advised to merely set forth some general equity principles, because resistance and political opposition by local elites would undermine any anticipated bottom-up organizing to create or influence reform. Instead, the central body must craft a more specific mandate, sufficient to substantially shift what is politically possible within the district and thereby to overcome such local resistance. As Boyd (1989) has argued, what is needed is a balanced approach to educational improvement using elements of top-down and bottom-up reform judiciously, "according to the characteristics and needs of the given policy problem" (p. 517; see also Fullan 1994, 2001; Huberman & Miles, 1984).

Thus, we argue that if equity-minded reforms are to be initiated, the context surrounding the reform effort must change. A top-down mandate, which would not be recommended by most authors of the change literature (see Tyack & Cuban, 1995), becomes an attractive option with this new perspective. The cases we have studied provide ample illustration. In none of the districts would detracking have risen to the top of the reform agenda, and even if it had, it would not have garnered the support of those who could ensure its successful implementation. Rather, the push for detracking came more from those who were adversely affected by the tracking system—the parents, students, and educators affiliated with low-track classes. In the end, these actors, by turning to the court system, helped to create a top-down mandate that would allow much-needed grassroots change to take place. But, as we have noted, the court orders are only one crucial component of the change process. In the following sections of this chapter we focus on what needs to happen at the school level before equity-minded, top-down mandates can be successfully implemented.

TAKING A NEW APPROACH TO BOTTOM-UP REFORM

The three cases we studied also make clear that top-down and bottom-up reforms are not dichotomous. Successful equity-minded reform requires a mix of both. Consider a hypothetical teacher who would like to move her school toward detracking. In 2002, she brings up the idea with some of her colleagues and is told, in no uncertain terms, that they like the present tracked system and have no interest in change. In 2003, a federal court, in response to a plaintiff's complaints of discrimination via the tracking system, issues an order requiring the district to detrack its schools. Now, in 2005, this teacher and others at the school site and at the community level, who before were unable to mount an effective reform effort, can move forward more confidently with their *bottom-up* ideas. The opponents of detracking may persist in their opposition, but their strategic position and their political power and influence have been moved by the court. Those who were once on the fringe—the teacher mentioned above as well as the plaintiffs in the case—now have more power to implement their ideas. By analogy, the boundaries of the playing field have shifted to include some who were previously on the sidelines. It is, perhaps, unlikely that they will overwhelm the more established players, but they are now in the fray (see Thompson, 1984, for an elaborated discussion of this point).[8]

According to many change theorists and researchers in the field of education, meaningful change requires buy-in by as many constituents as possible. To garner this buy-in, reformers often must be careful not to offend anyone involved in the change process. Consequently, researchers as well as change agents find themselves in wholly unfamiliar territory when collecting data on and writing about equity-minded reforms in education. For instance, White researchers usually squirm at the sound of the "r-word"; mid- to high-income researchers feel a hidden guilt when discussing issues of poverty; men hesitate to talk about gender issues; and only the bravest few traverse the taboo grounds of sexual orientation. Even in some of our best efforts, researchers and school leaders huddle behind all-inclusive, and nonspecific, words like "equity," "diversity," and "heterogeneity"—words that, without greater explication, may become little more than "window dressing for the same old beliefs and practices" (Oakes, 1995, p. 3). As a consequence, equity-minded reformers find little in the educational literature that offers guidance about how to confront and overcome powerful normative and political obstacles to changes that will upset the status quo in racially diverse schools.

Left standing in a theoretical and conceptual vacuum, only a few reform leaders at the schools we studied were able to begin deconstructing the hidden ideologies driving the opposition of anti-change forces and to operate accordingly. These educators often were able to unmask the opposition often because they were able to identify with the "standpoints" (Banks, 1995; Harding, 1993) of students and parents who were ill served by the tracking structure. This insight made them acutely aware that the opposition to detracking was driven not solely by rational thought, but also by nonrational "symbolic politics" (Sears & Funk, 1991).

Often because of past experiences, and sometimes because of their own social status, these educators had reached a level of "individual consciousness," enabling them to interpret their situation differently, thus allowing for a more penetrating critique of their opposition (Hill-Collins, 1991). However, even these educators, who moved beyond a neutral perspective regarding the reform, found themselves lacking in tools to help them apply their critique to the reform process. The following three sections offer some practical tools for equity-minded educators attempting to effectively detrack.

Moving Beyond Technical Approaches to Professional Development

Because of the unique obstacles standing in the path of equity-minded reform, staff development efforts should, in addition to providing assistance with instructional techniques and curricula, prepare teachers to confront important normative issues and to change instructional practices in detracked classes (see Welner & Oakes, 2000). Many teachers simply do not believe that all students should be academically challenged at a high level—that each child can learn. Many other teachers are, to a lesser degree, skeptical of the concept of such high universal expectations.

Some recent work, not often considered as part of the "school change" literature, may provide us with a theoretical head start toward understanding how educators and community members might come to understand and grapple more systematically with, and therefore implement more fully and positively, un-sought-after and often unwelcome equity-minded reforms. This work suggests that if changes are to be more than a refinement of the status quo—in terms of fundamental school goals and norms—then the status quo needs to be critically examined as part of that change process.

Sirotnik and Oakes (1986, 1990), for example, suggest a site-based "critical inquiry" process (discussed in greater detail below) whereby teachers systematically challenge their own beliefs and actions. They posit that through this process, educators undergoing reform can come more thoroughly to understand and critique deeply held beliefs and ideologies about intelligence, racial differences, social stratification, White supremacy, and elite privilege as powerful forces to be reckoned with inside and outside of schools. The need to delve deeply into these contentious issues is articulated clearly by many social theorists writing both inside and outside the field of education (see hooks, 1992; West, 1994). These scholars explain that social constructions such as race and class are not simply elements of society that are more pronounced in some institutions than in others, but that these elements actually help constitute our personal, societal, national, and international worlds (West, 1994).

The proposition underlying critical inquiry is that an active and forthright confrontation of these beliefs will enhance greatly the ability of school actors to overcome obstacles such as those that we witnessed in our study of the three school districts. For example, participants in critical inquiry continually remind themselves that the problems they face have a current and historical context, and that the routine problems of schooling—such as using time effectively, staff communication, and grouping students for instruction—must be situated in these contexts in order to be understood. "What are we doing now?" and "How did it come to be that way?" are questions that help frame this discussion. Such critical inquiry also asks participants to recognize and contend with embedded values and human interests in school practices, by asking, "Whose interests are (and are not) being served by the ways things are?"

Critical inquiry also demands that knowledge of all types—for example, results of research, newly developed professional practices, and participants' own multiple experiences and perspectives—be brought to bear on the matters under discussion. Critical inquiry is based on the premise that fundamental, democratic change is possible when people are accountable to one another, express themselves authentically, and negotiate common understandings that support collective action. The questions to ask at every opportunity are, "Is this the way we want things to be?" and "What are we going to do about it?"

The critical inquiry process can prompt teachers to re-evaluate debilitating beliefs and provide teachers with normative armor to shield against, and to counter, attacks by pro-tracking parents and others. By providing the opportunity for open and serious dialogue around these issues, this process directly targets long-held beliefs and understandings about students and their abilities that serve as barriers to successful detracking. For example, teachers participating in a critical inquiry focused on detracking would question explicitly and openly whether they believe all children can learn and would question whether they believe that White children have greater intelligence or better behavior than African American and/or Latino children. They also would question the bases of these beliefs. All these questions should be considered using an accepted ideal, such as social justice, as a touchstone. Thus, teachers also would question their beliefs about the nature of a just society and would contemplate how their own norms and behavior conform to that ideal. Critical inquiry's goal would not be to understand the culture and context of African American and/or Latino students; rather, the goal would be to explore and confront individuals' barriers to understanding and having high expectations for these students.

Importantly, while teachers using, for instance, a social justice touchstone would work toward providing an excellent education for all students, the critical inquiry process might prompt some probing of the foundation for achieving such a broad goal. That is, the broad goal would be unlikely to generate a neutral, "rising tide lifts all ships" approach to ensuring that all children are academically challenged. Instead, the participants would work to identify existing barriers to the goal and would critique their own role in erecting or failing to confront those barriers.

Critical inquiry, however, is no panacea. In many ways it is highly problematic, since the majority of teachers in most districts are not very open to this idea. For instance, many teachers of detracked classrooms acknowledge their classrooms' imperfections but lay the blame for those problems on a variety of external factors: the students' parents, culture, and race; the socioeconomic differences among students; and even the unwise decision to detrack. Thus, only a fraction of teachers may be open to engaging in such inquiry.

We have found, however, that each district typically contains a group of insightful teachers and administrators who have already begun confronting some of the enormous normative barriers to successful detracking. This group could be expanded by infusing such issues into the district's staff development activities. Accordingly, critical inquiry should still be pursued, as it remains a useful and direct way of confronting the beliefs that would undermine successful reform. An ongoing critical inquiry process could help to change schools' culture and, in combination with the other recommendations set forth below, could be a tremendous boon to the pro-equity-minded reform forces.

This discussion of critical inquiry highlights a point that is crucial for us as supporters of detracking: As an educational reform, detracking must consist of much more than the mere formation of detracked or heterogeneously grouped classrooms. Curriculum in the mixed-ability classes should be challenging for all students and should be project-based, allowing for individualization of assignments. Staff development should be available to help teachers adopt the revised curriculum and, if necessary, adjust their teaching styles to become more constructivist. Academic supports should be introduced for students, particularly those students formerly in undemanding, low-track classes. As noted by Clarke, Madaus, and Shore (Chapter 5, this volume), inequality is additive; the later the cycle is halted, the more acceleration is necessary. Finally, for detracking to be most successful, teachers must truly believe that each child in their classes should be academically challenged at a high level. In our experience, this element of detracking is the most difficult to achieve—but it is very, very important.

The central issue here is that effective detracking will result only from a change of the hearts and minds of many teachers who are burdened with stereotypes and biases against low-income students of color. While top-down mandates create the political space for this to happen, they are not enough in and of themselves.

Engaging in Democratic Public Discourse

Bottom-up support for equity-minded reform is unlikely to emerge, even from critical inquiry, without participation of all who have a stake in the reform. The reform process must include regular, public opportunities for diverse groups of parents and community members to discuss the schools' progress toward high-quality education for all students. Such forums should be designed not simply as a public relations effort, but as a genuine opportunity for public, community-wide deliberation concerning the normative and political issues raised by the reform, as well as the changes in structure and practice. The agenda for the forums should explicitly stress the goal of high-quality education for all, rather than focusing on, for example, improving the education of the poorest served or avoiding watering down the education provided to the highest achievers. All such issues are encompassed within the broader goal, and all concerns should be welcomed.

Such an approach to effective implementation of an equity mandate requires a deliberate and tenacious bottom-up effort to bring parents and community members from different racial groups and socioeconomic positions to the same venue to talk. Much care must be taken to ensure that all members of the community feel welcome, and that all have an opportunity to voice their opinions—the politically powerful should not be allowed to dominate the discussions or the agenda (see discussion of democratic deliberation in House & Howe, 1999). Such public discussions can help community members avoid the too-easy trap of responding to difficult reforms like detracking with blame—blaming uncaring or ill-trained teachers; competitive or self-serving parents; short-sighted administrators; a neglectful, uncaring community; government bureaucracy, and so on. Sometimes, the blame lands squarely on the very people who are themselves the objects of the inequality: students and groups of students who are thought to be unmotivated or not smart enough to learn.

Unless such views are examined in public, many will continue to see the inequality in opportunities and achievement that now plague the school system as logical, sensible, and inevitable. Only with the full participation of all segments of the community can educational change agents hope to engage schools in grappling seriously and effectively with the gap between the ideals of equity and the reality of educational failure for so many students.

Political Mobilization

In addition to providing for inclusive, public discussion of equity reforms, we recommend that steps be taken to ensure that all constituents have an effective political voice. True democratic deliberation requires responsiveness to all people, not just those with the loudest voices. On a practical level, each school should review the composition of its parent groups to ensure that they reflect enrollment. If they do not, the school should monitor agenda-setting practices, meeting times, locations, communications, outreach, and other procedures to increase the groups' accessibility to all members of the school community.

Just as important, further steps should be taken to ensure democratic deliberation within diverse parent groups. Low-income parents, African American and/or Latino parents, and parents of lower-achieving students should be welcomed into an environment wherein they can speak about what they want for their children, with as much confidence and sense of entitlement as wealthier parents, White parents, and parents of higher-achieving children. At the same time, educators also can assist in developing an environment wherein more-advantaged parents can struggle openly, and in the presence of those who are not White or middle class, with the schools' efforts to reform an education system that is politically and academically skewed in their favor. This type of effort brings the process of equity-minded reform, as well as the struggles inherent within that process, to the fore, where all community members can engage together in developing the best educational environment for all children.

CONCLUSION: SOCIAL MOVEMENT STRATEGIES TO FURTHER EQUITY-MINDED REFORMS

Equity-focused change projects demand explicit attention to the cultural and political dynamics of social and racial stratification. This attention is more likely to be generated and sustained when fueled by a revolutionary social movement than by the efforts of actors usually charged with preserving the status quo. Without attention to normative and political dynamics of change, hoped-for reforms are either abandoned entirely or implemented in ways that actually replicate (perhaps in a different guise) the stratified status quo. However, few reformers are equipped with the legal, strategic, or even moral capital to stand up to the cultural resistance and backlash that arise when reforms actually begin to redistribute schooling resources. Further, the vast majority of the literature on school reform does little to help reformers acquire such capital (see Welner, 2000).

Most of this literature—to the extent that it addresses reforms that aim specifically to benefit students with less power in schools and communities—assumes that school systems are filled with well-meaning educators who simply need some centralized assistance or prompting to help their bottom-up efforts achieve more equitable and efficacious pedagogies. As Hochschild (1984) explains, this assumption is grounded in the premise that racist practices and beliefs are at odds with basic American values, and therefore Americans will, if given the opportunity, naturally move away from past racist practices. However, the struggles faced by equity-minded reformers over the past 3 decades suggest that this rarely happens.

In this chapter, we have attempted to clarify the exceptional barriers that change agents encounter as they attempt to initiate and implement equity-minded and racially explicit school reforms. In the United States at least, struggles for equity for low-income children and children of color expose and challenge contradictions deeply rooted in American culture. This struggle is an integral part of the change process, in part because equity-focused changes are grounded in universal principles that are nonetheless highly context-dependent. Thus, the process of change cannot be transferred in whole cloth from one setting to another. These are local matters. What and how schools will change must be constructed in ways that make sense locally and must rely on collaboration with those who will enact and sustain the changes locally. Still, as we have noted, this does not mean that top-down mandates to change the status quo and redistribute opportunities and access are unnecessary. Indeed, we have found that such mandates are often essential.

The abstract principles of equitable education are deeply engrained in the cultural rhetoric of Western democracies. They permeate the rhetoric of schooling, and most educators and citizens espouse them. In the United States it is easy to find consensus around certain highly abstracted and universally sound principles—one current example being, *No child should be left behind*. However, making contextually appropriate changes based on equity principles requires that these principles must be moved beyond the abstract.

As the principles become locally and collaboratively defined—and made concrete in programs and practices—the unequal and stratifying consequences of the status quo replace consensus with conflict. This is exactly what one would expect when the potentially redistributional impact of equity-minded change is made concrete and explicit. Such explicitness reveals the fragility of the local agreement about equity; those advantaged and disadvantaged by the status quo rarely agree on the local specifics of equity and fairness for diverse groups of students. Moreover, since those currently advantaged nearly always have disproportionate influence over the conduct of schools—including their change efforts—the specifics, if not the abstraction, of equity-focused change are resisted by those with the power to halt them. This power inequality yields a process whereby the educational change effort loses consensus and becomes a cultural struggle.

Consequently, those who seek a redistribution of opportunities and outcomes perceived to be scarce, and who challenge practices that reflect racist and classist values, should look to strategies used in social and political movements, such as local organizing and combining constituencies (i.e., church, youth, service, and education). And we contend that these strategies additionally should be combined with engaging the courts as powerful, if not omnipotent, guardians of educational equity. Equity-minded reforms present daunting normative and political obstacles. Such reforms will meet with greatest success when change strategies are altered to directly confront these obstacles from both the bottom-up and top-down.

NOTES

Acknowledgments. The authors wish to thank Janice Petrovich, Amy Stuart Wells, and Susan Liddicoat for their helpful comments and assistance. However, the opinions and ideas expressed herein are solely the responsibility of the authors.

1. Successful equity-minded reform does occur from the bottom-up. Burris, Heubert, and Levin (2004) recently described a very successful detracking reform in Long Island, NY, for instance. However, this and other bottom-up efforts undeniably take place within larger policy contexts, often shaped in powerful ways by top-down policies. These contexts should not be thought to deterministically control bottom-up possibilities, but neither should their strong influence be underestimated.

2. For a more detailed discussion of these three cases, see Welner (1999, 2001a) and Welner, Oakes, and FitzGerald (1998).

3. *See People Who Care* v. *Rockford Board of Education School District No. 205, Vasquez* v. *San Jose Unified School District, Hoots* v. *Commonwealth of Pennsylvania.* Each of these cases has given way to subsequent decisions modifying the original

orders. Most notably, in Summer 2000, the presiding judge reaffirmed the *Rockford* decision, clearly stating that the within-school segregation evidenced in high school classes was unacceptable and must be fixed. But this was reversed by an appellate decision that essentially absolved tracking as a wrongful and harmful policy, instead attributing unequal outcomes to poverty, family size, "parental attitudes and behavior . . . and ethnic culture" (*People Who Care* v. *Rockford*, 2001, p. 1076). In 2000, in the case involving the East Pittsburgh community of Woodland Hills, the federal judge found that the district had complied with nearly all of the court's requirements, including some aspects of detracking, although he instructed it to continue to work to detrack its high school mathematics program. See *Hoots* v. *Commonwealth of Pennsylvania*.

4. We conducted more than 90 interviews with educators, policymakers, students, and community members, all during the 1996–97 school year.

5. Welner (2001b) proposes a litigation approach to turning high-stakes outcome standards into a basis for challenging low-track courses. In a nutshell, he argues that standards-based accountability systems leave no rational educational or legal justification for schools' provision of less demanding classes.

6. See the court's written opinions in all four *People Who Care* v. *Rockford Board of Education School District No. 205.*

7. See, for example, Oakes, and Wells, and associates (1996); Oakes, Wells, Yonezawa, & Ray (1997); Oakes, Welner, Yonezawa, & Allen (1998); Wells & Oakes (1998).

8. For a more detailed discussion of these ideas, see Oakes, Welner, Yonezawa, & Allen (1998). The authors thank Kluwer Academic for their kind permission regarding the use of this work.

REFERENCES

Banks, J. (1995). The historical reconstruction of knowledge about race: Implications for transformative teaching. *Educational Researcher, 24*(2), 15–25.

Boyd, W. L. (1989). Policy analysis, educational policy, and management: Through a glass darkly? In N. Boyan (Ed.), *Handbook of research on educational administration* (pp. 510–522). New York: Macmillan.

Burris, C. C., Heubert, J. P., & Levin, H. M. (2004). Math acceleration for all. *Educational Leadership, 61*(5), 68–72.

Elmore, R. F. (1993). School decentralization: Who gains? Who loses? In J. Hannaway & M. Carnoy (Eds.), *Decentralization and school improvement: Can we fulfill the promise?* (pp. 33–54). San Francisco: Jossey-Bass.

Elmore, R. F., & McLaughlin, M. W. (1988). *Steady work: Policy, practice, and the reform of American education.* Santa Monica, CA: Rand.

Firestone, W., & Corbett, H. D. (1989). Planned organizational change. In N. Boyan (Ed.), *Handbook of research on educational administration* (pp. 321–340). New York: Macmillan.

Fullan, M. (1994). Coordinating top-down and bottom-up strategies for educational reform. In R. Elmore & S. Fuhrman (Eds.), *1994 ASCD yearbook: The governance of curriculum* (pp. 186–202). Alexandria, VA: Association for Supervision and Curriculum Development.

Fullan, M. (2001). *The new meaning of educational change* (3rd ed.). New York: Teachers College Press.

Harding, S. (1993). Rethinking standpoint epistemology: "What is strong objectivity?" In L. Alcoff & E. Potter (Eds.), *Feminist epistemologies* (pp. 49–82). New York: Routledge.

Hill-Collins, P. (1991). *Black feminist thought: Knowledge, consciousness, and the politics of empowerment.* New York: Routledge, Chapman, & Hall.

Hochschild, J. L. (1984). *The new American dilemma: Liberal democracy and school desegregation.* New Haven, CT: Yale University Press.

Hoff, D. J. (2004, February 11). Utah panel votes to quit No Child Left Behind Act. *Education Week, 23*(22), 11, 16.

hooks, b. (1992). *Black looks: Race and representation.* Boston: South End Press.

Hooper, K. L. (2004, March 5). State joins protest of education law. *Indianapolis Star,* p. 1B.

Hoots v. Commonwealth of Pennsylvania, 545 F.Supp. 1 (W.D. Pa. 1981).

Hoots v. Commonwealth of Pennsylvania (W.D. Pa. 2000). Unpublished opinion, July 25.

House, E., & Howe, K. (1999). *Values in evaluation and social research.* Thousand Oaks, CA: Sage.

Hoxby, C. (2003). School choice and school productivity (or, could school choice be a tide that lifts all boats?). In C. Hoxby (Ed.), *The economics of school choice* (pp. 287–341). Chicago: University of Chicago Press.

Huberman, M., & Miles, M. (1984). *Innovation up close: How school improvement works.* New York: Plenum.

McLaughlin, M. (1990). The Rand change agent study revisited: Macro perspectives and micro realities. *Educational Researcher, 19*(9), 11–16.

Oakes, J. (1991). Grouping students for instruction. In M. Alkin (Ed.), *Encyclopedia of educational research* (6th ed.; Vol. 4, pp. 562–568). New York: Macmillan.

Oakes, J. (1992, May). Can tracking research inform practice? Technical, normative, and political considerations. *Educational Researcher, 21*(4), 12–21.

Oakes, J. (1995). *Rollinghills Middle School.* UCLA Graduate School of Education & Information Studies, Research for Democratic School Communities, Los Angeles.

Oakes, J., Wells, A. S., & Associates. (1996). *Beyond the technicalities of school reform: Policy lessons from detracking schools.* Los Angeles: Author.

Oakes, J., Wells, A. S., Datnow, A., & Jones, M. (1997, Spring). Detracking: The social construction of ability, cultural politics, and resistance to reform. *Teachers College Record, 98*(3), 482–510.

Oakes, J., Wells, A. S., Yonezawa, S., & Ray, K. (1997). Equity lessons from detracking schools. In A. Hargreaves (Ed.), *1997 ASCD yearbook: Rethinking educational change with heart and mind* (pp. 43–72). Alexandria, VA: Association for Supervision and Curriculum Development.

Oakes, J., Welner, K., Yonezawa, S., & Allen, R. (1998). Norms and politics of equity-minded change: Researching the "zone of mediation." In M. Fullan (Ed.), *International handbook of educational change* (pp. 952–975). Norwell, MA: Kluwer Academic.

People Who Care v. *Rockford Board of Education School District No. 205*, 851 F.Supp. 905 (N.D. Ill. 1994).

People Who Care v. *Rockford Board of Education School District No. 205*, 171 F.3d 1083 (7th Cir. 1999).

People Who Care v. *Rockford Board of Education School District No. 205* (N.D. Ill. 2000). Unpublished opinion, August 11.

People Who Care v. *Rockford Board of Education School District No. 205*, 246 F.3d 1073 (7th Cir. 2001).

Peterson, P. E. (1981). *City limits*. Chicago: University of Chicago Press.

Sears, D., & Funk, C. (1991). The role of self-interest in social and political attitudes. *Advances in Experimental Social Psychology, 24*, 1–95.

Sirotnik, K., & Oakes, J. (1986). Critical inquiry for school renewal: Liberating theory and practice. In K. A. Sirotnik & J. Oakes (Eds.), *Critical perspectives on the organization and improvement of schooling* (pp. 3–94). Hingham, MA: Kluwer-Nijhoff.

Sirotnik, K., & Oakes, J. (1990, Spring). Evaluation as critical inquiry: School improvement as a case in point. *New Directions for Program Evaluation, 45*, 37–59.

Slavin, R. (1990). *Achievement effects of ability grouping in secondary schools: A best-evidence synthesis*. Madison: Wisconsin Center for Educational Research.

Slavin, R. (1993). Ability grouping in the middle grades: Achievement effects and alternatives. *Elementary School Journal, 93*(5), 535–552.

Thompson, F. J. (1984). Policy implementation and overhead control. In G. C. Edwards, III (Ed.), *Public policy implementation* (pp. 3–26). Greenwich, CT: JAI Press.

Tyack, D., & Cuban, L. (1995). *Tinkering toward utopia*. Cambridge, MA: Harvard University Press.

Vasquez v. *San Jose Unified School District* (N.D. Cal. 1994). Unpublished stipulation, case no. C-71-2130.

Wells, A. S., & Oakes, J. (1998). Tracking, detracking, and the politics of educational reform: A sociological perspective. In C. A. Torres & T. Mitchell (Eds.), *Emerging issues in the sociology of education: Comparative perspectives* (pp. 155–180). Albany: State University of New York Press.

Wells, A. S., & Serna, I. (1996). The politics of culture: Understanding local political resistance to detracking in racially mixed schools. *Harvard Educational Review, 66*(1), 93–118.

Welner, K. G. (1999). They retard what they cannot repel: Recognizing the role that teachers sometimes play in subverting equity-minded reforms. *Journal of Negro Education, 68*(2), 200–212.

Welner, K. G. (2000). Change in complex and evolving schools. *Journal of Education for Students Placed at Risk, 5*(4), 447–451.

Welner, K. G. (2001a). *Legal rights, local wrongs: When community control collides with educational equity*. New York: State University of New York Press.

Welner, K. G. (2001b). Tracking in an era of standards: Low-expectation classes meet high-expectation laws. *Hastings Constitutional Law Quarterly, 28*(3), 699–738.

Welner, K., & Oakes, J. (2000). *Navigating the politics of detracking*. Arlington Heights, IL: Skylight.

Welner, K. G., Oakes, J., & FitzGerald, G. (1998). *Reforming for excellence and equity in Woodland Hills: A progress report on detracking*. Report prepared for the United States District Court for the Western District of Pennsylvania.

West, C. (1994). *Race matters*. New York: Vintage Books.

Wise, A. (1982). *Legislated learning: The bureaucratization of the American classroom* (2nd ed.). Berkeley: University of California Press.

5

Shaping the Future

Testing and Diversity in College Admissions

MARGUERITE CLARKE
GEORGE MADAUS
ARNOLD R. SHORE

In 1997, a University of California (UC) task force recommended that all UC undergraduate campuses drop the SAT-I[1] as an admissions requirement (Fletcher, 1997). The announcement was not unexpected. It came at a time when race-conscious affirmative action policies had been eliminated in the UC system and were under threat in several other states. Thus, many higher education officials were searching for ways to reduce the adverse impact of low standardized test scores on minority admissions. Specifically, the removal of the SAT-I was seen as a way to halt dwindling admissions rates for African American and Hispanic students to the most selective and prestigious UC campuses. While the proposal was limited to the UC system, it received national attention and sparked a vigorous debate. The reason is simple. This proposal resonated with a broader theme in educational policy and reform in the United States: the effort to balance the pursuit of equity (in terms of a fair distribution of educational opportunities and resources) and excellence (when narrowly defined as test scores) in education.

Over the years, equity issues have been a major focus of testing policy in the United States. Historically, test scores have been used to illustrate inequities in the education system, substantiate the need for new programs and policies, and evaluate the success of these efforts (Haney, Madaus, & Lyons, 1993). Yet at the same time, equity concerns have been central to discussions about the longitudinal effects of testing on educational access and opportunity. Simply put, from the time children enter kindergarten, testing is strongly implicated in their life chances, and over time it has an additive effect. Decisions made on the basis of test scores at the elementary level can influence the type of high school education one receives. Further, a student's high school test scores can open or close doors of opportunity at the college level. For those on the wrong side of these decisions, they result in an accumulation of disparities in access to educational opportunities and resources, including promotion to the next grade, graduation from high school, and admission to college. This additive process is especially relevant in the case of non-Asian minority students because their scores on standardized tests are generally lower than those of other students.

This chapter focuses on equity issues surrounding test use in college admissions and minority students' (mainly African American and Hispanic) access to higher education. This discussion should be particularly useful to college administrators seeking to understand the equity implications of their admissions policies, especially in light of the June 2003 U.S. Supreme Court ruling upholding the use of race in admissions decisions. We begin with a discussion of racial and ethnic group performance differences on the two most commonly used college admissions tests and a simulation of the impact of these differences on minority students' admissions rates to higher education in the absence of affirmative action programs. Next, we present the findings from two studies conducted by the National Board on Educational Testing and Public Policy and funded by the Ford Foundation.[2] Employing a qualitative methods approach in the first study, National Board researchers were able to examine, through in-depth interviews with admissions directors and admissions consultants, how the college admissions process actually works and the roles played by test scores and diversity characteristics, including, but not limited to, race and ethnicity. Using a quantitative approach in the second study, National Board researchers were able to model the effects of a race-blind admissions system on the racial and ethnic composition of the UC college population. The chapter concludes with reflections on the findings of these studies and some recommendations for the role of testing in an equitable system of education.

Two powerful themes emerge from these data. The first is that admissions directors believed that they were trying to accomplish a "balancing act" between equity (defined as underrepresented minority students' access to higher education) and excellence (defined as high test scores) in the college admissions process. This theme came through strongly in the qualitative study when admissions directors described the roles of testing and diversity in college admissions and the strategies they used to balance these two sets of goals. For instance, they noted that when they admit only students with high test scores, it promotes an atmosphere of academic excellence and an image of institutional quality. At the same time, they acknowledged that a diverse student body provides an enriched educational experience for all students and fulfills institutional social goals. Meanwhile, the quantitative study of admissions data for California shows what happens when policies aimed at creating racial and ethnic diversity are removed and admissions staff is forced to rely more heavily on test scores and other "objective" measures of excellence. The result—reduced access for African Americans and Hispanics to the most selective campuses in the UC system—makes it clear that too much emphasis on test scores upsets the balancing act that the admissions directors said they strove to achieve.

The second theme, already mentioned above, is the longitudinal and additive nature of inequity. This is seen most strongly in the quantitative study, which discusses the different rates of test taking, eligibility, and applications to college among minority and nonminority groups in California, and the negative impact of these differences on African American and Hispanic students in the UC admissions process. The longitudinal nature of inequity is also evident in the qualitative study in terms of the outreach strategies that admissions directors and admissions consultants described for preparing and encouraging underrepresented minority students to apply to college. These strategies are being employed at increasingly earlier stages in the K–12 system in order to reduce the gatekeeping effects of tests and other factors on minority students' access to college. Before discussing these two themes in more depth, we will provide some context for the issues involved by examining racial and ethnic group performance differences on college admissions tests.

GROUP DIFFERENCES ON COLLEGE ADMISSIONS TESTS

Decades of standardized testing in the United States have shown significant racial and ethnic group performance differences on almost any standardized measure of achievement and at every level of schooling (Jencks & Phillips, 1998). By the time students take a college admissions test, the differences are very large.

Trend data on racial and ethnic group performance differences on the two most commonly used college admissions tests make this point quite starkly. Figures 5.1 and 5.2 show trend data for the mathematics sections of the SAT-I and the ACT. The performance of White students for each year a test is taken is the zero point of the scale. Groups below the zero line perform worse than Whites, and groups above perform better. Differences between groups are expressed in standard deviation units, which means they can be compared across tests.

The trend lines show that Asian American high school seniors were the highest-performing group on both the SAT-I and ACT mathematics tests over the 20 years spanning 1976–77 to 1996–97. White high school seniors, the second-highest-performing group on both tests, achieved at average levels that were roughly 0.3 of a standard deviation unit lower than the levels for Asian American seniors. This places the average White student at the 38th percentile among Asian American students. In other words, only 38% of Asian American high school seniors scored as low as or lower than the average White high school senior.

The average performance of African American students was consistently lower than that of all other groups on both tests and stood well below that of Asian American and White students—roughly one standard deviation unit below Whites and 1.3 standard deviation units below Asian Americans on both tests. The one standard deviation unit difference alone places the average African American student at the 16th percentile among Whites. That is, only 16% of White high school seniors scored as low as or lower than the average African American high school senior. American Indian, Mexican American, and Puerto Rican high school seniors performed somewhat better than African American seniors on both tests, although there was still a considerable gap between them and their White and Asian American counterparts.

While much has been written on the reasons for these gaps, we do not go into them here.[3] We present these data merely to illustrate their magnitude and equity implications, particularly in an environment where 90% of colleges require applicants to submit SAT-I or ACT scores. Furthermore, these scores are often the second most important piece of information—after high school achievement—in making admissions decisions (Breland et al., 1995).

Still, it is difficult to isolate the effects of these score differences on minority admissions since colleges—both public and private—tend to use multiple criteria in making admissions decisions and are secretive about how they weigh each piece of information. The quantitative study discussed later in this chapter examines this issue in the context of the UC system. Here, we briefly describe another National Board study that used simu-

Figure 5.1. Trends in Racial/Ethnic Group Differences: SAT-I Mathematics, High School Seniors

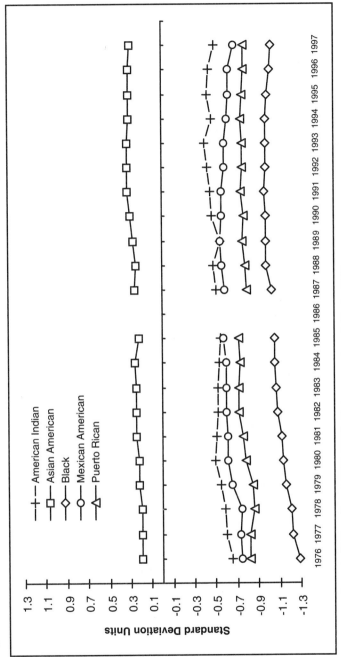

Source: Data from the College Board (1972–1997). Data were not available for 1986.

Figure 5.2. Trends in Racial/Ethnic Group Differences: ACT Mathematics, High School Seniors

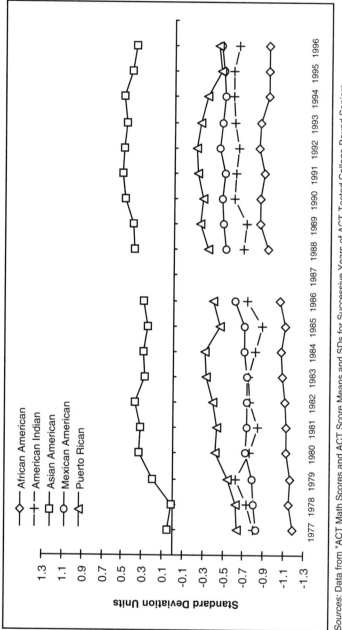

Sources: Data from "ACT Math Scores and ACT Score Means and SDs for Successive Years of ACT-Tested College-Bound Seniors 10% National Sample" (Iowa City: American College Testing, undated and unpublished tabulations); and James Maxey, American College Testing, personal communications (August–September 1997). Data were not available for 1987.

lated data to isolate the effects of test score differences on minority admissions rates in general (Koretz, 2000).

This simulation exercise involved creating a database that mirrored general patterns of African American and White student performance on college admissions tests and examining the effects of some simple admissions rules that were based solely on test scores.[4] Specifically, a succession of different cut scores was set on the test, and all students scoring above the cut were "admitted," while all those below it were "rejected." No other characteristics of students were considered. While these are overly simple admissions rules that no colleges follow, they are useful in that they isolate the effects of test scores.

When the cut score for admission was set at the overall mean for both groups, and equal numbers of African American and White applicants were used, African Americans were underrepresented in the admitted student body by roughly a factor of two relative to their representation in the pool of applicants. That is, although they constituted half of the applicants, they made up only 27% of the selected students. The simulation also shows that the effects become progressively more severe as the selectivity of admissions increases or as the proportion of African American applicants in the pool decreases. For example, when the cut score was set much higher—at one standard deviation above the overall mean score for both groups—but equal numbers of African American and White applicants were used, African Americans were underrepresented in the admitted student body by roughly a factor of eight relative to their representation in the pool of applicants. That is, although they constituted half of the applicants, they made up barely 6% of the accepted students. When the cut score was maintained at one standard deviation above the mean, but the number of African Americans was reduced to a more realistic 15% of the total applicant pool, the percentage of African American and White accepted students remained the same (because the cut score and the mean score for each group remained unchanged). However, the smaller number of African American applicants increases the homogeneity of the accepted student population. Thus, while the applicant pool is 15% African American, these students constitute only 1% of the accepted student body.

As will be seen below, an analysis of data for California indicates that race-blind admissions have a similar disproportionate effect on the profile of students admitted to the most selective institutions in the UC system. Before examining the California data in more depth, however, we first turn to the qualitative National Board study. This study provides an overview of the roles of both testing and diversity in college admissions as seen through the eyes of admissions directors and admissions consultants who work with or at selective public and private institutions.

BALANCING TESTING AND DIVERSITY
IN THE ADMISSIONS PROCESS

In the summer and fall of 1999, National Board researchers interviewed 13 admissions directors who worked at selective public and private institutions as well as four admissions consultants who had been hired by these and other institutions to aid in setting and meeting admissions goals (see Clarke & Shore, 2001). The aim of the study was to explore the roles that testing and diversity play in college admissions decisions from the perspective of those involved in the daily policy and practice of admissions. Testing was defined in terms of the standardized tests that students are required to take in order to apply to most U.S. colleges, namely the SAT-I and ACT. Diversity was defined broadly (i.e., race/ethnicity, gender, socioeconomic status, religion, geography, academic discipline, nonacademic talent, age, disabilities), although we were most interested in interviewees' views on the roles that race and ethnicity played in the admissions decision-making process.

Institutions were chosen to represent a range of selectivity levels as well as geographic locations.[5] Nonselective schools (those that accept 86% or more of all qualified applicants) were excluded. At each institution, we interviewed the director of the undergraduate admissions office. The 13 directors interviewed—one from each school—had between 18 and 30 years of experience in college admissions. The admissions consultants worked at private firms and were hired by college admissions offices to help them set and meet goals for the admissions process. These consultants had between 6 and 22 years of consulting experience with a variety of selective public and private colleges. In addition, they had worked between 12 and 15 years in various college admissions offices before becoming consultants.

Four main areas were covered in the interviews:

- *Admissions Factors*, including the organizational context of admissions; the types of information used in making an admissions decision; and the link between an institution's mission and the way it makes admissions decisions
- *Recruitment and Marketing*, including the goals and strategies of marketing and recruitment efforts; the use of financial aid and merit awards to attract students; and the influence of college rankings on admissions decisions
- *Diversity*, including definitions of diversity and the link between an institution's diversity goals and the way it makes admissions decisions
- *Affirmative Action*, including the institution's stance on this issue and the effects of recent court rulings on admissions decisions

While we gathered a wealth of information on admissions directors' and admissions consultants' views and knowledge in each of these areas, in this chapter we focus on what they said about the roles of test scores and diversity characteristics in admissions decisions. A fuller description of the study findings is provided in the National Board publication by Clarke and Shore (2001).

Table 5.1 shows the roles that test scores and diversity characteristics play in the various stages of the admissions process, according to the interviewees. Some of these roles are more evident in admissions to public than to private institutions (and vice versa), but mainly they occur in both domains. Also presented in Table 5.1 are existing or proposed strategies that

Table 5.1. The Roles of Test Scores and Diversity Characteristics in College Admissions

	Test Scores	*Diversity Characteristics*	*Balancing Strategies*
Before	• A focus for marketing and recruitment	• A focus for marketing and recruitment	• Improving the academic preparation of students in the K–12 pipeline • Encouraging minority and low-socioeconomic-status students to apply to college
During	• Information for decision making	• Information for decision making	• Basing the admissions decision on several kinds of information • Using a student's race, or proxies for race, as a factor in admissions decisions • Linking the way admissions decisions are made to the college's overall mission • Using an X percent rule
After	• A factor in financial aid decisions • A factor in selecting students for academic support programs	• A factor in financial aid decisions • A focus for retention efforts	• Preferential packaging of financial aid • Providing academic support for students who might have difficulties with college-level work • Providing nonacademic support for students • Finding different ways to measure success in college

Source: Clarke and Shore (2001).

the interviewees identified for balancing the effects of these roles on the academic quality and diversity of the student body. One of the reasons given for having these balancing strategies is that both test scores and diversity characteristics help institutions achieve excellence in terms of an academically strong and well-rounded student body. Still, a tension exists between the pressure on institutions to maintain a reputation of academic strength, which generally is measured in terms of test scores, and the need to create educationally beneficial diversity in the student population, which can lead to lower average test scores for those admitted. Thus, the admissions directors we interviewed had to struggle to find ways to balance both diversity and high test scores for their institution, a task made more or less difficult by the various national, state, or system policies in place.

For clarity, the roles and balancing strategies are organized into the time periods before, during, and after the period in which the decision is made to accept or reject a student's application (Table 5.1). "Before" refers to the period from when colleges start to recruit students and students start to inquire about colleges until a student decides whether and where to apply. "During" covers the period in which a college reviews the information a student has submitted and decides whether to accept or reject him or her. "After" covers the activities that colleges engage in after the admissions decision, such as the granting of financial aid to encourage students to enroll and the use of support programs to keep them in college. Let us consider each of these time periods in turn and focus on the roles and balancing strategies found in each. As we move through each stage, note the attempt to keep testing and diversity in balance throughout and how removing or de-emphasizing one or the other at any stage of the process can upset the outcomes that admissions directors are trying to achieve.

Before Students Apply

In the period before students actually apply to a college, student test score and diversity information helps focus many of the recruitment and marketing strategies used by colleges. In terms of recruitment, college admissions offices can obtain information on the test score and diversity profile of the national applicant pool from such sources as the College Board Student Search Service. The test score information comes from College Board-administered exams (e.g., the Preliminary SAT and the SAT-I) that many students take when applying to college. The diversity information comes from the forms students fill out when they take these exams. The College Board allows schools to request the names of students with certain test score and high school grade point average (GPA) combinations, further broken down by diversity characteristics such as racial and ethnic identity. Students that match the particular profile a college is looking for are then targeted through direct mailings from the college.

In terms of broader marketing strategies, colleges use the test score and diversity profile of their current student body to showcase their inclusive nature and academic standing to the general public as well as to prospective students and their parents. The diversity profile of an institution provides information on what the student body looks like in terms of gender, race, ethnicity, national origin, and so on. Students who are looking for a certain college environment may use this information to determine whether they would "fit in" at a particular institution. The test score profile, in the form of the institutional average or range, provides information on the SAT-I or ACT performance of the previous year's incoming class. Frequently, a college publishes the 25th to 75th percentile score range for the previous year's class in order to give prospective students an idea of the variation in test performance among students admitted to the institution. For example, if the 25th to 75th percentile score range for an institution is 1350 to 1540 (combined scores on the verbal and mathematical reasoning sections of the SAT-I test), this means that 50% of the admitted students scored between 1350 and 1540 on the test, 25% scored below this range, and 25% scored above this range. These score ranges are used by some students to assess their probability of admission to a particular institution.

The admissions directors and admissions consultants interviewed noted that the goal for many institutions at this stage of the process is to create as academically talented, but also diverse (e.g., race, ethnicity, cultural background, social class) an applicant pool as possible. They also noted that tensions exist because these desired characteristics do not always overlap at the applicant level. In particular, the available pool of academically qualified (in terms of test scores and GPA) African American and Hispanic applicants tends to be small, and many of these students are recruited aggressively by comparable institutions. In addition, external factors, such as institutional rankings that use test scores as one of the criteria, place pressure on colleges to attract high-scoring applicants at the expense of other types of qualified students.[6] The best known of these rankings is published annually by the magazine *U.S. News and World Report* (see Clarke, 2004, for an overview and critique). Research shows that a drop in an institution's position in the *U.S. News* rankings one year can negatively affect the quality of the applicants it attracts the following year (Monks & Ehrenberg, 1999). This places pressure on institutions to improve their performance on the indicators used to create these rankings (such as incoming students' test scores) so as to avoid a drop in rank and the subsequent negative impact on their applicant pool.

On the other hand, colleges also value diversity in their applicant pool since they recognize that employers like to hire graduates who can work effectively with people from different backgrounds. For example, when the U.S. Supreme Court decided to review two cases concerning the use of race in admissions decisions at the University of Michigan, numerous military leaders and CEOs of Fortune 500 companies filed friend-of-the-court briefs outlining the benefits of affirmative action and diversity in the workplace.

The admissions directors and consultants interviewed spoke of two sets of strategies that they or others in the education system used for balancing these tensions. The first set of strategies, which focus on *improving the academic preparation of students in the K–12 pipeline,* includes collaborative efforts by colleges and K-12 educators to increase the rigor of the precollege curriculum, particularly for minority and low-income students who tend not to take many college-track courses. These efforts may involve college faculty, administrators, or students visiting neighboring schools to help with curriculum development, teaching, or tutoring. They also may take the form of so-called summer-access programs in which high school students spend the summer on college campuses taking courses and improving their test-taking skills. The second set of strategies, which focus on *encouraging minority and low-socioeconomic-status students to apply to college,* may be incorporated into the aforementioned collaborative efforts between colleges and K–12 educators, or may involve stand-alone mentoring and recruitment programs designed by the college (in addition to whatever mentoring and counseling students receive at the high school level). The interviewees noted that while both sets of strategies may well lessen tensions between testing and diversity in the long run, they require time and resources before they become effective. In other words, such strategies require the colleges to commit to the long-term goal of changing the composition of the future applicant pool by expending current resources. It is also worth noting that these strategies, while not new, began to receive more attention and resources (particularly among public institutions) after the rise of race-blind admissions mandates in the mid-1990s. In fact, some of these mandates explicitly encourage outreach strategies as a way to increase the number of qualified minority students in the applicant pool.

During the Review of Student Applications

In the period when colleges are reviewing student applications, test scores and diversity characteristics are used as information for decision making. Generally, test scores are seen as a uniform way of comparing the academic merit of students from schools with nonuniform grading policies. Meanwhile, diversity characteristics are seen as information that enables a college to admit a well-rounded group of students. Both are seen as necessary for the creation of the optimal student body.

Still, there are tensions involved in balancing these two pieces of information when making admissions decisions. Due to a high volume of applications and limited staff, the common approach at public colleges and universities is to use test scores and high school GPA/class rank to make an initial cut in the very large applicant pool. Students with the highest test scores and GPAs are admitted right away, while those with low test scores and GPAs are rejected. Those in the middle are given further review. For students in the latter group, the admissions staff often takes diversity and other kinds of information (including the number of spaces available in the incoming class) into account before making final admissions decisions. Thus, only minority students who make it through to this stage of the process will benefit from the use of race or ethnicity-related information in the decision-making process.

Meanwhile, test scores take on less of a gatekeeping role in private colleges and universities. At these institutions, test scores tend to be used more subjectively and *concurrently* with other kinds of applicant information, including diversity characteristics, for making admissions decisions. For example, each student application (including test scores, high school transcript, high school GPA, letters of recommendation, essays, diversity information, and so forth) usually is read in its entirety by at least one member of the admissions staff, who then assigns a score to the student (e.g., from 1 to 10, with 1 being the best) based on a subjective evaluation of the information in his or her file. The student's test score and GPA might be used as the basis for an initial score (e.g., an SAT-I total of 1300 and a 3.8 GPA might earn a student an initial rating of 3), and then other information may be used to adjust that score up or down. For instance, if the student is an underrepresented minority student with strong leadership skills and good letters of recommendation, the rating might rise to a 1. After all files have been reviewed, the admissions staff confers and makes final decisions on whom to admit, whom to reject, and whom to place on standby. The number of students who fall into each of these categories may be based on the distribution of scores in the applicant pool (e.g., how many 1s, 2s, 3s, and so on, are in the pool), the number of spaces available, cutoff points already in place (e.g., all students below 6 may be rejected), or institutional preferences for students with certain talents or attributes (e.g., underrepresented minority applicants with scores as low as 7 may be admitted, while others with scores of 7 are rejected).

Importantly, the admissions directors at both public and private institutions as well as the admissions consultants interviewed identified four strategies for coping with the tensions between testing and diversity at this stage of the admissions process. As explained below, there are obvious differences in the extent to which these strategies are employed at public versus private institutions.

The admissions directors and admissions consultants noted that the first strategy—*basing the admissions decision on several kinds of information*—was critical because the more information a college admissions office has on a student, the less likely that office is to use any one item in determining admission. It is also less likely that any one group will be advantaged or disadvantaged in the admissions process. In addition, the interviewees argued that this strategy allows for a broader definition of excellence, one that is most likely to produce a well-rounded and academically strong student body, because it factors other talents such as musical or leadership ability into the decision. Admissions staff at private colleges tended to have more latitude to employ this approach to admissions. Those at public institutions were less likely to adopt this time-intensive approach due to higher applicant volumes and proportionately fewer admissions staff.

The second strategy was *the use of a student's race or proxies for race as a factor in admission decisions* with the specific aim of promoting racial and ethnic diversity (as opposed to other kinds of student diversity) in the admitted pool. When race was used as an explicit factor in the review process, this could mean that a student was given bonus points for being in a minority category that the institution wished to attract. Alternatively, the student's race might be used as a positive tipping factor in committee discussions about students who were on the borderline of being accepted or rejected. (It is worth noting here that in June 2003 the U.S. Supreme Court struck down the University of Michigan's undergraduate admissions policy, which automatically awarded bonus points to applicants from underrepresented minority groups, but upheld the University of Michigan's law school admissions policy, which gives general consideration to race in the individual review of each application.)

In instances when it was not possible to use race as a factor in admissions decisions, a proxy, such as socioeconomic status, might be used instead. This approach assumes that the proxy is sufficiently related to race that its use—even without knowledge of the applicant's race—will result in more minority students being admitted. For example, one proxy mentioned by interviewees was the "life challenges" a student had faced, which includes factors such as poverty, immigration, or homelessness, and could be used as the topic of an essay that applicants were required to submit. This information might be factored into the initial review of a student's application or used as a tipping factor later on.

In terms of differences between public and private institutions, admissions directors at private institutions were more likely to use race as a factor. Those at public institutions were more likely to use proxies due to legal rulings or system policies that restricted or prohibited the use of race. Admissions directors at these institutions reported that proxies were not particularly effective at producing a racially and ethnically diverse student body since they were just as likely to advantage students from nonminority groups, as discussed later in this chapter (see also Koretz, Russell, Shin, Horn, & Shasby, 2001).

The third strategy was *linking the way admissions decisions are made to the college's overall mission.* A college's mission is usually communicated to the public in the form of a written statement that summarizes the goals of the institution. For example, a mission statement could be: "To provide a superior liberal education to undergraduate students, attending not only to their intellectual growth but also to their development as adults committed to high ethical standards and full participation as leaders in their communities."[7] Since most college mission statements include social as well as academic goals, this strategy allows admissions staff to look at many types of information, including, but not limited to, test scores and diversity characteristics, when deciding whether to admit a student. While all admissions directors interviewed felt there was some link between their institutions' missions and the way admissions decisions were made, the admissions consultants interviewed felt that the link between mission and admissions was often weak in practice. They argued that this was because of both external and internal pressure on admissions staff to conform to a one-dimensional view of excellence—the institutional test score average for incoming students.

The fourth strategy, commonly known as *the X percent rule*, came into effect in California, Florida, and Texas in the late 1990s in response to, or concurrent with, the introduction of race-blind admissions in those states. Basically, this strategy means that the best students in each high school— that is, those who exceed a certain percentile in class rank—are automatically admitted to their state's public university system. For example, public universities in Texas must automatically admit any in-state applicant who ranks in the top 10% of his or her high school graduating class. The California and Florida percent plans automatically admit the top 4% and 20%, respectively, of each high school's graduates to the state university system (unlike in Texas, entry to a particular campus is not guaranteed). The Texas strategy essentially circumvents the use of test scores in admission decisions, instead using high school rank as an indicator of academic merit. While test scores are not used in determining admission to the California and Florida state university systems under those states' X percent rules, they are still considered in admission to individual institutions. It also should be noted that the California and Texas plans apply to in-state graduates of both public and private high schools, while the Florida plan applies only to graduates of the state's public high schools (see Horn & Flores, 2003, for a more detailed discussion of these percentage plans).

The admissions directors and admissions consultants interviewed noted that while these percentage rules use the de facto racial segregation of many high schools to help maintain the overall number of minority students enrolled in a state university system, they do not restore the numbers enrolled at the most selective institutions in these systems to pre-rollback levels. Overall, the interviewees felt that the best way to achieve both academic excellence and diversity in the admitted student pool was to use several kinds of information, including race, in making admissions decisions.

After Admission Decisions Have Been Made

In the period after admissions decisions have been made, both test scores and diversity characteristics are used as factors in financial aid decisions. For example, a minority student accepted by a particular school might receive a much better financial package than that offered to a nonminority student with the same financial need. Similarly, a student with high test scores (usually in conjunction with a good GPA or class rank) might receive a much better financial package than a student with a less stellar academic profile but similar financial need. In addition, there may be scholarships in place that provide monetary awards to incoming students with exceptional academic records or who are from certain backgrounds.

In this "after" stage, test scores also are used as a selection device for academic support programs. Admitted students with low test scores may be flagged as candidates for optional or mandatory academic support programs. These programs may run during the summer prior to students' official arrival on campus or throughout their college experience.

Meanwhile, diversity often becomes a focus for retention efforts. This means that students from certain backgrounds (e.g., racial, ethnic, English as a Second Language), particularly those who are not well represented on campus, may be targeted with support programs designed to make them feel welcomed and part of the campus community.

Unlike the other stages of the admissions process, in the "after" stage, the roles of testing and diversity overlap with the balancing strategies used. This is because the admitted pool represents the admissions staff's best efforts at maximizing both academic quality and diversity, and the roles of testing and diversity are intertwined with efforts to avoid any attrition to the pool that would upset this balance. Thus, the first three of the four balancing strategies discussed below represent extensions or combinations of the aforementioned roles.

The first strategy is *the preferential packaging of financial aid* to create an optimal balance of both test scores and diversity in the enrolled student body. The two examples given above (i.e., a minority student receiving a much better aid package than that offered to a nonminority student with the same need, and a student with high test scores receiving a much better financial package than a student with a less stellar academic profile but similar need) are simple cases. In the first instance, the institution is strategizing to attract the minority candidate and thus maximize diversity, while in the second example the institution is strategizing to attract the high-scoring candidate and thus maximize academic excellence. In the case where an accepted student is both a minority and has high test scores, the institution is meeting its goals in both areas and thus may offer an increase in financial aid in order to fend off competing institutions. What if there is a limited amount of financial aid and a decision must be made between a minority student with average test scores and a nonminority student with high test scores, both with similar need? The outcome will be influenced by several factors, including the profile of the admitted class, the profile of those who have already received financial aid, the broader mission of the institution, and other talents these students may have that meet institutional needs.

The next two strategies—*providing academic support for students who might have difficulties with college-level work* and *providing nonacademic support for students*—are focused primarily on retaining students once they have arrived on campus. Academic support may include the kinds of programs mentioned earlier, as well as tutoring, or even lengthening the college stay. For example, one admissions director who worked at a private institution explained that his college gave academically weaker students the option of entering a 5-year, instead of the standard 4-year, degree program. This allowed these students to take fewer courses each semester while still receiving financial help over the course of the 5 years. Nonacademic support may include financial support, peer mentoring, or counseling, as well as the fostering of a diverse campus environment and curricula so that students from different backgrounds feel welcomed and acknowledged. Admissions directors at both public and private institutions noted the need to provide such financial, emotional, and cultural support for underrepresented minority students in order to retain them. In addition, there was a good deal of anecdotal information suggesting the importance of a "critical mass of one's peers" in encouraging underrepresented minority students to stay in college.

The final strategy in this "after" period is not linked to any of the afore-mentioned roles, but focuses more broadly on *finding different ways to measure success in college*. The admissions directors and admissions consultants interviewed spoke of the need to identify and collect both short- and long-term information on the many ways—for example, academic, economic, social—in which students can be successful, both while they are in college and after they graduate. It was suggested that by defining different kinds of success in college and beyond, more varied types of information could be identified as useful in making admissions decisions. While this strategy offers intriguing possibilities for expanding the range of measures available to admissions offices, it appeared to be more wishful thinking than reality due to difficulties with finding easy-to-measure indicators.

Summary of Findings from the Interview Data

The findings from the qualitative interviews with admissions directors and admissions consultants shed light on the two central themes of this chapter—namely, the "balancing act" between equity and excellence and the longitudinal and additive nature of inequity. In particular, these interviews highlight the need to move beyond the false dichotomies and simplistic definitions—that is, excellence as high test scores and equity as racial preferences that result in underqualified minority students being admitted—that frame current conversations about college admissions. The admissions process described by these interviewees is far richer and more complicated. In particular, definitions of excellence are much broader, and admissions directors are cognizant of the wealth of talents and experiences that different students bring to the learning experience. In relation to the longitudinal and additive nature of inequity, the various balancing strategies described by the interviewees and listed in Table 5.1 indicate the necessity for colleges and state policymakers to enhance efforts to counter inequities in the K–12 pipeline as early as possible. Namely, these data call for vast improvements in the academic preparation of elementary and high school students, and ongoing efforts to address the issue of inequality throughout the college experience through academic and nonacademic support services on campus.

There is a third theme in these findings—namely, the layers of policies acting on the college environment and the extent to which top-down mandates or policies from the state can aid or impede the bottom-up policies or strategies of the college in terms of defining and achieving excellence and equity in the undergraduate admissions process. The different strategies employed by college admissions offices in an attempt to find a balance between the institutional need for high test scores and the need for diversity are a mix of national, state, system, and institutional policies and practices. It is evident that institutional balancing strategies can be reinforced or negated by system, state, or national policies or mandates. At the same time, admissions directors who are determined to find a way to maintain diversity goals can modify top-down policy at the school level. It is also evident that for colleges and universities to achieve the goal of creating a student population that is composed of high academic achievers who are also diverse, policies at each level—institution, system, state, and national—need to be compatible. The next section of this chapter provides a quantitative demonstration of what happens to institutional efforts to increase the racial and ethnic diversity of the admitted student population when system and state policies that require race-blind admissions are put in place.

THE CASE OF CALIFORNIA

In 1995, the UC Board of Regents enacted SP-1, stating that "the University of California shall not use race, religion, sex, color, ethnicity, or national origin as criteria for admission to the University or to any program of study." The following year, California voters approved Proposition 209, which banned the consideration of race, ethnicity, and gender in public employment, public contracting, and education. Taken together, these two policies meant that race could no longer be considered in admission to California's state system of higher education.

In response to these changes in California and other states, National Board researchers decided to examine how various approaches to college admissions—including race-blind or "race-neutral" policies—affect the diversity of the admitted student population. Since California was one of the main focuses of debate about the rollback of affirmative action, the analyses used data from that state and were modeled after the admissions procedures of the UC system. A brief summary of the study and its findings is presented here. A fuller description can be found in the National Board publication by Koretz and colleagues (2001) from which this summary is drawn.

Study Questions, Data, and Methods

Using a database of some 130,000 California students,[8] National Board researchers investigated the following questions:

- What are the effects of different stages in the admissions process—for example, a student's decision to take a college admissions test and apply, and the college's decision to accept an applicant—on the racial and ethnic composition of the student population?
- How does a race-neutral admissions model (a logistic regression model developed for this study that used only test scores and GPA to predict admission to college) compare with actual admissions before and after the elimination of affirmative action in the UC system?
- What are the effects of alternative admissions approaches that take into account factors other than test scores and grades, but not race or ethnicity, on the racial and ethnic composition of the student population?

The analyses required to answer these questions had three stages. In the first stage, a race-neutral admissions model was created for each UC undergraduate campus. Using data obtained from the UC Office of the President, these models estimated the probability of admission to each campus as a function of SAT-I scores and GPA. The eight campuses were then grouped into three categories based on the apparent selectivity of their admissions: highly selective (Berkeley and Los Angeles), moderately selective (Davis, Irvine, Santa Barbara, and San Diego), and least selective (Riverside and Santa Cruz). Within each category, the model from one campus was chosen to represent all of the schools in that category. The high-selectivity model was based on the Berkeley campus, the moderate-selectivity model was based on the Irvine campus, and the low-selectivity model was based on the Santa Cruz campus.

In the second stage, the three models chosen in the first stage were applied to student test score and background data (e.g., GPA, race/ethnicity) obtained from the College Board to estimate the racial/ethnic composition of the admitted pool under race-neutral admissions rules. These analyses used 1998 and 1995 data and were limited to students who attended high school in California at the time they took the SAT-I. The models did not predict acceptance or rejection for individual students; instead, they predicted the probability of admission for students in a given range of SAT-I scores and GPA. These probabilities were multiplied by the number of tested students in each range to obtain estimated counts of admitted students.

The UC selection process is made up of a series of screens that progressively reduce the applicant pool: (1) taking a college admissions test; (2) meeting UC system eligibility criteria based on test scores, course requirements, and GPA[9]; (3) applying to a campus at a given level of selectivity; and (4) being admitted to that campus. The race-neutral model described above represents a simplified version of the fourth of these screens. National Board researchers also simplified the first two screens in the UC selection process by considering only SAT-I[10] data for the first screen, and SAT-I and GPA data for the second. In addition, the records of all UC institutions to which each student had his or her SAT-I scores sent (obtained from the College Board) were used as a proxy for actual applications in the third screen. The effects of these four screens (individually and in combination) on the diversity of the surviving pool of students was examined, and the results compared with actual UC admissions data from 3 years: 1995 (before enactment of SP-1 and Proposition 209), 1999 (to represent full implementation of these policies), and 1997 (to represent the transitional period).

In the third stage of the analysis, the researchers examined the effects of a number of alternative admissions models on the racial and ethnic diversity of the admitted student population. These models used both individual variables (such as mother's education) and school characteristics (such as high school graduation rate). As part of this stage, a number of X percent rules also were modeled.

The results of stages one and two of the analysis provide answers to the first two study questions outlined above. These results are presented in the next section and are organized according to the selectivity level of the UC campus to which students applied (i.e., highly selective, moderately selective, or least selective). The results of stage three of the analysis provide answers to the third study question outlined above and are presented in the section that follows the one below. It should be pointed out that while all the findings are based on data for California, Koretz and colleagues (2001) conclude that they probably could be generalized "in broad brush" to other states.

Leaks in the Pipeline

Results for admissions to highly selective campuses are shown in Table 5.2. Following the progression of Asians through the filters, we see that:

- In 1998, 15% of graduates of California high schools were Asian.
- They constituted 23% of SAT-I test takers that year.
- 25% of those who were UC system eligible were Asian.
- 36% of those who both were eligible for the UC system and actually applied to a highly selective campus were Asian.
- Asians constituted 38% of those who were admitted to a highly selective campus under the race-neutral model.

Table 5.2. Racial/Ethnic Composition, Highly Selective Campuses: Actual and Estimated Using All Screens and SAT-I + GPA Admissions Model

	Asian, Asian American, Pacific Islander	Black or African American	Hispanic	White	Other	Decline to State
Graduates, 1998	15	7	31	45	1	NA
SAT-takers, 1998	23	7	19	42	6	3
UC eligible, 1998	*25*	*4*	*15*	*46*	*6*	*3*
Eligible and applied to high-selectivity school, 1998	*36*	*4*	*15*	*35*	*7*	*2*
Admitted by neutral model, 1998	*38*	*2*	*9*	*42*	*7*	*3*
1995 admitted class	36	7	19	31	2	5
1997 admitted class	38	6	15	33	2	6
1999 admitted class	41	3	10	35	2	9

Note: Race/ethnicity is based on student self-reports for all rows except the "Graduates" row, which is based on reports by school administrators. Estimates are italicized; other numbers are actual counts. Percentages may not sum to totals because of the exclusion of American Indian students and rounding.

Source: Koretz, Russell, Shin, Horn, and Shasby (2001). Estimates reflect National Board analysis; admissions figures are published figures from the UC system (http://www.ucop.edu/pathways/infoctr/introuc/prof_engin.html); counts of SAT-takers are based on National Board tabulations of data provided by the College Board; counts of graduates are from the California Department of Education, Educational Demographics Unit (http://data1.cde.gov/dataquest).

For the first research question—what are the effects of different stages in the admissions process on the racial and ethnic composition of the student population—we can see that for Asians, the effect is to overrepresent their relative percentages in the population at each progressive stage. In terms of the second research question—how the race-neutral admissions model compares with actual admissions before and after the elimination of affirmative action in the UC system—the answer can be found by looking at the last three rows in Table 5.2. If we look at the three entries for Asians in these rows, we can see that Asians constituted 36, 38, and 41% of the actual admitted class in 1995, 1997, and 1999, respectively. Thus, they approximated (in 1995 and 1997) and then exceeded (in 1999) the relative percentage predicted by the race-neutral model. In their discussion of these results, Koretz and colleagues (2001) note that this underprediction of Asians (as well as the overprediction of Whites in Table 5.2) may be due to differences in the proportions of students from these groups applying to selective private institutions in California as well as out-of-state institutions.

If we proceed through these screens for other racial/ethnic groups, we note that the percentage of African Americans and Hispanics decreases rather dramatically and that this starts to occur from early on in the admissions process. The first screen applied—students' decision whether to take the SAT-I—causes the biggest reduction in the percentage of Hispanic students, while the second screen applied—UC system eligibility—causes the biggest reduction in the percentage of African American students. The eligible-and-applied screen has a negligible impact on both groups. The race-neutral-admissions screen has a more substantial one. Comparing the percentages admitted by the race-neutral model—2% for African Americans and 9% for Hispanics—with the last three rows of Table 5.2, we see that the model underpredicts the representation of both groups in the 1995 and 1997 admitted classes, but closely approximates their percentages in the 1999 admitted class. These findings suggest that race played some role in admissions to highly selective UC campuses in 1995 and 1997 and that admissions post SP-1 and Proposition 209 are producing effects (at least for African American and Hispanic students) similar to those obtained with a race-neutral model that relied primarily on test scores and grades.

Results for moderately selective institutions are shown in Table 5.3. The first two screens applied—deciding to take the SAT-I and meeting UC system eligibility requirements—are the same for these moderately selective institutions as they are for the highly selective schools. Thus, the representation of non-Asian minority students falls considerably before use of the filter of application to a moderately selective campus.

The self-selection of eligible students to apply to moderately selective campuses affects the African American and Hispanic composition of the pool only slightly. For example, Hispanic students constitute 15% of the eligible pool but 13% of the eligible students who applied to such an institution. African American students, who constitute 4% of eligible students, made up 3% of those who were eligible and applied. In contrast to the findings for high-selectivity campuses, the race-neutral model has little effect on the racial and ethnic composition of the admitted student pool. In particular, the percentage of Hispanics decreases only from 13 to 12%, and that of African Americans drops from 3 to 2%.

Comparing the results from the race-neutral model with the last row of Table 5.3, it appears that by 1999, race was not a factor in admissions decisions for the moderately selective UC campuses. In other words, the composition

Table 5.3. Racial/Ethnic Composition, Moderately Selective Campuses: Actual and Estimated Using All Screens and SAT-I + GPA Admissions Model

	Asian, Asian American, Pacific Islander	Black or African American	Hispanic	White	Other	Decline to State
Graduates, 1998	15	7	31	45	1	NA
SAT-takers, 1998	23	7	19	42	6	3
UC eligible, 1998	*25*	*4*	*15*	*46*	*6*	*3*
Eligible and applied to moderate-selectivity school, 1998	*32*	*3*	*13*	*42*	*6*	*2*
Admitted by neutral model, 1998	*33*	*2*	*12*	*43*	*7*	*2*
1995 admitted class	35	3	14	42	4	2
1997 admitted class	36	3	13	44	3	5
1999 admitted class	36	2	11	41	2	8

Note: Race/ethnicity is based on student self-reports for all rows except the "Graduates" row, which is based on reports by school administrators. Estimates are italicized; other numbers are actual counts. Percentages may not sum to totals because of the exclusion of American Indian students and rounding.

Source: Koretz, Russell, Shin, Horn, and Shasby (2001). Estimates reflect National Board analysis; admissions figures are published figures from the UC system (http://www.ucop.edu/pathways/infoctr/introuc/prof_engin.html); counts of SAT-takers are based on National Board tabulations of data provided by the College Board; counts of graduates are from the California Department of Education, Educational Demographics Unit (http://data1.cde.gov/dataquest).

of the group admitted in 1999 was very similar to that predicted by the race-neutral model. In addition, the composition of the admitted classes changed very little from 1995 to 1999. These small changes, after affirmative action was terminated, suggest that racial/ethnic preferences had been much less substantial at the moderately selective campuses than at the highly selective campuses.

There are many similarities between the results for the least and the moderately selective UC campuses (Table 5.4). In particular, it is evident that admission of African American and Hispanic students to the least selective campuses also changed little from 1995 to 1999 and matched the race-neutral model reasonably closely in all years. This suggests that racial and ethnic preferences played little role in admission to these institutions in the years prior to, as well as after, SP-1 and Proposition 209.

Table 5.4. Racial/Ethnic Composition, Least Selective Campuses: Actual and Estimated Using All Screens and SAT-I + GPA Admissions Model

	Asian, Asian American, Pacific Islander	Black or African American	Hispanic	White	Other	Decline to State
Graduates, 1998	15	7	31	45	1	NA
SAT-takers, 1998	23	7	19	42	6	3
UC eligible, 1998	*25*	*4*	*15*	*46*	*6*	*3*
Eligible and applied to low-selectivity school, 1998	*23*	*3*	*16*	*38*	*7*	*2*
Admitted by neutral model, 1998	*33*	*3*	*15*	*39*	*7*	*3*
1995 Admitted class	33	3	15	39	7	3
1997 Admitted class	33	3	16	38	7	3
1999 Admitted class	24	4	16	46	6	3

Note: Race/ethnicity is based on student self-reports for all rows except the "Graduates" row, which is based on reports by school administrators. Estimates are italicized; other numbers are actual counts. Percentages may not sum to totals because of the exclusion of American Indian students and rounding.

Source: Koretz, Russell, Shin, Horn, and Shasby (2001). Estimates reflect National Board analysis; admissions figures are published figures from the UC system (http://www.ucop.edu/pathways/infoctr/introuc/prof_engin.html); counts of SAT-takers are based on National Board tabulations of data provided by the College Board; counts of graduates are from the California Department of Education, Educational Demographics Unit (http://data1.cde.gov/dataquest).

Because most states lack the system-eligibility screen used in California, Koretz and colleagues (2001) tested the generality of their findings by eliminating the UC eligibility screen from the aforementioned analyses. Removing this screen had little impact on the racial/ethnic composition of the groups admitted by the race-neutral model to the high-, moderate-, or low-selectivity campuses in the UC system.

The Difficult Search for Alternatives

Two sets of analyses were required to answer the third study question—the effects on diversity of alternative admissions approaches. In the first set, several X percent rules were modeled. As described previously, the X percent rule enables admissions staff to admit automatically a certain percentage of the state's graduating high school seniors based primarily on their high school rank. Each of the X percent rules modeled for this study ranked students solely on their high school GPAs (an approach that is consistent with the X percent policies implemented to date).

The first X percent rule ranked all students in public high schools statewide and automatically admitted the top 12.5%. This was viewed as the baseline against which to compare all other X percent models since UC undergraduate admissions policy is guided by the California Master Plan for Higher Education, which requires that the top one-eighth (i.e., 12.5%) of the state's high school graduates be eligible for admission to the UC system. The second X percent rule ranked all students within each school and automatically admitted the top 12.5% from each school. The third rule automatically admitted the top 6% within each school, and the fourth automatically admitted the top 4% within each school (California adopted a similar 4% plan after the passage of SP-1 and Proposition 209, but data on the effects of this rule on UC enrollment patterns were not available at the time of this study). To obtain an admitted group of students that represents 12.5% of graduating public school students in California, the third and fourth models also accept the top 6.5 and 8.5% of students statewide after removing the top 6 and 4% from within each school, respectively. The results of these analyses are shown in Table 5.5.

Given the baseline rule of attracting the top 12.5% across the state, automatically accepting the top 4% from each school before accepting the remaining top 8.5% statewide would not have much effect on the academic qualifications or diversity of the admitted students (see Table 5.5). Accepting the top 6% within each school also would have little effect on diversity and GPA, but it would reduce the mean SAT-I of accepted African American and Hispanic students by a noticeable amount. In contrast, accepting the top 12.5% within each school would have dramatic effects compared with the baseline condition of accepting the top 12.5% statewide. The percentage of admitted students who are African American or Hispanic would almost double. However, this would come at the cost of a large drop in the academic qualifications of these students. Most strikingly, the mean SAT-I scores of African American and Hispanic students would drop 135 and 127 points, respectively.

The second set of analyses explored the impact of a number of alternative admissions models that used both individual variables (such as mother's education) and school characteristics (such as high school graduation rate) as proxies for a student's race. In each of these analyses, the equivalent of a 200-point SAT-I bonus was awarded to students who came

Table 5.5. Modeled Results of Top 4%, 6%, and 12.5% Admissions Policies

	Asian	Black	Hispanic	White	Other	Total
Top 12.5% Across State (Baseline)						
% of Admitted Group	29	2	10	49	10	100
Mean SAT-I	1222	1136	1126	1211	1210	1204
Mean GPA	3.89	3.90	3.93	3.87	3.88	3.89
Top 4% Within High School						
% of Admitted Group	29	2	10	49	10	100
Mean SAT-I	1223	1117	1115	1214	1210	1204
Mean GPA	3.90	3.87	3.93	3.88	3.88	3.89
Top 6% Within High School						
% of Admitted Group	29	2	11	48	10	100
Mean SAT-I	1221	1091	1093	1216	1208	1200
Mean GPA	3.90	3.84	3.89	3.89	3.88	3.89
Top 12.5% Within High School						
% of Admitted Group	27	4	18	42	9	100
Mean SAT-I	1173	1001	999	1198	1168	1145
Mean GPA	3.88	3.60	3.68	3.87	3.85	3.83

Source: Koretz, Russell, Shin, Horn, and Shasby (2001).

from the most disadvantaged background in terms of one of these variables. The preference awarded for each step on a variable depended on the number of categories the variable had, as indicated in Table 5.6.

Table 5.7 shows the results of giving preference to each variable, first individually and then in combination (when combinations were used, the maximum impact was set to 200 points). Since school-level data were available only for public schools in California, these analyses were run on a reduced data set. The first two rows of Table 5.7 compare the results of the SAT-I and GPA-only models and illustrate that the reduced and full data set yielded about the same racial and ethnic mix of admitted students.

It is evident that giving preference to students based on any of the variables decreases the representation of Asian students and increases that of White and Hispanic students. None of the preferences have much impact on the representation of African American students. What is perhaps most striking (and troubling) about these results is that even the largest effects of giving preference to demographic variables do not come close to making the representation of African American and Hispanic students in

Table 5.6. Variables, Number of Levels, and Preference per Step Applied in Alternative Models

Variable	Levels	Effective SAT-I Point Boost per Level
Income	14	15.38 per step
Mother's Education	BA or beyond No BA	0 200
High School Graduation Rate	> 75% 50% to 75% < 50%	0 100 200
Free/Reduced Price Lunch	Continuous, from 0% to 95%	2.1 for each 1% increase in percent free lunch
School Location	Suburban/Other Urban/Rural	0 200

Source: Koretz, Russell, Shin, Horn, and Shasby (2001).

the admitted groups proportionate to their numbers in the pool of potential students.

Summary of Findings from the California Study

Similar to the interview study, the findings from this study shed further light on our two chapter themes. In particular, the analyses conducted by Koretz and colleagues (2001) and summarized here suggest that race-neutral admissions decisions have a large negative impact on African American and Hispanic rates of admission in highly selective academic environments. In other words, if race is not taken into account, fewer African American and Hispanic students are likely to attend the most selective universities. While this may seem due to the increased influence of test scores on the admission decision, it should be pointed out that the adverse impact does not stem from test scores alone. Making these admissions decisions based on high school GPA alone also would result in Hispanics and African Americans being substantially underrepresented in admissions to highly selective campuses since these students tend to have lower grades than other students. This fact, in conjunction with lower test taking, system eligibility, and application rates among these groups, suggests that there is a cumulative impact on minority access to higher education in terms of the choices made and opportunities available to students earlier in the education system.

Table 5.7. Students Admitted (%)

Modeled Variable	Asian	Black	Hispanic	White	Other	Decline to State
SAT-I + GPA Full Sample	38	2	9	42	8	3
SAT-I + GPA Reduced Sample	40	2	8	40	8	2
SAT-I + GPA + Income	33	2	11	46	7	1
SAT-I + GPA + Mother's Education	30	2	12	48	7	1
SAT-I + GPA + Location	29	2	10	49	7	3
SAT-I + GPA + Graduation Rate	31	2	9	49	7	3
SAT-I + GPA + Free Lunch	31	2	10	47	7	3
SAT-I + GPA + Income + Mother's Education + Location + Graduation Rate + Free Lunch	30	2	10	49	7	1

Source: Koretz, Russell, Shin, Horn, and Shasby (2001).

RECOMMENDATIONS

Both studies presented here demonstrate that test scores and diversity characteristics hang in a delicate balance and that placing more weight on one than the other in the admissions process can substantially change the academic and racial/ethnic composition of the admitted student population. As a result, the most important recommendations from these studies are framed by the two themes that run through this chapter, namely, the "balancing act" of equity and excellence and the additivity of inequity.

- Given the dynamics of inequity—small disparities grow larger and more consequential with time—significant effort should be put into the earlier segments of a student's educational career. Any notion of a head start on education needs to begin as early as practicable and stay in place through the early grades, where educational equity begins its yawning divide (see Schweinhart, Barnes, & Weikart, 1993).
- Given the additive nature of inequity, it is important to address all parts of the education system simultaneously while working to move away from ameliorating the later-stage effects of inequity (college admission and beyond) in favor of earlier efforts. As we have reported in our National Board studies, the tensions inherent in efforts to rectify later-stage effects are difficult, costly, and socially

divisive. It would be far better to resource—or even over-resource—efforts at the earlier grades and make explicit a strategy to reduce later-stage efforts as earlier-stage efforts take hold.

- Given the key role of resources (as pointed out in Chapter 2, this volume), there is a need to monitor equity in terms of educational inputs as well as in terms of educational outcomes at all levels of the system. Put differently, we need to be very careful that we do not measure educational outcomes (in terms of tests alone or even in terms of tests and other measures) without measuring educational inputs such as dollar resources, organizational arrangements, educational leadership, and the like. Otherwise, we may be measuring the effects of resource differentials more than student ability or achievement.
- Given the weaknesses inherent in testing technology, multiple measures of achievement should be used for students at all grade levels and most especially where the stakes are high. In particular, given the low predictive value of most standardized college and graduate school admissions tests, as well as the equity issues associated with their use, the range of measures of excellence and predictors of success used in making college admissions decisions should be broadened.

In offering these recommendations, we trust that researchers will continue to work hard to understand how educational equity actually operates in the classrooms and colleges of our nation. Solid applied research is necessary if we are to grapple successfully with the very precious resource of equitably well-educated future citizens.

NOTES

Acknowledgments. In addition to the authors listed, several individuals contributed to this chapter through their work on, or help with, the studies described in the text. These individuals include: Daniel Koretz, Michael Russell, David Shin, Cathy Horn, Kelly Shasby, Walter Haney, Joseph Pedulla, Susan Henderson-Conlon, and Steve Stemler. We are also grateful to Janice Petrovich and Amy Stuart Wells for their feedback on earlier versions of this chapter.

1. The SAT-I—also known as the SAT I: Reasoning Test or, more simply, the SAT—is a measure of verbal and mathematical reasoning skills. The test is developed and administered by the College Board and usually taken by high school juniors and seniors. Many colleges and universities use SAT-I scores as one indicator of a student's readiness to do college-level work. More information on the SAT-I and other College Board tests is available at www.collegeboard.com.

2. The National Board on Educational Testing and Public Policy, located in the Carolyn A. and Peter S. Lynch School of Education at Boston College, is an independent monitoring body created by a 1998 Ford Foundation grant. The National Board grew out of the earlier work of the Ford-sponsored National Commission on Testing and Public Policy (1990), which recommended the creation of an independent monitoring body for tests. The National Board was set up to monitor testing programs, policies, and practices; evaluate the benefits and costs of testing programs; and assess the extent to which professional standards for test development and use are met in practice. The National Board provides ongoing information on the uses and outcomes of educational testing for decision-making purposes, paying special attention to groups historically underserved by the education system. The applied research agenda proposed by the National Board has five priorities: (1) monitoring the effects of state-level testing programs; (2) designing state-level systems for accountability; (3) understanding the role of tests in standards-based education reform; (4) understanding how tests are used in college admissions; and (5) understanding the link between testing and technology. The National Board addresses a number of audiences, including policymakers and policy analysts; students, parents, and educators; the media; representatives of advocacy groups; test developers; and scholars. More information on the National Board is available at www.bc.edu/nbetpp.

3. Inquiries into the achievement gap have run the full gamut of themes. Chief among the explanations offered for this phenomenon have been family background (e.g., Kao, 1995), social and economic factors (e.g., Oakes, 1990), cultural factors (e.g., Ogbu, 1986), genetic differences (e.g., Herrnstein & Murray, 1994), language proficiency (e.g., Bradby, Owings, & Quinn, 1992), school organizational factors such as tracking (e.g., Oakes, 1985), course-taking patterns (e.g., McLure, Sun, & Valiga, 1997; Schiel, Pommerich, & Noble, 1996), societal stereotypes (e.g., Steele, 1997), and test bias (e.g., Jencks & Phillips, 1998).

4. Databases were created that had a mean difference of .80 standard deviation between African Americans and Whites—a difference slightly smaller than those found on the SAT-I. In line with the pattern shown in numerous studies, the scores of simulated African American students were made a little less variable than those of Whites. The distribution of scores used in all three scenarios was based on a population that is 15% African American and 85% White.

5. Selectivity levels for institutions were defined in terms of test scores, high school rank, and high school GPA ranges for enrolled first-year students, as well as acceptance rates. While we managed to achieve some variation in selectivity among the public and private institutions chosen, we did not find large differences in the way the admissions process worked at these different selectivity levels (*within* the public and the private domains). The biggest contrast we found was in the way admissions works at public versus private institutions. Thus, the main distinctions made here are between public and private ways of handling admissions.

6. One response by colleges has been to introduce "early decision" or "early action" programs, which allow high-achieving students to apply in the fall semester of their senior year and receive an admissions decision by about January of

the following year. These programs tend to increase the number of students with high test scores in the admitted pool, thereby raising the institutional average.

7. This is part of the mission statement for Duke University (not one of the institutions where we conducted our interviews). The full mission statement is available at www.duke.edu/web/president/mission.html.

8. The College Board provided complete data files for all California students who took the SAT in 1995 through 1998. These data included SAT-I scores, information identifying students' high schools and the colleges to which they had their scores sent, and background data (e.g., GPA, racial and ethnic identity, parents' education) from the Student Descriptive Questionnaire that students fill out when registering for the SAT-I. Aggregate data for the UC system on actual acceptances and enrollments by race/ethnicity, and on the probability of admission to specific campuses as a function of SAT-I scores and GPA, were taken from tabulations published by the UC Office of the President. Information on the characteristics of high schools was taken from the U.S. Department of Education's Common Core of Data for public school files and the California Department of Education DataQuest records. These were merged with student-level records using a matching of high school identifiers provided by the College Board.

9. UC system eligibility is based on three criteria. First, GPA and SAT-I scores are combined on a sliding scale to set minimum requirements. Second, students must take a set of required courses. Third, students must take three SAT-II tests (these are subject-matter tests in areas such as English literature and science), although they are not required to attain a specific score on these tests. The models used in this National Board study simplified UC system eligibility by applying the GPA and SAT-I criteria, but not the requirements for specific courses or for taking SAT-II tests.

10. Since 98% of students who apply to the UC system take the SAT-I (Geiser, 1998), considering only whether students take the SAT-I, not either the SAT-I or the ACT, has little impact on the student pool.

REFERENCES

Bradby, D., Owings, J., & Quinn, P. (1992). *Language characteristics and academic achievement: A look at Asian and Hispanic eighth graders in NELS: 88. Statistical analysis report* (NCES-92–479). Washington, DC: National Center for Education Statistics.

Breland, H., Maxey, J., McLure, G., Valiga, M., Boatwright, M., Ganley, V., & Jenkins, L. (1995). *Challenges in college admissions: A report of a survey of undergraduate admission policies, practices, and procedures.* American Association of Collegiate Registrars and Admissions Officers, American College Testing, College Board, Educational Testing Service, and National Association of College Admission Counselors.

Clarke, M. (2004). Weighing things up: A closer look at *U.S. News and World Report*'s ranking formulas. *College and University, 79*(3), 3–9.

Clarke, M., & Shore, A. (2001). *The roles of testing and diversity in college admissions.*

Chestnut Hill, MA: National Board on Educational Testing and Public Policy.

Fletcher, M. A. (1997, September 20). UC may drop SAT entry requirement; California system fears sharp decline in Black, Latino enrollment. *Washington Post*, p. A3.

Geiser, S. (1998). *Redefining UC's eligibility pool to include a percentage of students from each high school: Summary of simulation results*. Oakland: University of California, Office of the President.

Haney, W. M., Madaus, G. F., & Lyons, R. (1993). *The fractured marketplace for standardized testing*. Boston: Kluwer Academic.

Herrnstein, R., & Murray, C. (1994). *The bell curve*. New York: Grove.

Horn, C. L., & Flores, S. M. (2003). *Percent plans in college admissions: A comparative analysis of three states' experiences*. Cambridge, MA: Harvard University, Civil Rights Project.

Jencks, C., & Phillips, M. (Eds.). (1998). *The black–white test score gap*. Washington, DC: Brookings Institution.

Kao, G. (1995). Asian Americans as model minorities? A look at their academic performance. *American Journal of Education*, 10(2), 121–159.

Koretz, D. (2000). *The impact of score differences on the admission of minority students: An illustration*. Chestnut Hill, MA: National Board on Educational Testing and Public Policy.

Koretz, D., Russell, M., Shin, D., Horn, C., & Shasby, K. (2001). *Testing and diversity in postsecondary education: The case of California*. Chestnut Hill, MA: National Board on Educational Testing and Public Policy.

McLure, G., Sun, A., & Valiga, M. (1997). *Trends in advanced mathematics and science course-taking and achievement among ACT-tested high school students: 1987–1996*. Iowa City: American College Testing Program.

Monks, J., & Ehrenberg, R. G. (1999). *The impact of U.S. News and World Report college rankings on admissions outcomes and pricing policies at selective private institutions*. Cambridge, MA: National Bureau of Economic Research.

National Commission on Testing and Public Policy. (1990). *From gatekeeper to gateway: Transforming testing in America*. Chestnut Hill, MA: Author.

Oakes, J. (1985). *Keeping track: How schools structure inequality*. New Haven, CT: Yale University Press.

Oakes, J. (1990). *Lost talent: The underparticipation of women, minorities, and disabled persons in science*. Santa Monica, CA: Rand.

Ogbu, J. (1986). The consequences of the American case system. In U. Neisser (Ed.), *The school achievement of minority children: New perspectives* (pp. 19–56). Hillsdale, NJ: Erlbaum.

Schiel, J., Pommerich, M., & Noble, J. (1996). *Factors associated with longitudinal educational achievement as measured by PLAN and ACT assessment scores* (ACT Research Rep. 96–5). Iowa City: American College Testing Program.

Schweinhart, L. J., Barnes, H. V., & Weikart, D. P. (1993). *Significant benefits: The High/Scope Perry preschool study through age 27*. Ypsilanti, MI: High/Scope Press.

Steele, C. (1997). A threat in the air: How stereotypes shape intellectual identity and performance. *American Psychologist*, 52(6), 613–629.

6

Addressing Institutional Inequities in Education

The Case of Advanced Placement Courses in California

MAYA FEDERMAN
HARRY P. PACHÓN

Many educational policies are implemented with specific equity goals in mind and should be analyzed to determine their success or failure in promoting equity. Some policies, on the other hand, are implemented for other reasons, but may end up having important implications for equity in terms of opportunities for students of different racial, ethnic, and social class backgrounds. The advanced placement (AP) program is one such policy. Given the growing popularity of the AP program nationally and the critical role that AP tests now play in college admissions, it is important to evaluate the equality of opportunities that students of different races, ethnicities, social classes, and communities have to participate in this program.

Equality of educational opportunity has received increased attention in California in recent years. Specifically, the repeal of affirmative action in the state university system by the passage of Proposition 209 in 1996 has led to a re-examination of the effects of various aspects of the university admissions policy on the matriculation of underrepresented minority students and on equality of opportunity (see Chapter 5, this volume). Participation in AP courses can play an important role in admissions decisions in two ways: (1) by serving as an indicator that an applicant has taken a rigorous set of courses, and (2) by enabling a student taking AP courses (and other honors classes) to gain an additional grade point in the calculation of his or her high school grade point average (GPA) for college admissions.

In this chapter we evaluate the AP program in California through an equity lens, focusing on student access as measured by the presence and depth of the AP program at the high school level. We find that, after controlling for school size and other characteristics, schools enrolling a high proportion of African American and Hispanic students offer significantly fewer advanced placement courses. We also find that schools with higher rates of low-income students and schools in rural areas offer fewer of these courses, on average.

Thus, the AP program in California serves as a good case study for evaluating the equity effects of programs whose primary goal was something else. Additionally, looking at the AP experience in California provides important lessons for other states with increasing participation in the program or that may be experiencing an increase in the importance of AP course taking in their college admissions process. We begin the discussion by providing some historical background on the advanced placement program as well as recent changes in admissions at the University of California (UC) system. Next, we discuss our methodology and our findings on the inequalities of availability in AP programs across high schools in the state. Finally, we discuss the different legal and legislative efforts that, drawing on research such as this, attempt to address the inequities associated with this program, and we make suggestions for additional areas of action and evaluation.

HISTORY OF THE ADVANCED PLACEMENT PROGRAM

The advanced placement program was initiated during the early 1950s as a response to concerns about the educational needs of high-ability secondary school students and a perception that some of these students were repeating, during their first years of college, material they had learned in high school. Two related experiments led to the eventual creation of curriculum and exams to enable students to study college-level material in high school and receive college credit. In 1951, a study sponsored by the Ford Foundation's Fund for the Advancement of Education examined student coursework at three elite high schools—Exeter, Andover, and Lawrenceville—and at Harvard, Princeton, and Yale. The authors of the study found a great deal of overlap in the high school and college material and thus proposed the development of achievement exams that would allow colleges to give advanced placement credit to students. Around the same time, the Ford Foundation's Fund also sponsored a cooperative effort among 12 colleges and 12 secondary schools, known as the School and College Study of Admissions with Advanced Standing, to develop 11 college-level courses that then were offered in 18 secondary schools. The Educational Testing Service then helped in the development of course examinations. Finally, in 1954, the College Board assumed responsibility for the advanced placement program (College Board, 2001).

From the 1955–56 to the 1999–2000 school years the program grew from 104 to 13,253 participating schools and from 2,129 to more than one million exams administered. The program currently offers 33 distinct courses in 19 subject areas. California also has seen dramatic growth in the program. The numbers of exams given in the state increased from 78,379 in 1989 to 229,310 in 2000 (College Board, 2001).

ROLE OF AP COURSES IN COLLEGE ADMISSIONS
AND RECENT DEVELOPMENTS IN UC ADMISSIONS

While some advocates of the AP program focus on the ways in which these classes enhance the rigor and intellectual challenge of the high school curriculum, our focus in this chapter is on the role of the AP program in the college admissions and matriculation process. The advantage that AP courses provide students in this process has been at the heart of recent equity concerns regarding the AP program in California, especially as it relates to admission to the prestigious University of California system. Students taking AP (or other honors) courses (up to a maximum of 8 courses) in their junior or senior year are awarded extra points toward their GPA to reflect the greater difficulty of these courses (University of California, 2001). Thus, an A in an AP course is worth 5 points toward a GPA rather than the 4 points students receive for getting an A in a standard high school course. Having a diverse offering of honors and AP courses is helpful, because it allows students greater choice over which courses to take at an advanced level. It is common, therefore, for students in high schools with rich AP and honors course offerings to graduate with GPAs higher than 4.0. Of those students admitted to UC Berkeley in 2000, for example, 84% had a 4.0 or higher. In addition, admissions offices also consider the number of and performance in approved honors, advanced placement, and transferable college courses when selecting students (University of California, 2000). While it is recommended that reviewers take into account the availability of these courses at the applicant's school, in large systems such as the University of California, with hundreds of thousands of applicants, such high school level comparisons are challenging, to say the least.

The final potential benefit to participation in the AP program is the opportunity for students to earn college credit while still in high school. Students receiving a high enough score (a 3 or above in the UC system) on the AP examination administered by the Educational Testing Service earn college credits toward graduation. With the growth of AP course availability and enrollment, it is no longer uncommon for students to enter college with second-semester freshman or sophomore standing. This benefit potentially shortens the time for a college student to graduate and correspondingly lowers the costs of a college degree. This may be especially important at colleges where high overall enrollments may make it difficult for students to enroll in some courses they need as crowded classes get closed. This "impacting" may make it more difficult to finish college in the usual 4 years. Another benefit is that students entering with high numbers of AP courses have more flexibility in choosing courses and may be able to more easily complete a double major while in college.

The inequities in access to the AP program in high school take on increased importance given recent actions to eliminate the use of affirmative action in admission to the UC system and in other states. The University of California's Resolution SP-1, enacted by the UC Board of Regents in 1995, together with Proposition 209, passed by California voters in 1996, eliminated consideration of race and ethnicity in admissions. This change went into effect for first-year applicants in Fall 1998. In November 2001, the Regents voted to repeal SP-1 and to allow individual campuses more flexibility in admissions guidelines beginning in Fall 2002. Meanwhile, the U.S. Supreme Court ruled in two landmark cases involving the University of Michigan that race can indeed play a role in the admissions process. However, because Proposition 209 is still in effect, admissions officers on the UC campuses still cannot directly consider race or ethnicity in admissions (Barreto & Pachón, 2003).

This movement away from affirmative action in California has had an important effect on the admission of Latino and African American students into the UC system. Acceptance rates for both groups fell considerably between 1997, the last year before the change, and 2002. Across the UC system, the acceptance rate for Latino students fell from 64 to 47%, while acceptance rate for African American students fell from 56 to 36%. The declines were even more pronounced at the two most selective

UC campuses—UC Berkeley and UC Los Angeles—where acceptance rates fell by roughly half. At UC Berkeley, the acceptance rate for Latino students fell from 45 to 25% while the acceptance rate for African American students fell from 50 to 22%. At UCLA, the acceptance rate for Latino students fell from 41 to 22% while the acceptance rate for African American students fell from 38 to 19% (Barreto & Pachón, 2003). These dramatic changes in acceptance rates for African American and Latino high school graduates call for careful examination of inequities in the education system that influence admissions decisions in the absence of affirmative action policies. While inequities in the AP program are arguably not the most critical of the various inequities present in the education system, they are important to examine because they may play an important direct and indirect role in the admissions process. As importantly, AP courses serve as a symbol that highlights the educational inequities that are present in many school districts across the nation.

METHODS OF ANALYSIS

Given the significance of the AP program in the college admissions process and the potential benefits of this program to students in reducing college coursework and thus lowering their tuition costs, a natural question arises: Do students throughout the state of California have equal access to AP courses? A cursory look at the statistics suggested that this may not be the case. For instance, the average number of AP courses offered in California high schools is five; however, AP course offerings vary dramatically among individual high schools—from 0 to 18. We examined variations in AP course offerings to see whether student access to AP courses in high school is correlated with demographic characteristics of the student body or the school's location. In light of the concerns about reduced enrollments of underrepresented minorities in the UC system, we were particularly interested in assessing whether there is a correlation between schools with large numbers of underrepresented minority students—namely, African American and Latino students—and lesser offerings of AP courses. We use data from two sources: the California Basic Educational Data System (CBEDS) and School Fiscal Services, both from the California Department of Education. The data gathered are from Fall 1997 and include 870 public high schools in California.[1]

Because we were interested primarily in the issue of *access*, the main variable of interest is the number of AP *courses*—not classes—offered at a school. This is the number of *distinct AP courses*—for example, calculus

AB, English language and composition, and biology—offered at the school. Even though the total number of AP classes or sections offered might be of interest as well—and we do consider this too—we used the course measure in our initial analysis because we argue that a student has greater access to a diverse AP program in a school offering single classes of AP Spanish, AP English, and AP calculus than in a school offering three sections of AP Spanish. In addition to availability of a range of courses at the school, another important element to AP and, eventually, college access is how students are placed into courses and whether minority students are less likely to be encouraged to enroll in these courses. Unfortunately, the school-level data that we have do not allow us to measure this directly.

To analyze the factors associated with the availability of AP courses, we considered several demographic and contextual variables. The primary variable of interest was the racial/ethnic composition of the school, specifically the percentage of students who are Latino or Black—those students considered underrepresented minorities in the UC system. All statistical analyses presented in the tables pool Black and Latino students together; results for the two groups analyzed separately are similar. To analyze whether the number of courses offered is related to school characteristics, in particular the proportion of students who are Latino and black, we went through three steps. First, we looked at the average number of courses offered at schools of varying minority-student enrollments. Next, because we think another important factor, school size, is related to both the depth of course offerings and minority enrollments, we replicated the previous analysis but for schools of varying sizes. It was at this point in the analysis that a strong pattern emerged: Higher minority enrollments are associated with a much lower variety of courses offered. We also analyzed the relationship between AP course availability and the percentage of low-income students (measured by the percentage of students signed up for free or reduced price lunch) and whether there is variation in AP program availability by school location—urban, suburban, or rural. To distinguish between urban and suburban schools, we used the definition suggested by the California Department of Education: Cities with fewer than 100,000 people are considered suburban. (It should be noted that the use of this definition results in a recoding in the data of some schools' self-reported locations. For consistency, we chose to apply the suggested definition to all schools.) Finally, we employed a statistical technique called regression analysis, which allowed us to examine the relationship between course offerings and the school characteristics of interest, holding other school characteristics constant.

WHAT WE LEARNED

Availability of AP Courses

In 1997, 29 different types of AP courses were offered in California: 1 in music, 2 in computer education, 2 in English, 3 in art, 3 in mathematics, 4 in science, 7 in foreign language, and 7 in social science. Overall, a total of 4,369 courses in 739 California high schools were offered. As we noted above, the average number of distinct AP courses offered was five per high school, although, also as noted above, the number at each individual high school ranged from no AP courses to as many as 18.

Do schools with a higher proportion of minority students offer fewer AP courses? Table 6.1 presents a first look at the question of whether schools with higher percentages of minority students offer fewer AP courses. When considering just this attribute in isolation, it does not appear to be the case. If anything, having very few (0–10 %) or many (75–100%) Blacks and Latinos seems to be associated with a smaller number of AP course offerings, although the difference is small. It is important, however, to include an additional variable in the analysis—school size—which can be expected to strongly influence the number of courses offered. Schools with large enrollments should be able to offer a larger variety of all types of courses, including AP courses. This is confirmed in Table 6.2: Schools with over 2,000 students offer an average of 7.33 courses compared with 2.59 courses offered at schools with from 500–1,000 students, for example.

Because schools with high percentages of Latino and Black students are more likely to be large, the relationship between racial/ethnic composition and AP course offerings may be obscured if school size is ignored. Table 6.3 shows that predominantly minority schools are in fact more likely

Table 6.1. AP Courses by Enrollment and Percent Black and Latino

Percent Black and Latino	Courses Offered
0–10%	4.17
10–25%	5.27
25–50%	5.20
50–75%	5.37
75–100%	4.77

Source: TRPI analysis of California Department of Education, 1997 data.

Table 6.2. AP Courses by Enrollment

Enrollment	Courses Offered
1–500	0.65
500–1,000	2.59
1,000–1,500	4.45
1,500–2,000	5.48
2,000 +	7.33

Source: TRPI analysis of California Department of Education, 1997 data.

to be large. Almost half of the high schools with student populations that are more than 50% Black and/or Latino have 2,000 students or more compared with less than a third of the high schools with 10 to 25% Latino and Black students and approximately one-eighth of the schools with less than 10% Latino and Black students. Similarly, high schools with less than 10% underrepresented minorities are much more likely to be small; almost a third have enrollments of 500 students or less, compared with fewer than 8% of high schools with more than 50% minority enrollment.

Thus, once we controlled for enrollment size, evidence of a negative relationship between AP courses and underrepresented minority concentration emerged, as we show in Table 6.4. For large high schools—with 2,000 or more students—those with minority enrollments of 25% or more offer just under seven types of AP courses on average compared with nine courses for those schools with 10–25 % minorities and ten courses for schools with less than 10% minority populations. The relationship between fewer AP course offerings and higher minority-student enrollments is similar for high

Table 6.3. Distribution of High School Enrollment Size by Percent Black and Latino

Enrollment	0–10%	10–25%	25–50%	50–75%	75–100%
1–500	30.30	14.78	10.55	7.36	7.89
500–1,000	17.42	12.81	9.38	8.59	13.16
1,000–1,500	21.21	18.23	11.72	9.82	13.16
1,500–2,000	18.18	25.12	25.00	26.99	16.67
2,000 +	12.88	29.06	43.36	47.24	49.12

Source: TRPI analysis of California Department of Education, 1997 data.

Table 6.4. AP Courses by Enrollment and Percent Black and Latino

Enrollment	0–10%	10–25%	25–50%	50–75%	75–100%
1–500	0.70	0.57	0.78	0.50	0.56
500–1,000	3.56	2.12	2.46	2.64	2.07
1,000–1,500	5.00	4.86	4.60	3.56	3.07
1,500–2,000	5.38	5.53	5.63	5.70	4.42
2,000 +	10.12	9.07	6.77	6.81	6.75

Source: TRPI analysis of California Department of Education, 1997 data.

schools of other sizes. For instance, in high schools with 1,000–1,500 students, the average number of AP courses offered is five in schools with the lowest concentration of Black and Latino students compared with only three courses, on average, in schools with the highest concentration of these students. While a difference of two or three courses may not seem significant, these figures represent a roughly 30% difference in AP course offerings between low- and high-minority enrollment high schools. Thus, the answer to the question, "Do schools with higher proportions of minority students offer fewer AP courses," is yes, *once we control for student enrollment*. This is an important result: Students attending high schools with higher minority concentrations have less opportunity to enroll in these important gatekeeper courses than do students in schools of similar size with lower minority concentrations. It should be noted again that this measures only a portion of the inequality in course availability, the lack of access at the school level. To the extent that minority students are also less likely to be encouraged to enroll in the AP courses that are at their school, the inequality of opportunity grows.

Do schools with more low-income students offer fewer AP courses? Having a larger proportion of low-income students (as measured by the percentage of students signed up for free or reduced price lunch) also is correlated with fewer AP courses offered, although the differential is smaller than in the case of racial/ethnic composition. As shown in Table 6.5, high schools with less than 10% low-income students offer 6.5 AP courses on average compared with roughly 4.5 courses in high schools with more than 25% low-income students. Table 6.6 shows the average number of courses offered broken down by both proportions of low-income students and school size.

Does the availability of AP courses vary across locations? On average, urban and suburban schools offer roughly the same number of AP courses—

Table 6.5. AP Courses by Percent Signed Up for Free/Reduced Price Lunch

Percent Signed Up	Courses Offered
0–10%	6.59
10–25%	5.13
25–50%	4.38
50–75%	4.82
75–100%	4.37

Source: TRPI analysis of California Department of Education, 1997 data.

urban, 6; suburban, 6.4—while rural schools offer fewer courses, 2.5, on average. That rural schools offer fewer AP courses should not be surprising given that these are usually smaller schools. As will be seen in the results in the next section, however, rural schools offer fewer AP courses than urban and suburban schools *even after controlling for school size* and other factors as well. Additionally, for large schools (2,000 or more students), suburban schools do in fact offer more AP courses, controlling for size, racial/ethnic composition, and other factors.

Relationship Between the Number of AP Courses and School Characteristics

In this section, we use a statistical technique called regression analysis to examine the relationship between course offerings and each of the various school characteristics, holding the other characteristics constant.

Table 6.6. AP Courses by Enrollment and Percent Signed Up for Free/Reduced Price Lunch

Enrollment	0–10%	10–25%	25–50%	50–100%
1–500	0.63	0.95	0.71	0.50
500–1,000	5.20	2.30	1.90	2.42
1,000–1,500	5.90	4.08	3.91	4.17
1,500–2,000	6.20	5.30	5.46	5.17
2,000 +	9.19	7.52	6.26	7.43

Source: TRPI analysis of California Department of Education, 1997 data.

Table 6.7 presents such an analysis of the relationship between AP course offerings and the various demographic and location variables.

Racial/Ethnic Composition of the School. The negative correlation between the percentage of students who are Latino or Black and the number of AP courses offered is statistically significant at the 99% level. That means that we are 99% confident that the two variables are related. The coefficient of –.032 can be interpreted as indicating that a 50 percentage point increase in Latino/Black enrollment (going from 10 to 60% or 25 to 75%, for example) is associated, on average, with a decrease of 1.6 AP courses. This is a 32% reduction from the average school offering of five AP courses. The proportionate reduction is similar in magnitude for large and small schools. Thus, the larger coefficient for schools with more than 2,000 students corresponds to a higher average number of courses offered. For instance, for high schools with more than 2,000 students, a 50 percentage point increase in minority enrollment is associated with a decrease of 1.8 AP courses on average. For schools with fewer than 2,000 students, a 50 percentage point increase in Black or Latino student enrollment is associated with one less AP course on average.

Table 6.7. Correlates/Predictors of AP Course Offerings OLS Regression Results

	All Schools	*2,000+ Schools*	*< 2,000 Schools*
% Black and Latino	–.032**	–.036**	–.021*
% Free/Reduced Price Lunch	–.012*	–.011	–.010
Enrollment Size	.0022**	.001**	.003**
Suburban Location	.832	2.55**	–.111
Rural Location	–1.77**	.482	–1.50*
% Black/Latino—Suburban	.004	–.027*	.004
% Black/Latino—Rural	.035**	–.008	.022†
Schools in District	.006	–.002	.011
LAUSD	2.33**	3.64*	1.57*
Constant	2.65**	4.23**	2.00**
Adjusted R^2	.463	.271	.392
Sample Size (*n*)	856	319	537

*p ≤ .05; **p ≤ .01; †p ≤ .10

Source: TRPI analysis of California Department of Education, 1997 data.

Low-Income Enrollments. The percentage of low-income students measured by the percentage signed up for free or reduced price lunch also is
negatively correlated with the number of AP courses offered, although the
effect is considerably smaller than for minority enrollment.[2] A 50 percentage point increase in low-income student enrollment is associated with a
decrease of AP courses offered of .6, a decrease of 12%.

School Size and Location. Enrollment size also is strongly correlated
with AP course offerings, as expected. The coefficient of .0022 implies that,
on average, an increase of 1,000 students is associated with a 2.2 course
increase in the number of types of AP courses offered. This also is statistically significant at the 99% level. Additionally, an independent rural effect remains after controlling for other variables. Compared with schools
of similar size and demographic characteristics, rural schools offer 1.8 fewer
AP courses on average. This is an important result in that it implies that
rural schools offer fewer AP courses more generally, not just because they
are smaller. This has important equity implications for those students living in rural areas. Finally, among large high schools with 2,000 or more
students, suburban schools offer more AP courses, an additional 2.55
courses, on average. Meanwhile, for smaller schools with fewer than 2,000
students, there is no difference in the number of AP course offerings between urban and suburban schools.

Interactions Between Racial/Ethnic Composition and Location. The analysis presented in Table 6.7 also allows us to examine the issue of whether the
relationship between the racial/ethnic composition of students enrolled
and the number of AP courses offered varies by location. For example, use
of the interaction term "% Black/Latino* Suburban" allows us to measure
the additional effect of higher minority concentration that is specific to the
suburbs. For large high schools with more than 2,000 students, there is a
statistically significant *negative* interaction between suburban location and
percent Latino and Black. This implies that, for large schools, the difference in course offerings between low- and high-minority concentration
schools is larger in the suburbs. That is, the coefficient measuring the effect of higher minority enrollments is –.063 (–.036 + –.027) as opposed to
only –.036 in the nonsuburban areas. The other way to interpret this coefficient is that, for large schools, the "suburban advantage" is far less in
suburban high schools with more underrepresented minorities. Using the
same reference of a 50 percentage point increase in minority enrollment,
the suburban advantage of 2.55 courses is reduced to 1.2. Again, it should
be noted that this additional effect is observed only in large high schools.

For rural high schools, on the other hand, there is a statistically significant *positive* coefficient on the interaction with minority concentration (% Black/Latino* Rural). This coefficient is of roughly equal magnitude to the coefficient of minority concentration alone (% Black and Latino). As these are added together to find the total effect for rural schools, it implies that, among rural schools, minority concentration is not correlated with average AP course offerings.

District Characteristics. Finally, regression analysis can address the question of whether the average number of AP courses offered varies with the number of schools in the district. This could be the case if high schools in districts with many other high schools found it easier to expand their course offerings, perhaps because they learned about the program from other schools or there were greater opportunities for district support. This does not seem to be the case, however, as the coefficient is small and is not statistically significantly different from zero, implying that there is not a relationship between AP courses offered and the number of schools in the district. Still, high schools in the state's largest district, the Los Angeles Unified School District (LAUSD), do seem to offer more courses. After controlling for size and demographic characteristics, schools in LAUSD offered on average two more types of AP courses. This is perhaps related to recent attempts to expand the AP program in Los Angeles schools. Another issue worth noting when considering the Los Angeles Unified School District (and many other California school districts) is the large number of multitrack, year-round schools. This can have the effect of reducing the number of AP courses available for a student in a given track. Because the data for all tracks in these schools are cumulated, it is difficult to analyze the tracks separately. One option is to divide the number of courses offered by three, the number of tracks. If this is done, it is also necessary to divide the total enrollment by three. The estimates obtained after making these changes are almost identical to the original estimates, including the estimate of the LAUSD effect. It would be useful, however, to have additional data available reporting AP course availability (and size and demographic information) separately for each track. More work should be done examining the impact of multitrack schools on the equality of opportunity to enroll in AP programs.

Average Number of Sections Offered per Course

An additional measure of interest is the average number of classes offered per distinct course, which we call the average number of "sections" that a student has to choose from for each course. We see this as a measure of *participation* and *demand* as well as *access*, because once a high school has the teacher and curriculum to offer a particular course, it may well be that the number of sections of the course offered largely reflects the demand for the course by the students and their parents. Thus, number of sections also may be a partial measure of the intensity of recruitment efforts by the administration and/or teachers to encourage students to enroll.

The average number of sections per course for schools that offer AP programs is 1.58 overall (1.73 in larger schools and 1.46 in smaller ones). This means that, on average, there are roughly three sections for every two AP courses. For example, a school that has AP English and AP calculus will, on average, offer two sections of one of these courses and one section of the other.

Table 6.8 presents a regression analysis of the relationship between the number of sections per AP course and the various demographic and location variables for those schools that have an AP program. Not surprisingly, the number of sections is positively related to school size. On average, an increase of 1,000 students is associated with an increase of .24 section per AP course overall, a 15% increase.

Table 6.8. Predictors of AP Sections (Defined as the number of classes/number of courses) OLS Regression Results

	All Schools	2,000+ Schools	< 2,000 Schools
% Black and Latino	−.0007	−.003	−.002
% Free/Reduced Price Lunch	−.0027†	−.002	−.0035†
Enrollment Size	.0002**	.00034**	.00014†
Suburban Location	.34*	.448**	.329
Rural Location	.18	−.045	.247
% Black/Latino—Suburban	−.005*	−.0063*	−.0046
% Black/Latino—Rural	.0004	.002	−.0017
Schools in District	−.0015	.004	−.0079
LAUSD	.164	−.048	.253
Constant	1.10**	.923**	1.17**
Adjusted R^2	.101	.168	.020
Sample Size (*n*)	736	310	426

*p ≤ .05; **p ≤ .01; †p ≤ .10 (Only schools offering at least one AP course are included in the "sections" analysis.)

Source: TRPI analysis of California Department of Education, 1997 data.

In comparing large high schools with more than 2,000 students in urban and suburban contexts, we found that more sections of AP courses are offered in suburban schools. Indeed, we found that, on average, suburban schools offer .45 section more per course. This number is statistically significant. Also, among large suburban schools, the higher the percentage of Latino or Black students enrolled, the fewer AP course sections offered. This result holds only for large suburban schools, and it is still the case that high-minority-concentration suburban schools still offer more sections, on average, than their urban counterparts.

For smaller high schools, we found that the school characteristics of interest explain very little of the variation in the number of sections offered. There is a small negative relationship between the proportion of low-income students and the number of sections offered; this relationship is statistically significant at the 90% level.

IMPLICATIONS OF OUR FINDINGS

Addressing Inequity in California

Because of the importance of AP courses in the college admissions process and the increased attention paid to issues of equality of opportunity for students applying to the University of California systems as well as growing evidence of inequality in AP course availability, civil rights lawyers and activists have begun to draw attention to African American and Latino students' unequal access to AP classes. Some initial actions have been taken to begin to address the situation. In 1999, the American Civil Liberties Union of Southern California filed a class-action lawsuit (*Daniel v. State of California*) against the Inglewood Unified School District and the California State Department and Board of Education accusing the state of denying equal educational opportunity in violation of the Equal Protection Clause and the California State Education Code. Data analysis reported in this chapter was used in support of the ACLU case. The education code states that "it is the intent of the Legislature that each public high school shall provide the full precollegiate program, provide adequate course selections in precollegiate programs to accommodate all its pupils and regularly counsel pupils to enter those programs and courses" (California State Education Code, 1991).

Many agree that variations in the availability of curriculum by race/ ethnicity, income level, or location should not occur in a system with a goal of equality of opportunity, especially in the case of courses that play a significant role in the college admissions process. In fact, Ward Connerly, a

UC Regent opposed to the use of affirmative action, applauded the ACLU lawsuit (Associated Press, 1999). In response to the lawsuit, new state funds were dedicated to expanding AP opportunities to address the inequities across schools in 2000. Senate Bill 1688 earmarked $30 million for expanding AP availability, including funds for grants to 550 high schools to develop AP courses, train teachers to implement pre-AP and AP courses, and tutor underserved students. The bulk of the money goes to high schools that offer few or no AP courses and have low college-going rates or a high number of low-income students. Additional funds went to the UC College Prep Initiative (UCCP) begun in Spring 1999 to provide online AP and honors courses to students with limited opportunities for these courses at their high schools. Also, schools with limited or no AP courses were given priority for new funding provided for buying computers. This has allowed many schools to give students access to online courses in addition to increasing the number of AP courses they offer on campus.

These changes are an important (and symbolic) step in addressing inequities in the education system stemming from variations in access to AP programs. An important follow-up will be to evaluate the implementation of this policy to see the impact it has on expanding the accessibility of quality courses to a diverse student population. There are two important parts to this. The first is to see that the expansions at the high school level are made in such a way as to reduce the observed inequities in access across high schools of varying characteristics. The second is to ensure that the newly expanded curricula do in fact reflect expansions or additions of "quality" courses. Labeling more courses as advanced placement or honors will in fact increase the availability of gatekeeper courses, but on its own will not guarantee that the new courses will be of higher quality. For example, initial results for online courses were mixed as many students had difficulty with the level of independent work. The UCCP has worked to address this, however, by making changes, including hiring local teachers to work with students. Finally, expansion of AP course offerings must be approached in the context of overall education and equity improvements. Expansion of the advanced placement program must be built on a foundation of improved education and achievement in the pre-AP curriculum.

Further, additional work should be done to expand the diversity of students served within high schools with AP programs, as many students technically may have access (as measured by availability) but may not be encouraged or receive adequate preparation to take advantage of existing AP programs. In California and across the nation, Hispanics and African Americans generally participate in AP classes at rates substantially below their share of total school enrollment (California State University Institute for Education Reform, 1999). Finally, the state and local schools should increase efforts to educate students and parents early on about the importance for college admissions of programs like advanced placement.

Equity vs. Excellence Implications

Some observers express concern about the efficacy of working to increase AP programs and participation in schools. If the reason why schools do not offer the programs, or students do not enroll, is lack of preparation, ability, or interest, then attempts to expand equity would lead to a decline in excellence in the programs. It is likely, however, that this supposed trade-off between excellence and equity is overstated or does not exist. There are many reasons why schools choose not to offer these programs and students do not take them, including lack of information and encouragement. Some recent efforts to expand AP programs in underserved schools have been successful and have demonstrated the possibility for successful implementation even in schools where teachers and administrators initially do not believe that the students are adequately prepared. One such example is the Dallas (Texas) Public Schools Advanced Placement Incentive Program, founded and funded by a private local foundation to improve AP participation and performance at local schools. Between 1993 (before implementation of the program) and 1999, the number of AP exams taken in math, science, and English in the Dallas Public Schools increased from 300 to 2,143. Pass rates also were considerably higher than national and state averages (U.S. Department of Education, 2000).

There also have been some recent efforts at the federal level to expand participation in AP programs among disadvantaged students. In 2000, the U.S. Department of Education increased funding from $4 million to $15 million for the development and expansion of programs to increase AP program participation targeting primarily low-income students.

Equity Issues in Changes to the AP Program Elsewhere

Recently, there have been other changes in state and local policies related to the expansion of advanced placement programs that should be evaluated from an equity standpoint. Some states have promoted the AP program as a tool for school reform. As we have seen here in the case of California (and in other chapters of this book), policies created for other reasons related to "excellence" can have important implications for equity that should be evaluated and addressed. State and local support for AP programs ranges from paying exam fees to staff development to teacher bonuses. Examples include Texas, which helps fund exams, teacher training, and teaching costs, and Florida, which provides financial assistance for exam costs. In addition to assisting with fees, South Carolina requires all schools to offer AP courses and all public colleges to give course credit to students who have achieved high AP scores (Lively, 1993). On the local level, Oklahoma City provides teacher incentives, staff development, materials, reduced exam fees, and a financial bonus for AP teachers (Steller & Lambert, 1996). From 1989, when that policy was put in place, to 1994, the percentage of Oklahoma City students receiving passing grades on their AP exams jumped from 13% to 56%. While these state and local policies may succeed in increasing student participation in AP courses and enabling more students to earn college credit in high school, potential equity implications should not be ignored. Because of the possible advantages in terms of college admissions afforded students in AP programs, policymakers should try to ensure that expansion of these programs does not increase the *inequality* of opportunity for students. Further, these program expansions could be specifically targeted to actually decrease inequities elsewhere in the education system.

If advanced placement programs continue to gain prominence in high school curricula and in college admissions, as is likely to happen, further attention should be paid to the processes by which students are selected into or encouraged to take these classes. There is some evidence that high schools have been using the SAT or PSAT as a filter when placing students in AP classes (Chenoweth, 1998). Such practice exacerbates already existing inequities that result from the emphasis on standardized testing in some college admissions processes.

AP Access and Participation in the Overall Equity Discussion

Advanced placement was not a program designed to address equity. Rather, it was a program implemented for other purposes, primarily to allow high school students the opportunity to receive college credit for college-level work done in high school. As the program has grown in importance both in terms of high school curriculum and college admissions policies, concern has been raised about the impact that unequal access to and participation in the program has on the educational opportunities of disadvantaged students, especially poor students of color. The question becomes, how can we better equalize opportunity in this context where advanced placement courses play such an important role in current educational practice? When we view the issue this way, we see that increasing access to AP courses can be an important tool to address inequities in the current system.

It is also important to balance attempts to increase equality in AP offerings with other efforts to enhance equity and educational opportunity.

The advantage that large schools may have in their ability to offer greater variety in their curriculum should, for example, be balanced against other advantages that smaller schools have. As another example, our findings on rural schools and their more sparse AP course offerings should not necessarily lead to an argument for greater consolidation of small rural high schools. Such schools also could investigate alternatives to full-fledged, on-campus courses, including online or distance learning courses. An example of such an online program is Apex, in which students are taught by experienced AP instructors. Students turn in assignments and tests and receive feedback and evaluation as well as interact with their teacher and other students via computer (U.S. Department of Education, 2000).

Finally, it is important to remember that access to and participation in AP courses is but one issue in the broader equity debate. Thus, efforts to expand AP programs to reach more disadvantaged students and promote greater equity in the existing system should not be supported with resources taken away from other important equity policies. Improving access to AP programs should be an additive solution, enhancing other policies that improve educational resources and opportunities for disadvantaged students. Additionally, in the equity reform debate, the expansion of AP programs should not be viewed as a long-term tool that is *the* answer to the general problem of inequality. Rather, it should be seen in context as an important policy change that seeks to remedy a specific case of institutional inequality manifested in the current system.

CONCLUSIONS AND FUTURE RESEARCH DIRECTIONS

Advanced placement courses were designed to provide high school students with challenging coursework and enable students to earn college credit while in high school. Currently, AP courses play an important role in the college admissions process and can provide advanced standing and improve students' chances of on-time graduation. Given the recent elimination of affirmative action in the University of California system and the resulting decline in acceptance rates for Latino and African American students, examining and ameliorating the inequities in the AP program are of increased importance. Using California as a case study, we have examined variations in course availability across high schools of varying demographic characteristics. We find that, after controlling for other characteristics, high schools enrolling a higher proportion of African American and Latino students offer significantly fewer AP courses. The proportion of low-income students at the school also is negatively related to the number of AP courses offered, although the effect is smaller. Rural schools offer fewer AP courses, on average, even after controlling for their smaller size. Among larger high schools, we found important contextual differences, with suburban schools offering more AP courses than their urban counterparts.

It can be argued that inequities in AP course offerings reflect the larger inequities in our public school systems. Not only is the lack of AP courses possibly affecting African American and Latino students' chances of being considered for admission at higher education institutions, but it also reflects their lack of access to rigorous precollegiate courses that would better prepare them to succeed in their college coursework.

It is important to note that we have focused on inequities in AP course access and participation, measured at the school level, in only one state. Another potentially significant source of inequality arises from differences across racial/ethnic groups in terms of actual enrollment in advanced placement and other honors courses *within* a school building. In addition, with the advent of year-round schooling in certain urban school districts, researchers need to examine student access to AP courses across the various tracks. More work is needed to analyze the sources of these differences to help determine how best to address them.

The benefits to students of AP courses in terms of potentially more rigorous curriculum and improved access to college are clear. Ensuring that all students can receive these benefits regardless of race or ethnicity fulfills the stated goal of the American public school system: equal educational opportunity for all.

NOTES

1. Schools identified as special education, county community schools, California youth authority, opportunity schools, juvenile court schools, alternative opportunity schools, continuation schools, community day schools, and so on were not included. For two of the 870 schools in the sample, 1999 AP course data were used, since 1997 data were not available. For ten schools, 1998 race/ethnicity enrollment data were used, and no race/ethnicity enrollment data were available for two schools. Several schools also are missing data on the percentage of students who are low income.

2. Because of measurement error, we cannot tell for sure that the relationship with race/ethnicity is in fact stronger than the relationship with income. The income measure available measures only the percent of students above or below a single income threshold and therefore only picks up some of the variation in income status. It is possible that some of the effect of income might be picked up by the race/ethnicity measure.

REFERENCES

Associated Press. (1999, July 28). Students sue state claiming they are denied advanced college prep classes. *Associated Press State & Local Wire*.

Barreto, M., & Pachón, H. P. (2003). *Impact of University of California System's SP-1 (Eliminating Affirmative Action)*. Claremont, CA: Tomas Rivera Policy Institute.

California State Education Code. (1991). Chapter 1198, Section 66204.

California State University Institute for Education Reform. (1999). *The advanced placement program, California's 1997–98 experience*. Sacramento, CA: Author.

Chenoweth, K. (1998). The College Board decries preparation gap. *Black Issues in Higher Education, 15*(15), 24–25.

College Board. (2001). College Board online. Retrieved September 24, 2001 from www.college.board.org/ap.

Daniel v. State of California. (1999, July 27). California Superior Court, County of Los Angeles, Case No. BC214156.

Lively, K. (1993). More states encourage advanced placement courses for college credit: Saving money is one goal. *The Chronicle of Higher Education, 39*(38), A21–A22.

Steller, A. W., & Lambert, W. K. (1996). Advanced placement: Helping to achieve system wide reform in urban schools. *NAASP Bulletin, 80*(576), 96–103.

University of California, Office of the President. (2000). Guidelines for implementation of university policy on undergraduate admissions. Retrieved March 14, 2001 from http://www.ucop.edu/sas/adguides.html.

University of California, Office of the President. (2001). Freshman selection criteria. Retrieved September 24, 2001 from http://ww.ucop.edu/pathways/infoctr/introuc/select.htmlucophome/commserv/psat.html.

U.S. Department of Education. (2000). *Dispelling the culture of mediocrity: Expanding advanced placement*. Washington, DC: Author.

PART III

Education Reform Since the 1980s: Excellence Trumps Equity

The chapters in this part examine reforms instituted since the 1970s for the purpose of enhancing education quality by allowing parents to choose the school for their children among many new alternatives. Government policies have supported an increase in the number of options available to parents and school districts by encouraging the burgeoning of for-profit and nonprofit educational providers and educational management companies, and encouraging entrepreneurship on the part of communities to develop their own schools. Educational decision making has, at some levels, devolved to parents and teachers by giving public funds (and increasingly, private scholarships) to families to be used for education, and by creating charter schools that provide varying levels of authority to parents and teachers. The expectation is that educational quality will be enhanced by the competition between these many alternative education models and by centralized systems of accountability through testing.

Chapter 7 recounts the development of new school models through the New American Schools (NAS). NAS was created in the early 1990s by corporate leaders who wanted to foster "break the mold" schools and thus transform public education through whole-school reform designs. Although originally intended to provide new models of restructuring all public schools, NAS has been directed mostly toward urban public schools with high proportions of minority students, in part because of the availability of federal Title I funds in such schools to support the NAS whole-school reforms. In this chapter, Mark Berends, Susan Bodilly and Sheila Nataraj Kirby describe the complexities in implementing whole-school reform designs through NAS. The authors found that school reform designs by themselves did not transform schools and that intensive assistance was required. Even then, faithful implementation of a design was hard to achieve and was most effective in localities that had stable and supportive district leadership and union support. Finally, the study found that NAS's initial goal of dramatically raising student performance had not been achieved after 9 years. The authors conclude with a word of caution to policymakers and reformers who believe that a school reform model by itself can deal with the complex environment of urban high-poverty schools often characterized by unstable educational leadership, demoralized teachers, and a fluctuating reform agenda.

Within the environment of increasing educational choices, California's governor pushed for legislation in the late 1990s that resulted in the opening of single-gender academies. In Chapter 8 Amanda Datnow and Lea Hubbard examine their development. As is the case with NAS discussed in the preceding chapter, the research shows that implementation of the new program was very uneven. The authors found that school personnel for the most part were not knowledgeable or enthusiastic about implementing single-gender academies. Rather, they saw the funding that was attached to the legislation as an opportunity to address other educational needs of the low-income students that formed their student bodies. The research demonstrates, as does RAND's study of NAS, that more educational choices do not, in and of themselves, create better schools in the absence of clear leadership and assistance for effective implementation.

Charter schools, which receive public funding to operate more autonomously from their school systems, have been, since the early 1990s, the fastest-growing alternative to promote public school quality. Chapter 9 summarizes the results of a study of California charter schools that set out to explore their potential to improve education for minority and poor children. Amy Stuart Wells, Janelle Scott, Alejandra Lopez, and Jennifer Jellison Holme found that the greater autonomy afforded to charter schools has enabled some members of disenfranchised communities to create schools that present their history and culture within the school curriculum. Nevertheless, most charter schools need more funding than provided by the government, forcing them to seek outside and private funds. In addition, the ability of schools to innovate is curtailed by the imposition of state-mandated tests. The data also suggest that not only do parents choose charter schools, but the schools themselves also select parents and students, and in the process more-privileged students are favored. Thus, even though charter school reform offers some potential to empower minority communities and address cultural and linguistic needs, inadequate funding and conflicting state mandates actually may help exacerbate the gap between the rich and the poor.

In Chapter 10, Thomas Shapiro and Heather Beth Johnson present data on how parents choose schools for their children. Historically, parental choice has been exercised largely through the selection of the community in which the family lives. In recent decades, however, we see that choices of schools increasingly are limited by family resources and by the existing residential patterns in this country, which are highly segregated by race and class. Data from interviews of White and Black families suggest that families use their financial resources to move to more prosperous and less diverse communities. The proportion of White children in the schools largely defines the choices, premised on the existence of "better-quality" schools in predominantly White communities. The authors conclude that educational vouchers that provide public funds to individual families to pay for their children's schooling have the potential for increasing segregation by race and class.

Martin Carnoy and Patrick McEwan's research, which appears in Chapter 11, demonstrates that Shapiro and Johnson's fears for voucher systems in the United States indeed were played out in Chile. As a country that instituted a system-wide voucher system in 1980, Chile provides an important example with ample data to test the premises of vouchers. The authors found that following the implementation of vouchers that could be used for both public and private schools, private-school enrollments grew rapidly. However, low-income pupils became more highly represented in public schools, which were of lower status than private schools. Their data suggest that the voucher program did not improve the quality of the education system; the academic achievement of students from the same income groups was not statistically different whether students attended public or private schools. Thus, vouchers led to an increasingly stratified education system with little discernible increase in quality. The authors also examine data from the limited U.S. voucher programs that have been targeted toward low-income students and see similar patterns.

And finally, on a more hopeful note, Chapter 12 presents Michael Rebell's analysis of the role of constituency building in the Campaign for Fiscal Equity's (CFE) successful lawsuit for school finance equity in New York State. Prior chapters show that the policies that pursue equity are not sufficient to ensure a high-quality education and those attempting to promote excellence can undermine social justice. Rebell's chapter leads the much-needed discussion of "now what?" CFE's experience with grassroots organizing around the legal and political issues that were central to the court case offers a model of a double strategy of both top-down policy and bottom-up grassroots mobilization efforts to bring equal funding and resources to the students of New York City's public schools. This case has successfully combined the quest for resource equity with the goal of educational excellence. CFE's experience will serve as a valuable model for other finance equity cases across the United States. Although CFE has won the court case, at this writing the state is delaying required action, as has happened in many other states. The need for an active constituency to help define the parameters of an adequate education and ensure its effective implementation will remain. The success of CFE should provide inspiration and a road map for those committed to bringing equity back.

7

Reforming Whole Schools

Challenges and Complexities

MARK BERENDS
SUSAN BODILLY
SHEILA NATARAJ KIRBY

In the past decade, the educational landscape has seen the development and expansion of reforms to improve the academic achievement of all students. As Chapter 1 of this book explains, during the 1980s and 1990s "excellence became the rallying cry of the country's political leadership, leaving equity in the dust." National educational goals focusing on improving the performance of students emerged during the late 1980s, stemming in part from such gatherings as the 1989 meeting of former President Bush and state governors. These goals were written into federal legislation as part of President Clinton's Goals 2000 legislation.

One such "excellence" reform initiative—New American Schools (NAS) —entered the policy landscape in the early 1990s. Beginning in 1991 and funded by the private sector, NAS sought to engage the nation's best educators, businesspeople, and researchers in the task of creating, testing, and fostering the implementation of whole-school designs that were not constrained by existing regulations, work rules, and conventions. These whole-school designs were meant to transform entire schools to dramatically improve the performance of students across the nation.

Bringing Equity Back: Research for a New Era in American Educational Policy. Copyright © 2005 by Teachers College, Columbia University. All rights reserved. ISBN 0-8077-4576-6 (cloth). Prior to photocopying items for classroom use, please contact the Copyright Clearance Center, Customer Service, 222 Rosewood Dr., Danvers, MA 01923, USA, tel. (978) 750-8400.

Indirect federal support for the NAS initiative was provided by the Goals 2000 legislation, passed in 1994, and its agenda of furthering standards-based reforms to improve the education outcomes of all students (Smith & Scoll, 1995; Smith, Scoll, & Link, 1996). The subsequent 1994 reauthorization of the Elementary and Secondary Education Act (ESEA), called Improving America's Schools Act, allowed schools to use Title I compensatory education money for "school-wide programs" that served all students as opposed to pull-out programs targeted only toward low-income students. However, it was not until 1997, with the passage of the Comprehensive School Reform Demonstration (CSRD) legislation and later President Bush's 2001 reauthorization of ESEA, the No Child Left Behind Act, that the federal government more directly funded whole-school designs like those at the center of NAS.

Meanwhile, federal, state, and local policymakers have embraced the comprehensive or whole-school reforms, such as those that were part of NAS, as an effective strategy to improve the learning conditions of students in high-poverty settings in particular. The purposes and approaches of NAS and its design teams are now consistent with those for Title I school-wide programs and the CSRD program, also known as Obey-Porter.[1] For example, CSRD is intended to help schools "identify and adopt high-quality, well-defined, and research-based comprehensive school reform models that show the promise of preparing children to meet challenging state content and performance standards" (U.S. Department of Education, 2001, p. 4). Currently, more than 2,000 schools receive CSRD funding to implement whole-school reforms such as NAS designs (see Berends, Kirby, Naftel, & Sloan, 2001; Kirby, Berends, Naftel, & Sloan, 2001).

Thus, more than a decade after the creation of NAS, the impact of this initiative has been impressive, affecting thousands of high-poverty schools that are now engaged in whole-school improvement efforts. In several instances, such designs are mandated at the state level (e.g., New Jersey) or made possible through federal funding.

The purpose of this chapter, therefore, is to draw on nearly 10 years of RAND research examining NAS, the largest-scale effort to implement whole-school reform programs nationwide. Currently operating in about 4,000 schools, NAS offers many popular whole-school reform designs, such as Accelerated Schools, and was previously associated with Success for All.[2] In this way, the findings from our study shed light on the feasibility and viability of a growing trend in the United States.

In what follows, we address the complexities and challenges underlying reform of high-poverty schools through whole-school designs, using insights gained from the RAND assessment of New American Schools. Our NAS research offers some sobering lessons for policymakers who are looking to comprehensive school reform as *the* panacea for failing schools in high-poverty areas. For instance, our findings reveal that although NAS was not originally an equity-minded reform, the NAS design teams ended up assisting low-performing, urban schools serving mostly low-income students and students of color. These schools face a number of challenges that schools in more-affluent communities often do not have to face, such as large numbers of very poor students with special needs and low test scores, and the lack of principal leadership, teacher efficacy, and school capacity for change. Meanwhile, the NAS schools attempted reform in environments fraught with uncertainty, as federal, state, and district policies increased performance demands on schools via standards-based reforms and high-stakes accountability systems.

Given these circumstances and the social context of the NAS reform, it is not surprising that we found considerable variation within *and* across schools, districts, and design teams in the level of implementation achieved 2 years into the 5-year, scale-up effort. In addition, we learned that the goal of dramatically improving student achievement through the NAS whole-school reform model was overly ambitious and too often naive about the contextual factors that we found to be so important to a school's ability to implement these reforms. Still, this chapter is not an indictment of whole-school reform designs; rather, it is an appeal to those who have supported such reforms as the necessary solution to problems in public schools—especially urban public schools—to consider the many factors that affect the degree of "excellence" in education. We realize that writing such as this creates a real danger that whole-school reforms, despite their promise and possibilities, will be cast aside because they did not provide a quick and easy fix for the problems facing high-poverty schools. Yet another way to look at it is to say that the broader inequality in our society—an inequality that is reflected in our public schools—and the lack of equity-minded public policy to address this inequality may provide the greatest hindrance to the most well-intended excellence reforms.

RAND ASSESSMENT OF NAS

Since it was established in 1991, NAS contracted with RAND to provide analytic support and feedback.[3] From 1995 to 2000, RAND conducted an evaluation of the scale-up of NAS designs to many schools and addressed three major questions.

- What is the level of implementation in NAS schools?
- What impedes or facilitates that implementation?

- Does the adoption of a NAS design result in any changes in student and school outcomes?

Over this time period, RAND's program of studies has included several phases:

1. A longitudinal sample of over 100 NAS schools that began implementing whole-school designs early on in the scale-up phase and included data on school performance
2. Case studies in 40 schools to analyze implementation and the role that districts play in impeding or enabling comprehensive school reform
3. A description of how designs have evolved from the initial proposal stage to implementing across a large number of the nation's schools
4. Analyses in one urban school district of how designs promote changes in classroom instruction, teaching and learning, and individual student achievement scores
5. An analysis of performance differences in high-implementing NAS sites
6. Ongoing discussions with NAS staff and design team leaders

As part of this program of studies, RAND conducted a comparative descriptive analysis of classroom practices and instructional strategies in NAS and non-NAS schools in Texas (Berends, Chun, Schuyler, Stockly, & Riggs, 2002). This analysis focused on 4th-grade students in San Antonio and relied on a variety of data-collection methods, including principal and teacher surveys, classroom observations, collection of student work, and administration of the Stanford Achievement Open-ended Reading Test (Version 9).

There are some important limitations of this research that need to be kept in mind. First, the schools analyzed here were, for most design teams, the first schools the teams provided assistance to in implementing their designs on a fee-for-service basis. There were many changes in both the designs and the assistance provided as the teams and the schools gained experience (for an analysis of the evolution of these designs, see Bodilly, 2001). Second, the fact that designs were evolving over time as educators gained experience implementing them and adapting them to local contexts makes a longitudinal evaluation difficult, so findings regarding progress in implementation over time need to be interpreted with some caution. Third, the school-level measures we used to compare performance in NAS schools with that of the district as a whole are also subject to important limitations. For example, these aggregated measures might fail to capture changes at the end of the spectrum of change or miss some significant achievement effects that might be captured if student-level data were available and comparable across jurisdictions. (See Berends, Kirby, Naftel, & McKelvey, 2001, for a detailed discussion of the shortcomings of monitoring student achievement gains using school-level test scores.)

The rest of this chapter is divided into several sections. First, we provide an historical description of NAS as a private-sector effort. Second, we provide an overview of the districts and schools that attempted to use NAS comprehensive school designs to improve their performance from 1995 to 1998. We show that these schools were primarily high-poverty, low-achieving schools. Third, we briefly describe the general findings of the RAND evaluation in terms of the progress the NAS schools made in implementing the whole-school designs and improving school performance from 1995 to 1998. Fourth, we examine the factors that are related to implementation in our sample of schools. We end the chapter with some lessons learned from the NAS experience and policy implications for current federal, state, and local programs targeting high-poverty schools.

NEW AMERICAN SCHOOLS: A PRIVATE-SECTOR INITIATIVE

In July 1991, in conjunction with President Bush's America 2000 initiative, the New American Schools Development Corporation (NASDC) was established as a nonprofit corporation funded by the private sector to create and support design teams capable of helping existing schools transform themselves into high-performing organizations by using whole-school designs. The aim was to improve all schools to provide an excellent education for all, as indicated by dramatically improved test scores.

In its original request for proposals, NASDC (1991) was direct in communicating its promotion of excellence, as the following statements suggest:

> NASDC is not interested in incremental changes that promise, at best modest improvements in student achievement compared to conventional classrooms or schools. The achievement of students in the New Generation of American Schools will be measured against world class standards. (p. 20)

> At the end of the five-year [scale-up] period, NASDC anticipate that a proven capacity will be in place to support communities as they seek to develop the high-performance educational systems that America needs. (p. 15)

NAS leaders argued that the best way to accomplish the goal of improving student achievement was through "break the mold" whole-school designs that could be adopted by communities around the nation. This NAS strategy was based on a core premise that all high-quality schools possess a de facto design that allows school staff to function to the best of their abilities and integrates research-based practices into a *coherent* and *mutually reinforcing* set of effective approaches to teaching and learning for the entire school. It "articulates a school's vision, mission, and goals; guides the instructional program; shapes the selection and socialization of staff; and establishes common expectations for performance and accountability among students, teachers, and parents" (Glennan, 1998, p. 11). The adoption and adept use of coherent, interrelated, and mutually reinforcing practices would be the antithesis of the fragmented programs and idiosyncratic teacher practices often found in schools. In addition, designs were to be for all students. They were not special programs targeted to specific populations, to be added to the school's repertoire.

Given NAS's unique approach to school reform, grounded in business principles such as efficiency and accountability, the announcement of its creation fostered a mix of support and condemnation. As the following quotations demonstrate, opinions were divided over the value of a private-sector reform initiative:

> It is wrong-headed to suggest that the greatest problem in education is not knowing what to do and that we must wait for privately-funded design teams to come up with ideas. (Timpane, 1991, pp. 19–20)

> I cannot comprehend why the Secretary and the President consider a private research effort to be the centerpiece for system changes for the most important function of government—education. (Ambach, 1991, p. 39)

> Schools are highly constrained by various laws, regulations, nongovernment policies (e.g., SAT and the Carnegie units), and organizational rigidity. The New American Schools Development Corporation is needed to break loose from these impediments. (Kirst, 1991, p. 38)

Despite the warnings, the NAS effort was a dramatically different way of initiating and disseminating large-scale educational improvement. From the outset, NAS's vision was of a large scale-up effort to transform thousands of schools, not just a handful. Not only did the emphasis on eventual scale-up set it apart, but so too did the involvement of the private sector and the choice of school designs as the vehicles for reform. This scale of private-sector involvement was unique in K–12 education, as was the venture capital notion of deliberate development of designs. Private-sector contributions to education reform traditionally have come in the form of relatively small amounts of funding or materials to individual schools in "partnership" programs to help promote specific activities such as reading or science. To a large extent, this is true of many reform efforts even today.

To make its goal of improving student achievement a reality, NAS saw itself as a several-year R&D effort. For instance, it initially organized its work into several phases (see Figure 7.1).[4]

- A competition phase to solicit proposals and select designs
- A development phase of 1 year to develop the ideas in the proposals in concrete ways
- A demonstration phase of 2 years to pilot the designs in real school settings
- A scale-up phase in which the designs would be widely diffused in some as yet unspecified fashion

In its competition phase, NAS selected 11 teams with unique designs. After a year of design, NAS funded 9 of the 11 teams to demonstrate and implement whole-school designs in real schools during the 1993–94 and 1994–95 school years. During this time, the number of NAS schools grew to 147. From 1995 to 1998, NAS led a scale-up phase in 10 jurisdictions across the country (for more details, see Bodilly, 2001). By that time, only seven designs remained.

Figure 7.1. Phases of the New American Schools Reform Initiative

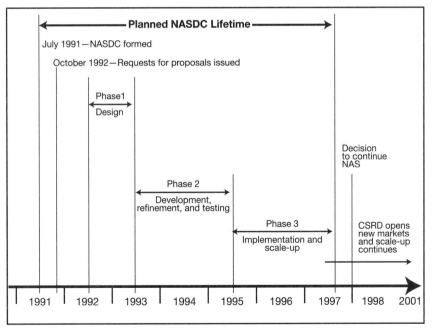

After the scale-up phase, the NAS Board decided not to go out of business as the leaders originally had envisioned, but rather to transition NAS into a new organization. It currently has 10 primary teams that work for the improvement of whole-school reform efforts and their successful adoption nationwide. NAS leaders also recruited other design models to become a part of its network. Reportedly, its designs are now associated with over 4,000 design-based schools.

The distinguishing features—involvement of the private sector, the choice of school designs as the vehicle for reform, and the ambitious goal of scale-up across the country—set NAS apart from other reform efforts. (See Table 7.1 for an overview of the original NAS principles and concepts.) The involvement of the private sector drove two important principles. The design teams, while needing some initial investment funds, would transition within 3 to 5 years to self-sufficiency using a fee-for-service system. Schools adopting designs might need some initial investment funds, but sustaining design implementation would not incur additional costs over the normal operating budget.

It is also important to point out that NAS was different in many respects from other types of reforms because initially the leaders did not want design teams to target specific populations, grades, or schools with peculiar characteristics. NAS did not focus specifically on equity per se, in the sense of focusing on students who had not been well served by the education system. Rather, NAS emphasized excellence for all students, provided by private-sector sponsorship of a new business—namely, design teams and the assistance they offered schools. Only one NAS design, Roots and Wings, was developed specifically to meet the needs of high-poverty schools, and it was the only one that developed any materials for schools addressing significant proportions of students with English as a second language. Yet, as NAS and the designs evolved, it became clear that Title I money for poor schools provided a significant source of funding for the fees the schools had to pay for the designs. Roots and Wings had experience with this Title I federal funding source and paved the way into this market for the other NAS designs.

As NAS entered the scale-up phase, there were seven design teams.[5]

- Audrey Cohen College (currently renamed Purpose-Centered Education)
- Authentic Teaching, Learning, and Assessment for All Students
- Co-NECT Schools
- Expeditionary Learning Outward Bound
- Modern Red Schoolhouse

Table 7.1. Original NAS Principles and Concepts

Principle	Description
Private Funding	Initially, the effort was privately funded and supported—it was not a local, state, or federal government mandate. Ideally, schools and districts would enter into a relationship with a design team on a voluntary and well-informed basis.
Whole School	Designs were to be for "whole schools." This notion had two parts. First, the designs would be coherent, thoughtful sets of school-level policies and practices. The adoption and adept use of coherent, interrelated, and mutually reinforcing practices would be the antithesis of the fragmented programs and idiosyncratic teacher practices often found in schools. In addition, designs were to be for all students. They were not special programs targeted to specific populations, to be added to the school's repertoire.
Adaptive Approach	NAS designs were not supposed to be perspective molds for model schools to ensure uniformity of practice. Designs were to adapt to local conditions and were to enable local communities to create their own high-performance schools.
Design Teams	Teams were deliberately created organizations of experts. NAS intended that teams would develop coherent designs and then work with schools in further ground-level product development to perfect those designs. Later, they would promote the use of their designs in schools across the nation. Nearly 700 potential teams responded to the RFP. The 11 initially chosen were mostly private nonprofit organizations connected to universities or research organizations. The exceptions were one for-profit firm, two districts, and one nonprofit without a research or university connection.
Multiple Designs	There was no one best school design, but many, depending on the needs of individual schools. Multiple teams would be supported, allowing schools a choice of designs.
Reasonable Costs	While it was understood that transforming schools might require investment funding, the operating costs of the schools after transformation were to be equivalent to those for the "typical" school in that community. In other words, break the mold designs were to be no more costly in daily operation than other schools, making them affordable to all districts.
Market Driven	NAS would not be a self-perpetuating organization. From the beginning, it planned to "go out of business" after it had accomplished its purpose. One consequence of this was that design teams had to become financially self-sufficient over time, creating their own client base to support their work. Thus, teams over the 5-year time line to which NAS originally committed (1992–1997) would need to transform themselves from visionaries to product developers to entrepreneurial organizations.

- National Alliance for Restructuring Education (currently renamed America's Choice Design Network)[6]
- Roots and Wings (RW)

While each design has unique features, the designs tend to emphasize school change in the following areas: organization and governance, teacher professional development, content and performance standards, curriculum and instructional strategies, and parent and community involvement.

One of the most important lessons learned during the demonstration phase was that designs, by themselves, could not transform schools. Schools needed significant amounts of professional development, technical assistance, and materials geared to the design. This "design-based assistance" (Bodilly, 1996) became a key component of the NAS initiative and distinguishes it from the more traditional approaches to school reform. Such design-based assistance includes providing participating schools: (1) a choice of designs to partner with; (2) specified designs that clarify both the hoped-for outcomes as well as the intermediate implementation steps; and (3) assistance from the team in the form of professional development, training, materials, conferences, networks, curriculum and instruction packages, and so forth. In return for this assistance, the participating schools pay the NAS team. Thus, NAS emphasizes the role of the external agent in enabling whole-school transformation, but the design teams also rely on fees to pay for those assistance services.

As NAS moved into the scale-up phase, it was clear that school transformation would not occur unless there was strong district support. Therefore, NAS decided to partner with a limited number of districts to develop "markets" for the designs. Ideally, these markets were to be in jurisdictions supportive of the NAS initiative. In particular, NAS sought jurisdictions that would commit to 5-year partnerships with NAS and the design teams to create an environment conducive to whole-school reform. NAS required that the partnering districts also commit to transforming 30% of their schools using design-based assistance within a 5-year period; the NAS leaders thought that this percentage, although somewhat arbitrary, would establish a significant core of schools to propel further changes in districts and schools.

Another lesson learned by NAS was the extent of investment funding a school might need in order to implement a design. This varied among designs from approximately $40,000 to $150,000 per year for 3 years (see Keltner, 1998). Although the exact cost of this scale-up phase was not known at the outset, it was obvious that schools or districts would need significant discretionary funds to adopt designs using a fee-for-service basis. The greatest source of discretionary funding available to poor schools and districts was and still is the federal Title I funding provided to high-poverty schools. More particularly, NAS was scaling up just as the afore-mentioned changes to the Title I program were being implemented in the 1990s to give schools in which more than 50% of the students were poor the option of using their Title I funding for school-wide programs. Thus, the NAS strategy of whole-school designs fit well as a reform strategy under the new federal funding formula for Title I.

It should be no surprise then that all of the districts that responded to NAS's request for partners had at least one of two things in common. They were in states that had adopted or were moving to adopt standards and accountability systems that required districts and schools to show improvement on student assessments; and/or they had some discretionary resources, often Title I resources, available for investment. The result was that NAS partnered with 10 jurisdictions at the beginning of its scale-up phase: Cincinnati, OH; Dade County, FL; Memphis, TN; Pittsburgh, PA; Philadelphia, PA; San Antonio, TX; San Diego, CA; and several districts in Kentucky, Maryland, and Washington State.

While there was initially some negotiation about the costs of the designs and how those costs would be paid, the districts agreed to pay the fees for design team services, with one important caveat—they all insisted that the participating schools meet district or state standards and that students be assessed against district- and state-mandated tests. In addition, given the states' requirements to show improved test scores within a 3- to 5-year period, most jurisdictions insisted that NAS schools be judged on their test score increases after the third year of implementation. NAS's leaders and the design teams were concerned about the alignment of these state content and performance standards and assessments with design team standards, assessment, curriculum, and instruction, but these concerns were not shared by the participating districts. Despite the possible flaws in the existing assessment regimes, the districts' insistence on improved student performance as measured by district- or state-mandated assessments prevailed, and NAS and the design teams accommodated this position.

We now turn to the actual scale-up experience and the RAND findings concerning implementation and outcomes.

AN OVERVIEW OF NAS SCALE-UP SCHOOLS

While NAS initially intended to provide break the mold designs for all schools across the nation, what unfolded was a reform movement that served only a certain segment of the nation. In particular, NAS designs in the scale-up districts ended up assisting schools serving disproportionate numbers of poor, minority, or low-achieving students. Available funding opportunities through Title I support and the need to see improved performance in low-scoring schools, given the state policy contexts, were the two primary reasons for this development.

As a result, most of the schools receiving design team assistance could be considered socially and academically disadvantaged in terms of poverty, racial ethnic composition, climate, and academic achievement scores. Thus, the NAS sites in our sample were below "average" on several measures of student need and academic performance when a number of school characteristics were compared with national norms (Berends, 1999). For example, NAS schools in Cincinnati, Dade, Memphis, Philadelphia, Pittsburgh, and San Antonio were serving mostly poor student populations, with more than two-thirds of the students eligible for free/reduced price lunch at these sites. Meanwhile, the NAS schools in Kentucky and Washington State were more affluent than the national average. If the latter schools were excluded from the sample, the school poverty composition of the NAS sample would increase to 68%.

The NAS schools in our sample also served a disproportionately high number of students of color. For example, about 35% of the nation's students were categorized as racial/ethnic minorities. In contrast, 57% of students in NAS schools were students of color. Excluding the Kentucky and Washington schools, over 80% of the students in NAS schools were minorities.

In terms of school climate, NAS principals reported greater problems with absenteeism and school readiness when compared with what is reported nationwide by school administrators (for details see Berends, 1999). Some of the design teams, such as Roots and Wings and Expeditionary Learning, were in schools where the reported problems of readiness were more severe. School readiness was measured by principal reports about problems such as students coming to school with poor nutrition, poor health, and apathy. These students were deemed as unprepared to learn.

In general, our data indicate that the majority of NAS sites were in low-income communities in urban school districts. Not surprisingly, within these districts and with few exceptions, the NAS design teams found themselves assisting schools that were scoring at or below the district average on mandated tests. The NAS sites were some of the lowest-performing schools within school districts that were primarily low-performing when compared with state averages (Berends, 1999). There are two exceptions. First, the NAS sites in Washington State tend to be more affluent and generally higher-performing than other schools in their districts. Second, many of the Kentucky schools are not urban schools, and they tend to score at or close to the state average on the state-mandated test. Thus, in the other states, it seems fairly evident that low-performing urban school districts partnered with NAS for a single reason: the promise of raising test scores for their student populations.

As we mentioned above, in the initial stages of development, only one of the design team developers (Roots and Wings) had significant experience in working with students in high-poverty and high-needs settings, and had developed materials to address the needs of non-English-speaking students in the districts serving such students. The other NAS design team developers had little experience working with schools that were predominantly poor and enrolled mostly students of color.

One way to view the experience of the NAS scale-up phase is to attempt to understand whether the design teams and their designs were effective in these settings. We turn now to the major findings from the RAND research to better understand this issue.

FACTORS RELATED TO IMPLEMENTATION IN NAS SCHOOLS

The most important finding of both the case study and the quantitative research was that schools varied considerably in the level of implementation achieved 2 years into the 5-year, scale-up effort. Generally, about half of the schools examined in the case study research were implementing at targeted levels—those desired by design teams, NAS, and districts—while the other half were below these levels (Bodilly, 1998). The following findings from the longitudinal analysis by Berends, Kirby, Naftel, and McKelvey (2001) of 104 NAS schools help to explain these distinctions across sites:

- Large differences in implementation across both jurisdictions and design teams due to a myriad of social, economic, and political factors
- Stability in implementation over time
- Considerable variability in implementation within schools

We learned in this study of 104 NAS schools that the implementation of a particular design at a particular school site is affected by a myriad of social, economic, and political factors. In other words, the process of changing entire schools to improve student learning opportunities is complex and difficult, because so many actors are involved and so many factors have to be aligned to support change. Several factors emerge from our research as fostering high-quality and coherent implementation in the types of schools in the sample: teacher expectations, school characteristics and principal leadership, design team support and clear communication, and district support.

Teachers: Importance of High Expectations and Support for the Design Team

In the implementation of any educational program, teachers are the "street level bureaucrats" (Weatherly & Lipsky, 1977). They are the ones who are at the end of the line affecting implementation in the classrooms where students spend most of their days. In our analyses, we found that teacher perceptions of students and their readiness to learn were significantly related to teacher-reported levels of implementation. Thus, the teachers who reported a higher level of implementation were the same teachers who were less likely to argue that their students' lack of basic skills was a hindrance to their academic success or to see a lack of student discipline or parent support as a problem. At the same time, these teachers also said that students can learn with the resources available. In addition, the teachers who reported greater support for the design team assisting their school also reported higher levels of design implementation. Teachers who held very different views—for example, that lack of basic skills, parent involvement, or resources was a problem—reported lower levels of design implementation. Given that these are conditions commonly reported in urban schools, these findings highlight the importance of getting teachers behind the adopted model and providing them with supports and resources to allow them to teach to high standards.

School Characteristics: Importance of Size, Level, and Leadership

Taking into account other factors related to teachers, design teams, and districts, we found that school size and level were related to implementation. For instance, teacher-reported implementation levels were higher in smaller schools and elementary schools compared with large and secondary schools. These findings are consistent with our case study research as well as other research on school organizations. For instance, Perrow (1986) notes that larger, secondary schools are more complex organizations and are likely to resist organizational change. Moreover, these large schools may be more bureaucratic rather than communitarian, resulting in a climate where teachers are less likely to collaborate around the common, whole-school missions and visions embraced by the NAS designs (see Bryk & Driscoll, 1988; Lee & Smith, 1995, 1997; Lee, Bryk, & Smith, 1993).

Schools with strong principal leaders also reported higher levels of implementation than those schools lacking such leaders. Principal leadership in our analysis was measured by aggregated teacher reports about principals who clearly communicated what was expected of teachers, were supportive and encouraging of staff, obtained resources for the school, enforced rules for student conduct, talked with teachers regarding instructional practices, had confidence in teachers' expertise, and took a personal interest in the professional development of teachers. The importance of principal leadership for establishing effective schools has been emphasized by researchers for decades (Edmonds, 1979; Purkey & Smith, 1983; Rosenholtz, 1985), so it is not surprising that such leadership is important for the implementation of NAS designs. While not surprising, the importance of principal leadership should not be overlooked when adopting and implementing whole-school reforms.

Our discussion has focused thus far on the net influence of each factor, controlling for other important measures. However, it is important to emphasize that schools often face a multiplicity of challenges, and the interaction among these factors can set these schools back considerably in their attempts to implement school designs. Bodilly (1998) found, for example, that schools that were beset with a combination of two or more negative factors, such as internal tensions, leadership turnover, forced adoptions of designs, or poor understanding of designs, ranked very low on implementation. Thus, schools need stable leadership, and capacity and commitment on the part of the teachers, to make the designs work.

Related to these first two factors of implementation—teacher buy-in and school-level variables and leadership—we learned that not only does implementation vary between schools, but most of the variability in implementation lies *within* schools. In fact, we found that only about 28% of the total variation in implementation lies *between* schools, leaving as much as 72% of the variance in implementation to factors within schools.

While such findings are not uncommon in analyses of school contextual effects on student and teacher outcomes (see Gamoran, 1992; Lee & Bryk, 1989), this is an important finding for the NAS initiative. When considering school reform and the effects of schools on students, it is critical to understand that most of the differences in critical outcomes—whether in implementation factors or "results"—are likely to occur *within* schools rather than *between* them. This implies that conditions in these schools did not favor transference of practice from design teams to teachers and that, after several years, a significant percentage of teachers were not implementing the desired practice. These attempts at whole-school reform did not affect the *whole* school. Related to this finding we learn that not only are the educators and school characteristics important, but there are also some design team characteristics that are important to the implementation of whole-school reform.

Design Teams: Importance of Clear Communication and Support to the School

Bodilly (1998) identified five elements related to design teams that were important contributors to design implementation.

1. A stable team with the capacity to serve a growing number of schools
2. Ability to communicate the design well to schools
3. Effective marketing to the district and ability to gain needed resources
4. Greater relative and immediate emphasis on core elements of schooling (curriculum, instruction, student assignment, student assessment, and professional development) rather than emphasis on planning, governance, or integrated social services
5. Stronger implementation support to schools in the form of whole-school training, facilitators, extensive training days, quality checks, and materials

The case study findings were reinforced by earlier quantitative work that highlighted the importance of design team support and clear communication to schools and teachers in encouraging high levels of implementation (Berends, Kirby, Naftel, & McKelvey, 2001; Kirby, Berends, & Naftel, 2001).

Comparisons among design teams reveal that Co-NECT Schools, Roots and Wings, and National Alliance for Restructuring Education ranked comparatively high on our measure of implementation, while Modern Red Schoolhouse generally ranked the lowest. However, in terms of differences in means, none of these differences was statistically significant.[7]

District Support: Importance of Stable Leadership, Resources, and Support

As we showed earlier, the level of implementation varied significantly across districts. Bodilly (1998) also identified several district and institutional factors that contributed to implementation. These were leadership backing and stability at the district level; centrality of the NAS initiative to the district's agenda; lack of crisis situations; history of trust and cooperation; availability of resources for transformation; school-level authority and/or autonomy; union support; and district accountability and assessment systems that were compatible with those of the designs. Figure 7.2 shows differences in implementation by school district. The overall mean

Figure 7.2. Overall Implementation Index by Jurisdiction, Spring 1998

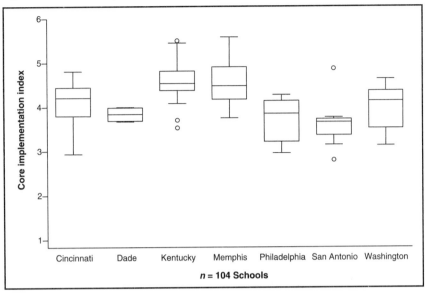

Notes:

Sample sizes are Cincinnati ($n = 16$), Dade ($n = 4$), Kentucky ($n = 20$), Memphis ($n = 29$), Philadelphia ($n = 7$), San Antonio ($n = 9$), Washington ($n = 19$).

Implementation was measured by a summative scale of teacher responses as to the degree to which the following described their school (on a scale of 1–6, with 1 = does not describe my school, and 6 = clearly describes my school): parents and community members are involved in the educational program; student assessments are explicitly linked to academic standards; teachers develop and monitor student progress with personalized, individualized learning programs; student grouping is fluid, multiage, or multiyear; teachers are continual learners and team members through professional development, common planning, and collaboration; and performance expectations are made explicit to students so that they can track their progress over time.

The results in this figure are portrayed with box-and-whisker diagrams, which show the distribution of the particular indicator being examined. In a box-and-whisker diagram, the line in the box is at the median value—half the values fall above the line and half fall below. Each "box" captures the middle 50% of the distribution. The lines, called "whiskers," at each end of the box show the range of scores beyond the upper and lower quartiles. Outliers are indicated by the circles. The box-and-whisker plot thus allows us to compare the centers (median or center of the box), spread (measured by the interquartile range or the height of the box), and tails of the different distributions.

for the sample schools was 4.20, with a standard deviation of 0.58. Kentucky and Memphis ranked relatively high on this index, with means of 4.56 and 4.49, respectively, while Philadelphia and San Antonio ranked the lowest (means of 3.73 and 3.60, respectively). The differences between the highest and lowest jurisdictions were all statistically significant.

Districts played several important roles in fostering/hindering implementation, including:

- Initial matching and selection
- Resource support of the design team
- Creating an environment with supportive political leadership and regulatory policies

Initial Matching and Selection. Districts played a strong role in determining the initial and sustained viability of the relationship between the school and the team. In every district in the sample, schools had complaints about poor planning and lack of time for making decisions, issues brought up in other assessments of the adoption of school-wide programs (Wong & Meyer, 1998). Several districts forced schools to accept a particular design, which proved self-defeating. These schools were well behind on implementation and complained bitterly about the treatment they had received from the district. Several districts negatively influenced the matching process in less visible ways.

- Failing to provide information about choices and how to make them, the level of resources available for implementation, designs, and time lines for making choices and implementing them in a thoughtful, timely manner
- Implementing policies that called for the rotation of principals to other schools on a cyclical basis (every 3 to 6 years, depending on the district)
- Failing to recognize severe problems in certain schools—for instance, poor leadership, political infighting, extremely low capacity in the school due to systematic resource allocation to other schools, or, in one instance, alleged malfeasance

Thus, the districts played a crucial role in the matching and selection process. A match thought to be suitable and well informed by both design and school did not guarantee high levels of implementation. But clearly unsuitable matches or unprepared schools guaranteed very low implementation levels.

Resource Support. In addition to this matching and selection role, we also found that the districts played a crucial role in determining the design team support. Instances of poor support by specific design teams to schools were often the fault of teams and resulted from poor planning, lack of resources, and leadership turnover. However, the districts also played an important role. For instance, it was the district, not the schools, that negotiated the contract for design team services and determined how much to pay the teams. Some districts recognized that assistance to transform an entire school would be more costly than assistance needed to implement a single program within a school. Other districts attempted to get a cheaper package, more in line with what they were used to paying for individual, fragmented programs. Unfortunately, cheaper was indeed what districts and schools got in these instances. Our data indicate a strong positive relationship between the level of implementation and the amount of money a district dedicated to professional development and teacher planning.

Thus, our findings highlight the importance of adequate resources for implementation. These resources are spent on the following types of costs: payments to the design teams for assistance; personnel costs within the school, such as a facilitator or a coordinator; training and planning time for teachers; and materials and conference costs. Resources can come from different sources, depending on the districts.

Other RAND research suggests that resource availability is more an issue of resource allocation. Keltner (1998) found that of the cost to implement a design during the 1996–97 school year, nearly 40% was met through reallocation of budgets for personnel, substitute teachers, and materials. The remaining 60% came from resources external to the school—for example, Title I, district, or grants. Thus, the issue is for schools and districts to rethink existing funding streams to support whole-school reform (Bodilly & Berends, 1999; King, 1994, 1999). Yet, as Odden (1997) notes in his analysis of NAS design costs, reallocation of funds is not always a straightforward exercise "because it usually involves 'trading in' or redefining the positions of current educational specialist staff for the needed NAS ingredients; however in terms of actively promoting and sustaining real reform, it is the most powerful and effective approach" (p. 11).

Attention to resources—whether funding for materials, professional development, assistance providers, or time—will continue to be an issue even with the support of the federal Title I whole-school program. While the funds provided no doubt will further the demand for NAS designs and other design-based assistance organizations, many funding issues remain. For instance, districts and schools control many resources that can supplement the federal funds, and some reallocation will be necessary (Berends, Bodilly, & Kirby, 2002; Keltner, 1998).

Political and Leadership Support. In addition to the above-mentioned factors, higher average levels of implementation were found in districts that had a stable district leadership that placed a high priority on the effort, that lacked a major budget crisis or other crisis, and that had a history of trust between the central office and the schools. School-level respondents directly linked these factors to greater efforts at implementation. When these factors were missing, as is common in challenged urban schools, school respondents reported that their own efforts stalled or were less intense.

For example, in Pittsburgh, the superintendent announced the district's 5-year commitment to the NAS effort at approximately the same time she announced her retirement in 2 years. Teachers and principals reported this sent them a "mixed message" about what level of effort they should give the initiative. In our interviews, many teachers asked why they should commit to the superintendent's initiative when the superintendent was not going to be around long enough to see it through. In the first year of implementation, the same district put a redistricting initiative on the agenda that would have closed several of the schools implementing the designs and reassigned students to others. In the second year of implementation, a severe budget crisis hit. Schools revised their budgets accordingly. Promised money for design team implementation did not arrive, and attention of the central office support team for NAS was drawn to more pressing political problems. Again and again, teachers and principals indicated that they interpreted these actions as showing that the district did not place a high priority on the NAS effort. Thus, they followed suit. It is no wonder then that the schools in this district showed low levels of implementation after 2 years. In fact, in our longitudinal study of schools, Pittsburgh schools were dropped from the final analysis because too few reported implementing a NAS design (see Berends, Kirby, Naftel, & McKelvey, 2001).

Regulatory Support. While crucial, central office political support and attention also must be buttressed by significant changes in regulatory practices. Comprehensive school reform is not confined to the adoption of a new curriculum or a few new instructional strategies. Instead, it requires the rethinking and adoption at the school level of a whole new curriculum and instructional package that may be quite different from those the district has mandated or approved for all its schools. In turn, the curriculum and instructional package cannot be developed or implemented without significant changes in resource allocation for instructional positions, materials, technology, professional development, and so forth. Thus, schools attempting comprehensive school reform to address their particular problems must have, minimally, increased site-level control over their curriculum and instruction, their budgets, their positions and staffing, and most essentially their mission.

In our sample, districts varied significantly in their understanding and response to these school-level needs for transformation. In those districts that provided modest budgetary support and some autonomy for schools, implementation progressed. In those that did not, implementation lagged.

While we focus primarily on the central office, union actions or policies also can prohibit implementation.

San Antonio offers an example of the problem of how directions and support from the district office may result in conflicting mandates at the school and classrooms levels. The district originally had provided extensive school-level control over curriculum and instruction and had the support of a strong superintendent committed to NAS designs but also to raising the test scores of students in the district, which were abysmal. The district leadership introduced the NAS initiative to schools with hopes that the marketed break the mold designs would enable teachers and administrators to engage enthusiastically in comprehensive school reform. The thought was that external model providers would be more successful at pushing and sustaining change than the central office ever could be by itself. The district had every intention of fully supporting its NAS schools in all ways—including professional development, site-based facilitators (called Instructional Guides), and other resources for the schools to implement the designs.

The manner in which the district leaders chose to increase test scores, however, proved to run counter to the implementation of the designs. The district established an Office of Curriculum and Instruction responsible for developing a sequential, standards-aligned curriculum across grade levels in all schools throughout the district. The district leadership then required schools to implement specific mathematics, reading, and language arts programs in addition to the NAS designs. In Spring 1996, all schools were implementing *Everyday Mathematics*, developed by the University of Chicago School Mathematics Project. The district leaders expected all schools throughout the district to follow a similar pace, and developed pacing guides to ensure that this would happen. In addition, the district leaders required San Antonio elementary schools to begin implementing a reading initiative that involved a 90-minute block of time. During the 1998–99 school year, the district required two 90-minute blocks of uninterrupted instructional time for reading and math, respectively, and teachers to manage time within these blocks in prescribed ways. Although not to the same degree, the district structured language arts activities (spelling, grammar, and writing) as well, totaling approximately 70 minutes of instructional time per day. Thus, the district leadership mapped out roughly 4 hours of instructional activities for every elementary school teacher to follow. (Roots and Wings teachers were exempt from implementing the district's reading initiative).[8]

Within this context, the district leadership provided a substantial amount of professional development to teachers. Much of the inservice training revolved around the district's reading and mathematics initiatives. Because NAS teachers were obligated to attend as many of these various inservices as their colleagues in non-NAS schools, the amount of training activities served only to heighten frustrations. All of the designs, except for Roots and Wings, required teachers to develop units and write curriculum. Thus, although the district leaders encouraged schools to implement NAS designs, they simultaneously constrained the educators' ability to do so by telling teachers what to teach and how.

What we observed in San Antonio is not unique among high-poverty districts and schools faced with high-stakes accountability mandates from their states. Many schools are suffering the burden "of having a torrent of unwanted, uncoordinated policies and innovations raining down on them from hierarchical bureaucracies" (Fullan, 2001, p. 22). In a recent survey of schools in districts in California and Texas, Hatch (2000) reported that two-thirds of the schools were working with three or more improvement programs; over one-fifth were working with six or more. In short, barriers imposed by district leaders can significantly inhibit innovative ideas and reforms. Leaders must actively restructure existing mandates and regulations in order to allow whole-school instructional reforms to flourish.

Related to these issues of mandates and regulations, in many instances, the districts we studied had state-mandated standardized tests that increasingly are used to evaluate principal and teacher performance. In these cases, implementing schools are drawn to skill and drill techniques and strict content coverage to ensure the test scores on which they will be judged. Teachers indicate that this testing accountability regime leads to lower levels of implementation of designs, as students are drilled for several weeks prior to the high-stakes tests.

In other instances, we found that district or union control over staffing and position assignment was a barrier to implementation. For example, in one district at the end of 2 years, school-level teacher/facilitators who had left the classroom to provide the day-to-day coaching to support design implementation ran up against a union rule that did not allow teachers to remain "out of the classroom" for more than 2 years. The waiver process seemed to be decided in a somewhat idiosyncratic fashion, depending on who attended the union meeting.

And finally, another dimension of regulatory control that sometimes was lessened was control over budgets. In fact, several districts in our study claimed to have increased school autonomy over the budget. However, often this was limited to decisions on how to spend within particular, highly specified categories of funding, or stovepipes, but not between stovepipes. Thus, stovepipes were narrow and fragmented, making coherent school improvement policy illusive.

Regulatory barriers, then, can significantly inhibit innovative ideas and reforms. The whole-school design reforms often have to accommodate to the existing mandates and regulations of school districts, and thus their implementation may ebb and flow over time.

In short, district-level politics, policies, and practices could promote or derail the effort to transform schools using comprehensive school reform models. Schools looked to district leadership, climate, and regulations to determine whether it was worth their time and effort to invest in transforming. Schools in some districts judged it was not, and did not invest their efforts in reform. In others, schools received the support they needed to begin a legitimate effort at implementation.

PERFORMANCE IN NAS SCHOOLS

The results of our study show that the NAS goal of dramatically improving the achievement of large numbers of students was overly ambitious, especially in a short period of time. In total, of the 163 schools for which we had data during the first few years of the scale-up phase, allowing comparisons in performance relative to the district or state, 81 schools (50%) made gains relative to the average district gain in mathematics and 76 schools (47%) made such gains in reading. Among the four jurisdictions with 10 or more implementing NAS schools, Memphis and Kentucky schools appeared to be the most successful in terms of improvement in mathematics, while Cincinnati and Washington did better in reading.

The results by design team varied across mathematics and reading tests. For example, for the eight Audrey Cohen College schools, five made progress relative to the district in mathematics, but only two did so in reading. With the exception of the Authentic Teaching and Expeditionary Learning schools, about half of the schools working with each design team made progress relative to the district in mathematics; in reading, fewer than half of Audrey Cohen College, Co-NECT, and National Alliance for Restructuring Education schools made gains relative to the district. Roots and Wings was consistent, with 10 out of 21 schools making progress in both reading and mathematics relative to the district. Of the 11 Modern Red Schoolhouse schools, seven made progress in mathematics and eight in reading.

While each design has unique characteristics, these uneven outcomes suggest that the wide variation in implementation conditions and strategies, as well as school and district environments, diminishes the possibility of consistently robust performance results across the NAS sites. Note that these gains include *any* gains relative to the district average gain over the early years of implementation; we did not have information to test the statistical significance of these gains. Better and longer-term performance data are needed in order to make conclusive judgments about designs and their effects on school performance.

However, our implementation analysis showed that the overall level of implementation increased modestly over time, but there was ongoing within-school variation in implementation. If the NAS approach to school improvement is the best method for turning around failing schools, at least in theory, then weak implementation will lead to weak impacts on student performance. Our findings suggest that we cannot expect stronger performance results unless the implementation process across school sites and district contexts significantly improves.

A detailed classroom study of San Antonio allowed us to examine whether variation in instructional conditions was related to student achievement, controlling for other student, teacher, classroom, and school characteristics. Similar to other analyses of school-wide reforms, we found that

- Strong principal leadership, as reported by teachers, had significant positive effects on students' state test scores in reading and mathematics.
- Instructional conditions promoted by reforms such as NAS—including teacher-reported collaboration, quality professional development, and reform-like instructional practices—were not related to student achievement net of other student and classroom conditions.
- In general, early implementation of NAS designs in a high-poverty district within a high-stakes accountability system did not result in significant effects on student achievement.

THE LINK BETWEEN IMPLEMENTATION AND PERFORMANCE

Given that we do not have good, sustained, and coherent measures of student performance that are comparable across jurisdictions and across design teams, it is not surprising that our data do not show any clear linkage between implementation and performance in NAS schools. This was disappointing and runs counter to conventional wisdom. If the theory of action underlying comprehensive school reform is valid and if these models are implemented in a sustained, coherent fashion, then higher implementation should be related to improved outcomes. As Stringfield, Millsap, and Herman (1997) conclude in *Special Strategies for Educating Disadvantaged Children*, "We know that some programs, well implemented, can make dramatic differences in students' academic achievement" (p. 43). Yet, Stringfield and colleagues go on to point out the critical challenge in education reform that has existed in this country for decades.

> After a third of a century of research on school change, we still have not provided adequate human and fiscal resources, appropriately targeted, to make large-scale program improvements a reliably consistent reality in schools serving students placed at risk. (p. 43)

We offer two hypotheses for the failure to find a link between implementation and performance. First, despite schools reporting implementation of designs, our research was conducted too early to find deep implementation that would dramatically affect performance gains. As Sizer (1984) points out, "Schools are complicated and traditional institutions, and they easily resist all sorts of well-intentioned efforts at reform" (p. 224). Moreover, as several design developers and school reformers have pointed out, schoolwide change programs can take more than 5 years to take hold in a school and make a difference in the lives of educators or students (Darling-Hammond, 1988, 1995, 1997; Hess, 1995; Levin, 1991; Sizer, 1992).

Some of the design team developers emphasize that it takes several years for implementation to make a difference in a school (Bodilly, 1998; Smith et al., 1998). Only with coherent implementation would one expect school test scores to consistently increase throughout the school. Our analysis shows a large number of NAS schools near the midlevel implementation points on scales for the wide array of indicators considered here. Moreover, there is a great deal of variation among teachers within the NAS sites. Our case studies support these quantitative findings (Bodilly, 1998). Over time, with more specific test score information and additional measures of implementation, the empirical link might be observed. This remains an open question.

Second, the nature of our dependent variable—a simple dichotomous (0/1) variable indicating whether or not a school made gains relative to the district—does not allow for any gradations in student performance. Had we been able to calculate effect sizes, perhaps we would have seen a link between implementation and performance, but most districts were unwilling to provide this more detailed information.

Some have argued that perhaps our analysis sample may have failed to find evidence of the link between implementation and student performance because of measurement error in our indicators. Additional research and longitudinal data addressed the relationship of implementation and performance in NAS schools—using matched comparison schools and more specific data on student performance, observational data, and specific implementation indicators gathered at the classroom level (see Berends,

Chun, et al., 2002; Chun, Gill, & Heilbrunn, 2001). The findings of these supplemental studies did not change our overall conclusion that in most NAS schools implementation was never deep enough to expect a relationship to school performance.

POLICY IMPLICATIONS OF THE NAS INITIATIVE

NAS, a business-oriented, not-for-profit organization, entered into the school reform arena with a useful goal of raising student performance by the use of comprehensive and coherent whole-school designs. Its goal was ambitious: to dramatically improve the performance of schools by the use of these designs. After a decade of experience, the record on results is mixed. For the most part, the teams failed to meet the very high expectations— dramatic transformation across whole districts—set for them by the business leaders. We have pointed to several reasons why. Nonetheless, each design team worked with at least some challenging schools where it implemented the design at relatively high levels, and the schools experienced some achievement gains. In the end, the effort produced several self-sustaining design teams that are experiencing increased demand generated by federal legislation geared to building school capacity for comprehensive school reform.

When federal Title I funding was made available to schools engaged in school-wide or whole-school reform as well as federal Comprehensive School Reform Demonstration funds, more schools and districts throughout the country attempted NAS-like reforms. Schools that attempted comprehensive school reforms faced many obstacles during implementation, and because of this, whole-school design developers continue to confront challenges in significantly raising the achievement of all students. This is particularly important to remember when setting expectations for school improvement under new federal, state, and local policies and programs.

Because the targets of federal CSRD funds were primarily high-poverty schools, model developers and educators often encountered very fragmented and conflicting environments, difficult and changing political currents, new accountability systems, trenchant unions, lack of resources in terms of teacher time, demoralized teachers (given the fluctuating reform agenda), and the very difficult task of improving student performance under these types of conditions (for a description of CSRD schools, see Kirby, Berends, Naftel, & Sloan, 2001).

Given this, federal and state policymakers need to think critically about their current stance of simultaneously promoting high-stakes testing, comprehensive school reforms that promote innovative curriculum and instructional strategies, and multiple other concurrent reforms. The implementation of high-stakes testing regimes—the outcome of many standards-based reforms—might preclude the adoption of rich and varied curricula that challenge students and motivate them toward more in-depth learning experiences. It certainly prevents it when other, more skill and drill reforms are mandated on top of the design-based curriculum. Our interviews with teachers and principals clearly indicate that high-stakes tests are a two-edged sword in this environment. On the one hand, high-stakes tests motivate schools to increase performance and often to seek out new curriculum and instructional strategies associated with comprehensive school reforms. On the other hand, those very same tests provide disincentives to adopt richer, more in-depth curriculum, as teachers feel incredible pressure to teach to the tests.

Our findings are consistent with Porter's and Clune's schemes for better educational policy (see Clune, 1998; Porter, 1994; Porter, Floden, Freeman, Schmidt, & Schwille, 1988). They posit that educational policies such as comprehensive school reform that are specific, powerful, authoritative, consistent, and stable are more likely to influence teachers and students. *Specificity*, or depth, is the extent to which the comprehensive school reform provides detailed guidance or materials to help schools and teachers understand what they are supposed to do (e.g., materials that describe the stages of implementing the design and ongoing, clear assistance strategies to further promote implementation). *Power* refers to the rewards or sanctions attached to the whole-school reform, such as teachers receiving bonuses or greater autonomy if they comply with implementing the design. *Authority* means the degree to which the reform policy is seen as *legitimate* and as having the *support* of those who are responsible for implementation. If respected groups or policymakers have strong positive views toward whole-school reform and if teachers support its implementation, the design is likely to have greater influence in changing teaching and learning. *Consistency*, or *alignment*, refers to the extent to which the set of whole-school interventions and strategies are aligned with a common mission and vision, both within the school and the district. *Stability* means that the reform is sustained over time in a coherent, consistent manner. Policymakers and educators should use these dimensions as a means for thinking critically about a comprehensive school reform under consideration and whether the conditions exist for it to flourish.

Consistent with Porter's and Clune's suggestions, we offer the following suggestions to help schools and policymakers create an environment that makes it more likely for the CSRD and Title I school-wide reform to flourish and bring about the desired effects on student performance:

- Ensure teacher buy-in and support. Without willing and able school staff who embrace reform, believe their students can achieve, and provide the necessary leadership and energy, no reform can be enacted. As Fullan (2001) succinctly stated, educational change depends on "what teachers do and think—it's as simple and as complex as that" (p. 117).
- Improve the capacity of principals and teachers and the quality of teaching through incentives, professional development, and training.
- Emphasize clear communication and design-based assistance from model developers to support the implementation of the designs.
- Encourage supportive state and district policies and environments aligned with comprehensive school reforms.
- Promote, encourage, and support the free flow of information and funding throughout the system, thus developing more informed consumers at the school level by disseminating information about models, costs in terms of both resources and time, initial selection and matching, and funding.

These issues are even more important in schools that have high proportions of children in poverty because such schools already face a host of challenges. Thinking carefully about the factors necessary to promote high-quality implementation and coherence with other educational policies and reforms and ensuring that these factors are present and aligned in these schools is the only way in which comprehensive school reform can succeed in improving the learning opportunities of students in these high-poverty settings. In short, easy fixes to the equity issues in our schools are not possible. Rather, equity can be achieved only through systematic, sustained reform of the educational infrastructure.

NOTES

Acknowledgments. We thank the Ford Foundation and the Atlantic Philanthropic Service Company for their support of this research on New American Schools. We are also grateful to the teachers and principals in the schools who gave of their time to respond to our questions, the staff in districts and states who helped us piece together relevant data, and the design teams who clarified issues along the way. Several members of RAND's research team contributed to the studies informing this chapter, including JoAn Chun, Brian Gill, Tom Glennan, Joann Heilbrunn, Brent Keltner, Christopher McKelvey, Scott Naftel, Susanna Purnell, Robert Reichardt, Gina Schuyler, Sue Stockly, and R.J. Briggs. We thank the members of the Research Advisory Panel (funded by the Annenberg Foundation) who provide critical guidance to RAND's research on NAS. Members include Barbara Cervone, Paul Hill, Janice Petrovich, Andrew Porter, Karen Sheingold, and Carol Weiss. Of course, any errors remain the responsibility of the authors and not of these individuals or agencies.

1. To further the implementation of comprehensive, whole-school reforms, the Comprehensive School Reform Demonstration program, also known as Obey-Porter, was established in November 1997. These appropriations committed $145 million to be used to help schools develop comprehensive school reform based on reliable research and effective practices. The majority (83% in FY98 and 77% in FY99) of the funds are committed to Title I schools. Part of the money ($25 million in FY98 and FY99) was available to all public schools, including those ineligible for Title I, as part of the Fund for the Improvement in Education (FIE) program. Approximately 1,800 schools received at least $50,000 per year for 3 years under the CSRD program, beginning in FY98. There was an increase of $75 million for FY00 ($50 million in Title I/Section 1502 funds and $25 million in FIE funds) over the $145 million appropriated for FY98 and FY99, which allowed 1,000 additional schools to undertake comprehensive reform (see Kirby, Berends, Naftel, & Sloan, 2001).

2. This count includes all schools in which designs were ever implemented, including schools that dropped designs or changed to a different design. For example, with the transition of National Alliance to America's Choice, several schools in Kentucky dropped the NARE design and did not switch to America's Choice. These schools are still included in the total count. Moreover, NAS recently expanded to ten teams. For example, by adding Accelerated Schools to its portfolio, it added roughly 700 schools.

3. See Berends, 1999, 2000; Berends, Bodilly, & Kirby, 2002; Berends, Chun, Schuyler, Stockly, & Riggs, 2002; Berends, Kirby, Naftel, & McKelvey, 2001; Bodilly, 1996, 1998, 2001; Bodilly, Purnell, Ramsey, & Smith, 1995; Glennan, 1998; Kirby, Berends, & Naftel, 2001; Mitchell, 1996.

4. A more detailed description of the history of the NAS initiative and the design teams appears in Berends, 2004; Berends, Bodilly, & Kirby, 2002; Berends, Kirby, Naftel, & McKelvey, 2001; Bodilly, 1998; Glennan, 1998; Stringfield, Ross, & Smith, 1996. See also Ball, Camburn, Cohen, & Rowan, 1998; Datnow, 2000; Datnow & Castellano, 2000; Datnow & Stringfield, 1997, 2000; Desimone, 2000, 2002; Herman et al., 1999; Ross, Sanders, Wright, & Stringfield, 1998; Ross et al., 1997; Stringfield & Datnow, 1998.

5. NAS's portfolio of teams has changed significantly since RAND's programs of studies began in the scale-up phase. For instance, another design—Urban Learning Centers (ULC)—was being implemented in the Los Angeles area during the development phase of NAS, but when scale-up began, this design team was not included in the NAS portfolio because the team had not shown the capacity to go to scale. Since that time, ULC has shown this capacity and is currently being marketed by NAS as one of its designs. Moreover, Audrey Cohen did not show during scale-up the progress that NAS desired, and this team was dropped from the portfolio. Finally, for the past few years, America's Choice and Success for All have not

been affiliated with NAS. At this writing, NAS has 10 teams in its portfolio: Accelerated Schools, ATLAS Communities, Co-NECT, Different Ways of Knowing, ELOB, Leonard Bernstein Center, Modern Red Schoolhouse, The National Institute for Direct Instruction, Turning Points, and Urban Learning Centers. Readers can find information on these design teams at http://www.newamericanschools.org/.

6. NARE's development into America's Choice reflected a major change in the design, from NARE's emphasis on changing the school system (e.g., organization and governance, and assessments) to America's Choice's additional emphasis on curriculum, instruction, and professional development changes within classrooms and schools. Despite this change, the school principals in the sample analyzed in our study continued to report that they were implementing the principles of the NARE design.

7. The results for the core implementation index by jurisdictions and design teams are consistent with findings from examining a wider set of indicators separately (see Berends, Kirby, Naftel, & McKelvey, 2001). In addition, we also did sensitivity analyses of our results by constructing more diverse and more inclusive indices of implementation (see Berends, 2000, for an example of a larger index). The results were quite consistent across these different indices.

8. In San Antonio, the RW design was never fully implemented. The schools we studied were interested in the Success for All reading portion of the RW design only.

REFERENCES

Ambach, G. (1991). The essential federal role. In *Voices from the field: 30 expert opinions on America 2000, the Bush Administration strategy to "reinvent" America's schools* (pp. 39–40). Washington, DC: William T. Grant Foundation on Work, Family, and Citizenship and the Institute for Educational Leadership.

Ball, D. L., Camburn, E., Cohen, D. K., & Rowan, B. (1998). *Instructional improvement and disadvantaged students*. Unpublished manuscript, University of Michigan, Ann Arbor.

Berends, M. (1999). *Monitoring the progress of New American Schools: A description of implementing schools in a longitudinal sample*. Santa Monica, CA: Rand.

Berends, M. (2000). Teacher-reported effects of New American Schools' designs: Exploring relationships to teacher background and school context. *Educational Evaluation and Policy Analysis, 22*(1), 65–82.

Berends, M. (2004). In the wake of *A Nation at Risk*: New American Schools' private sector school reform initiative. *Peabody Journal of Education, 79*(1), 130–163.

Berends, M., Bodilly, S., & Kirby, S. N. (2002). *Challenges of whole-school reform: New American Schools after a decade*. Santa Monica, CA: Rand.

Berends, M., Chun, J., Schuyler, G., Stockly, S., & Riggs, R. J. (2002). *Challenges of conflicting school reforms: Effects of New American Schools in a high-poverty district*. Santa Monica, CA: Rand.

Berends, M., Kirby, S. N., Naftel, S., & McKelvey, C. (2001). *Implementation and performance in New American Schools: Three years into scale-up.* Santa Monica, CA: Rand.

Berends, M., Kirby, S. N., Naftel, S., & Sloan, J. S. (2001). *The status of standards-based reforms in Title I schools: First-year findings from the National Longitudinal Study of Schools.* Washington, DC: U.S. Department of Education.

Bodilly, S. (1996). *Lessons from New American Schools Development Corporation's demonstration phase.* Santa Monica, CA: Rand.

Bodilly, S. (1998). *Lessons from New American Schools' scale-up phase: Prospects for bringing designs to multiple schools.* Santa Monica, CA: Rand.

Bodilly, S. (2001). *New American Schools' concept of break the mold designs: How designs evolved over time and why.* Santa Monica, CA: Rand.

Bodilly, S. J., & Berends, M. (1999). Necessary district support for comprehensive school reform. In G. Orfield & E. H. DeBray (Eds.), *Hard work for good schools: Facts not fads in Title I reform* (pp. 111–119). Cambridge, MA: The Civil Rights Project, Harvard University.

Bodilly, S., Purnell, S., Ramsey, K., & Smith, C. (1995). *Designing New American Schools: Baseline observations on nine design teams.* Santa Monica, CA: Rand.

Bryk, A. S., & Driscoll, M. E. (1988). *The high school as community: Contextual influences and consequences for students and teachers.* Madison: University of Wisconsin–Madison, Wisconsin Center for Education Research.

Chun, J., Gill, B., & Heilbrunn, J. (2001). *The relationship between implementation and achievement: Case studies of New American Schools.* Santa Monica, CA: Rand.

Clune, W. (1998). *Toward a theory of systemic reform: The case of nine NSF statewide systemic initiatives.* Madison: University of Wisconsin–Madison, Wisconsin Center for Education Research.

Darling-Hammond, L. (1988). Policy and professionalism. In A. Lieberman (Ed.), *Building a professional culture in schools* (pp. 57–77). New York: Teachers College Press.

Darling-Hammond, L. (1995). Policy for restructuring. In A. Lieberman (Ed.), *The work of restructuring schools: Building from the ground up* (pp. 157–175). New York: Teachers College Press.

Darling-Hammond, L. (1997). *The right to learn: A blueprint for creating schools that work.* San Francisco: Jossey-Bass.

Datnow, A. (2000). Power and politics in the adoption of school reform models. *Educational Evaluation and Policy Analysis, 22*(4), 357–374.

Datnow, A., & Castellano, J. (2000). Teachers' responses to Success for All: How beliefs, experiences, and adaptations shape implementation. *American Educational Research Journal, 37*(3), 775–799.

Datnow, A., & Stringfield, S. (Eds.). (1997). *School effectiveness and school improvement, 8*(1).

Datnow, A., & Stringfield, S. (2000). Working together for reliable school reform. *Journal of Education for Students Placed at Risk, 5*(1), 183–204.

Desimone, L. (2000). *Making comprehensive school reform work.* New York: ERIC Clearinghouse on Urban Education, Teachers College.

Desimone, L. (2002). How can comprehensive school reform models be successfully implemented? *Review of Educational Research, 72*(3), 433–479.

Edmonds, R. R. (1979). Effective schools for the urban poor. *Educational Leadership, 37*, 15–24.

Fullan, M. G. (2001). *The new meaning of educational change* (3rd ed.). New York: Teachers College Press.

Gamoran, A. (1992). The variable effects of high school tracking. *American Sociological Review, 57*, 812–828.

Glennan, T. K., Jr. (1998). *New American Schools after six years.* Santa Monica, CA: Rand.

Hatch, T. (2000). What does it take to "go to scale"? Reflections on the promise and the perils of comprehensive school reform. *Journal of Education for Students Placed at Risk, 5*(4), 339–354.

Herman, R., Aladjem, D., McMahon, P., Masem, E., Mulligan, I., Smith O'Malley, A., Quinones, S., Reeve, A., & Woodruff, D. (1999). *An educators' guide to schoolwide reform.* Washington, DC: American Institutes for Research.

Hess, A. G. (1995). *Restructuring urban schools: A Chicago perspective.* New York: Teachers College Press.

Keltner, B. (1998). *Resources for transforming New American Schools: First year findings.* Santa Monica, CA: Rand.

King, J. A. (1994). Meeting the needs of at-risk students: A cost-analysis of three models. *Educational Evaluation and Policy Analysis, 16*(1), 1–19.

King, J. A. (1999, May). *Making economically-grounded decisions about comprehensive school reform models: Considerations of costs, effects, and contexts.* Paper presented at the National Invitational Conference on Effective Title I Schoolwide Program Implementation, Laboratory for Student Success at Temple University Center for Research in Human Development and Education, Arlington, VA.

Kirby, S. N., Berends, M., & Naftel, S. (2001). *Implementation in New American Schools: Four years into scale-up.* Santa Monica, CA: Rand.

Kirby, S. N., Berends, M., Naftel, S., & Sloan, J. S. (2001). *Schools adopting comprehensive school reform demonstration models: Early findings on implementation.* Washington, DC: Rand.

Kirby, S. N., Sloan, J. S., Naftel, S., & Berends, M. (2001). *Title I schools receiving Comprehensive School Reform Demonstration (CSRD) program funds: Recent evidence from the National Longitudinal Survey of Schools.* Washington, DC: U.S. Department of Education.

Kirst, M. (1991). Toward a focused research agenda. In *Voices from the field: 30 expert opinions on America 2000, the Bush Administration strategy to "reinvent" America's schools* (p. 38). Washington, DC: William T. Grant Foundation on Work, Family, and Citizenship and the Institute for Educational Leadership.

Lee, V. E., & Bryk, A. S. (1989). A multilevel model of the social distribution of high school achievement. *Sociology of Education, 62*(3), 172–192.

Lee, V. E., Bryk, A. S., & Smith, J. B. (1993). The organization of effective secondary schools. *Review of Research in Education, 19*, 171–267.

Lee, V. E., & Smith, J. B. (1995). Effects of high school restructuring and size on early gains in achievement and engagement. *Sociology of Education, 68*(4), 241–270.

Lee, V. E., & Smith, J. B. (1997). High school size: Which works best and for whom? *Educational Evaluation and Policy Analysis, 19*(3), 205–227.

Levin, H. M. (1991). *Learning from Accelerated Schools.* Pew Higher Education Research Program, Policy Perspectives. Philadelphia: Pew Charitable Trusts.

Mitchell, K. (1996). *Reforming and conforming: NASDC principals discuss school accountability systems.* Santa Monica, CA: Rand.

New American Schools Development Corporation. (1991). *Designs for a new generation of American schools: Request for proposals.* Arlington, VA: Author.

Odden, A. (1997). *How to rethink school budgets to support school transformation.* Arlington, VA: New American Schools.

Perrow, C. (1986). *Complex organizations: A critical essay* (3rd ed.). New York: Random House.

Porter, A. C. (1994). National standards and school improvement in the 1990s: Issues and promises. *American Journal of Education, 102*(4), 421–449.

Porter, A. C., Floden, R., Freeman, D., Schmidt, W., & Schwille, J. (1988). Content determinants in elementary school mathematics. In D. A. Grouws & T. J. Cooney (Eds.), *Perspectives on research on effective mathematics teaching* (pp. 96–113). Hillsdale, NJ: Erlbaum.

Purkey, S. C., & Smith, M. S. (1983). Effective schools: A review. *The Elementary School Journal, 83*(4), 427–452.

Rosenholtz, S. J. (1985). Effective schools: Interpreting the evidence. *American Journal of Education, 93*, 352–388.

Ross, S. M., Sanders, W. L., Wright, S. P., & Stringfield, S. (1998). *The Memphis restructuring initiative: Achievement results for years 1 and 2 on the Tennessee Value-Added Assessment System (TVAAS).* Unpublished manuscript, University of Memphis.

Ross, S., Troutman, A., Horgan, D., Maxwell, S., Laitinen, R., & Lowther, D. (1997). The success of schools in implementing eight restructuring designs: A synthesis of first year evaluation outcomes. *School Effectiveness and School Improvement, 8*(1), 95–124.

Sizer, T. R. (1984). *Horace's compromise: The dilemma of the American high school.* New York: Houghton Mifflin.

Sizer, T. R. (1992). *Horace's school: Redesigning the American high school.* New York: Houghton Mifflin.

Smith, L., Ross, S., McNelis, M., Squires, M., Wasson, R., Maxwell, S., Weddle, K., Nath, L., Grehan, A., & Buggey, T. (1998). The Memphis restructuring initiative: Analyses of activities and outcomes that impact implementation success. *Education and Urban Society, 30*(3), 296–325.

Smith, M. S., & Scoll, B. W. (1995). The Clinton human capital agenda. *Teachers College Record, 96*(3), 389–404.

Smith, M. S., Scoll, B. W., & Link, J. (1996). Research-based school reform: The Clinton administration's agenda. In E. A. Hanushek & D. W. Jorgenson (Eds.), *Improving America's schools: The role of incentives* (pp. 9–27). Washington, DC: National Academy Press.

Stringfield, S., & Datnow, A. (Eds.). (1998). *Educational Urban Society, 30*(3).

Stringfield, S., Millsap, M. A., & Herman, R. (1997). *Special strategies for educating disadvantaged children: Findings and policy implications of a longitudinal study.* Washington, DC: U.S. Department of Education.

Stringfield, S., Ross, S., & Smith, L. (Eds.). (1996). *Bold plans for school restructuring.* Mahwah, NJ: Erlbaum.

Timpane, M. (1991). A case of misplaced emphasis. In *Voices from the field: 30 expert opinions on America 2000, the Bush Administration strategy to "reinvent" America's schools* (pp. 19–20). Washington, DC: William T. Grant Foundation on Work, Family, and Citizenship and the Institute for Educational Leadership.

U. S. Department of Education. (2001). *High standards for all students: A report from the national assessment of Title I on progress and challenges since the 1994 reauthorization.* Washington, DC: Author.

Weatherley, R., & Lipsky, M. (1977). Street level bureaucrats and institutional innovation: Implementing special education reform. *Harvard Educational Review, 47*(2), 171–197.

Wong, K., & Meyer, S. (1998). Title I schoolwide programs: A synthesis of findings from recent evaluation. *Educational Evaluation and Policy Analysis, 20*(2), 115–136.

8

School Choice in the Foreground, Gender Equity in the Background

AMANDA DATNOW
LEA HUBBARD

In 1998, California became the first state to experiment with single-gender public education on a large scale. Six districts opened single-gender academies (both boys and girls) at the middle and high school levels as a result of former California Governor Pete Wilson's legislation and funding for a single-gender academies pilot program in the public school system. This chapter examines California's pilot program, using findings from a qualitative case study of the single-gender academies. We discuss why, how, and for what purposes the California's single-gender schooling experiment was implemented, and what the consequences of this school choice movement were for gender equity.

The single-gender academies in California, as we will explain, were not created to systematically address gender equity, which we define here as the removal of gender barriers, bias, and stereotyping for females and males, and a conscious acknowledgment of gendered power relations in society. Instead, from the perspectives of state policymakers, the single-gender academies were created as part of a larger school choice agenda. From the perspective of educators and officials in local school districts and schools, the single-gender academies were created as a way to garner additional resources, reduce distractions between boys and girls, and, in some instances, address the underachievement of low-income students and students of color in separate academies of their own. Despite the name of the policy and the gendered characteristics of the schools' enrollments, this did not reveal itself to be an equity-minded reform at the policy, school, or classroom levels. Rather, like many of the other reforms discussed in this book, California's single-gender public schooling experiment symbolized the "choice" policy ideologies of the 1980s and 1990s.

We want to point out that the California legislation uses the term *single gender*, yet one could argue that *single sex* is a more appropriate term to describe the separation of boys and girls. Typically, the terms *sex* and *gender* refer to the biological and social characteristics, respectively, of being male and female. As Pamela Haag notes in a publication of the American Association of University Women (AAUW), "Schools with all girls are not necessarily single gender because they may include students with both masculine and feminine identities" (AAUW, 1998b, p. 36). However, for the purposes of this chapter, we use the term *single gender* to maintain consistency with the language of the California experiment, and occasionally use the term *single sex* to refer to prior research.

In order to provide some context for our study, we begin this chapter with a brief framework on gender equity and single-sex schooling and then discuss the particulars of California's pilot program.

GENDER EQUITY AND SINGLE-SEX SCHOOLING

Many studies over the past 25 years have documented gender bias against girls in coeducational classrooms (see AAUW, 1992, 1998a, for reviews). Girls receive less teacher attention than boys, feel less comfortable speaking out in class, and face threats of sexual harassment in school (AAUW, 1993; Sadker & Sadker, 1994). Although the achievement gaps between boys and girls are closing in some areas, girls' achievement still lags behind boys' in math and science, and most significantly in computer science and technology majors and careers (AAUW, 1998a, 2000). There is also concern that gender equity solutions have reached girls of different ethnic groups unequally. For example, Latinas perform less well than other racial and ethnic groups of girls in several key measures of educational achievement (Ginorio & Huston, 2001).

While gender equity has long been discussed in terms of remedies designed to raise girls' achievement, more recently some scholars have begun to ask, "What about the boys?" (Gurian, 1998; Pollack, 1998). Public discourse has centered on a "crisis" for boys, focusing on their lower reading and language test scores and higher rates of special education referrals as compared with girls (Kleinfeld, 1999), as well as boys' greater propensity to be involved in violent crimes (Gilbert & Gilbert, 1998). All boys are seen as at risk for these problems, but most notably boys of color. Increasing dropout rates and higher rates of incarceration are particularly salient for African American boys and men (Leake & Leake, 1992).

Meanwhile, many feminist researchers believe that gender equity is still problematic for *girls* in the United States after 20 years of weak enforcement of Title IX, which prohibits discrimination in public educational programs on the basis of sex (Campbell & Sanders, 2002; Marshall & Anderson, 1995). These researchers argue that at the policy level, "today, gender equity is no longer seen as a priority. . . . The gender problem in education has been reduced to the academic performance of women in certain disciplines and delinked from contestation of ideological messages sustained by schooling" (Stromquist, 1997, p. 69).

As these arguments make clear, gender bias is now understood as affecting both girls and boys, as neither group is immune to societal pressures and expectations. For feminist educators and researchers, achieving gender equity in schools means acknowledging that gender bias exists in both subtle and overt forms, eliminating sexist language and stereotyping regarding girls and boys, and offering a socially critical and gender-inclusive curriculum (Kruse, 1996; Murphy & Gipps, 1996). Many argue that educators must address how a social and political agenda benefiting males is embedded in school structures and practices, and make pedagogical, organizational, and curricular changes to even the playing field (Kenway, Blackmore, Willis, & Rennie, 1996; Marshall & Anderson, 1995; Murphy & Gipps, 1996). Such educational changes are seen to benefit both girls and boys and society as a whole.

Single-sex schooling is seen as one possible vehicle for improving the education of girls and boys, although of course not all single-sex schooling experiments are driven by the gender equity goals noted above (Datnow & Hubbard, 2002; Herr & Arms, 2002; Sanford & Blair, 2002). What does the research on single-sex schooling tell us? A comprehensive review of studies of Catholic single-sex and coeducational schools finds academic achievement benefits for girls and low-income and minority boys attending single-sex schools (Riordan, 1990). Some studies find that girls who attend all-girls schools are more apt to adopt leadership roles, to become engaged in math and science, and to show improvements in self-esteem (Moore, Piper, & Schaeffer, 1993). Single-sex schools also are looked upon as more comfortable spaces for girls to learn (Streitmatter, 1999). Research on gender in the 1980s (Belenky et al., 1986; Gilligan, 1982), arguing that women learn differently than men, also has helped to provide justification for all-female schooling.

All-boys classes or schools also have been looked upon as ways to improve literacy achievement and discipline (Gilbert & Gilbert, 1998) and are said to improve character development (Hawley, 1993). Advocates of all-male, Afrocentric academies in public schools argue that the presence of African American role models and a focus on multicultural curricula can be beneficial in developing leadership skills and improving achievement for African American boys (Hopkins, 1997). Proponents of single-sex education also argue that the separation of the sexes is the most effective way to manage classroom behavior by eliminating distractions and peer pressures for both boys and girls (Pollack, 1998). Clearly, the reasons behind the recent establishment of single-sex schools are no longer simple; they represent efforts to address not only gender bias, but also racial and cultural issues.

While some research finds in favor of single-sex schools, other studies have questioned the academic and social advantages offered by single-sex schooling, arguing that school factors contribute more to positive outcomes than does gender separation (Lee, 1997). Other researchers also argue that single-gender educational settings promote stereotypical gender roles and attitudes toward the opposite sex (AAUW, 1998b; Lee, Marks, & Byrd, 1994). A significant limitation is that most studies of single-sex schooling have been conducted in the private sector and therefore may not generalize to public schools in the United States (see Mael, 1998, for a review). This raises important concerns for the validity and relevance of research findings. As Pamela Haag asks, "Do students achieve because of a school's sex composition or because the schools draw from economically and educationally privileged populations?" (AAUW, 1998b, p. 15).

In recent years, public schools in at least 15 states experimented with single-sex education, most often in the form of separate math or science classes for girls (Streitmatter, 1999), but we still know little about the outcomes. Other manifestations of public single-gender schooling include Afro-centric academies for boys in Detroit, Baltimore, and Milwaukee, and the Young Women's Leadership schools in Harlem and Chicago. Many of these experiments have been found to be in violation of Title IX and have been forced to close or become coed (Salomone, 2002). In the late 1990s, Senator Kay Bailey Hutchison (R-Texas) attempted to pass a Senate bill to allow public school districts to experiment with federally funded single-gender education (Hutchison, 1999; Richards, 2000). Although this bill did not pass, recently there has been a relaxing of Title IX guidelines at the federal level to allow for and even encourage experiments with single-sex public schooling. Thus, while most instances of single-sex schooling still occur in the private sector in the United States, we might expect to see more single-sex public schools in the future.

It is in this policy and reform context that California began the single-gender academies pilot program. This 2-year pilot program was legislated by the governor in 1996 and was funded by the state of California from September 1997 to June 1999. The program allocated funding to six local school districts and county offices of education to operate a girls' academy and a boys' academy. This chapter presents findings from a 3-year case study of these single-gender academies in six districts in California. The purpose of the study was to assess the consequences of single-gender schooling in the public sector. A major goal was to examine the equity implications of the California experiment. We conducted over 300 extensive interviews with educators, policymakers, and students, and school and classroom observations. It is the most comprehensive study of single-gender public schooling conducted in the United States to date.

THE CALIFORNIA SINGLE-GENDER
PUBLIC SCHOOLING EXPERIMENT

California's single-gender academies legislation was the brainchild of then-Governor Pete Wilson. In Wilson's 1996 "State of the State Address" he argued that single-gender academies were a way to provide public school students more options, more choice, and better preparation for real-world opportunities (California Department of Education, 1998). Later, in a speech we observed at one of the single-gender academies, Wilson stated: "Kids need options . . . and single-gender academies will stimulate competition and give kids opportunities they currently do not have because they are trapped in their schools and they need another approach." Expanding school choice was the key motivation for Wilson. This goal is quite different from the motivating forces behind some of the single-gender public schooling experiments we discussed earlier.

When single-gender schooling was proposed, the political climate across the nation and in California in particular was ripe for the expansion of school choice. California was the second state to pass charter school legislation in 1992, and the number of charter schools was growing steadily. In 1994 (and again in 2000), there were state ballot initiatives for school voucher programs, although neither passed. These movements to introduce more parental choice into the public system signified a belief that the solution to solving the ills of public schools was to gear schooling toward the needs and wants of particular groups and to force schools to compete for students. The single-gender schooling experiment, designed as an optional program, fit well within the political mood of the state.

According to staff members we interviewed at the Department of Education and the governor's office, Wilson initially presented a plan for all-male academies as magnet schools for at-risk boys, and all-female schools focused on math and science. His expectation was that sex separation would allow for the establishment of strong disciplinary climates for boys and more attention for girls in traditionally male-favored subjects. His initial plan for the single-gender academies raised concerns among legal advisors and feminists alike. Wilson's attorneys pointed out that attending to perceived gender differences could violate constitutional law, specifically Title IX. Feminist groups that had long fought for integration and equality saw the separation of the genders as a move toward inequality.

As a result, Wilson's initial vision for different types of academies for boys and girls was compromised in the final legislation. While his choice plan remained, what changed was that the academies had to be identical for girls and boys. The legislation passed in 1996 as part of Assembly Bill 3488 stated that while the single-gender academies would be tailored "to the differing needs and learning styles of boys as a group and girls as a group, . . . if a particular program or curriculum is available to one gender, it shall also be available to those pupils in the other gender who would benefit from the particular program or curriculum" (Education Code Section 58520-58524). In other words, there had to be "equal opportunities at both boys' and girls' academies." These equality provisions were important to ensuring equal access for boys and girls to the schools established by this new school choice option. After all, the primary goal of the legislation was to "increase the diversity of California's public educational offering" (Education Code Section 58520-58524).

The legislation instructed the California Superintendent of Public Instruction, under the pilot program, to award grants on a competitive basis to "10 applicant school districts for the establishment of one single gender academy for girls and one single gender academy for boys, in each of those selected school districts" at the middle or high school levels (Education Code Section 58520-58524). In other words, a district that opened a school for one gender must open a second school for the other. Moreover, both schools had to provide equivalent funding, facilities, staff, books, equipment, curriculum, and extracurricular activities, including sports. Finally, while a single-gender school could be located on the campus of another school, it had to be a complete school, not just a single-gender class or program. These legal guidelines reflected an effort to stem legal challenges against single-gender public schools.

The push for equal opportunity was apparent in the allocation of funds. California's law allowed the school districts to receive $500,000 to operate single-gender academies at the middle or high school levels. The grant was to be divided equally between a district's boys' and girls' academies. The funding was intended as a development grant to schools; they would be able to use the money as they wished, but the expectation was that after 2 years they would fully fund themselves through average daily attendance money. The single-gender academies would operate as magnet schools pursuant to the California Education Code. The legislation gave the responsibility of oversight of the single-gender academies to the State Department of Education. Management of the program was assigned to the office of educational options since this was "the basis on which this is being offered in California," explained a staff member. No extra funding was provided by the legislation for the administration of these new schools.

Two experienced staff members at the California Department of Education were charged with writing the request for proposals (RFP) based on the legislation and subsequently reviewing the proposals that were submitted. Initially, 24 districts expressed interest in proposing single-gender academies. Disappointingly, according to one Department of Education official, only eight school districts submitted proposals for funding. The grant opportunity apparently was not well marketed. The timing of the grant application posed a problem for some potential applicants, as there were only 2 months between the release of the RFP and the proposal deadline. A state official said that administrators in some districts also were concerned about the legalities of single-gender public schooling, despite assurances from attorneys that the legislation met the standards of Title IX. Of those eight that submitted proposals, one district's proposal was rejected because the design was not appropriate, and a second district pulled out of the review process because of legal concerns. In the end, only six districts in California were funded to start single-gender academies. These districts were not particularly unusual in any way and represented a broad range in terms of demographics, district size, location, and prior success at obtaining grant funding. Table 8.1 includes a description of each district's academies.

One Department of Education staff member explained that districts were encouraged to create single-gender academies that were "mirror images, and the only difference was the gender of the students. Same teaching materials, access to the same caliber of teachers, not necessarily of the same sex, you know." He added: "We tried to make it as equal as possible." He was careful to say, however, "We stayed out of curriculum. . . . This was their baby. . . . It was somewhat of an experimental type of activity." Another staff member explained: "They were required to be absolutely equivalent. So we worked with applicants to be certain that . . . there was no indication that they were planning to do very different types of things for boys and girls."

Table 8.1. Characteristics of the Single-Gender Academies in 1997–98

District	Location	Grades Served/Type	Student Population	Approximate Ethnic Distribution*
Palm	Urban	Grades 7–12 Self-contained alternative schools.	60 boys; 30 girls Students had a history of truancy, gang violence, or substance abuse.	80% Latino 12% Asian 8% White
Evergreen	Rural	Grades 7–8 Schools within a K–8 school; ⅔ of middle school students were in academies.	28 boys; 30 girls Students were very low income. Most relied on public assistance.	88% White 9% Latino 3% Native American
Cactus	Suburban	Grades 7–8 Schools within a K–8 school; ½ of middle school students were in academies.	36 boys; 50 girls Students were a mix of upper-middle, middle, and low income.	65% White 14% Black 9% Asian 8% Latino 3% Pacific Isl.
Birch	Urban	Grade 9 (expanded to grade 10 in 1998–99) Schools within a high school.	18 boys; 22 girls Students were predominantly low income.	32% Latino 27% Black 12% White 14% Asian 10% East Indian 5% Pacific Isl.
Pine	Urban	Grades 5–8 Self-contained schools.	90 boys; 50 girls Students were low income and at risk due to academic, health, and human service needs.	46% Latino 38% Black 18% Pacific Isl.
Oak	Urban	Grades 6–8 Schools within a middle school.	67 girls; 46 boys Students were predominantly low income.	32% Asian 27% Black 16% Latino 13% White 11% Other non-White

* Some percentages do not add to 100 due to rounding.

In sum, the single-gender academies pilot program in California was a school choice initiative designed to ensure equal opportunity for boys and girls. The above statements reveal that policymakers' intent to ensure equality for boys and girls was translated into sameness of facilities, curriculum, and resources. While the legislation placed such "equality"— defined in terms of resource parity only—at the forefront of the agenda, one staff member was concerned that it did not actually address gender in a meaningful way.

> To me, gender is such a fundamental underlying issue of social organization that to equate these academies as just another choice is to ignore that larger context. And I think the actual context for these academies needed to be viewed from an educational basis as an issue of discrimination and bias. . . . And then they become an option for a reason.

However, most of the policymakers and the legislation itself did not acknowledge gender bias in society in these ways, nor did they see the legislation as a vehicle for addressing it. The primary goal from the outset was increasing school choice.

IMPLEMENTING SINGLE-GENDER PUBLIC SCHOOLS: WHY, HOW, AND FOR WHOM?

In our interviews with educators and community members, we asked about why they started single-gender academies. We were interested in finding out which students the educators were hoping to serve in the academies, what problems they were aiming to address, and how the design of the academies would help them meet their goals. Of course we also were interested in the degree to which a desire for achieving gender equity influenced the educators' visions and, more generally, how their ideologies about gender, race, and class influenced the establishment of single-gender schooling.

We found that many administrators sought the $500,000 because of the resources and opportunities that it would provide for students who were not successful in their school systems. In other words, instead of seeing the single-gender academies as primarily an opportunity to address gender inequities (as one might predict), most educators saw the grant as a way to help address the more typical educational and social problems of low-achieving students. In most cases, these were low-income students, primarily those of color. This is perhaps not surprising when one considers that the legislation stated that the academies needed to be designed with the "unique educational needs" of their students in mind, pushing some to focus on specific at-risk populations.

To be sure, all of the educators sought to increase school choice and decrease distractions among boys and girls, and many sought to improve students' self-esteem. However, none of the proposals showed evidence that the single-gender academies were designed to address systemic gender bias. Thus, although one might assume that funding for single-gender public schools would provoke genuine interest from educators who held a commitment to single-gender education and a strong theory for why they were doing it, in the majority of cases, the reality proved to be quite different.

Educators' purposefulness in applying for the monetary grant was evident from their comments. The principal of the single-gender academies in one district said, "Why do I go for the single gender? What's so great? It's a great opportunity. It's also money. I can do something. If you have a traditional school . . . you've got to get extra money." With the grant she was able to purchase the technology for Web TV, which provided students with access to online curriculum at home. A school administrator in charge of another district's academies explained: "My main interest? Honestly, the gender part of it wasn't huge. I didn't really think about gender bias and all those sorts of things." Instead, the academies were seen as a way to improve the achievement of low-income and minority students—an option for "incoming ninth grade student populations that have shown a high potential to attend college but have achieved only poor grades in middle school" (Birch Single Gender Academies Proposal, p. 2).

The above examples point to the power of money in motivating district or school administrators to start single-gender schooling in their communities. The single-gender funding was a chance to provide new opportunities for students. With the grant funding, educators planned to develop social and academic support structures to address the problems of their particular student populations, such as low achievement, truancy, poverty, violence, or geographic isolation. As a result, the students the academies attracted, and the curricular plans, organizational arrangements, and special services, differed somewhat from site to site. Common among them, however, was a wealth of resources not typically available in public schools.

For example, the educators in one district located in an isolated rural area of the state wanted to broaden students' experiences and opportunities. They purchased vans to transport students to San Francisco and Sacramento and other places of cultural and historic interest. The grant also provided for reduced teacher–student ratios, computers, and much-needed lab equipment. Even in places where school funding was perhaps not as scarce, educators found that they could use the single-gender academies funding to lower class size (not just in the single-gender academies, but effectively across the whole school) and purchase technology not formerly available to them. In sum, the funding allowed schools to provide a new educational option with increased academic supports and resources.

Two of the six districts also saw the grant funding as a way to address the needs of boys and girls in their communities. However, these districts differed notably from the others in that they had prior experience with single-gender education, and thus the grant was not the initial motivator. One district operated a school for at-risk boys for 2 years prior to the grant funding becoming available. The school opened as a result of the super-intendent's concern for boys of color in the community, whom she saw as lacking male role models and subject to involvement in violent crimes at a young age. The school initially was established as a safe haven for at-risk, very low-income boys where they would be provided with "tough love," structure, mentoring from adult males, and basic skills. The single-gender academies funding led the district to expand its single-gender academies, opening them to girls as well as boys (as required by the legislation), and enhance the social and academic support services it offered on site.

Notably, a middle school in another district piloted two single-gender classes for 60 boys and girls in the 2 years prior to the grant becoming available. The impetus for these initial classes was concern about the low self-esteem of adolescent girls, documented in *How Schools Shortchange Girls* (AAUW, 1992) and *Reviving Ophelia* (Pipher, 1994). A teacher explained, "The whole idea behind [the initial experiment], particularly for the girls, was to give them enough strength emotionally, socially, and intellectually so that they can hold their own . . . in mixed classes." However, instead of serving a randomly selected, heterogeneous group as in the past, the grant-funded, single-gender academies would aim to serve underachieving students with small class sizes, two full-time counselors, and additional classroom resources. Here again, even in this district, the state grant became a vehicle for educating low-achieving students, shifting from the original vision of improving gender equity.

In sum, well-intentioned educators, many of them responding to economic and social realities in their schools and communities, found ways to use single-gender education as a vehicle for meeting needs through this new school choice option. Most commonly, educators sought to address the pressing academic and social issues of the low-achieving students in their communities. The grant money allowed them to address these needs through reduced class sizes, teacher teaming, academic support programs, counseling, and increased technology.

Not surprisingly, the vision, design, and target population of the various single-gender academies strongly influenced who enrolled when the academies opened in 1997–98 (see Table 8.1). Thus, while the California single-gender academies pilot program was constructed largely as a vehicle for expanding public school choice, who attended was largely predetermined. In at least four of the six districts, at-risk students of color were strongly recruited by educators to join the single-gender academies, instead of freely choosing to attend. As a result, a number of the California single-gender schools became a mechanism by which to educate these youth. On the other hand, White, average, or higher-achieving students were more likely to freely choose to attend, and this occurred primarily in two districts where parents were more savvy about the resources offered by the new option.

Many students were attracted by the special offerings of the academies, and less so by their single-sex nature. In several districts, the academies (either for boys or girls or for both) operated under capacity due to insufficient public interest or to difficulties in marketing the choice option (Datnow, Hubbard, & Woody, 2001). Thus, our findings suggest that the single-gender academies did not all provide equal access, as in some cases the academies were oriented to particular target populations and students were recruited based on their characteristics, whereas in other cases they freely chose to attend. Our findings also reveal that the single-gender academies did not necessarily provide the same education to girls and boys, as we will explain below.

HOW EDUCATORS' BELIEFS ABOUT GENDER
INFORMED CLASSROOM PRACTICE

We investigated whether and how classroom practices and school organization in the single-gender academies led to a confrontation of gender bias and broadening of gender role expectations, as gender equity experts might suggest, or a reinforcement of gender stereotypes. We examined the influence of educators' beliefs about gender on curriculum and instruction in the single-gender academies. No doubt, teachers' ideologies arise from experiences in a society that socializes individuals to learn appropriate gender roles early on (Thorne, 1993; Weitzman, 1975), and in schools and elsewhere men occupy positions of higher status and women face constraints due to their gender (Acker, 1989; Datnow, 1998; Hubbard & Datnow, 2000). Just as in coeducational school environments, teachers' ideologies about gender influence their actions in single-gender settings (Streitmatter, 1999).

Curriculum and Instruction

As we explained, the single-gender schooling legislation in California stated that the single-gender academies should be tailored "to the differing needs and learning styles of boys as a group and girls as a group," as well as provide "equal opportunity in both boys and girls academies" (Education Code Section 58520-58524). These dual and ambiguous goals raised tensions about providing something "separate" on the one hand, but "equal" on the other. In keeping with the legislation, teachers and administrators were very concerned about spending resources equally and offering the same curriculum to boys and girls. As the superintendent in one district explained: "We wanted to be Title IX clean, on track. I mean, if somebody got a number 2 pencil, the other academy got the same one. There was not going to be a difference." Similarly, in response to the question, "To what extent is gender included in your plans for curriculum?" an administrator of one set of academies responded: "At this point in time, it isn't. We're strictly following the grant guidelines, which indicate that we will do exactly the same for boys as for girls and vice versa."

Teachers in another district explained that the same literature, social studies, and science lesson plans were used in both the boys' and girls' academies. When asked to define gender equity, one educator responded: "Equality between the sexes, between the genders. Equality of opportunity." Most teachers believed that everything that was taught to one gender must be taught to the other, and thus they attempted to make the curriculum "gender neutral." In practice, this sometimes meant that the curriculum was oriented toward the males, as teachers were very concerned about maintaining order in the all-boys classes and thus chose topics or materials that they thought the boys could relate to. In one instance, a principal explained, "We are going to do video conferencing in Denmark this month, and both the boys and girls will learn how to design a car."

Some teachers, however, said that they geared the curriculum toward students' interests, which just "naturally" varied by gender. For example, at one school, students were given the opportunity to choose novels (from a list of acceptable books) in their English literature classes. In the girls' academy, the students chose to read *Pride and Prejudice*. In the boys' academy, the students chose to read *All Quiet on the Western Front*. One teacher explained: "The girls tend to choose the romantic spiel . . . and the guys tend to go for the action."

When students in one district's academies were studying the early history of the United States and the migration of settlers to the west, boys took a survival skills class from a young male teacher, and girls studied quilting and sewing, taught by middle-aged women teachers. These elective class offerings appeared to be driven by teachers' gendered identities and personal interests as well as by the students' interests. At another school, a male teacher said he used examples from sports to clarify ideas for his male students because "guys can kind of relate to that." In sum, it appears that when teachers geared the curriculum to respond to students' interests, they perhaps unintentionally reinforced traditional gender roles. In most cases, teachers did little to change student choices by suggesting alternative books or topics that potentially might challenge gendered dispositions.

Often educators also attended to the perceived gender-based needs of students by adjusting their instructional methods. Echoing the beliefs of many teachers we spoke to, a male teacher at one school stated that he believed that boys are "much more kinesthetic; girls are a little more linguistic," and that this was "just a natural thing." The director of the single-gender academies at another site said that while the curriculum was the same for the boys and the girls, the instructional methods needed to be gender specific.

> The girls do much better cooperatively. . . . And they can spend a lot more time on [an activity] and they won't lose much interest. And the boys, if they throw a little bit of competition in there they'll get it done. And I know those are stereotypes that we hear about how girls and boys learn differently, but they seem to be true.

Similarly, a science teacher explained, "When I'm talking with the boys, my examples might be slightly different, more mechanical. . . . And with the girls, on some things they seem more interested, sometimes, in detail." We did find a few teachers who believed that addressing gender bias was necessary to achieving gender equity, and they felt single-gender classes were particularly well suited for this purpose. They tended to be women teachers who were enlightened to issues of sexism in society, typically through their own education or life experiences, and who chose to address such issues in their classes with girls. For example, one veteran woman teacher who had experienced discrimination as a woman scientist, prior to becoming a teacher, explained that with her girls, "We talk about what the statistics [are]. Female lawyers have three times the miscarriage rate that other working professionals have. That's a fact. That's stress. . . . I said, 'There are just things that make it hard.'" This teacher felt compelled to promote gender equity among her students and, for her, it meant addressing the challenges young women might encounter in the workplace.

For the most part, these female teachers did not give the same messages to boys; they taught to presumed differences. In fact, very few teachers addressed the issue of sexism when they taught boys. Men teachers, with the exception of perhaps one, tended not to have gender equity as an expressed goal of their classes. When they did have discussions about gender in society, which was seldom, these discussions tended to be only with boys (not with girls) and focused on how to be a productive adult male, which reflected rather traditional conceptions of gender roles. Discussing the conversations he had with the boys in his class, one male teacher stated:

> I talk to the boys. I say, you know, "Guys, what does it mean to be proud of the way you look? Don't you want to be strong enough to help your mother do things? Don't you want to be a man that's respected?" And I told them, "What does a man who's respected look like? What does he feel like?" We talked about strength, and we talked about self-control and being able to control your emotions and making sacrifices for others.

This teacher said that when he tried to have discussions with girls about the role of women in society, it did not work well; he and the students were less comfortable with such conversations because he was a man. However, this viewpoint seems to reify gender differences. Some argue that men teachers cannot be absolved from responsibility for gender equity solutions simply because they are men (Sanders, 1996). Only one male teacher, who said he grew up in a home with "anti-sexist" parents, said he talked with his male students about off-color language being a form of sexual harassment or sexism. He felt that single-gender classes allowed him to address these issues with students, whereas coeducational settings did not lend themselves as easily to such discussions.

One teacher, a young feminist woman, included gender equity and the deconstruction of traditional gender roles as a goal for both her boys' and her girls' classes. She said: "I think that's where it's at. I think that this is the age group for it." She talked about an activity where students were broken into groups and asked to come up with their ideal man or woman. She then led the students in a deconstruction of these ideals. While she did this activity with both boys and girls, she said, "I feel like I've gotten a bit further with the girls in terms of being able to demystify image. . . . With the boys, I think they get it, but I don't think it's very cool to get it." However, she also used the Columbine incident to expose the fact that violence is the way boys sometimes express themselves. "Instead of crying tears, boys cry bullets," she explained to the students. She believed that single-gender education might allow both boys and girls to develop "a sense of self" that deconstructed stereotypical gender roles.

We found that enlightenment about power differences between men and women (and a deconstruction of traditional roles)—in the few instances where it did occur—took place far more often in classes in the girls' academies than in the boys' academies. In the boys' academies, traditional gender roles appeared to be reinforced and definitely not questioned. One teacher at a boys' academy stated that for the boys, "it's been kind of fun to sit around and have guy talk, talk about hunting and fishing." As Kruse (1996) argues, teachers concerned with sexism should deal with boys, with their gender identity, and with their concepts of masculinity: "Focusing only on girls will result in imposing on them the whole responsibility for change, and it will underpin the assumption that 'boys are boys' and there-fore cannot change" (p. 179). By focusing only on traditional notions of masculinity or adopting a gender-blind approach, many teachers (both men and women) reinforced traditional gender roles.

Gender Differences in Discipline

Educators' ideologies about gender also influenced their management approaches in all-boys and all-girls classes. Most educators operated on the assumption that boys needed discipline and girls needed nurturing. When boys misbehaved or when girls were academically focused (and some students fit these models because of the population the schools were designed to serve), educators' beliefs were reified. Teacher–student inter-actions and school policies then institutionalized the wisdom of treating boys and girls in different ways and did little if anything to challenge gen-der stereotypes along these lines.

As we explained, some of the academies drew their male population of students from district referral lists of boys who had either poor academic achievement records, excessive absences, unresolved health and human services needs, or repeated discipline problems. The result was that many boys were perceived as "tough." One male teacher in a boys' academy reported that, "for the first 3 months of school, [his] job was basically just to keep kids [boys] quiet and sitting down and not throwing chairs at each other." Teachers at another set of academies geared toward a more tradi-tional public school clientele reported similar assessments of boys, suggest-ing they were "talkative, loud, and could not sit still." Some educators expressed the belief that their at-risk population of boys was difficult and, in retrospect, would have benefited more from an "academic boot camp," which ideally would be taught by male teachers.

Male students often agreed with their teachers' descriptions of their behavior. They admitted that they (as opposed to girls) made "all the ruckus." Boys admitted that they were "not real good" and that teachers "kept sending [them] down to the counselors and stuff." When asked why, they reported it was "because we were running wild." Academy boys were made to feel that they were more poorly behaved than their nonacademy male peers. Clearly many of the boys who enrolled in some of the academies already had disciplinary problems, but many did not, yet all boys seemed to be treated as if they did. The situation was exacerbated by the constant comparisons that some teachers made between the boys and girls. These comparisons pitted boys and girls against one another and reinforced gender stereotypes of boys as "bad" and girls as "good" (Woody, 2002).

Most educators believed that girls needed a much softer approach to discipline. One administrator explained that he had to "learn to communicate with the girls" not by yelling at them, but rather by showing respect. At several schools, when girls misbehaved in their classes generally, it was interpreted as "girls being catty" or "gossipy." These were behaviors that teachers felt were "normal" for girls. One female teacher indicated that her 7th-grade girls did not need the strict discipline prescribed for boys. In fact, if "her girls" were referred to the detention room, she wouldn't let them go because the experience was too humiliating and she felt that it was unnecessary. Instead, she protected her girls in a very nurturing way. She gave them much more freedom in the classroom than did her colleagues in the boys' academy, some of whom admitted to running their classes in "military style."

In sum, we found that educators typically made sense of the ambiguous goals of the legislation by offering the same curriculum and equal resources in both boys' and girls' academies, but employing different instructional techniques and electives, as well as initiating different modes of discipline and class management to respond to what they perceived to be gender-specific needs. Most curriculum and pedagogy, by being gender neutral or even differentiated, reinforced traditional gender roles and did little if anything to advance gender equity.

Overall, there was little time for deep inquiry about gender among educators, and a general lack of discussion about what it meant to be teaching boys and girls in single-sex classrooms. Even though almost all of the districts had planned staff development sessions to raise gender awareness (as part of their academy proposals), very few opportunities actually were provided. Even if these opportunities had been provided, evidence suggests that gender equity workshops tend to be quick fixes that do little to change teachers' attitudes about gender, which are formed over the course of a lifetime (Sanders, 1996).

THE ABSENCE OF A THEORY AND THE DEMISE OF THE SINGLE-GENDER ACADEMIES

By and large, the public single-gender academies lacked a strong theory of single-gender education. The single-gender academies we studied were located in districts (and sometime schools) where gender bias, and gender issues in general, simply were not "on the radar screen" of most school administrators. As one teacher remarked: "Any acknowledgment of gender would be a step in the right direction. Because I never hear it. I never hear it at all."

Within 2 years, the lack of district support for gender-based reform, the politics surrounding the legislation, and the resource constraints of district and school administrators coalesced to structure the demise of most of the single-gender academies. Through a series of political actions at the state level, the single-gender academies did not receive the additional funding that they were expecting the third year. Governor Wilson had allocated $2 million in the state budget to support existing sites and $3 million to support the start-up of six new pairs of academies. However, during a legislative hearing that was held to consider these allocations, a state senator who was philosophically opposed to single-gender schools staged a campaign against them, bringing in a representative from the American Association of University Women to testify against the policy by citing research that suggested that single-gender schools were not better than coed schools. Subsequently, the single-gender academies funding was quietly stripped from the budget. This coincided with Wilson's replacement in January 1999 by Governor Gray Davis, who introduced his own new plan for reforming the state's public education system.

All of the single-gender academies remained in operation during the 1998–99 school year. Administrators in all of the schools were angry and disappointed about the political process and that more funding would not be coming their way. Some wrote letters to senators and lobbied in their communities. When future state funding was uncertain, most academies lost status locally, reinforcing that financial interests motivated their opening initially, not a real commitment to single-gender education.

The opinions of students, parents, and teachers held little weight against those of powerful district administrators who made decisions about the future of the academies, typically without any stakeholder participation at all. Most district administrators argued that there were no "hard data" to show gains in student achievement and that, moreover, the AAUW *Separated by Sex* report (1998b) did not offer support for single-gender schools. Despite their supposed interest in "objective indicators" about the effectiveness of single-gender education, most administrators admitted that if the academies had received additional grant funding, they would have continued.

At the beginning of the 1999–2000 school year, four of the six districts closed their academies; a fifth district closed its academies at the end of the year. Even the district that had single-gender classes prior to the advent of the legislation chose not to continue the academies. Quite simply, most administrators were not willing to put themselves on the line in front of school boards to advocate for single-gender academies, particularly in the face of other competing priorities. Meanwhile, the single-gender academies in one district remained open as of 2004, largely because, according to a state administrator, the academies in this district are the superintendent's "baby" and "she is the only superintendent in any of these districts who has the level of commitment needed." Of course, the academies at this site also serve a very at-risk population of students who are referred from schools elsewhere in the district, making them politically more popular with educators in those schools trying to get rid of troubled youth.

CONCLUSION AND IMPLICATIONS

One might assume that the single-gender academies legislation would have provoked applications from educators genuinely interested in single-gender education and remedying gender bias. In reality we found that the impetus for most of the single-gender academies was the generous state grant. To be sure, all of the educators sought to increase school choice and decrease distractions among boys and girls, and many sought to improve students' self-esteem. However, none of the proposals showed evidence that the single-gender academies were designed to address systemic gender bias. When well-meaning educators at the local level in California implemented single-gender academies in accordance with the legislation, schools were organized to respond to more pressing issues salient in each local community, such as low achievement, poverty, violence, and geographic isolation. For most administrators, single-gender schooling was a vehicle for meeting these needs, or an opportunistic moment, and not an end in itself. Overwhelmingly, educators' and policymakers' conceptions of gender, race, and class informed the legislation and its subsequent implementation.

The primary goal of the single-gender academies legislation was to increase the diversity of California's public educational offerings. However, we found that parental choice was limited from the outset and attendance was determined by the districts' target populations and goals for the academies. In most cases, districts designed their single-gender schools for at-risk students who were actively recruited to join. In a few instances, efficacious parents were attracted by the additional resources available in the academies and sought to enroll their students. Overall, however, public interest in the choice of single-gender public schooling was not as intense as policymakers might have thought, and some schools struggled to fill their classrooms.

Moreover, as we have seen in other chapters in this volume (see Petrovich, Chapter 1; Gittell, Chapter 2), our study provides further evidence that school choice, like other reforms that have arisen in the accountability movement, is not by itself very successful in achieving either equity or excellence. We found that when educators in the single-gender academies tailored curriculum and instruction to meet the different educational needs of boys and girls (as the legislation suggests), they did not, despite their best intentions, offer a gender-equitable education to boys or girls. Both boys and girls lost out, but in different ways. Rather than finding a setting filled with possibilities, we found that many teachers shaped curriculum, instruction, and discipline in ways that reinforced gender stereotypes. Most teachers were unable or unwilling to challenge traditional notions of gender, finding it difficult to move from a biological to a social construction of gender. Encouragingly, however, we found a few occasions when the single-gender schools in this study were successful in expanding opportunities for students and challenging traditional gender roles. While such experiences were the exception, their significance points to the effect teachers can have on students' understanding when teachers have a gender equity agenda.

We conclude that neither boys nor girls had the full opportunities that could have been provided to them through single-gender education. Kruse (1996) states: "Sex segregated education can be used for emancipation or oppression. As a method, it does not guarantee an outcome. The intentions, the understanding of people and their gender, the pedagogical attitudes and practices, are crucial, as in all pedagogical work" (p. 189). Kruse also argues that in addition to promoting self-esteem, gender identity, and enhanced achievement, one of the pedagogical purposes for single-sex classes should be to "raise the political awareness of anti-sexist issues in light of trying to alter socially constructed gender patterns" (p. 181). Addressing gender bias was not a goal of the policymakers who established or implemented the single-gender schooling legislation, nor was it a goal of many of the administrators who started the schools in their communities. The absence of a strong guiding theory for single-gender education is all the more apparent in light of the fact that five of the six districts did not sustain their academies for more than 2 years.

Our findings from the single-gender experiment in California should give pause to policymakers considering implementing single-gender schooling under the policy framework that existed in California. In fact, our research leads us to conclude that unless future policies or legislation for single-gender public schools explicitly addresses gender equity and provides guidelines for how it might be achieved, these schools may fall short of their expected outcomes. As Gittell (Chapter 2, this volume) and Welner and Oakes

(Chapter 4) indicate, a top-down mandate may be necessary for meaningful equity reform, yet our findings suggest that a top-down reform effort related to gender is not truly an equity reform unless the policymakers and educators who implement the reform consider gendered power relations.

A further implication of this study is the worrisome conclusion that many policymakers and educators see the gender "problem" in schools as essentially solved. This is evidenced by the fact that the single-gender academies in California were promoted under the umbrella of school choice, not as a way to address gender inequities. This also appears to be true of new federal laws allowing for more flexibility for single-sex public schooling. In addition, on a broader scale, many believe that boys and girls now have equal opportunities in schools and point to the narrowing of the achievement gap between girls and boys, with girls actually achieving better outcomes than boys in some areas (Riordan, 1998). Moreover, attention seems to be converging on the problems that boys are experiencing, refocusing efforts away from the unresolved issue of the imbalance of power between males and females in this society.

Yet we know that gender is a strong shaping principle of social and power differentiation, with women still on unequal footing in many professions, including teaching and school administration (Apple, 1994; Shakeshaft & Perry, 1995). If schools pursue a gender-blind approach under the guise of equal opportunity and choice, and if policies refocus attention on the plight of boys without a careful analysis of gender inequality, the gendered culture of schooling and society is likely to continue.

Acknowledgments. The work reported herein was supported by grants from the Ford Foundation and the Spencer Foundation. However, any opinions expressed are the authors' own and do not represent the policies or positions of the funders. We wish to thank the participants of our study who kindly invited us into their schools, districts, and state offices and who were very generous with their time. We are also greatly appreciative of Betsey Woody, Gilberto Conchas, Barbara McHugh, and Jennifer Madigan for their research assistance. Our sincere thanks to our advisory board members Patricia Gandara, Peter Hall, Pedro Noguera, and Amy Stuart Wells for their insights throughout the study.

REFERENCES

Acker, S. (1989). *Teachers, gender, and careers.* London: Falmer Press.

American Association of University Women. (1992). *How schools shortchange girls.* Washington, DC: Author.

American Association of University Women. (1998a). *Gender gaps: Where schools still fail our children.* Washington, DC: Author.

American Association of University Women. (1998b). *Separated by sex: A critical look at single sex education for girls*. Washington, DC: Author.

American Association of University Women. (2000). *Tech-savvy: Educating girls in the new computer age*. Washington, DC: Author.

American Association of University Women Educational Foundation. (1993). *Hostile hallways: The AAUW survey on sexual harassment in America's schools*. Washington, DC: Author.

Apple, M. W. (1994). Is change always good for teachers? Gender, class, and teaching in history. In K. Borman & N. Greenman (Eds.), *Changing American education: Recapturing the past or inventing the future?* Albany: State University of New York Press.

Belenky, M. F., Clinchy, B. M., Goldberger, N. R., & Tarule, J. L. (1986). *Women's ways of knowing: The development of self, voice and mind*. New York: Basic Books.

California Department of Education. (1998). *Fact sheet: Single gender academies pilot program, Enclosure A*. Sacramento: Author.

California State Education Code. (2004). Available: http://www.leginfo.ca.gov/cgi-bin/calawquery?codesection=edc&.

Campbell, P., & Sanders, J. (2002). Challenging the system: Assumptions and data behind the push for single-sex schooling. In A. Datnow & L. Hubbard (Eds.), *Gender in policy and practice* (pp. 31–46). New York: RoutledgeFalmer Press.

Datnow, A. (1998). *The gender politics of educational change*. London: Falmer Press.

Datnow, A., & Hubbard, L. (Eds.). (2002). *Gender in policy and practice*. New York: RoutledgeFalmer Press.

Datnow, A., Hubbard, L., & Woody, E. (2001). *Is single gender schooling viable in the public sector? Lessons from California's pilot program* (Final report). Toronto: Ontario Institute for Studies in Education.

Gilbert, R., & Gilbert, P. (1998). *Masculinity goes to school*. London: Routledge.

Gilligan, C. (1982). *In a different voice*. Cambridge, MA: Harvard University Press.

Ginorio, A. M., & Huston, M. (2001). *Sí, we puede! Yes, we can: Latinas in school*. Washington, DC: American Association of University Women.

Gurian, M . (1998). *A fine young man: What parents, mentors and educators can do to shape adolescent boys into exceptional men*. New York: Putnam.

Hawley, R. (1993). The case for boys schools. In D. K. Hollinger & R. Adamson (Eds.), *Single sex schooling: Proponents speak* (pp. 11–14). Washington, DC: U.S. Department of Education.

Herr, K., & Arms, E. (2002). The intersection of educational reforms: Single gender academies in a public middle school. In A. Datnow & L. Hubbard (Eds.), *Gender in policy and practice* (pp. 74–89). New York: RoutledgeFalmer Press.

Hopkins, R. (1997). *Educating black males: Critical lessons in schooling, community, and power*. Albany: State University of New York Press.

Hubbard, L., & Datnow, A. (2000). A gendered look at educational reform. *Gender and Education, 12*(1), 115–130.

Hutchison, K. B. (1999, October 6). Senate floor speech on single-sex classrooms amendment. Proceedings and debates of the 106th Congress, first session. Retrieved November 15, 2004 from http://www.senate.gov/hutchison/speech11.htm.

Kenway, J., Blackmore, J., Willis, S., & Rennie, L. (1996). The emotional dimensions of feminist pedagogy in schools. In P. Murphy & G. Gipps (Eds.), *Equity in the classroom: Towards effective pedagogy for girls and boys* (pp. 242–259). London: Falmer Press.

Kleinfeld, J. (1999). Student performance: Males versus females. *The Public Interest, 134*, 3–20.

Kruse, A. M. (1996). Single sex settings: Pedagogies for girls and boys in Danish schools. In P. Murphy & G. Gipps (Eds.), *Equity in the classroom: Towards effective pedagogy for girls and boys* (pp. 173–191). London: Falmer Press.

Leake, D., & Leake, B. (1992). Islands of Hope: Milwaukee's African American immersion schools. *Journal of Negro Education, 61*(1), 24–29.

Lee, V. E. (1997). Gender equity and the organization of schools. In B. Bank & P. M. Hall (Eds.), *Gender, equity, and schooling* (pp. 135–158). New York: Garland.

Lee, V., Marks, H. M., & Byrd, T. (1994). Sexism in single sex and coeducational independent secondary school classrooms. *Sociology of Education, 67*, 92–120.

Mael, F. (1998). Single sex and coeducational schooling: Relationships to socioemotional and academic development. *Review of Educational Research, 68*, 101–129.

Marshall, C., & Anderson, G. (1995). Rethinking the public and private spheres: Feminist cultural studies perspectives in the politics of education. In J. Scribner & D. H. Layton (Eds.), *The study of educational politics* (pp. 169–182). Washington, DC: Falmer Press.

Moore, M., Piper, V., & Schaeffer, E. (1993). Single sex schooling and educational effectiveness: A research overview. In D. K. Hollinger (Ed.), *Single sex schooling: Perspectives from practice and research* (pp. 7–68). Washington, DC: U.S. Department of Education.

Murphy, P., & Gipps, G. (Eds.). (1996). *Equity in the classroom: Towards effective pedagogy for girls and boys.* London: Falmer Press.

Pipher, M. (1994). *Reviving Ophelia: Saving the selves of adolescent girls.* New York: Putnam.

Pollack, W. (1998). *Real boys: Rescuing our sons from the myths of boyhood.* New York: Random House.

Richards, C. (2000, November 15). Public funds for experimental single-sex ed? *Women's News.* Retrieved November 15, 2004 from http://www.womensenews.org/article.cfm?aid=160&context=archive.

Riordan, C. (1990). *Girls and boys in school: Together or separate?* New York: Teachers College Press.

Riordan, C. (1998, August). *Student outcomes in public secondary schools: Gender gap comparisons from 1972 to 1992.* Paper presented at the annual meeting of the American Sociological Association, San Francisco.

Sadker, M., & Sadker, D. (1994). *Failing at fairness.* New York: Touchstone.

Salomone, R. (2002). The legality of single sex education in the United States: Sometimes "equal" means "different." In A. Datnow & L. Hubbard (Eds.), *Gender in policy and practice* (pp. 47–72). New York: RoutledgeFalmer Press.

Sanders, J. (1996). How do we get educators to teach gender equity? In P. Murphy

& G. Gibbs (Eds.), *Equity in the classroom: Towards effective pedagogy for girls and boys* (pp. 214–227). London: Falmer Press.

Sanford, K., & Blair, H. (2002). Engendering public education: Single-sex schooling in Western Canada. In A. Datnow & L. Hubbard (Eds.), *Gender in policy and practice* (pp. 90–108). New York: RoutledgeFalmer Press.

Shakeshaft, C., & Perry, A. (1995). The language of power versus the language of empowerment: Gender differences in administrative communication. In D. Corson (ed.), *Discourse and power in educational organizations* (pp. 136–155). Cresskill, NJ: Hampton Press.

Streitmatter, J. L. (1999). *For girls only: Making a case for single sex schooling.* Albany: State University of New York Press.

Stromquist, N. P. (1997). Gender policies in American education: Reflections on federal legislation and action. In C. Marshall (Ed.), *Feminist critical policy analysis: A perspective from primary and secondary schooling* (pp. 54–72). London: Falmer Press.

Thorne, B. (1993). *Gender play: Girls and boys in school.* New Brunswick, NJ: Rutgers University Press.

Weitzman, L. (1975). Sex role socialization. In J. Freeman (Ed.), *Women: A feminist perspective* (pp. 105–144). Palo Alto, CA: Mayfield.

Woody, E. (2002). Constructions of masculinity in California's single gender academies. In A. Datnow & L. Hubbard (Eds.), *Gender in policy and practice* (pp. 280–303). New York: RoutledgeFalmer Press.

9

Charter School Reform and the Shifting Meaning of Educational Equity

Greater Voice and Greater Inequality?

AMY STUART WELLS
JANELLE T. SCOTT
ALEJANDRA LOPEZ
JENNIFER JELLISON HOLME

Perhaps one of the best sites in which to explore the changing meaning of educational "equity" is a currently popular reform known as charter schools. Clearly, in so many ways the charter school movement, which provides public funds for schools to operate autonomously from the education system, attempts to address parents' and educators' frustration with the traditional public school system. In many instances, these frustrated parents and educators are advocates for low-income students and students of color. Their dissatisfaction with "regular" public schools often is grounded in experiences with an inherently unequal education system and a set of so-called "equity" reforms—mostly created in the 1960s and 1970s—that attempt to provide disadvantaged students with additional resources or greater access to services and opportunities. These reforms, as helpful as they have been in terms of targeting resources, have, for the most part, failed to deal with the cultural aspect of schooling—namely, whose knowledge and experiences were valued and whose cultural capital was rewarded in the schools (see, for example, Shujaa, 1996).

Through charter school reform, therefore, advocates for poor students and students of color have been able to create schools that speak to some of these cultural and social needs. It has given some members of disenfranchised communities greater voice in how their children are educated and how their history and culture are presented and discussed within school curriculum. Yet, at the same time, these charter schools, with their progressive agendas and their more ethnocentric curriculum, exist within a policy framework and political context that is highly regressive in terms of redistributing resources, access, and services (see Wells, 2002; Wells, Lopez, Scott, & Holme, 1999).

In other words, charter school reform provides the policy space to create community-based schools that respond to the needs and desires of children who often have not been well served in regular schools. Yet, at the same time, most state charter school laws offer little support or reward for groups creating such schools. In fact, in most instances, charter schools receive less public funding than regular public schools because they must pay for their facilities out of their per-pupil money. Meanwhile, the greatest demand for such charter schools is often in those communities where the public, per-pupil funding is low compared with more affluent suburban communities. In some states charter schools receive a statewide average per-pupil amount, which, obviously, is lower than the average for the wealthiest districts. In other states the per-pupil funding is tied to local, district per-pupil expenditures, which vary a great deal across district lines.

This means that while charter schools may have the potential to meet the cultural and curricular needs of low-income students and students of color in ways the reforms of the 1960s and 1970s often failed to do, they frequently lack the resources that the prior policies provided. As the history of education has taught us, this lack of material support too often undermines the pedagogical promise of schools.

This policy framework of greater freedom but fewer resources means that poor communities struggling to make charter school reform work for them must choose between either running under-resourced schools or connecting with private for-profit or nonprofit corporations—called "educational management organizations"—to support them (see Scott, 2002). Often, these educational management organizations, or EMOs, are owned, operated, and staffed by people who are not from the schools' local communities. Furthermore, while charter school founders and educators have greater freedom to shape their curriculum around the culture and experiences of their students, in the end they are supposed to be evaluated by the same state-mandated standardized tests, which reward adherence to a more traditional curriculum.

This chapter provides a bit of insight into these layers of complicated and thorny equity issues. Essentially, we argue that charter school reform may well provide educators, parents, and students the opportunity to shape their own school communities, but they will be forced to try to make these schools work within a reform that pushes the education system toward greater inequality in term of resources. Meanwhile, in most states, charter schools are being held accountable to high-stakes and narrowly defined tests, further minimizing their autonomy in terms of curriculum.

Our deep understanding of these complex dilemmas emerged from our 2½-year study of charter schools in 10 school districts, housing 39 charter schools, in California—the state with the largest charter school enrollment (UCLA Charter School Study, 1998). Furthermore, other, more recent studies confirm these findings in other states.

In the end, we fear that while charter school reform may help empower some parents, students, and educators in low-income communities by allowing them to engage in a politics of identity, it simultaneously may lead to greater inequality and stratification in the education system overall by forcing greater reliance on private resources. Such resources are generally more plentiful in wealthy as opposed to low-income communities. Thus, even as low-income communities can gain more community control via charter school reform, such control, in some instances, may be a pyrrhic victory as these schools are forced to survive with inadequate funds or rely on benefactors and management companies from outside their communities for necessary resources (see Scott, 2002).

And finally, there are important equity issues related to student access in the midst of a reform that offers no outreach or recruitment of students and gives charter schools a great deal of autonomy in whom they admit. This means that because charter schools have more autonomy to create their own communities through admissions criteria and selective recruitment, even when they serve low-income students they tend to exclude those low-income students who have the least-involved parents.

This chapter also will discuss some of the inherent contradictions between the themes of free-market, deregulatory reforms such as charter schools and the cry for local, community control of schools in poor neighborhoods. We argue that such contradictions may well lead to a fracturing of the fragile political coalition of right-wing ideologues and low-income desperate parents supporting efforts to increase school "choice" or alternatives, while increasing inequality in the education system. Using charter school reform as a lens through which these themes are explored, we raise important issues about how equity is defined and advanced in an era of greater deregulation and school choice. We begin with an historical overview of equity-based reform efforts and place charter schools within this context.

CHARTER SCHOOL REFORM—AN ALTERNATIVE TO WHAT?

Charter school legislation, perhaps the most popular education reform of the past decade, has been passed in 40 states, the District of Columbia, and Puerto Rico, opening the door for more variation in educational services while letting malcontents exit the regular public schools. Thus, libertarians in Arizona, members of the religious right in Colorado, home schoolers in California, progressive educators in Minnesota, Afrocentric scholars in Washington, DC, and teachers' union activists in Hawaii are all drawn to this new form of independence from state-run schools. Yet each group sets out to accomplish dramatically different educational ends. Indeed, with 42 distinct pieces of charter school legislation and more than 2,700 charter schools across the country enrolling more than 600,000 students, there is no single "grand narrative" of charter school reform.

Therein lies both the beauty and the central tension of charter school reform. It delivers autonomy to people choosing to design and run unconventional schools, but does not bind them to any shared set of principles regarding which conventions they shun or why.

According to the fourth-year report of a federally funded study of charter schools in 27 states, the number one reason why people start charter schools is to "realize an alternative vision" different from that of existing public schools. The second most-cited reason for starting a charter school, according to this survey of 971 charter school operators, is to gain more flexibility and greater autonomy from laws and regulations governing regular public schools (U.S. Department of Education, 2000).

What makes the study of charter schools highly significant, therefore, is that it allows researchers to better understand not only what new and different approaches to education charter schools provide, but also what aspects of the traditional public system charter school founders disfavor. Such dissatisfaction, however, must be examined in light of efforts in the past 4 decades by the federal and state governments to create policies that alleviate inequalities within the education system. Obviously, many of these policies have received a great deal of criticism, and these critiques often come from the very people the policies are supposed to help (e.g., Bell, 1987; Dempsey & Noblit, 1996; Shujaa, 1996). Other times, the criticism comes from more advantaged groups that do not benefit directly from such policies and that are fed up with government equity-based interventions that they see as fostering "reverse discrimination" or providing an "unfair advantage" for people not like them (Edsall, 1991; Lelyveld, 2001).

To the extent that charter schools present a thoughtful critique of the shortcomings of these decades-old equity policies and demonstrate more successful ways of serving disadvantaged children, there is a great deal to be learned from these new and innovative schools. But we also must consider whether, at the same time, charter school reform opens the door for an era of educational policies in which the government does not play a role in redistributing resources and educational opportunities in the direction of those who have the least. We have evidence from our research and other studies to suggest that both phenomena are occurring.

Therefore, we discuss what we call "established" conceptions of equity issues within educational policies of the 1960s and 1970s. These conceptions have led to the identification of disadvantaged or at-risk students on the basis of broad categories—for example, poverty, race, and disability. We also examine some of the educational policies developed over the past 40 years to ensure that these categories of disadvantaged students receive extra resources and better educational opportunities. We juxtapose these more broadly accepted categories of "disadvantaged" students with other, alternative and more contextualized ways of understanding who is "at risk" in the education system and why.

ESTABLISHED CONCEPTIONS OF EQUITY: THE REDISTRIBUTIVE POLICY PARADIGM

In the 1960s and much of the 1970s, the policy discourse surrounding equity issues in education was grounded in the belief that the public schools should provide opportunities to learn and excel for all students, regardless of race, poverty, language, disability, gender, or the educational level of their parents (see Chapter 1, this volume; Wise, 1979).

Thus, categories of students defined as at risk or disadvantaged were identified in these equity-minded policies as needing extra services or support from their schools or court-enforced access to educational institutions. Those categories include race, social class, disability, language, and gender. For instance, U.S. Supreme Court rulings such as *Brown* v. *Board of Education* and federal legislation such as the Civil Rights Act of 1964 strengthened the role of the federal government in ensuring equal protection of all citizens and thus denied local educators, parents, and politicians their "rights" to segregate and discriminate against Black children.

In terms of poor students, the Elementary and Secondary Education Act of 1965 provided school districts serving students from low-income families, compensatory education funds under Title I. It also provided the "carrot"—namely, federal funding—to coerce schools to comply with the Civil Rights Act of 1964 (Cross, 2004). Many states also developed compensatory education programs to supplement the federal dollars. In addition, several state-level finance equity cases have attempted to redistribute public funding for education toward school districts serving the poorest students. Furthermore, bilingual education services were created to serve children from households in which English is not the first language and who would be at-risk of failure in an English-language-based education system and society. Other categorical programs that grew out of a combination of equity-based court cases and legislation include special education for students with special needs and Title IX programs to help create equal opportunities for female students (see Cross, 2004; Rabe & Petterson, 1988; Yudof, Kirp, & Levin, 1992).

Lawyers and advocates called on the federal government to force local educators to provide more equal educational opportunities for these various "categories" of students who faced discrimination in the public system. This movement led to federal court rulings and legislation designed to ensure that powerful political actors at the school and district level were impeded from systematically denying poor and minority students, in particular, educational opportunities (Guthrie, 1996; Wise, 1979). In other words, the federal response to inequality under this old policy paradigm was to mandate top-down reforms and create targeted programs designed to infuse resources to support students who traditionally were denied educational opportunities within a more decentralized education system.

Thus, one of the consequences of the equity-based policies of the Civil Rights era was a centralization of decision making and power within an otherwise highly decentralized education system (Elmore, 1993). Through this new federal presence, the Civil Rights era brought about greater centralization of educational governance in the name of democratic principles such as liberty and justice (Lewis & Nakagawa, 1995; Plank & Boyd, 1994). In other words, in many cases these court rulings and laws wrestled control away from local schools and districts to correct the history of negligence of at-risk students in a more decentralized system (Tyack, 1990).

Still, it is important to note that despite this movement toward greater centralization, the U.S. education system has a far more fragmented governance structure than that of most Western nations. Yet even after the increased influence of the federal government in the 1960s and 1970s and the growth of state departments of education in the 1980s, local school districts are still the fundamental governance agencies in education, by tradition and practice. Indeed, many important decisions about how equity-based policies are implemented, and which schools and students have access to the federal and state resources, are made at the school district level (Elmore, 1993).

The major programs targeting federal and state resources toward broad categories of disadvantaged students have been in place for the past 30–40 years. Yet, as the focus of educational policy discourse shifted in the 1980s toward issues of excellence and away from an emphasis on equity, many of the equity-based policies, such as bilingual education, were scaled back or reconfigured to fit the new policy emphasis on so-called "excellence." For instance, Title I funding for poor students is now the main "carrot" in the No Child Left Behind Act, which supports harsh accountability measures and sanctions. Many of the old equity-minded policies of the 1960s and 1970s have endured in some shape or form and have continued to be directed, for the most part, toward the same groups of students—for example, students with special needs, poor students, and limited-English speakers. Still, inherent in the more recent deregulatory reforms such as charter schools is the ongoing critique of the old policies.

Criticisms of Redistributive Equity Policies

There are at least two sides to the critique of these aging equity-based policies. The first comes from more-advantaged people who are not the targets of these reforms, and the second comes from educators and less-advantaged people, who are supposed to benefit from these programs. The criticism that more-advantaged people tend to espouse is rooted in a long history of demand for local control and less government interference to support disadvantaged people. For instance, in the 1950s and 1960s the call for greater local control usually came from White southerners who strongly resisted the federal government's effort to desegregate their schools or to ensure African Americans the right to vote. Since that time, the relationship between local control and the constitutionally guaranteed rights of Blacks and other disenfranchised groups has been suspect as the federal government periodically has used its power to push for greater access and equity (Orfield, 1988; Plank & Boyd, 1994).

The current popularity of deregulatory reforms such as charter schools that restore greater local control is, to a large extent, a backlash against the federal and state governments' more interventionist role of the 1960s and 1970s. Many White working-class and wealthy Americans have become increasingly critical of the cost of federal policies and programs designed to create greater equality. Furthermore, some more-advantaged Americans do not want to pay taxes to support services for other people's children, and thus they shun the government's redistributive role (Brands, 2001; Edsall, 1991; Sniderman & Piazza, 1993). According to Edsall (1991), in a very important book on this topic, "The race and tax agenda effectively focused majority public attention onto what government takes, rather than onto what it gives" (p. 11).

This focus has in turn fueled a powerful and pervasive sentiment— particularly among Americans who are not the beneficiaries of these programs—that the government should not be in the business of redistributing resources and opportunities (Brands, 2001). Recent court cases challenging race-based admissions to magnet schools and university affirmative action programs are good examples of how more White Americans have grown tired and disillusioned with such policies.

The second critique of equity-based policies comes from some educators and advocates who represent less-advantaged students—the intended beneficiaries of these policies. Thus, at the same time that whiter and wealthier members of society have embraced an anti-government message, poor parents of color who live in the inner city are voicing their demands for greater local control of schools as a pathway to community empowerment.

This criticism often centers around the more subtle, cultural aspects of schools and schooling—what happens, for instance, inside desegregated schools when African American and Latino students get off the bus (Shujaa, 1996). Indeed, rarely do equity-based policies such as desegregation court orders deal with the fact that students often are tracked into racially distinct and unequal classes or that they encounter teachers who hold significantly lower expectations for them than for White students. Similarly, court orders cannot mandate that teachers value the life experiences and cultural understandings that non-White students bring with them to school (Bell, 1987; Schofield, 1989; Wells & Crain, 1997).

Similar criticisms exist of Title I compensatory education programs as well as bilingual education and special education. These critics argue that poorly designed pull-out or add-on programs often fail to address cultural equity issues and generally are not used to ensure that all students are achieving (see Shujaa, 1990; Darling-Hammond, 1997).

ALTERNATIVE CONCEPTIONS OF EQUITY:
THE CULTURAL PARADIGM

This second, advocacy-based critique of traditional equity policies targeting specific categories of students with programs that may or may not affect their classroom experiences is shaped by recent and long-running arguments over reframing the concept of "equity." Overlapping and inter-twined with policies that redistribute educational resources toward the most disadvantaged students, via categorical programs and court orders, are al-ternative and often more subtle conceptions of what constitutes equity in education. These more cultural understandings of equity are less focused on broad categories of students and more interested in how particular cate-gories of at-risk factors play out in the lives of individual students.

This critique focuses on school curriculum that reflects the history and culture of our diverse society and on instructional strategies that help stu-dents who traditionally have not succeeded in public schools. Rather than make universal claims about all African American students or all poor stu-dents, an alternative view of who is at risk and why would consider the sociocultural context of each student and question how these categories interact with a particular school environment to place some students at greater risk in spite of Title I funding or court orders (see, for instance, Boateng, 1990; Delpit, 1995; Faltz & Leake, 1996; Foster, 1997).

Proponents of this view argue that while the policy paradigm of re-distributing resources and programs is important, it is only part of the answer to meeting the needs of at-risk students or ensuring that all stu-dents have equal educational opportunities and can achieve to a high stan-dard. This discussion reflects recurring arguments in education that the concept of equity should include the more cultural dimensions of school-ing—for example, the school curriculum, teachers' attitudes and under-standings, and instructional styles and strategies—to help students who traditionally have not succeeded in public schools (see Delpit, 1995; Fos-ter, 1997).

Freedom from federal, state, or school district regulation, from this perspective, means freedom to create a curriculum that reflects the history and culture of the students served, to create an environment that respects the integrity of the individual students and diverse cultures, and to create partnerships and bridges among educators, students, parents, and the local community. This also may mean the freedom to hire and train teachers who have high expectations for students who come to a school with different ways of knowing the world.

The demand for such freedom on the part of disadvantaged schools and communities is not new, of course. In fact, as history has taught us, this is an ongoing and recurring struggle within many communities. For instance, in the 1960s and 1970s, when the federal government was attempt-ing to ensure that some rights of African Americans and other disenfran-chised groups were protected through top-down policies and court orders, grassroots coalitions were demanding greater community control of the schools in their neighborhoods (see Fantini, Gittell, & Magat, 1970).

These community control movements, leveled against school boards and district administrators who were seen as unresponsive to the needs of low-income and minority students, led to "fragmented centralization" as local school districts were under attack from two sides—the federal government and community coalitions. Both efforts, in most cases, focused on empowering those who traditionally had been disenfranchised from the political power structure and giving them a greater say in how extra resources would be used (Lyke, 1970; Tyack & Hansot, 1982).

This fragmented centralization mirrored other War on Poverty efforts of that era as the government initiated policies promoting maximum feasible participation of low-income community members in federally funded programs such as Head Start and Community Action Programs. In this way, the federal government used public policy and tax dollars to try to increase the political, social, and economic power within poor, urban communities (Lewis & Nakagawa, 1995). Rather than anti-government in nature, this movement relied on the federal government to fight discriminatory practices through the courts and redistribute resources and opportunities by targeting poor, urban, and mostly African American communities with funded work and job training programs run by and employing people who lived there.

Thus, it is important to distinguish between those who call for greater local control from a Reagan-era new federalism perspective and the more liberal view of community control as a form of empowerment in the 1960s. The first standpoint is generally taken by those who already have social, economic, and political power and are thus resentful of the government's infringement on their right to exercise that power. Those who subscribe to the second view are generally people who have little power to begin with and thus seek public policies that will make local control more meaningful to them through the redistribution of resources.

Thus, while charter school reform offers the possibility of creating conditions for community control of schools in low-income communities, charter school policies, as they currently are constructed in most states, are more directly descended from an anti-government stance and related to the demand for local control (see Wells, 2002).

DECENTRALIZATION REFORMS: CHARTER SCHOOLS AS POSSIBILITIES AND THREATS

Charter school reform, therefore, has many historical and political roots, including critiques of equity-based policies from the 1960s and 1970s. Still, there are other, related but distinct roots of charter school reform, including the so-called market metaphor for school improvement that captured the attention of so many policymakers in the 1990s (Wells, Grutzik, Carnochan, Slayton, & Vasudeva, 1999).

Briefly, the market metaphor, which is articulated most thoroughly in Chubb and Moe (1990), states that bureaucratic, regulated, "monopolistic," and socialistic public schools are the antithesis of so many core principles of this country—for example, free markets, competition, deregulation, and individualism. The argument is that education systems, particularly in large urban school districts, represent a form of inefficient and wasteful "big government" that competitive economies can no longer afford (see Frank, 2000; Torres, 1995). In this way, the market metaphor both echoes and incorporates the political backlash against the redistributive policies of the Civil Rights Movement.

Indeed, some of the most popular such free-market education reforms have been deregulation of the student assignment process via greater parental choice and privatization of the system via contracting out with private for-profit and nonprofit firms to run schools. Thus, much of charter schools' popularity and appeal derive from the fact that these autonomous schools of choice more strongly resemble competitive, deregulated institutions than other publicly funded schools (see Finn, Bierlein, & Manno, 1996).

Charter school reform is also a product of systemic reform, which promised greater school-level autonomy at a time when many states across the country were implementing new standards and assessments designed to hold all schools accountable. The concept of systemic reform, as it shaped federal legislation such as Goals 2000 and the 1994 reauthorization of the Elementary and Secondary Education Act (ESEA), was yet another effort to create fragmented centralization. In other words, the idea behind systemic reform was to centralize standards and assessments at the state and national level while decentralizing governance and decision making to the individual school level (O'Day & Smith, 1993). Thus, a central aspect of systemic reform is greater autonomy for individual schools. Similarly, a fundamental goal of this reform is to free local communities and their schools to maximize opportunities for their particular students. According to O'Day and Smith (1993), each school must be free to choose "the instructional strategies, language of instruction, use of curricular materials, and topics to be emphasized" (p. 263).

And while the systemic reform vision of standards-based accountability systems has been compromised by the reauthorization of ESEA—the No Child Left Behind Act—with its more punitive and test-driven focus, charter school reform still provides hope of more autonomy for individual schools. Accordingly, this movement reflects both historical frustrations and more recent initiatives aimed at addressing inequities in the education system.

Charter Schools and the Cultural Paradigm

Grounded in and supported by both free-market and systemic reform ideology, charter school reform promises to release talented educators and community members to address the needs of students by moving the decision making down to the school level. Theoretically, this will allow educators the freedom to use public funds in new and different ways to better meet the needs of their students.

Indeed, in our study of charter schools in 10 California school districts, we saw some evidence that this was happening. For instance, within the urban, ethnocentric, and grassroots charter schools we studied, we saw the potential for educators, parents, and students to create sites of resistance where they could question and reject Eurocentric culture and historical perspectives (see Haymes, 1996; Wells, Lopez, Scott, & Holme, 1999).

For example, a woman who helped to found one such ethnocentric charter school in our study explained that the decision to start the school was made at a community meeting when "speaker after speaker—older adults as well as young—thought that maybe we need to have our own schools. We need to decide our own curriculum. We can decide how our children are going to learn, what they are going to learn" (see Wells, Lopez, et al., 1999, p. 193).

Some of these localized urban schools create "homeplaces" for those who have been disconnected from and disempowered within the traditional, state-run system (hooks, 1990). For instance, a founder of a charter school serving a Latino community explained that one of the motivating forces behind the effort to start the school was the way in which Latino students with limited English were being treated in the public schools. She noted that some students were put into English as a Second Language (ESL) programs with huge classes, even when they were close to fluency in English, and sometimes they never progressed out of ESL (see Wells, Lopez, et al., 1999).

Furthermore, as with the community control movement of the 1960s, urban grassroots charter schools have the potential to be politically empowering for formerly disconnected and disempowered parents. The process of organizing and founding a charter school can help low-income parents and community members of color create and sustain new social networks that can be used for political organizing and political voice within the larger society. This process also promises to forge connections between disempowered parents and the education system by enhancing their participation in their children's education in ways that are enriching for both the parents and students. But our research found that the community involvement potential of charter schools was not always realized for a whole host of reasons, including the fact that there was often a huge gap between the educators and the parents in terms of know-how about running a school, or because the educators had to rely so heavily on people from outside the community to support the school. Thus, the extent to which charter schools are parent-run and locally controlled varied greatly from site to site.

For instance, in one of the urban charter schools serving low-income students that we studied, parents sat on every decision-making committee or council in the school. The most involved parents, in particular, were able to voice their opinions and influence the course of the school. Yet, in two other urban charter schools in poor communities, parents said they had less voice than they had hoped because the educators were still seen as the experts making the decisions (Wells, Lopez, et al., 1999). In one urban charter school, it was mostly the representatives of corporations that supported the school, and not the parents from the nearby low-income community, who made the most important decisions about resources, growth, and staffing.

Still, many teacher-led charter schools offer the possibility of a liberatory and even emancipatory reform to the extent that these educators have embraced curricular and pedagogical practices that are more successful with and inspirational to the students they serve. For instance, some charter school educators saw the need to develop a more culturally relevant curriculum for low-income students of color, thereby offering a critique of a more Eurocentric curriculum (Wells, Lopez, et al., 1999).

Indeed, many of the charter school educators we interviewed spoke of the power of the autonomy they gained through charter school reform, including the ability to restructure their school year and day. Furthermore, founders and leaders of every charter school we studied stressed the significance of being able to hire their own teachers outside their districts' personnel policies (see UCLA Charter School Study, 1998).

Others talked about being able to make democratic and collaborative decisions at their school sites. These were educators who valued the autonomy they gained through charter school reform to use their professional knowledge and background to make decisions about serving children. Of course, not all the charter schools were as democratic or collaborative, but still it appears that in general the governance processes in charter schools are a bit more inclusive in terms of teacher voice—but not always parent voice—than many traditional public schools (UCLA Charter School Study, 1998; Wells, Lopez, et al., 1999). Still, as Scott's (2002) work demonstrates, it is quite possible that this is less true for most charter schools operated by EMOs.

To the extent that charter schools lived up to their potential to be culturally more relevant and politically more inclusive, they could, theoretically, play a significant role in overcoming some of the inequalities that exist in the public education system. Yet there are several other issues that threaten the potential contribution of charter school reform to alleviating current and prevalent inequalities. Indeed, it is where the promise of community-controlled charter schools meets the harsh reality of an educational free market in a highly unequal society that things become much more complicated.

Charter Schools in a Highly Unequal Free Market

What the proponents of charter schools and other deregulatory reforms do not talk about is that the education system is circumscribed by highly unequal economic, social, and political conditions. Moreover, thanks to active lobbying on the part of conservative organizations such as the Center for Education Reform, most charter school laws in this country do nothing to try to counteract this inequality. In other words, most state charter school laws emphasize the quantity of charter schools over quality, force charter schools to rely heavily on private resources and to operate outside the public education system, and lack equity provisions to redistribute funds and support to charter schools in low-income communities. Thus, as these more autonomous schools arise, they exist, in many circumstances, outside the system of old equity-based policies and procedures intended to enhance disadvantaged students' access to schools, programs, and resources.

This is truly unfortunate from an equity perspective because resources appear to be an important factor in efforts to empower low-income parents and communities through decentralization. In the 1960s and 1970s, for instance, community control models in low-income Black communities, in particular, often failed in part because of inadequate funding (Fantini & Gittell, 1973). According to Cohen (1990):

> If decentralization is to work, the schools and neighborhoods most sorely in need of improvement will need a major, long-term infusion of new political and organizational resources. Lacking that, some opportunities will languish, and others will be seized by existing political agencies. Those agencies that already have power will accumulate more. This too has happened before. (p. 366)

We certainly found this to be true in our study of California charter schools, which varied tremendously in terms of both the public and private resources they garnered and required. For instance, in terms of public funding, we learned that although the California state law is pretty straightforward in stating that charter schools should be funded on a per-pupil basis, exactly how that per-pupil amount is calculated varied tremendously across and within school districts (see Slayton, 2002). This was due in large part to the political context of the school districts, including the attitude of board members toward charter schools, and the savvy and knowledge—or lack thereof—of charter school administrators. Thus, the more well-connected—especially with school district officials—and well-informed charter school administrators we studied used their knowledge of the law and available resources, or their ability to apply political pressure, to ensure that their schools received all of the public funding to which they theoretically were entitled (Slayton, 2002).

Furthermore, some of these well-connected educators were able to draw additional revenue or benefits from their host districts. Meanwhile, other, less well-informed or less politically powerful charter school administrators were unable to claim the same level of support from their districts. This finding demonstrates that this is not simply an issue of charter schools in different school districts receiving different amounts of public support. We found that sometimes charter schools within the *same* school district can and do receive different amounts of public support. Indeed, these findings raise concerns about whether charter schools are being funded equitably in relation to one another or in relation to other public schools (Slayton, 2002).

In addition to these issues of operating costs, charter schools in most states do not receive capital funding or building space from their district or state. Instead, most are required to borrow or raise money to purchase or lease buildings and space. As the federal study of charter schools demonstrates, the number one barrier to success cited by charter school operators in 27 states is lack of start-up funds. The second most-cited barrier is inadequate operating funds; inadequate facilities ranked fourth (U.S. Department of Education, 2000).

Obviously, well-connected charter schools and those serving more-affluent communities will be in a better position to raise these private resources. For instance, some charter schools actually may have buildings and equipment donated by wealthy people or corporations. Other charter schools may lack the political or social connections to such individuals or institutions. Clearly, we saw such discrepancies in our study of California charter schools (UCLA Charter School Study, 1998).

Using data from the UCLA Charter School Study, Scott and Holme (2002) argue that the processes charter schools use to garner private resources are circumscribed by the social status and the social networks of their local school communities. In fact, these authors contend that the high-status networks—personal and professional connections to people with money and political power—are even more critical to private resource accumulation than the particular strategies used to acquire resources.

Thus, Scott and Holme (2002) argue that understanding the social context of schools is critical to understanding why the same processes or strategies of private resource accumulation net such disparate results for different charter schools. More specifically, they see vast, disturbing inequities emerging within and across charter school reform—inequities that mirror the wealth and poverty of the communities that house these schools. For instance, they note that at many urban charter schools serving low-income students in our study, there was no time or staff to pursue grants and fund raising, and yet the schools were greatly in need of resources. They cite a principal from one such low-income charter school serving students of color within an extremely old and dilapidated facility that regularly was without heat in the winter.

> Our biggest challenge right now is finding a site. This is not a good area. It isn't. We need to find a site that's safer for our students, plus we need our own gym. We need to meet those needs for the students as well as, we need to work on a lot of things. Our problem now is because we are so limited with money, and people are literally betting on us closing. It's kind of hard, but we're hoping that some rich, wealthy person will say, "Hey, I'll give you a couple of million dollars." And then at least some of our challenges will be met and settled, and somehow, it doesn't look like it. (p. 121)

Scott and Holme (2002) conclude that policymakers should attend to these inequities by targeting start-up funds and technical assistance to charter schools in low-income communities. In the absence of such government efforts to further support charter schools in poor neighborhoods, many charter schools in low-income communities will be forced to partner with private, for-profit or non-for-profit EMOs because of the financial support these groups offer. While these organizations provide necessary financial support, they may or may not allow the schools to be truly community-based or grassroots (see Scott, 2002).

In addition to the problems associated with resources, there are also important student access issues. Charter schools, for instance, generally have a great deal of autonomy in terms of admitting students. Granted, most state charter school laws stipulate that charter schools must be nonsectarian, may not charge tuition, and may not discriminate on the basis of race, ethnicity, national origin, religion, or gender. Still, most states do not specifically prohibit charter schools from instituting admissions requirements based on such criteria as students' prior achievement, expressed interest in the charter school's theme, or parental involvement requirements.

Also, because individual charter schools in most states and districts are autonomous to run their own recruitment and admissions process, they are free to send out information and applications to whatever target audience they choose. Unlike magnet schools, which usually are advertised and applied to through a centralized district office where some effort is made to balance schools along racial/ethnic lines, charter schools make their own decisions about who will be allowed to attend.

What we have learned is that perhaps the most salient manifestation of charter schools' autonomy to create school communities is the freedom they have to allow their shared values and beliefs to shape their understanding of which students and parents "fit" into that school community and thus who should attend. Furthermore, charter school operators have much more power than most regular public school educators to act on these preferences. That is, through the use of several mechanisms that shape charter schools' recruitment, admissions, and disciplinary processes, charter school operators can exclude students who do not fit the culture or norms of the school. Thus, alongside the community-building and mission-shaping aspects of charter school reform, lies a set of more difficult issues related to student access (see Lopez, Wells, & Holme, 2002).

In our study, we documented many charter school operators' efforts to form distinct school communities grounded in shared values and beliefs—what we refer to as "identity-building" efforts—in terms of how they distinguish themselves within the context of their school districts and local communities. Furthermore, we discovered that these distinctions relate to which students and parents are "desirable" in the eyes of charter school operators. We also found that even though many charter school operators say they greatly value diversity in their schools, their distinctions about who is desirable and who is not are often related in subtle, cultural ways to the social class, race/ethnicity, disability, and/or primary language of the students. And finally, we described how charter schools, unlike most regular public schools, are able to act on these distinctions by using specific mechanisms to structure who attends and who remains (see Lopez et al., 2002).

In other words, our data suggest that charter schools are making as many—or more—choices about which students and parents will attend as parents and students are making choices about which charter schools they would like to attend. We argue, therefore, that while charter schools provide some families with new educational opportunities, they frequently add another layer of selectivity to an already highly stratified public education system. Indeed, even in cases where charter schools are located in predominantly low-income communities, they tend to recruit, attract, and retain families who are relatively privileged, with greater resources compared with other families in these communities (Lopez et al., 2002).

For instance, we studied an urban elementary charter school located in a low-income community that had fairly strict parental involvement and student conduct contracts. Educators at this school regularly "counseled out" students who were not behaving in accordance with these contracts. At one of the school's governing board meetings, the staff and parents who were present voted to approve a strict attendance policy whereby students could be asked to leave the school if they were tardy to or absent from school more than a certain number of days in one semester. It is important to note that this charter school, like many others, did not provide its students with any transportation to and from school. Thus, parents must either drive the students every morning and afternoon or rely on mass transportation.

Still, many of the educators and most of the parents on this board said that the charter school was not for everyone, and if parents could not live up to the expectations, they needed to find another school. In this way, even though the school is in a low-income neighborhood, it probably is not serving the most needy students from that area of the school district. In fact, many of the parents we interviewed lived far from the school in a more working-class and middle-class section of the metropolitan area. As one person we interviewed put it, the parents who hear about and choose this charter school are not those on the "bottom of the barrel" in terms of involvement in and support of their children's education. Likewise, a teacher at this charter school pointed out that a child who was disruptive would not do well in that educational community (Lopez et al., 2002).

Although this phenomenon is not unique to charter schools, they, unlike other public schools, have the freedom to make requirements of students and parents—particularly in terms of behavior and school involvement—and these requirements affect admissions decisions. As a result, often even when charter schools are developed in low-income communities, they tend to serve students who are relatively privileged—that is, have the most involved parents, the greatest access to financial and in-kind resources, and so on—compared with others in the same community.

At another urban charter school that also served a low-income population, the parent contract is strictly enforced, helping to define who does not belong at that school. In fact, six families were asked not to re-enroll one fall because they had not fulfilled their required "volunteer" hours. Similarly, a parent at a suburban charter school told us that she was forced to take her children out of the school, in part because she could not fulfill the parent involvement requirement. She said, "The main thing was the time commitment, I did not have the time." This parent also pointed out that the parents who were most involved at the charter school were the stay-at-home moms. "They are very lucky. I wish I could do that, but I can't right now. It makes you wonder if charter schools can work in an inner city area where all the parents have to work" (Lopez et al., 2002, p. 138).

In other words, many of the shared values and beliefs that shape charter schools are strongly influenced by deep cultural and structural barriers. For instance, parents who can afford to be involved in certain ways or give more resources to the charter schools are often more highly valued simply because they have time and money. Furthermore, parents who historically have succeeded in school and thus have been treated well by educators probably have a more positive orientation toward involvement in schools than parents who have had fewer such positive experiences in the past (Lopez et al., 2002).

While 19 of 40 charter school laws have some form of racial/ethnic balance guidelines, these guidelines vary from specific mandates about charter school enrollment reflecting that of the local school district as a whole to requirements that charter schools abide by existing school desegregation orders (see Frankenberg & Lee, 2003). And while half of the states have no such racial/ethnic balance provisions, our study of California suggests that even when such provisions exist, they rarely are monitored and enforced (see UCLA Charter School Study, 1998). In addition, half of the states with charter school laws lack even basic provisions for charter schools to transport students from other neighborhoods. We are concerned that housing patterns that are segregated by race and social class, prevalent in most cities and towns in the United States, combined with the lack of transportation for charter school students in several states, make it difficult for charter schools to be multiracial or socioeconomically mixed, even when their organizers want them to be.

Given these cultural and structural issues and the fact that we live in a very unequal society, it is difficult to create "homogeneous" school communities without creating further separation along racial/ethnic, socioeconomic, linguistic, and other cultural dimensions. Indeed, Wells, Holme, Lopez, and Cooper (2000) demonstrate that early evidence from various states with large numbers of charter schools suggests that this is indeed the trend—charter schools are more segregated by race and social class than the already segregated public schools. In other words, although the national, aggregated data on the racial/ethnic makeup of charter school enrollments show that charter schools are similar to the general public school population overall in the states in which they exist, when the data are broken down to the state, district, local community, and school level, charter schools are seen to be highly segregated—even more so than the regular public schools. More recently, Frankenberg and Lee (2003) found in their study of data on 1,855 charter schools that 70% of all Black charter school students attend "intensely" segregated minority schools. Results were more mixed for White and Latino students.

Yet, it is important to note that the greater autonomy charter schools have in terms of admissions does not always raise equity issues. Indeed, some charter schools are specifically designed to recruit and serve students who have not succeeded in the regular public education system. According to the U.S. Department of Education's (2000) Fourth-Year Report, the third most popular reason cited for starting a charter school was to serve a special population of students. Such special populations conceivably could include at-risk language minority, disabled, or ethnic and racial minority students. Still, we do not know enough about how the educational opportunities in charter schools for at-risk students vary from those in other charter schools or other public schools. We argue that there are significant pedagogical issues related to not only whether charter schools serve at-risk students but also how they define "at risk" and how they choose to serve these students. Our study of charter schools in California, as well as some research on Texas charter schools (School of Urban and Public Affairs, 2000), suggests that charter schools targeted toward the students that no other schools want to serve may have the lowest-quality programs and the least challenging curriculum.

Thus, to the extent that charter schools offer yet another layer in a highly unequal education system, they have not solved the problems faced by the students on the "bottom" in terms of access to a better-quality education. Furthermore, to the extent that exclusionary charter schools exist, it is important for research on charter schools to document this and raise questions about its implications for the rest of the education system.

Lack of Real Curricular Autonomy in an Age of High-Stakes Tests

One of the central paradoxes of the systemic reform movement that helped to foster charter schools is that it promises to give schools greater autonomy and freedom, while at the same time holding them accountable for student outcomes. Yet, as we witness the proliferation of state standards and assessment systems under systemic reform's central pieces of federal legislation—Goals 2000 and the No Child Left Behind Act—we see that in some ways schools have less autonomy over their curriculum and instruction because they must all, within a given state, teach to the same tests. It is difficult to imagine charter schools, which must administer those same state assessments as part of their accountability systems, having much freedom to devise their own anti-establishment curriculum. How far afield can these schools really afford to go when their success or failure is measured by a state-mandated exam?

Another argument states that wholesale deregulation has the potential of reintroducing social injustices if schools are controlled locally by political groups that do not choose to serve students with special needs or those who are politically disenfranchised and thus discriminated against (Tyack, 1990). According to Plank and Boyd (1994), "The withdrawal of federal or judicial supervision of policies aimed at improving the relative standing of minorities, in these and other instances, might lead to the reassertion of majority control and the reversal of policies that favor minority interests" (p. 269).

Wise (1979) writes that the centralization of educational policy in the 1960s and 1970s was designed to address equity issues and overcome problems that the local schools were unwilling or unable to solve, such as segregation or the rights of disadvantaged students. He argues that these equity problems of access to resources and programs should not be decentralized to the local level because "community control and citizen participation tend to serve the dominant political interests within the community" (p. 209).

In other words, images of grassroots autonomous charter schools with ample resources and the curriculum and pedagogy to serve the most-disadvantaged students in the public system in a culturally relevant way are very much pie in the sky unless charter school laws are amended to recreate some of the fragmented centralization we saw in the 1960s.

CONCLUSION

All of the issues discussed in this chapter suggest ways in which a more decentralized and deregulated education system could exacerbate instead of alleviate inequalities within the system. Given the history of educational policy in the United States, many civil rights advocates are skeptical that the empowerment of poor people will occur simply through granting greater autonomy to schools—especially in an era when equity rarely is mentioned in policy debates over education reforms.

In fact, the history of the community control movement of 30 years ago offers some interesting and important lessons—regarding not only resources but also empowerment—that should inform the current movement toward decentralization. Reformers of that era noted that "decentralization in and of itself is only an administrative device, a reaction to the inefficiency and unreality of a massive bureaucracy. It does not necessarily result in a more responsive system or one in which the community has a determining voice" (Fantini, Gittell, & Magat, 1970, pp. 97–98). Nor does decentralization alone necessarily force educators to focus on their failure in dealing with the poor and, more particularly, with Black children (Fein, 1970, p. 85).

Indeed, our study of charter school reform in California suggests that this is the case today as it was more than 30 years ago. Despite its potential to allow the space and freedom for educators and communities to address the cultural issues related to oppression and inequity, charter school reform— born of an era of market metaphors and systemic reform and backlash against existing equity-minded programs—fails to address the growing gap between rich and poor schools. In fact, it may help to exacerbate it.

ACKNOWLEDGMENTS

We are greatly indebted to the Annie E. Casey and Ford Foundations for their support of our California charter school research. We would also like to thank the Spencer Foundation for providing fellowship support to members of our research team during the course of this study. While the support of these organizations was instrumental to our work, the views expressed here are those of the authors and not necessarily those of the foundations.

In addition, we would like to thank the other members of the UCLA Charter School Study research team: Ligia Artiles, Sibyll Carnochan, Camille Wilson Cooper, Cynthia Grutzik, Julie Slayton, and Ash Vasudeva. Further, we would like to thank the members of our Advisory Board— Richard F. Elmore, Michele Foster, Annette Lareau, Pedro Noguera, and Kenneth Wong—for their extremely thoughtful feedback and encouragement. And most importantly, we want to thank each and every educator, parent, community member, and policymaker whom we interviewed.

REFERENCES

Bell, D. (1987). *And we are not saved: The elusive quest for racial justice.* New York: Basic Books.

Boateng, F. (1990). Combating deculturalization of the African-American child in the public schools. In K. Lomotey (Ed.), *Going to school: The African American experience.* Albany: State University of New York Press.

Brands, H. W. (2001). *The strange death of American liberalism.* New Haven, CT: Yale University Press.

Chubb, J., & Moe, T. (1990). *Politics, markets and America's schools.* Washington, DC: Brookings Institution.

Cohen, D. K. (1990). Governance and instruction: The promise of decentralization and choice. In W. H. Clune & J. F. Witte (Eds.), *Choice and control in American education* (Vol. 1, pp. 337–386). New York: Falmer Press.

Cross, C. (2004). *Political education: National policy comes of age.* New York: Teachers College Press.

Darling-Hammond, L. (1997). *The right to learn: A blueprint for creating schools that work.* San Francisco: Jossey-Bass.

Delpit, L. (1995). *Other people's children.* New York: New Press.

Dempsey, V., & Noblit, G. (1996). Cultural ignorance and school desegregation: A community narrative. In M. J. Shujaa (Ed.), *Beyond desegregation: The politics of quality in African American schooling* (pp. 115–137). Thousand Oaks, CA: Corwin Press.

Edsall, T. B. (with Edsall, M.). (1991). *Chain reaction: The impact of race, rights, and taxes on American politics.* New York: Norton.

Elmore, R. F. (1993). School decentralization: Who gains? Who loses? In J. Hannaway & M. Carnoy (Eds.), *Decentralization and school improvement: Can we fulfill the promise?* (pp. 33–54). San Francisco: Jossey-Bass.

Faltz, C. J., & Leake, D. O. (1996). The all-black school: Inherently unequal or a culture-based alternative? In M. J. Shujaa (Ed.), *Beyond desegregation: The politics of quality in African American schooling* (pp. 227–252). Thousand Oaks, CA: Corwin Press.

Fantini, M., & Gittell, M. (1973). *Decentralization: Achieving reform.* New York: Praeger.

Fantini, M., Gittell, M., & Magat, R. (1970). *Community control and the urban school.* New York: Praeger.

Fein, L. J. (1970). Community schools and social theory: The limits of universalism. In H. M. Levin (Ed.), *Community control of schools* (pp. 76–99). Washington, DC: Brookings Institution.

Finn, C. E., Bierlein, L. A., & Manno, B. V. (1996). *Charter schools in action: A first look.* Washington, DC: Hudson Institute.

Foster, M. (1997). *Black teachers on teaching.* New York: New Press.

Frank, T. (2000). *One market under God: Extreme capitalism, market populism, and the end of economic democracy.* New York: Doubleday.

Frankenberg, E., & Lee, C. (2003). *Charter schools and race: A lost opportunity for integrated education.* Cambridge, MA: The Civil Rights Project, Harvard University.

Guthrie, J. W. (1996). *Reinventing education finance: Alternatives for allocating resources to individual schools.* Paper presented at the annual meeting of the American Education Finance Association, Salt Lake City, UT.

Haymes, S. (1996). *Race, culture and the city: A pedagogy for black urban struggle.* Albany: State University of New York Press.

hooks, b. (1990). *Yearning: Race, gender, and cultural politics.* Boston: South End Press.

Lewis, D. A., & Nakagawa, K. (1995). *Race and education in the American metropolis: A study of school decentralization.* Albany: State University of New York Press.

Lelyveld, J. (2001). Introduction. In Correspondents of *The New York Times, How race is lived in America* (pp. ix–xix). New York: Times Books.

Lopez, A., Wells, A. S., & Holme, J. J. (2002). Creating charter school communities: Identity building, diversity, and selectivity. In A. S. Wells (Ed.), *Where charter school policy fails: The problems of accountability and equity* (pp. 129–158). New York: Teachers College Press.

Lyke, R. F. (1970). Political issues in school decentralization. In M. W. Kirst (Ed.), *The politics of education at the local, state, and federal levels* (pp. 111–132). Berkeley: McCutchan.

O'Day, J., & Smith, M. (1993). Systemic reform and educational opportunity. In S. H. Fuhrman (Ed.), *Designing coherent educational policy* (pp. 250–312). San Francisco: Jossey-Bass.

Orfield, G. (1988). Race and the liberal agenda: The loss of the integrationist dream. In M. Weir, A. S. Orloff, & T. Skocpol (Eds.), *The politics of social policy in the United States* (pp. 313–356). Princeton, NJ: Princeton University Press.

Plank, D. N., & Boyd, W. L. (1994). Antipolitics, education, and institutional choice: The flight from democracy. *American Educational Research Journal, 31*(2), 263–281.

Rabe, B. G., & Petterson, P. (1988). The evolution of a new cooperative federalism. In N. J. Boyan (Ed.), *Handbook of research on educational administration* (pp. 467–485). New York: Longman.

Schofield, J. W. (1989). *Black and white in school*. New York: Teachers College Press.

School of Urban and Public Affairs. (2000, July). *Texas open-enrollment and charter schools: Third year evaluation* (Part 2). Arlington: University of Texas at Arlington.

Scott, J. (2002). *Charter schools, privatization and the search for educational empowerment*. Doctoral dissertation, University of California at Los Angeles.

Scott, J., & Holme, J. J. (2002). Public schools, private resources: The role of social networks in California charter school reform. In A. S. Wells (Ed.), *Where charter school policy fails: The problems of accountability and equity* (pp. 102–128). New York: Teachers College Press.

Shujaa, M. J. (1990). Policy failure in urban schools: How teachers respond to increased accountability for students. In K. Lomotey (Ed.), *Going to school: The African American experience* (pp. 85–102). Albany: State University of New York Press.

Shujaa, M. J. (1996). Introduction. In M. J. Shujaa (Ed.), *Beyond desegregation: The politics of quality in African American schooling* (pp. 1–4). Thousand Oaks, CA: Corwin Press.

Slayton, J. (2002). Public funds for California charter schools: Where local context and savvy meet formula. In A. S. Wells (Ed.), *Where charter school policy fails: The problems of accountability and equity* (pp. 77–102). New York: Teachers College Press.

Sniderman, P. M., & Piazza, T. (1993). *The scar of race*. Cambridge, MA: Belknap Press of Harvard University Press.

Torres, C. (1995). State and education revisited: Why educational researchers should think politically about education. In M. W. Apple (Ed.), *Review of research in education* (pp. 255–331). Washington, DC: American Educational Research Association.

Tyack, D. (1990). Restructuring in historical perspective: Tinkering toward utopia. *Teachers College Record, 92*(2), 170–191.

Tyack, D., & Hansot, E. (1982). *Managers of virtue: Public school leadership in America, 1820–1980*. New York: Basic Books.

UCLA Charter School Study. (1998). *Beyond the rhetoric of charter school reform: A study of ten California school districts*. Los Angeles: Author. Available: www.gseis.ucla.edu/docs/charter.pdf.

U.S. Department of Education. (2000). *The state of charter schools: Fourth-year report 2000*. Washington, DC: Author.

Wells, A. S. (2002). Why public policy fails to live up to the potential of charter school reform: An introduction. In A. S. Wells (Ed.), *Where charter school policy fails: The problems of accountability and equity* (pp. 1–28). New York: Teachers College Press.

Wells, A. S., & Crain, R. L. (1997). *Stepping over the color line: African American students in white suburban schools*. New Haven, CT: Yale University Press.

Wells, A. S., Grutzik, C., Carnochan, S., Slayton, J., & Vasudeva, A. (1999). Underlying policy assumptions of charter school reform: The multiple meanings of a movement. *Teachers College Record, 100*(3), 513–535.

Wells, A. S., Holme, J. J., Lopez, A., & Cooper, C. W. (2000). Charter schools and racial and social class segregation: Yet another sorting machine? In R. Kahlenberg (Ed.), *A notion at risk: Preserving education as an engine for social mobility* (pp. 169–222). New York: Century Foundation Press.

Wells, A. S., Lopez, A., Scott, J., & Holme, J. J. (1999, Summer). Charter schools as postmodern paradox: Rethinking social stratification in an age of deregulated school choice. *Harvard Educational Review, 69*(2), 172–204.

Wise, A. E. (1979). *Legislated learning: The bureaucratization of the American classroom*. Berkeley: University of California Press.

Yudof, M. G., Kirp, D. L., & Levin, B. (1992). *Education policy and the law*. St. Paul, MN: West Publishing.

10

Race, Assets, and Choosing Schools

Current School Choices and the Future of Vouchers

THOMAS M. SHAPIRO
HEATHER BETH JOHNSON

Despite the historic promise that public education would serve as the "great equalizer," evening out opportunity and rewarding meritocracy, more often than not schools reinforce the link between children's family backgrounds, their communities, and their life chances. In the United States, school districts are structured by funding and location based on residential patterns that are highly segregated by race and class (Massey & Denton, 1993; Orfield & Yun, 1999). The result is that children growing up with the most hardships typically live in the most deprived communities and overwhelmingly attend the weakest schools. In this way, class and race are deeply embedded in the structure of schooling, and thus must be addressed and examined in any effort to reform the public education system to expand opportunities.

Indeed, student achievement, school success, and educational failure closely track both race and class, with affluent White and Asian students coming out on top. And while no one set of statistics can fully tell this complex story, numbers provide snapshots of the extensive inequalities. For instance, our analysis of Panel Study of Income Dynamics data shows that the high school dropout rate is nearly 10 times higher for poor students than for students from top-income families. The fact that students from high-income families are seven times more likely to complete bachelor's degrees than students from poor families is but one of many measures of extensive educational stratification and inequality in our society (Mortenson, 2000).

Failure in school and lack of education are modern-day scarlet letters that practically ensure other difficulties later in life, including lower employment rates and earnings. The payoff for finishing college is great. The median annual salary of a college graduate is about $20,000 higher than that of a high school graduate. Similarly, the median earnings of families headed by college graduates are approximately $24,000 greater than those of families headed by high school graduates. A quick glance at wealth data from the Survey on Income and Program Participation shows how this payoff translates handsomely into financial assets—college-educated families possess $41,000 more net worth ($75,000 versus $34,000) and nearly 10 times as much in liquid assets ($20,000 versus $2,500) than high school-educated families. Today, college education is more vital and, perhaps, more valuable than at any time in our past. In this context, school reform takes on special significance in attempts to create opportunity and decrease inequality in society at large.

However, when we consider race as well as class in our analysis of total financial assets (as opposed to annual income alone), we see that college-educated Whites possess about four times as much wealth as college-educated Blacks—$67,000 compared with $15,000 (Oliver & Shapiro, 1997, 2001). Furthermore, in a classic 1968 sociological work, Duncan noted that more-affluent and economically successful Black families did not pass along their status to their children, in stark contrast to the ability of Whites to pass status along to the next generation. More than 30 years after Duncan's findings, we are revisiting this dilemma, and we find that the tale of two mobilities is a continuing story. Oliver and Shapiro's *Black Wealth/White Wealth* 1997 speculated that this was the case because Black families lacked the wealth assets necessary to optimize their children's life chances. In addition, Jencks and Phillips (1998) found that the test scores of children from affluent Black families still lagged far behind those of White children from similarly affluent families.

A central question of our current work is whether it is indeed true that Black families are less able to pass on wealth and success from one generation to the next and, if so, how and why this is still happening. Our fundamental premise was that the education system is a prime institutional site for passing along inequality from one generation to the next. Over the past several years, we have collected data through in-depth interviews with White, Black, and Latino families about what they think of their schools, the educational dilemmas and choices they face, their educational options, and the ultimate school choices they make. We examine how families with financial assets use them in the process of interacting with and negotiating the school system to get what they want for their children. The data we have collected, therefore, shed light on the thorny issue of how families currently are choosing schools for their children. We find that families with wealth—even in limited amounts—use their assets in a very calculated fashion to pass along advantage to their children through high-quality and highly selective schooling. At the same time we see how those without assets struggle to attain opportunities for their children and to keep them from falling further behind.

These rich data put us in a unique position to describe and gain some valuable insight into parental behavior under school choice policies, such as tuition vouchers. We believe our research findings provide valuable insights that should inform the debate over the future of school choice and voucher programs in American educational policy and the role of race and class in this process.

THE VOUCHER SOLUTION

The documented connections between family resources, school environments, and educational achievement have led researchers and policymakers to consider school reforms that will provide children from disadvantaged families greater access to better schools. Some people think that the best way to break this nexus is by introducing a market model of parental choice into the education system, whereby parents "vote with their feet" by choosing which schools their children attend. This chapter focuses specifically on the issue of the potential impact of one such school choice reform model—school voucher programs. Voucher plans are government programs that enable public school students to attend schools of their choice, public or private (Cookson, 1994).

Despite the fact that voucher policies have long been proposed and considered, and in some cases implemented, we know very little about the potential impact of large-scale voucher plans. Empirical evidence is scant, in part, because practical experience with voucher programs is so limited. In the United States very few government-created and -funded voucher plans have been enacted, and those—for example, the Milwaukee Parental Choice Program and the Cleveland Scholarship and Tutoring Program—have been small and experimental and researchers have lacked data from the private schools that students attend. (Indeed, Chapter 11 of this volume provides detailed and very valuable information on the much larger-scale voucher policy in Chile.) Still, despite the lack of evidence of the impact of vouchers in the United States, the efficacy of such a reform has been hotly debated. Scholars, educators, legislators, and the public alike have passionately championed and contested the implementation of voucher programs. As Caroline Hoxby (1999) has noted: "The question, 'If parents were given greater choice, how and what kind of schools would they choose?' is central to the debate over school choice. It is contentious because little is known about how parents actually choose among schools" (p. 281).

According to its advocates, this competitive school choice model of public funding for private schools will force failing public schools to enforce higher standards and improve their outcomes in order to attract and retain students. Schools that fail to be competitive will be closed down or will drop out of the competition and close. These supporters argue that the competition will improve the whole system because parents will choose "academically excellent" schools, as defined by some objective and clear measures of excellence, and will not consider other factors, such as the location of a school or the racial or social class makeup of the students enrolled. In fact, some proponents of such school choice proposals argue that they will lessen pervasive racial and social class segregation in the education system by opening up more schools to students of different racial/ethnic/social class backgrounds from outside the local neighborhood.

Meanwhile, opponents of vouchers argue that such a private school choice policy will only sort and stratify students further and will not result in increased educational quality overall. This argument is based on the observation that parents who currently have the ability to choose schools for their children often make these choices based on factors other than some objective measure of academic excellence. For instance, critics have noted that factors such as the racial makeup of the student population, social class exclusiveness of the school, athletic programs, and other extracurricular offerings available at the school seem often to be used by parents in choosing schools for their children (see Holme, 2002; Peterson & Hassel, 1998). They also note that when it comes to most of the private schools and many of the highly popular public schools, it is the schools that sort and select the students as much as—or more so—the parents choosing the schools (see Chapter 9, this volume, for instance).

We think that our research has something to offer this debate because we have focused on the many ways in which families choose schools absent a voucher policy. Thus, while a dominant theme in the debate over school choice is that with access to vouchers, families will be making school "choices" for the first time, we have been documenting the ways in which many families have been making critical educational choices for a long time. In particular, exercising educational choices is not a new phenomenon for those families who have the financial capacity to select schools for their children—either by paying private school tuition or buying a home in a school district of their choice. Indeed, it is in great part due to such freedom of choice that the education system—both public and private schools—has come to be so separate and unequal along race and social class lines. School choice, then, is not new but is now occurring in a rapidly changing, more highly charged context in which the outcomes will have even greater consequences than at any time in our past. Unfortunately, these sociological forces that affect the context within which people make choices will likely be too potent for a market-based reform such as vouchers to overcome. In other words, our data suggest that a bold effort on the part of the government to subsidize parental choice in education via tuition vouchers will only exacerbate this inequality by giving well-resourced parents a discount on their cost of procuring what they see to be the best education for their children, while draining resources from the public schools that will continue to enroll the vast majority of poor students and students of color.

Furthermore, we see from our data that even a targeted voucher program that provided funds only for low-income students or those in the worst schools, unless funded at an extremely high level—for example, about 10 times the size of the very small vouchers offered in places like Milwaukee and Cleveland—would not even come close to overcoming the asset gap between poor families of color and White and affluent families. In other words, even under the scenario of a $15,000-a-student voucher plan targeted exclusively toward low-income students in high-poverty neighborhoods, there would still be the issue of whether the voucher recipients could even gain access to the "better" schools—public or private—and, if so, how they would get to such schools on a daily basis. Given that there is nearly zero political support in this country for voucher plans that provide poor students with this much public tuition money and guaranteed access to their high-status school of choice (not to mention the daily transportation to get there), we argue that voucher programs, as currently constructed and conceptualized, will not alleviate the growing gaps between the educational "haves" and "have-nots." Indeed, our findings strongly suggest these programs will only exacerbate these problems.

RESEARCHING CURRENT SCHOOL CHOICES:
THE ASSETS AND INEQUALITY PROJECT

Our data come from a qualitative research study in which we interviewed nearly 200 Black and White families from three U.S. cities (Boston, St. Louis, and Los Angeles). The families interviewed represent a broad socioeconomic spectrum ranging from poor to working class to middle and upper-middle class. Each family included at least one school-aged child living in the home. Parents were asked in-depth questions about where they send their children to school and their school choice process. Interviews were conducted with couples and single heads of households, took place in the participants' homes or in another place of their choosing, and lasted from 1 to 3 hours each. In addition to questions about their school selections, we also asked parents about their assets, income, family background, and choice of neighborhood. The interviews took place between January 1998 and June 1999 and amount to over 7,000 pages of transcribed text. We masked individual identities by using pseudonyms and creative license with demographics. This qualitative data set is the first of its kind and well suited to provide insight into how families make decisions about where to send their children to school, what goes into these decisions, and how, in the minds of parents, school quality actually is defined.

Our interviews provide data that we believe to be especially relevant to the public voucher debate in the form of some significant knowledge about, and insights into, how parents frame school decisions when they have the kinds of "choices" that derive from wealth, assets, and financial resources. More specifically, these data allow us to examine two critically important issues that have strong bearing on the current voucher discussion.

1. We can explore the potential implications of vouchers for school diversity by examining the kinds of schools parents, who already have the private resources to make choices, are sending their children to.
2. As an integral part of parental decision making in this context, we can provide an analysis of how these parents construct school quality when choosing schools for their children.

Accordingly, our data offer insight into whether voucher plans and the deregulated form of parental school choice they facilitate would constitute the type of public policy needed to overcome the existing racial and social class inequality in the education system.

WHAT SCHOOL CHOICES ARE PARENTS MAKING NOW?

Like the communities in which they exist, and despite decades of court orders, America's schools remain widely segregated by race and class. A recurring theme of our interviews—that families with the assets to do so typically move to more prosperous, Whiter, and less diverse communities—

provides important insight into this process. We explore how families employ their resources to place their children in what they perceive to be the richest possible public and private educational environments. Under the current system, the primary way a family employs "school choice" is through picking where they live. Families often move to meet growing space needs when children are young as well as when their children first go off to school. At these critical times in the life course, assets become central in allowing families to strategize and negotiate residential and school landscapes imbued with racial hierarchy, and their decisions typically reinforce this racial inequality (Holme, 2002). The interviews reveal not only how and why families consciously look for homes according to school jurisdictions and reputations, but also the lengths to which parents with assets and wealth will go to get their children into the schools they want. Of course, financial resources allow them to do this.

It is clear from our interviews that when parents talk about their hopes for their children, they often disclose deep-seated class and racial anxieties. In fact, too often, the race and social class makeup of a school becomes a proxy for school quality, with White and affluent schools seen as the best in the absence of any concrete evidence of what is taking place within a school. Thus, for those who can afford to make such decisions, determining where to live or buy a home is a prime way in which inequality is passed along from generation to generation. In the present context of residential segregation and thus separate and unequal education systems, inequality often is reinforced by parents' choices of what they think is best for their children. The families we interviewed approach school decisions in an individualistic, market-like manner. Low-income families, White and Black, typically maneuver to overcome their own disadvantages and struggle to gain educational opportunity for their children. In contrast, families that are more affluent—and more likely to be White—use their resources to seek competitive educational advantages for their children and therefore pass their own status along. Our interviews reveal the ways these individualized family decisions are affected by and have impacts on dynamics of race and class inequality, and suggest the many ways in which a voucher program may well exacerbate the inequality within the system.

For instance, Mary Masterson, a single mother, lives in St. Louis with her two daughters, ages 12 and 7. Mary works as a child care center administrator. Her annual income is $18,480, net worth is $98,000, and net financial assets total $24,900. Mary grew up in a White, middle-class family and continues to receive financial support from her parents. This assistance has allowed Mary to have school options for her children that she otherwise would not have, given her income.

Mary and her daughters used to live in University City, a racially and socioeconomically integrated section of St. Louis County. But Mary started to get worried about what she was perceiving as an "edgy attitude," and she began to feel that she "needed to be out of U. City." Specifically, she wanted to get her daughters out of the schools there. She says, "It just feels like there's a, an edgy sort of attitude problem. The, the kids that were causing me the most concern were the kids who had the huge egos and the huge attitudes, and I just sensed danger." Mary says that she was particularly worried about crime and violence in the University City schools, especially in the junior high and high schools. She wanted to get her daughters out of the University City schools before her oldest reached junior high school age. With financial help from her parents, Mary was able to move her family out of University City and buy a house in Kirkwood—a predominantly White middle- to upper-middle-class suburban neighborhood of St. Louis.

Mary chose Kirkwood because she considers the schools there to be excellent. When asked what in her mind make these schools "excellent," she says she likes the "class" of people living there. Whiteness and affluence of a school population are markers of school quality for Mary. The reason she gives for being happy with the Kirkwood schools is that she likes "the reputation and economic class of this area." Mary says she is glad to have "escaped" University City and is clear about her intent having been to move her daughters to a Whiter, more affluent area so that they would be going to school with other children from "middle-class" families. She succeeded in this goal. Her daughters now attend a suburban public school with a White, middle- to upper-middle-class student population. In reflecting on her move, Mary says, "I'm glad they had the multicultural exposure in University City, um, but I'm sure they're getting a, a decent middle-class American education now. For what that's worth."

Mary's decision to move to Kirkwood for its schools was motivated primarily by her desire to place her children in Whiter, wealthier schools, not necessarily schools with higher academic standards. She is not alone or extraordinary in this view. In interview after interview we see a clear pattern emerge for White, middle-class parents. When it is possible, these families are using their financial resources to place their children in Whiter, wealthier, and less diverse school environments. These parents want high-quality education for their children, but their school choices are situated in social contexts thick with race and class perceptions and inequalities. Often White families purposefully choose the Whiter schools, and their decisions are racially motivated and racially charged as well as based on the perception (often accurate) that the Whiter, wealthier schools are of higher quality.

Families without the kinds of financial resources that make school choices possible are not able to act on their desires for their children's education in the same powerful ways. These families, a disproportionate number of whom are Black, are constrained by their lack of assets. They do not have the same mobility that other families have.

The Bryant family lives in Boston in a professional Black neighborhood. They have a 4-year-old son. Alice works as an upper-level administrative assistant for a local corporation. Her husband Bob is a freelance photographer. Their combined annual income is $51,500, their net worth is $17,000, but their net financial assets total negative $5,000. Alice and Bob cannot rely on their parents for financial help. In fact, the opposite is true: They often have to help out their parents financially.

When Alice and Bob had their son they felt they needed to move in order to access a good public school district for their son. They wanted to move to a suburban school district. They explain, though, that their financial constraints limited their options, and they ended up not being able to move to the kind of place where they really wanted to be—a place they thought had the better schools. Instead, they found that they could afford only the kinds of neighborhoods with "halfway decent schools." The neighborhood they moved into is in a working-class area of the city with schools that have fewer resources than those in more affluent suburban school districts. Alice and Bob wish that they could have moved further out to the suburbs where the schools are known to be better. Alice says, "I didn't have enough money to buy where I would really like to be." She goes on to explain the consequences she sees as a result of this: "He [her son] will not get the best education, not what most people would call the best education. He's going to get the best that we can afford to give him. There are schools that probably will give a lot better education, but we can't afford to send him there."

Alice and Bob have done the best they can for their son, but they can't compete with the advantage that Mary Masterson has from the financial support of her parents. Our interviews with Black families and families with low levels of financial resources show the stark contrast to families with more leverage. Families who are better off—families that are more likely than not to be White—simply have more school options. They have more mobility. They have real choices and they act on them.

The way families frame their options and subsequent actions centers around the ways in which they construct school quality. Parents say they are looking for "good schools." But what, to them, is a "good school"? How do parents define school quality when they make choices about where to send their children to school?

CONSTRUCTING SCHOOL QUALITY IN BLACK AND WHITE

In December 2000, the U.S. Department of Education published a report by the National Center for Education Statistics on school quality indicators. Based on a comprehensive review of recent research, the report identifies 13 key indicators of school quality thought to directly and indirectly affect student learning. These indicators of school quality are school leadership, school goals, professional community, discipline, academic environment, teacher academic skills, teaching assignment, teacher experience, professional development, course content, pedagogy, technology, and class size (National Center for Education Statistics, 2000). These are the characteristics that educational experts have identified as indicators of a good school. How do parents identify a good school? Do parents define school quality in ways related to the indicators? As families make school choices for their children and seek out good schools, how do they define school quality?

When choosing schools for their children, some of the parents we interviewed did consider school characteristics similar to some of the indicators of school quality identified by the Department of Education. One White middle-class mother explained what she and her husband had looked for in a school for their daughters.

> Smaller classrooms, a lot of parent involvement in the schools, I think that makes a big difference in the quality of education, the staff, the look and feel of the campuses, what kind of um, you know, what extracurricular things they have in the classroom. Computers, music, PE, the things that I would consider basic. . . . That's what I was looking for.

Another White middle-class parent, when asked what she was looking for, said, "I want small classrooms. I guess number one, I want good teachers. I think that is the most important thing. I want it to be safe. I want them to have good equipment."

Clearly, for these parents and some others, characteristics such as class size and technology resources help determine what a good school is. But, overwhelmingly, the parents we interviewed—especially the White parents—did not mention characteristics such as those identified by the Department of Education as indicators of school quality. Our interviews strongly suggest that other characteristics far outweigh such indicators and are much more at the forefront when these parents make school choices.

Over and over parents noted "reputation" as a key determining factor in where to send their children to school. Families with the resources
to make it happen often moved to particular residential areas based solely
on the local school district's reputation.

> *Interviewer:* How did you make the decision to send your children
>   to the Pierce School?
> *Don:* Well, generally Brookline schools have a better reputation
>   than Boston, which is why we moved here in the first place.

White middle-class parents often explained that "the prestige" of a
school and a school's "reputation of being a good school" were the reasons they chose it. But what, in the minds of parents, contributes to a good
reputation? Our interviews reveal that school reputation often is conflated
with characteristics quite different from the Department of Education's
school quality indicators. Rather, school reputation usually is tied directly
to the race and class composition of the student population. More often
than not we found that choosing a certain school, especially for most White
families, is really about avoiding other schools—particularly urban public
schools with high minority populations and low socioeconomic levels.
According to one parent:

> We specifically avoided the city because we did not want to have to
> deal with public education in the city. We avoided Hancock school
> district for the same thing, not that the education was any worse but
> that the, um, people that my children would have to associate with
> were not, um, up to par, as far as I'm concerned. It's like, city. Um,
> lower-class people.

School quality, for many White parents, is determined not by academic
excellence, teacher skills, or classroom curriculum, but by who sits next to
their child. Shauna Ferguson, a mother of two from St. Louis, says: "You
wouldn't want to send a child to the neighborhood schools." When asked why,
Shauna says, "The kids aren't getting great educations," because "anybody
and everybody goes there." Other schools, though, she explains, are different. They are better because they are more exclusive; not just "anybody and
everybody goes there." Public schools in "nicer areas" and private schools
are considered "good schools." Shauna, like many of the parents interviewed,
explains her reasoning for defining these as the good schools, as follows:

> The parents really have made the decision to go there, and they put
> more effort into their kids. That's really what it is. There's involve-

ment at home with the kids. So the kids come from an environment where the parents are interested in education, and support education. So the kids have a higher learning expectation, achievement level, etc.

Good schools often are defined by parents as those where "good" children from "good" families go to school. School quality becomes a proxy for student body composition as parents actively seek out schools for their children. Avoiding city schools seems to be specifically an attempt to avoid "urban" (i.e., African American and poor) populations more than it is an attempt to access high-quality academic facilities. A White working-class family from St. Louis, the Browns, also explain their school choice for their two young children as an attempt to avoid the city schools. Mike says, "Neither one of us wanted the kids to go to city schools." The Browns continue:

Mike: An underlying factor there, as far as the school that the kids would be going to is . . . it is in a probably 98% Black area.
Kim: Well it's around the projects, isn't it?
Mike: Right. It's not about the race, it's about the—it may even be the financial aspect of the people. The fact that they are in the projects. It's all subsidized housing, things like that. . . . So, like I say, while race may be an underlying factor, the Patrick Henry School, with the 10-foot fences with the barbed wire on top—that just doesn't sit well with me.

Despite what the Browns say about race versus social class, it was clear from our interviews that for them and many families like them, school quality is not just about a school's social class composition, but also explicitly about its racial composition. Specifically, often these parents purposely avoid sending their children to schools with large numbers of Blacks—even if it means compromising academics. The Staymans explained that they moved their daughter, Amy, out of a school they thought was academically quite excellent solely because of race.

Ginny: Well, Baldwin Hills School was 99% African American.
Matt: But, but I think that was actually a better school than Westside in terms of what they were demanding.
Ginny: Academically, right, but it was—I think Amy was the only White person in the classroom.

Our interviews suggest that the race and class atmosphere, in terms of who is attending schools, are key determining factors in how all families, but especially White families, choose schools. While parents actively avoid certain schools based on race and class composition, they also actively seek out other schools for the same reason. School quality, as defined by parents, often is based explicitly on the race and class identity of the residential areas where schools are located and the student populations schools serve. For instance, one father from Los Angeles discussed how he determines a "good school."

> *David:* Actually the public elementary school is almost as good or better than some of the private schools in the LA area, because it's such a nice area. The parents care, and some of the real rich people that live farther up the mountain, their kids go there, and [the] city councilman's kids go [to] that school. So, if it's good enough for him, it's a good school. The concern would be once they get out of the elementary school into the middle school, and especially the high school. Everyone is [in] one high school, so everyone from the whole town mixes together in high school, which is the bad elements of everywhere. So he [his son] would be exposed to more undesirable things and people.
>
> *Interviewer:* What are the undesirable things and people?
>
> *David:* Oh, probably some of the kids that are in gangs. Drugs. From the areas of South Monrovia where they have had drug problems, and you see graffiti, and you see old junker cars leaking oil in the street and trash all over, and beer cans on the grass. Whoever those people are, if they are going to the same high school, it makes you concerned, wonder if the kids are exposed to all of that. Whatever all of that is.
>
> *Interviewer:* Do you think those elements affect curriculum in any way?
>
> *David:* It would affect the atmosphere of the school, I guess.

When parents define school quality, the school "community," the "atmosphere," and who goes there are often more important than the actual academic quality. These characteristics often come first in the minds of parents, and the actual education—the academics—comes second. Jennifer Perrotto, a mother from Los Angeles who chose a private Catholic school for her children, explains what makes it a good school in her mind: "There's other mothers there that have the same desires as I do, and they all have the same faith." She goes on:

> I want my children to marry someone Catholic, so I need to expose them to other Catholic children. They also, their family values are

the same. And to me it's no longer education, it's the community
that it brought. . . . So there is education there, but the number
one thing is the community that I receive from there. And then
education.

Black families interviewed often spoke of similar considerations when
discussing their desires for schools for their children. Yvette Medina, a Black
middle-class mother from St. Louis, explains where she would like to send
her children to school and why she thinks the schools there are good.

> *Yvette:* If we were talking about the neighborhood that I really
> wanted to move in, it would probably be down further on
> Lindbergh in Maryland Heights. Those are some really nice
> homes. And I think that's the Parkway school district, which
> probably is a better school district.
> *Interviewer:* And what's the school district?
> *Yvette:* I'm not sure if it's Parkway or one of the other school
> districts. But I'm sure it's a pretty good school district, because
> they have really, really nice homes.
> *Interviewer:* You just assume the schools are better because the
> homes are better?
> *Yvette:* Probably so . . . I mean, it's West County. Everybody out
> there is rich. My doctor's kids go there. And I know he's got
> money. He's a specialist. . . . So I know he's got plenty of
> money.

Angela Slater, a Black middle-class mother from Los Angeles who
sends her children to a private school, explains how important the "environment" of the school is.

> It's not only the academics that I'm concerned about. You know I
> have to be concerned about the environment, the community, you
> know? Because who is to say where [their] attention will lie, you
> know? I have hopes that it will lie on the books and academics but
> they're kids, you know? They are influenced by their peers. So I
> have to be concerned about that as well.

Angela goes on to explain that by controlling where children go to school
parents can control who their peers are, the "element" they are exposed to.

> You can control the element by who can afford to go there. I mean
> you know, you know, for example, it costs ten to fifteen thousand

dollars a year for children to go to elementary school. So there is only a certain element that is going to be there. You know what I'm saying? So yea, it is controlled by that.

While Black families were in many ways similar to White families in the kinds of schools they were seeking for their children, they were different in other ways. An overarching theme of our interviews with Black families was "diversity," which they consistently brought up as an important factor in their school choice decisions. Black families, like White families, didn't want their children in all-minority schools. But unlike White families, Black families purposefully sought some racial and cultural diversity; they didn't want their children in all-White schools. Susan Molloy explains why she thinks her children's school is a good school: "Well, it's a very diverse school—economically, socially, and racially—and I like that a lot." Meta Joseph, a Black middle-class mother from Boston, explains why she thinks her daughter's school is a good school: "Diversity. A lot of kids from lots of different places—which I like . . . she's made a lot of friends from a lot of different places, and I like that. Black, White, Asian, Hispanic. I like that. I think that's important." For Black families, "diversity"—meaning not all-White, but also not all-Black—is an important characteristic in determining where to send their children to school. This contrasts with White families, who often seek out all-White schools and purposefully avoid diversity.

Both Black and White families focus intently on the atmosphere of the school, the environment, and who goes there. This often becomes of the utmost concern, a priority even above the academic quality of a school. Families who can afford to act on their conceptions of school quality place their children in schools that match these conceptions. A White middle-class mother explains her decision to send her children to private schools in the suburbs: "Quite frankly, neither my husband or I would want to see our children in the city school system. There's just too many problems that we know too much about. And we're able to afford it, so that's what we do."

Families with resources to do so use their assets to ensure advantageous schooling environments for their children. Because of the relationship between race and assets, these actions—sometimes intentionally and sometimes not—further perpetuate and increase class and racial segregation because parents with resources choose communities and schools that are more homogeneous and less diverse. This was especially true of the choices made by White parents, while Black parents were more likely to seek out racially diverse schools if they could find them and gain access to them. Such choices, in turn, further perpetuate educational inequity and exacerbate race and class inequalities.

SCHOOL CHOICES IN THE REPRODUCTION
OF CLASS AND RACE INEQUALITY

Our data show how elite and financially well-off parents—as they have historically—use their financial assets to ensure privileges for their children. Middle-class and White families organize their assets in an effort to attain educational advantages for their children. Meanwhile, poor and African American families attempt to gain a piece of the American dream by acquiring educational opportunities that are often out of their reach in a highly segregated society.

One clear consequence of this process, as signaled by our data, is that it increases both class and racial segregation at the cost of equity and diversity. In other words, our data raise the specter of increasing resegregation and more inequality in schools created by the choices made by parents with assets. We argue that White families in particular use their resources and their associated neighborhood and school choices to sort their children into communities and schools that are "better" in their view, which, not coincidentally, are Whiter and more affluent. Finally, under current circumstances, we are convinced that White and affluent families simply will use voucher-type plans to further exacerbate class and race inequalities in a more systematic and government-subsidized fashion. Meanwhile, although Black parents may seek out more-diverse schools, we have learned that it is often difficult for them to do so. A small voucher that is less than a third of the per-pupil funding in elite public schools or less than a third of the tuition at an elite private school—the size of vouchers in existing plans— will do virtually nothing to help these families move to the schools they most desire for their children.

The growth and dispersion of wealth over several decades along with the transition to a service economy and a diminishing civic role of the state have heightened the salience of wealth in determining opportunities, life chances, and capacities. Federal and state budget cuts over the past 20 years have weakened and diminished further the public role in developing basic civic capacities. The power of the political right and the acquiescence of others have reduced and weakened the state's role in education, housing, and health care. It costs families more to provide shelter, education, and health care, and with a shrinking state presence the differences must be made up by family resources. For those who lack such resources, those differences often are not made up at all. This changing context places a greater burden on family assets to provide opportunities and, typically, the unequal distribution of these opportunities becomes the source of further inequality.

Given our research findings and the present context, we conclude by bluntly raising a disturbing question: Should the public be subsidizing initiatives and experiments that foster less opportunity and diversity by instituting a publicly funded voucher system? One of the strongest findings from our interviews is that White families, in particular, who can afford to, choose to send their children to schools that are more segregated by race and class. If vouchers are adopted on a more widespread basis, our data indicate that the choices parents make will lead to even more segregated, Whiter, more affluent schools. Universal voucher programs that provide vouchers for all families in spite of income will only facilitate the process, with the state more fully subsidizing a movement to less diversity. Others also have argued that proposals for private school vouchers are likely to lead to greater, not less, economic stratification in schools and to reduce equality of opportunity (see Chapter 11, this volume; Kahlenberg & Leone, 2001). But here we provide more than simply an argument; our data reveal the consequences of the current school choices that families are making. Our findings indicate that race, as a determinant of perceived school quality, is key to how parents who currently have choices are choosing schools for their children. The implications and consequences of the choices have widespread predictive ramifications for the future use of vouchers in this society. Vouchers, we argue, would only create extensions of the patterns we see now—namely, greater segregation and stratification created by parents who have the assets to make the school choice system work for them. Voucher plans simply will allow these better-endowed parents to make the same "better" choices, but with a government-subsidized discount. Such evidence, we argue, should inform the current voucher debate and the policy decisions we make as we try to bring equity back to the reform agenda.

To understand the implications of our findings, one does not need to believe that the large majority of parents are acting from a racist stance—although some clearly are. Rather, we must consider their actions and assumptions about schools in the context of the increasing importance attached to a high-quality education for economic success in the global economy. In this context, a highly stratified education system and middle-class social apprehension combine to produce an environment where parents feel compelled to gain more and more opportunities or advantages for their children. Parents then make individual, rational decisions that make the most sense to them. Families act in racialized ways because the structure rewards them for doing so. We suggest that the current parental frenzy over children's schooling has broad implications. In the process of seeking educational advantages, Whites often resegregate themselves and their children in schools and communities that look like them, and pass inequality along. If we, as a society, make this easier for them and even subsidize these actions, then we facilitate the reproduction of class and race inequality.

Many parents have choices now. They are making "good" choices in their opinion. They are choosing what they conceptualize as the good schools (even if their perception of school quality often rests primarily on the characteristics of the students who attend a school). Indeed, because of a context in which poor and minority-populated educational environments are disproportionately underfunded and suffering from lack of resources, these parents choose what are, by most standards, the "better" schools. Still, we find that parents too often use the race and class of the student population as a proxy for school quality, and thus the social consequence of these structurally framed individual actions is that we recreate, reconstruct, and remake inequity (educational, economical, social, and political). The research presented here tells us that if the future era of reform is a future of vouchers, we will be doing the opposite of bringing equity back to American educational policy.

REFERENCES

Cookson, P. W., Jr. (1994). *School choice: The struggle for the soul of American education*. New Haven, CT: Yale University Press.

Duncan, O. D. (1968). Inheritance of poverty or inheritance of race. In D. P. Moynihan (Ed.), *On understanding poverty* (pp. 85–109). New York: Basic Books.

Holme, J. J. (2002, Summer). Buying homes, buying schools: School choice and the social construction of school quality. *Harvard Educational Review, 72*(2), 177–205.

Hoxby, C. M. (1999). The effects of school choice on curriculum and atmosphere. In S. E. Mayer & P. E. Peterson (Ed.), *Earning and learning: How schools matter* (pp. 281–316). Washington, DC: Brookings Institution.

Jencks, C., & Phillips, M. (Eds.). (1998). *The black–white test score gap*. Washington, DC: Brookings Institution.

Kahlenberg, R., & Leone, R. (2001). *All together now: Creating middle-class schools through public school choice*. New York: Century Foundation Press.

Massey, D. S., & Denton, N. A. (1993). *American apartheid: Segregation and the making of the underclass*. Cambridge, MA: Harvard University Press.

Mortenson, T. (2000). *Bachelor's degree attainment by age 24 by family income quartiles, 1970 to 1999*. Washington, DC: Postsecondary Education Opportunity. Available: http://www.postsecondary.org.

National Center for Education Statistics. (2000, December). *Monitoring school quality: An indicators report*. Washington, DC: U.S. Department of Education.

Oliver, M., & Shapiro, T. M. (1997). *Black wealth/white wealth: A new perspective on racial inequality*. New York: Routledge.

Oliver, M., & Shapiro, T. M. (2001). Wealth and racial stratification. In N. J. Smelser,

W. J. Wilson, & F. Mitchell (Eds.), *America becoming: Racial trends and their consequences* (Vol. I, pp. 222–251). Washington, DC: National Academy Press.

Orfield, G., & Yun, J. T. (1999). *Resegregation in American schools.* Cambridge, MA: The Civil Rights Project, Harvard University.

Peterson, P. E., & Hassel, B. C. (Eds.). (1998). *Learning from school choice.* Washington, DC: Brookings Institution.

11

Do School Vouchers Lead to Greater Social Equity?

MARTIN CARNOY
PATRICK J. McEWAN

Expanding school choice to include private schools is now part and parcel of America's social equity debate. The idea that educational choice could equalize opportunity is not new. In the 1960s and early 1970s, academics on the left, such as Christopher Jencks (1966), argued that the vast differences between the quality of public schooling for inner-city Blacks and suburban Whites could not be resolved within the structure of a residentially segregated public education system (see also Coons, Clune, & Sugarman, 1970). Jencks advocated a policy concept introduced by Milton Friedman (1955) more than a decade earlier—namely, offering public funds to families that could be used in any educational institution, public or private. Such "vouchers" would serve to give families increased choice in the kind of education their children received. Friedman saw vouchers as a way to break the "monopoly" of the public sector over education and increase consumer choice and hence economic welfare. Jencks saw vouchers as a way of improving educational opportunities for a group historically discriminated against within American society. Both shared a distrust of the state—Friedman of the bureau-centric state interfering with "democratic" markets, Jencks of the class/race-centric state reproducing inequality through public education.

Voucher advocates consistently have claimed that because public education is a government monopoly, it inherently denies consumers free choice in their children's education (Chubb & Moe, 1990; Friedman, 1955, 1962). This leaves them worse off than they would be under competitive conditions, for two reasons. Many consumers are less than optimally satisfied and would choose an educational alternative if they could, and schools are not compelled to produce as much output as they would (for the same cost) if they faced competition. Providing vouchers to students allegedly would solve both of these problems. Vouchers would induce private education providers to compete for public school students, giving consumers educational opportunities not previously available. They would force poor-performing public schools simultaneously to improve or lose students.

Friedman also argued that private providers would supply the same quality schooling at a lower price than the public sector. He derived this argument from his claim that the public education system is a monopoly, providing schooling at a higher price than would prevail under competition. For Friedman, "monopoly excess profit" accrues to teachers as higher wages per hour than they would receive if schooling were competitive and privatized. Indeed, the potentially cost-lowering impact of vouchers has always been central to Friedman's position, whereas Jencks's support for vouchers focused on the increased effectiveness of autonomous public and private schooling, especially in low-income urban areas. Today's voucher advocates, from a Friedman free-market position, have incorporated Jencks's argument that private schools are more *effective*—namely, that they are able to deliver higher educational achievement than public schools—into Friedman's claim that they are more efficient, as they can do so at lower cost per pupil (Chubb & Moe, 1990; Howell, Wolf, Peterson, & Campbell, 2000).

Nearly 4 decades after Friedman's proposal, the voucher debate is still embedded in this complex political mixture of conservatives who want to dismantle the public education system altogether and advocates for long-suffering urban minorities, who want a better education for poor and minority children. Several new ingredients have been introduced into this mixture. First, the U.S. Supreme Court ruled in *Zelman* v. *Simmons-Harris* (2002) that vouchers are constitutional—at least under the U.S. Constitution. Second, voucher proponents in the United States have pushed their idea much further into the public's political consciousness, and some members of minority groups have themselves taken up the voucher cause (for example, Howard Fuller in Milwaukee). Third, several countries and a number of localities in the United States have implemented voucher plans, based on both public and private funding, and researchers have tested their effects empirically. These evaluations provide insight into whether the hopes of voucher proponents can be realized.

In light of these recent developments, which point in the direction of more, not fewer, U.S.-based voucher programs in the near future, our main concern in this chapter is whether vouchers produce greater social equity— namely, more equal educational opportunity and a greater sense by consumers of educational services that they are being treated equally. Thus, we examine evidence from U.S. voucher programs and an extensive and long-running voucher policy in Chile, where we have conducted extensive research. We conclude that there is little systematic evidence that voucher programs promote greater social equity and that the context and specifics of these programs make a significant difference in how effective the programs are in improving educational quality.

Still, voucher advocates claim that these programs promote equity in at least four ways.

1. Vouchers provide educational choice to low-income families who do not have the resources to move to higher-income neighborhoods or send their children to private schools. Greater choice increases the satisfaction that low-income parents feel, and hence makes them feel better off.
2. Vouchers provide access to higher-quality (more academically effective) private schools for low-income pupils currently attending low-quality public schools. Access to private schools increases the academic gains that children from low-income families achieve, leading to higher educational attainment and higher incomes.
3. Vouchers increase competition for public school pupils, inducing low-performing public schools to improve, and thereby improving education for children in all schools.
4. Vouchers increase the public resources available for expanding schooling services because most private schools educate students at lower cost than most public schools. Theoretically, then, this more efficient system and its reduced schooling costs also should provide the resources to expand education or improve it.

In fact, voucher advocates argue that all four effects would help close the educational achievement and attainment gaps between low- and high-income pupils, and hence lead to greater social equity. Some of these claims have been tested in small-scale settings in the United States, and they provide empirical results on whether low-income students do better academically in private than in public schools. But despite some positive aspects of small-scale, quasi-experimental and experimental studies analyzing the effects of vouchers, they also have serious limitations (for a summary of experimental studies, see Benveniste, Carnoy, & Rothstein, 2002; Carnoy, 2001; Howell et al., 2000; McEwan, 2001). Since only small numbers of low-income students participate in these experiments, they tell us little about the supply response of private education to vouchers. They also tell us nothing about the potential impact of competition on the performance of students in public schools (Neal, 1998), and nothing about whether private schools would produce outcomes at lower cost than public schools. The little information we have on costs in voucher schools (for example, in Milwaukee) suggests the schools quickly demand a voucher amount equal to costs per pupil in public schools.

Until now, voucher experiments in the United States have been *targeted*—limited to low-income students—mainly because many low-income families are dissatisfied with their neighborhood public schools and because in urban areas there is considerable excess capacity in existing religious schools. Evaluations have been carried out with a specific focus on the gains to such students. But this masks another political reality. Most voucher advocates, including Milton Friedman, are politically committed to more widespread use of vouchers. They believe that public funding of private school choice should be available to every American family. Indicative of that commitment are the two statewide voucher initiatives in California and one in Michigan that would have made vouchers available to all students regardless of income level. Even though all three of these initiatives failed at the ballot box—because of suburban voters' support for their public schools—the fact that they got on the ballot demonstrates a political commitment in those states to the universal voucher idea.

Thus, it is important to remember that the voucher issue in the United States has been deeply embedded both in a broader, conservative, anti-public school ideology, and simultaneously in the practical demands of low-income parents for better schooling—public or private. Still, from the perspective of the more conservative market reformers, vouchers make all parents and children better off because of choice and competition, and thus private school choice should be made available to all parents, regardless of income. Indeed, because this is the long-term goal of many who support vouchers in the United States, it is critical that parents, educators, and policymakers understand the implications for social equity of *general* voucher plans, not just targeted ones.

We can gain insights into these issues by examining the limited and targeted U.S. experiments more carefully and by looking outside the United States to school systems where vouchers have been implemented on a large scale, and where private school supply has increased substantially. Chile is probably the single best example, worldwide, for studying the effects of vouchers, although the New Zealand case rightfully has also gained recent attention (Fiske & Ladd, 2000; Lauder & Hughes, 1999).

VOUCHER EXPERIMENTS IN THE UNITED STATES

Although an earlier voucher experiment was funded by the Nixon administration in the 1970s in northern California's Alum Rock school district, the current push for vouchers in the United States began in Milwaukee in 1990–91. Since then, other voucher experiments have been legislated in Cleveland (1996, Florida (1998), and Washington, DC (2003), and privately funded voucher experiments initiated in a number of cities, notably New York, Washington, DC, and Dayton, OH (1999), Charlotte, NC (2000), and San Antonio (2000). Over the past decade, voucher experiments have been evaluated or are being evaluated in Milwaukee, Cleveland, New York City, Dayton, Washington, DC, Charlotte, and San Antonio. Florida also has a voucher plan in place, but only a few vouchers have been issued in two "failing" public schools. Wisconsin's Supreme Court has found in favor of the Milwaukee's expanded plan, which also awards vouchers that are being used mainly in religious schools. Meanwhile, the Ohio and Florida Supreme Courts found those states' voucher plans unconstitutional because publicly funded vouchers were being used in religious schools. The Cleveland case was appealed to the U.S. Supreme Court, which agreed to hear it and then ruled in the summer of 2002, in *Zelman* v. *Simmons-Harris,* that channeling public money to parents who choose among a variety of schooling options, including religious schools, does not violate the Establishment Clause of the First Amendment to the U.S. Constitution (see Kemerer, 2002). Yet as Kemerer points out, the long-term implications of this landmark ruling are not yet known and could vary greatly from state to state given many state constitutional prohibitions against the use of public money for religious education.

Thus, the action remains at the state level, where, other than in the expanded Milwaukee program, the existing voucher plans are small in the number of students reached and limited to very low-income families. Furthermore, the evaluations to date have focused on parent satisfaction with choice and the relative achievement gains of students who receive vouchers and use them to attend private schools. No matter whether the evaluators are neutral or pro-vouchers, their results show that families receiving vouchers are significantly more satisfied with their children's new schools than parents who did not receive vouchers and had to keep their children in public school. This is not surprising. Parents who apply for vouchers, whether they are chosen to receive them or not, are highly dissatisfied with their children's public school and want a change. Switching their children to a private school is likely to make them feel that their children are better off.

Achievement Gains in the Milwaukee Choice Program

The results for academic achievement gains are more mixed, and often depend on whether the researchers are voucher advocates. The first experiment, in Milwaukee, initially involved seven private schools and a few hundred very low-income students, chosen by lottery from a larger number of applicants. Although 1,500 vouchers of $2,500 were offered, private schools made available a fraction of this number of places (the schools had to be secular in the original Milwaukee experiment). In a few years, however, under pressure from private schools themselves, the amount of the voucher rose to the level of per-pupil spending in Milwaukee public schools, about $5,500, a figure close to the primary school public cost per pupil when special education costs are accounted for. As the voucher amount rose, so did the number of schools and the number of places. More than 800 students participated in the 1995–96 school year.

The Wisconsin state legislature commissioned University of Wisconsin professor John Witte and his colleagues to evaluate the experiment over a 5-year period. They found no significant differences in reading and math score gains between voucher—"choice"—students and a sample of students from similar socioeconomic backgrounds in Milwaukee public schools. The only effect that approached statistical significance was a negative relative gain in reading score for those who had been in private schools for 2 years (Witte, Sterr, & Thorn, 1995).

In 1996, Harvard professor Paul Peterson and his colleagues used the same data to compare voucher students with those who applied but did not receive vouchers. The Peterson group (Greene, Peterson, & Du, 1996) found that voucher students made significantly larger gains in both reading and math by their third and fourth years in private schools. Witte (1997) responded by arguing that large numbers of nonrecipients had disappeared from the sample by the third and fourth years, and others entered private religious schools under a privately financed scholarship program but were not in the comparison group. This, Witte argued, explained the Peterson result.

Princeton public policy professor Cecilia Rouse then redid the analysis yet a different way, accounting for student "fixed effects" (student attributes that do not change over time, such as race, gender, ethnicity, socioeconomic background, and what she calls "native ability"). She found some math score gains for voucher recipients in the third and fourth years but no reading gains (Rouse, 1998a). She also found that low-income students in a group of experimental public schools with lower class sizes outperformed voucher students in private schools (Rouse, 1998b).

In 1997 the Wisconsin legislature expanded the voucher program to 15,000 low-income students, and included religious schools. Initially, after this expansion, about 8,000 students took up the vouchers, which continued to be worth about the cost of Milwaukee's per-pupil spending on primary education ($5,500 in 1997). In the first year, about one-third of voucher takers under this expanded program were already in private schools but qualified because of their low family incomes. Even so, the supply of new schools to take advantage of a fairly large voucher materialized rather slowly. Private schools not in operation when vouchers were offered had to be approved, limiting the supply of new schools. Only 8,000 pupils had taken vouchers by the year 2000. Also, most voucher pupils were in kindergarten and first grade. By the school year 2001–02, about 10,000 children had used vouchers at over 100 mostly religious private schools (Williams, 2000). In 2002–03, the number grew to almost 12,000, a significant fraction of Milwaukee's 100,000 public school students and 25,000 private school students. Even if only 6,000 of the voucher students transferred from public schools, the voucher program shifted almost 6% of Milwaukee's public school students to private schools.

This suggests that given a large enough voucher, many low-income families will take advantage of it, and at least some new schools will come into the market. However, no one knows whether voucher students are performing better in this expanded program because, unlike public school students, they are not required by the legislature to take state tests, and no evaluation program is written into the legislation. We also know little about how many students who took up vouchers returned to public schools within a year or two in a private school.

Achievement Gains in Cleveland's Voucher Plan

A similar conflict emerged between researchers over the academic gains achieved by students in Cleveland's voucher program, which was approved by the Ohio legislature in June 1995 and began in the 1996–97 school year with a maximum voucher of $2,500. The Cleveland program differed from the Milwaukee experiment in several important aspects. In Cleveland, more than twice as many vouchers were offered as in Milwaukee (3,700 versus 1,500). Unlike in Milwaukee, Cleveland families had to add funds to the voucher in order to attend private schools, both because the voucher covered only part of the tuition and because private schools could charge higher tuition than the voucher amount. As in Milwaukee, the program got off to a slow start, with only about 1,500 students taking advantage of the vouchers. Many of the children receiving vouchers were scheduled to enter kindergarten in 1995, just as Cleveland abolished full-day kindergarten in the public schools. This could have influenced parents to take vouchers. About 25% of Cleveland's vouchers were offered to families with children already in private schools, and vouchers in Cleveland could be used in religious schools, as they later were in the expanded Milwaukee program. About 80% of families in the Cleveland program sent their children to Catholic and other parochial schools. Almost all the others went to Hope Schools—two private for-profit schools created by David Brennan, a wealthy entrepreneur, especially to take advantage of voucher availability. Brennan had been instrumental in getting the voucher program through the Ohio legislature, but was unable to raise the value of the voucher once he realized that his schools were losing money at the $2,500 level. He subsequently converted the Hope Schools into charters to take advantage of higher levels of financing. This left almost all voucher students attending religious schools.

Evaluations of Cleveland vouchers are in even greater disagreement than the Milwaukee analyses. The Peterson group (Greene, Howell, & Peterson, 1997) focused on the two Hope Schools and looked at students in all grades. They found higher levels of parent satisfaction in the Hope Schools, and significant test score gains from Fall 1996 to Spring 1997 by students who started in one of the four grades in 1996 . The Ohio legislature contracted researchers from Indiana University, headed by Kim Metcalf, to conduct the state's evaluation. The researchers (Metcalf et al., 1998) chose to base their evaluation on 3rd-grade students and continued to follow them into 4th grade. Like in Milwaukee, the attrition rate from private schools was substantial from the first to the second year of the program. Between year 1 and year 2, 26 third graders in non-Hope Schools did not return to the program (approximately 20%). These were students who achieved significantly lower than other voucher students in 3rd grade even though all had statistically similar 2nd-grade test results. All left the Cleveland school district.

Keeping attrition in mind, second-year results showed that 4th-grade voucher students in the established, non-Hope private schools scored significantly higher in language and science, but not in other subjects, than public school students. Students in the Hope Schools, however, scored significantly lower in all subjects than either public school students or students in non-Hope schools (Metcalf et al., 1998). The differences in scores between voucher students in non-Hope schools and public school students were smaller when socioeconomic differences were taken into account, but Hope students still had significantly lower scores. As in the case of Milwaukee, Metcalf et al. (1998) found that private school classes had fewer students per teacher than classes in public schools.

Randomized Voucher Trials in Four Cities

The latest round of voucher evaluations focuses on privately financed "scholarship"—that is, voucher—programs for low-income children to attend private schools in Dayton, New York City, and Washington, DC (Howell et al., 2000). The programs established lotteries for parents who applied, gave applicants a baseline test, awarded scholarships to applicants at random, then later tested children who did and did not receive them. Some families who got vouchers did not actually send their children to private school, either because they could not come up with the extra tuition or because they could not find conveniently located private schools to accept their children. These programs differ from the Milwaukee experiment but are like the Cleveland program. Private schools in Milwaukee are not allowed to charge tuition above the voucher, but they are allowed to in Cleveland. The studies estimated test score differences over time between all students who received vouchers and those who did not, and between students who used vouchers and those who did not receive them and remained in public schools.

Results for Dayton, New York, and Washington, DC show no significant test score gains for Hispanic and White voucher recipients after 1, 2, or 3 years in private schools. Reading and math gains for African Americans using vouchers in private schools were found to be statistically significant in New York and Washington, DC, after 2 years. In Dayton, only reading gains were statistically significant, and then just marginally. Reported gains for African Americans were largest in Washington, DC, after 2 years. However, in the third-year follow-up, only African American students in the New York City experiment showed significant gains. Such a small number of voucher students remained in Dayton private schools by the third year that statistical tests were meaningless. The Washington, DC gains, largest in year 2, evaporated in year 3 (Howell & Peterson, 2002).

The second-year follow-up findings were widely hailed by voucher supporters across the political spectrum as proof that private schools could solve a problem public schools apparently could not—raise the lagging achievement of low-income, inner-city Black children. But soon after the second-year results for Dayton, New York, and Washington, DC were presented, a member of the Peterson team, the contractor for the New York City part of the research, openly challenged Peterson and colleagues' interpretation, arguing that the New York second-year results did not show voucher students—even African Americans—with a statistically significant advantage (Zernike, 2000). Most of the citywide gain reported by Peterson and colleagues for the New York City sample of African American voucher students in private schools came from one relatively small group of African Americans in the experiment, namely, 5th-grade voucher recipients. That group had made large and statistically significant gains in the first year of the experiment and maintained them in the second year. In the third-year follow-up, voucher proponents could point to some significant gains in math scores for New York City voucher users in other groups, such as African American students who were in 4th grade in the first year of the experiment and stayed in private schools for the full 3 years. Added to the 5th-grade cohort, which had maintained its gains into the third year, the proponents used the third-year follow-up to make even greater claims for vouchers, no less than eliminating the Black–White test score gap (Howell & Peterson, 2002). These claims were made despite the evaporation of gains in Dayton and Washington, DC, and the study's failure to show any significant differences for Latino voucher recipients.

Closer scrutiny of the main three voucher evaluations, including the evaluation in New York City, reveals problems other than the great variability of results across grades, across ethnic/racial groups, and across cities. For example, all the studies were characterized by relatively large numbers of students who dropped out of the sample and were not tested after the first year. The researchers made some attempt to correct the results for such losses, but without knowing whether the many African American voucher students who left private schools after the first year were those with the greatest academic problems, it is impossible to tell how biased the third-year results are. This and other issues should make us hesitant about the accuracy of the results (Carnoy, 2001). The controversies over earlier voucher studies in Milwaukee and Cleveland, where researchers other than the Peterson group had access to the data, seem to support this more skeptical view.

Summary of U.S. Findings

The results of the U.S. voucher studies to date suggest that there may be some small academic gains to low-income students who switch from public to private schools thanks to vouchers. These gains seem limited to African Americans, and they seem to occur only when students enter *existing* private schools, usually in small numbers in each school. Almost all such schools are religious schools. The second phase of the Milwaukee voucher plan suggests that when vouchers are targeted, new private schools are willing to enter a market for low-income students, but we have no information about the quality of these schools. Most of them are non-

Catholic religious schools. In Milwaukee, the voucher is valued at essentially the full per-pupil cost of a public primary school education, so there is no cost savings to the public sector from the voucher program. Yet the voucher is large enough to attract newly formed private schools into the market, some of them nonreligious. In the most recent voucher experiments in Dayton, New York, and Washington, DC, the value of the voucher is no higher than $1,700, far below public school per-pupil cost in those cities. The Hope Schools in Cleveland were one of the few nonreligious schools to accept low-value vouchers, capped at $2,500. But they quickly opted to become charter schools, qualifying for the full public school per-pupil amount, when the Ohio legislature refused to raise the value of the Cleveland voucher. The Cleveland experiment suggests that only existing religious schools are willing to participate in a low-value voucher program, and then mainly to fill vacant places.

According to voucher advocates, U.S. results imply major improvements in social equity from vouchers, especially for African Americans. However, this would mean that the academic gains found in the most optimistic versions of these studies would have to be duplicated in much larger groups of students shifting from public to private schools, if such private schools were willing to provide education to the students wishing to shift. Voucher researchers admit that they have no evidence whether this would be the case (Howell et al., 2000).

Yet there exist other voucher plans that can give us clues to the results for social equity and overall academic gains when vouchers are offered on a large scale. The largest program is in the South American country of Chile, and it can teach us lessons about the equity effects of vouchers that voucher experiments in the United States cannot.

THE CHILEAN VOUCHER PLAN

Influenced by Milton Friedman's proposal (Valdes, 1995), in 1980 Chile's military government transferred responsibility for public school management from the national Ministry of Education to local municipalities and began financing public and most private schools with vouchers (for descriptions of the Chilean reforms, see especially Gauri, 1998; Jofre, 1988; and Parry 1997a, 1997b).

Education Reform in Chile

In order to understand how the Chilean education system came to be controlled and financed in this way, it is important to look back historically to the early 1970s and the military regime that ruled the country at that time.

The Military Regime, 1973–1980. At the time of the military coup d'etat in 1973, Chile's education system was one of the most developed in Latin America. It had achieved near-universal enrollment in primary education, a feat that still eludes much of Latin America (Castaneda, 1992; Schiefelbein, 1991). A *dirigiste* Ministry of Education assumed exclusive responsibility for administering the public schools. One-fifth of Chile's primary school students attended private schools. About half of these schools were under the auspices of the Catholic Church (Espinola, 1993). Following a long tradition of public support of private education, many also received partial subsidies from the national government that covered about 30% of costs in 1980 (Larranaga, 1995).

Upon assuming power in 1973, the military government disbanded the teachers' union and fired teachers with leftist views (Parry, 1997a, 1997b). It also initiated a massive administrative reorganization, dividing the country into 13 regions, and the latter into provinces and over 300 municipalities. For each level of the government, the President appointed governors and mayors, drawn mainly from the ranks of the military. During the 1970s, the Ministry of Education, in addition to other ministries, devolved some powers to Regional Ministry Secretariats, which were charged with administrative and supervisory duties formerly performed by the central ministry. Despite the apparent move toward decentralization, the system often functioned as a military chain of command, organized to implement central government directives (Parry, 1997a). Mayors of municipalities would not be elected democratically until 1992.

The Education Reform, 1980–1990. In 1980 the military government initiated a sweeping reform. It first transferred responsibility for public school management from the Ministry of Education to local municipalities. Once transferred to municipalities, schools were placed under the control of one of two kinds of institutions. Most opted to manage their schools with a Departmento de Administración de la Educación Municipal (DAEM). DAEMs exist under the larger umbrella of the municipal bureaucracy and, as such, are governed by municipal rules. Corporations are a second form of municipal schools. They are nonprofit organizations that are not subject to direct mayoral control, although the mayor does preside over a governing board. Their operations are generally subject to fewer regulations. In contrast to DAEMs, the corporation head is not required to be a teacher, and corporation employees are not subjected to rules regarding the hiring and remuneration of municipal employees.

Furthermore, school buildings and land, which had been owned by the national government, were signed over to municipal control (Gauri, 1998; Parry, 1997a). Initial transfers proceeded rapidly, encouraged by financial incentives, and by 1982 around 84% of schools were operated by municipalities. Municipalities received an overhead grant of 3–5% of total municipal wages and salaries as an inducement to begin administering schools (Parry, 1997a; Winkler & Rounds, 1996). The process was interrupted by an economic crisis in 1982 when the central government was unable to cover the costs of transfers, but by 1987 all schools had been transferred (Jofre, 1988).

As schools were transferred to municipalities, public teachers were offered severance pay and became municipal rather than national employees (Castaneda, 1992). Instead of conforming to the national Escala Única de Remuneraciones, their wages and working conditions were henceforth governed by the more flexible Código de Trabajo that governed private-sector employment and was even less supportive of employees than the minimal protections accorded American workers under U.S. labor laws. Teachers, therefore, lost guarantees of job security, the right to salary during vacations, standard wage scales, a 30-hour work week, and the right to collectively bargain (Rojas, 1998). Teachers in private schools also lost some legal protections, including minimum wage guarantees and a system of annual salary adjustments.

Coupled with decentralization, the government drastically altered how public and most private schools were financed. Prior to 1980, as in much of Latin America, school budgets were largely determined by the need to sustain existing teachers and facilities. If budgets adjusted in response to the level of student enrollments, they did so only at a sluggish pace. Many private schools were already being subsidized by the government before 1980, meeting the rest of their costs with tuition payments and Church support—about 14% of students attended mainly Catholic, subsidized schools and another 6%, high-cost, nonsubsidized private schools.

Under the reform, the Ministry of Education began disbursing monthly payments to municipalities based on a fixed voucher multiplied by the number of students enrolled in their schools; private schools received equivalent per-pupil payments if they did not charge tuition. Thus, payments to public and private schools began fluctuating in direct proportion to student enrollments.

The law established a base voucher level, which varies according to the level of education and the location of the school. Chilean law specifies a factor by which the base voucher is adjusted for students at every grade level. Furthermore, selected municipalities receive ad hoc "zone assignments" to compensate for high poverty or isolation. Since 1987, rural schools within municipalities have received upward adjustments (for details, see Parry, 1997a). Although the real value of the voucher originally was intended to keep pace with inflation, following the deep recession of the early 1980s it was no longer adjusted by the cost of living index. Over the course of the 1980s, as copper prices fell, the real value of the per-pupil voucher declined precipitously, reaching its lowest point in 1988. It rebounded thereafter with improved economic growth and has continued to rise since. In 1999, the voucher (public spending per pupil) for a basic education (grades 1–8) was valued at 332,000 Chilean pesos, or about $550 per year.

The voucher plan precipitated a massive redistribution of enrollment across private and public schools. At the beginning of the 1980s, around 15% of students were enrolled in private voucher schools, and almost 80% in public schools. By 1996 around 34% of enrollments were in private voucher schools, and by 2003, about 37%. This growth occurred mostly at the expense of public schools (González, 2001). Throughout this period, 5–9% of students were enrolled in elite private schools that charged high tuition, with the higher percentage in the most recent years. As family incomes rise in Chile, a still small but increasing proportion of students are enrolling in elite private schools.

Return to Democracy, 1990. The military ceded power to a democratic government in 1990. The form and function of Chile's voucher system were largely maintained, although new policies were grafted onto the existing system. The government focused on improving the quality of poor primary schools through direct resource investments. The "900 Schools Program," referred to as P-900, was targeted at high-poverty and low-achieving schools (Garcia-Huidobro, 1994), and was financed by the Swedish government and subsequently by the World Bank. Classrooms received a package of basic teaching materials and infrastructure improvements, while teachers received additional inservice training. Funds also were provided to train and employ local secondary graduates as tutors for the lowest-achieving students. Eventually, P-900 expanded to include about 2,300 schools. In 1992, the Program to Improve the Quality and Equity of Preprimary and Primary Education was initiated with World Bank financing. More ambitious in scope than P-900, it sought to endow all publicly funded schools with textbooks, libraries, and some infrastructure improvements (Cox, 1997).

The proportion of Chilean children attending public schools and the different types of private schools stabilized once the democratically elected regime took over the reins of government (González, 2001). In the 1990s, about 58% of pupils attended municipally run public schools, considerably down from the 80% who attended public primary schools in 1980. These continued to be largely financed by vouchers. About 33–34% of Chilean pupils attended private voucher primary (K–8) schools in the 1990s, compared with 14% in 1980. One-third of private voucher schools are religious (almost all Catholic), and approximately two-thirds are nonreligious, for-profit schools. For-profit schools account for much of the 20-percentage-point growth of private voucher school enrollment after 1980. About 8% of students in the 1990s attended expensive independent private schools that do not take vouchers and fund themselves completely through tuition and private contributions, like independent private schools in the United States. Fifty-five percent of primary pupils still attend public schools.

The return to democracy in 1990 brought renewed political pressures from teachers seeking improved wages and working conditions. Negotiation between the government and teachers resulted in the passage of the 1991 Estatuto Docente, a national law that subjected the teacher labor market—particularly for public school teachers—to additional regulation (Rojas, 1998). Wage floors were set for teachers with various levels of experience and training. Limits on hiring and firing of public teachers also were introduced. Public school teachers could be hired as either tenured (*titulares*) or contracted (*contratados)* teachers. Tenured teachers were to be hired through public contests in each municipality, and severe restrictions were placed on their firing or reassignment. Contracted teachers had fewer restrictions placed on their hiring and firing, but could account for no more than 20% of a municipality's teacher work force. The contracts of private school teachers were still governed by the Código de Trabajo, which permitted significantly more flexibility in hiring and firing.

Lessons from the Chilean Voucher Plan

The Chilean voucher plan was supposed to improve Chilean education and make Chilean parents feel better off because they had a wide choice of where to send their children to school, including the option of private education. The Chilean data provide important insights into a privatized choice reality. Chile's reforms encouraged a rapid growth in private school enrollment in the 1980s that was driven by an expansion of nonreligious, for-profit voucher schools. After 20 years, what can we learn from Chile about the effects of vouchers on parent choice, student performance, the effects of competition, and educational costs? What, in turn, was the impact of each of these effects on educational equity?

Who Chooses Private Schools and Why? The growth of enrollment in private education was not uniform throughout Chile. By 1996, more than

50% of K–8 pupils in Santiago went to some type of private school, voucher or nonvoucher. Low-income pupils were much more likely to attend a public municipal school. In the rest of the country, containing about two-thirds of the school population, only 20% of pupils attended private schools. Again, low-income pupils generally went to public schools. Ninety of 340 municipalities had no private schools at all in 1996. These municipalities are mainly rural and low-income, with more widely dispersed populations.

Thanks to good data in Chile on parents and where they send their children to school, we were able to estimate how families choose schools. The data show that higher-income parents are much more likely to choose a private school for their children, and those in the top 20% of the family income distribution, to choose a private *paid* school that does not take vouchers. When we analyzed school choice further, we found that in choosing a school, parents with less schooling themselves place less value on higher test scores and the average schooling of other parents with children in the school—even when we controlled for the decreased availability of higher-scoring schools in geographic areas populated by less-educated parents (McEwan & Carnoy, 1998). So even when private voucher schools offer higher average test scores and a student body with better-educated parents at the same cost as the neighborhood municipal school, less-educated parents are less likely to take that offer.

Yet we have no hard data that explain *why* parents with different levels of education seem to choose differentially among public and private voucher schools, given equal access to them. We do not think this means that less-educated parents are "irrational." Rather, one explanation is that they might have less information about schools than do more-educated parents. And even with the relevant information, members of lower social class groups might perceive that their children do not "belong" in schools with children of somewhat better-educated parents (Wells & Crain, 1992). Less-educated parents' perceptions of their position in the social structure may prevent them from making choices to send their children to higher-status schools.

Schools whose pupils have more-educated parents also may reinforce these perceptions by dissuading less-educated parents from placing their children there. This would be rational behavior on the part of schools if they believed that bringing in lower-status children could affect the school's desirability to other parents, especially those with more education.

The fact that less-educated parents choose lower-status public schools, and better-educated parents choose higher-status private voucher schools, may not mean much if public schools raise pupils' academic achievement the same as or more than private voucher schools. But even so, lower-income children may be penalized in terms of both *peer effect* (the contribution of fellow students to a child's academic achievement) and *attainment* (the number of years of schooling the child actually completes) by attending schools of lower socioeconomic status. Higher-status schools have, on average, higher-scoring students and build "cultural capital" that raises students' academic expectations for a given level of academic achievement (Cookson & Persell, 1985). So even if private voucher schools do not do any better than public schools in raising academic achievement—an issue we explore below—better-educated parents may still be rational in choosing private schools. These better-educated parents may not get higher "value added" (the school's contribution to their child's achievement) from sending their children to a private school. But they may gain a positive effect on their child's academic outcomes from being with higher-achieving students who have higher expectations about how far they will go in school. Studies in Chile and elsewhere show that peer effects are important in explaining differences in test scores between private and public schools (McEwan, 2001; Somers, McEwan, & Willms, 2001).

Do Pupils in Private School Score Higher on Tests than Pupils in Public Schools? Our estimates using extensive data on pupil test scores in Chile in the 1980s and 1990s show that, on average, students in for-profit privately run schools score lower on achievement tests than students of similar socioeconomic background (SES) in municipal (public) schools (see Figure 11.1). Further results suggest that the lower the SES of students, the worse students in nonreligious, for-profit private voucher schools do compared with students in municipal (public) schools (McEwan & Carnoy, 2000).

In contrast to nonreligious, for-profit voucher schools, Catholic voucher schools (enrolling about one-third of all private voucher school students and 11% of all primary school students in the 1990s) are more effective than public schools at producing achievement for similar students.

These results are inconsistent with advocates' claims that, on the whole, privately managed voucher schools produce significantly higher achievement than public schools for pupils with similar socioeconomic backgrounds. *Indeed, for pupils of low socioeconomic background, attending private, for-profit voucher schools appears to be related to lower achievement gains than those for students attending public schools. This suggests that providing vouchers as a policy measure actually may have made the poor worse off in terms of achievement, possibly resulting in decreased access to educational quality for low-income students.*

Did Competition Promoted by Vouchers Improve Average Test Scores in Public Schools? We used data on test results and the density of private

Figure 11.1a. Chile: Fourth-Grade Spanish Achievement Differences Between Public
DAEM and Other Types of Schools, Adjusted for Pupil SES, 1990–1996

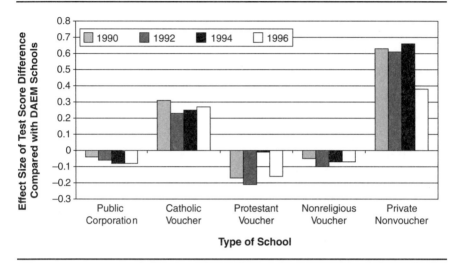

Figure 11.1b. Chile: Fourth-Grade Math Achievement Differences Between Public
DAEM and Other Types of Schools, Adjusted for Pupil SES, 1990–1996

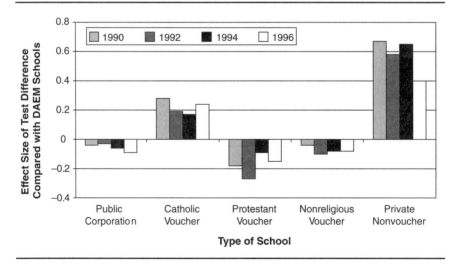

schooling at the municipal level from the early 1980s to the mid-1990s to estimate the possible effect that increased competition from private education might have had on public school performance and overall educational performance (McEwan & Carnoy, 1999). We tried to estimate competition by measuring the net effect on pupil test scores in public schools in municipalities with higher densities of private education. If competition has a positive effect on student performance, students attending public schools in municipalities with a higher concentration of private schools should have greater gains in test scores than students in municipalities where there are relatively few private schools.

We found that the effect of competition is positive in the Santiago Metropolitan Region, although not statistically significant. When other possible influences on student performance are accounted for, public school students in municipalities with a higher density of private schools gain roughly 0.2 of a standard deviation in test scores over a 15-year period. These overall gains appear to be driven by public schools in which parents have lower-middle or middle levels of educational attainment. Outside the Metropolitan Region, where three-quarters of Chile's primary students live, competition has slightly negative effects. *Our results suggest therefore that effects of competition may exist in some contexts, but not in others.* The most logical contextual effect is that public schools in the district would have to be concerned enough about losing students and money to competing private schools to implement changes that raise student scores. As important, public schools probably lose the more motivated parents in a competitive voucher environment, and therefore would have to raise test scores above the negative effects on average test scores caused by losing more-involved parents and their children.

Voucher proponents often presume that vouchers can be implemented just as described in planning memoranda. However, our study of the Chilean experience suggests that many stakeholders will seek, often with great success, to alter the form and function of voucher policies in ways not predicted by voucher proponents. For example, the military government—not subject to democratic elections—was unwilling to close neighborhood public schools even when the enrollment in those schools dropped considerably as families shifted their children to competing private schools. Closing neighborhood public schools is politically very difficult, even for a military government. In essence, such closings symbolize denying a public service, long considered a political right, to a local neighborhood. As another example of unpredicted consequences the association of private voucher schools in Chile recently became a major lobbyist for raising the value of the voucher, when the government proposed to require all schools to implement a 6-hour school day (to replace the 4-hour, 2-shift day). This modifies the incentives and constraints faced by public school managers and, ultimately, the effects that vouchers will have on student outcomes. This latter action was mirrored in the successful effort by private voucher schools in the Milwaukee experiment to raise their voucher from the initial $2,500 in 1991 to $5,500 (the average per-pupil cost in Milwaukee's public schools) by 1994.

Between 1980 and 1990, the Chilean voucher plan was "unusual" in that it was implemented during a dictatorship. Its provisions during that first decade met many of the conditions favored by voucher advocates in the United States—for example, the abolition of teachers' unions and unregulated expansion of for-profit private schooling. If the effect of competition on public education was attenuated in Chile's political context, it seems likely that it also would be attenuated in politically democratic societies, where political opposition to vouchers would flourish.

We observed in Chile that competition is only one of several potential effects that vouchers may have on schools and students. Vouchers also encourage a large-scale sorting of students across public and private schools. This certainly occurred in Chile and may explain why vouchers did not achieve the greater equity promised by reformers at the inception of the voucher plan. Low-income and higher-income pupils were at least as segregated by school after the voucher plan as before. Our data suggest that private school choice produced "cream skimming," in which able or privileged students were the first to exit public schools (Gauri, 1998; Parry, 1996). If peer effects are important (McEwan, 2001; Somers et al., 2001), then the exiting of these students negatively affected the outcomes of students remaining in public schools. There is some evidence that public school test scores in the 1980s fell relative to private school test scores for lower-income and lower-middle-income pupils (Carnoy, 1998; Prawda, 1993). This suggests that cream-skimming effects, which tend to concentrate more-able students with other more-able students, and less-able with other less-able students, were the main result of the voucher plan. Cream skimming increases inequity of results.

This is confirmed by two studies of the New Zealand choice plan (Fiske & Ladd, 2000; Lauder & Hughes, 1999). Those studies did not have access to student achievement data. They used survey analysis to show that choice among private and public schools financed by vouchers tended to concentrate the children of better-educated parents in one group of schools and the children of less-educated parents in a different group of schools. Although all parents received vouchers, "better" schools tended to select applicants from better-educated families, and it was those families who were more likely to apply.

Do Private Schools Cost Less than Public Schools? Although they produce somewhat lower test scores for students of similar social background, nonreligious private voucher schools produce achievement scores at a lower cost than public schools. This means that for-profit private voucher schools are more cost-effective than public schools. Catholic schools spend more per pupil than public schools (they charge higher tuition, on average, and have more expensive, largely donated facilities), but because they apparently add more academic value, they are about as cost-effective as public schools in producing achievement. Such results deliver a mixed message, suggesting that more money may be needed to produce higher student achievement even in private schools, but that private schooling (or deregulation) may save money.

However, the lower costs of for-profit voucher schools should be interpreted carefully when thinking about lower costs of schooling more generally. For-profit voucher schools in Chile lower costs by hiring, on average, younger teachers, who, because they have less seniority, are paid lower salaries. Public municipal schools retain their teachers longer; hence average seniority is higher and so are average salaries. Many younger teachers start out teaching in private schools, then compete to get into public schools for more permanent employment. Private schools in urban areas, particularly in Santiago, are able to "free ride" in other ways on the public education system, which provides the main employment draw for individuals into the teaching profession and an employment and pay "base." Enough public school teachers moonlight in private schools to allow private schools much greater teacher salary flexibility. About 30% of teachers in private schools are part-time, double the percentage in public schools.

Although it would be difficult to argue for a strategy that reduces costs per pupil at the expense of student achievement, poor school districts and countries with limited resources may find vouchers attractive. However, it would be naive to assume that a struggling democracy could—or should—implement a voucher plan as swiftly and decisively as Chile. Even if most parents support choice and privatization, as they probably did in Chile, reality in most democratic countries would make Chilean-style implementation difficult. After all, the Chilean plan was implemented by an authoritarian regime that systematically and violently squelched opposition, including forcibly dismantling teachers' organizations. In addition, our results provide little support for voucher advocates' argument that vouchers would save substantial public resources.

Another interesting aspect of these results is what they tell us about how private schools operate. Catholic schools in Chile—most predating the 1981 voucher reform—are able to achieve higher test scores than public schools, even when we account for pupil social class differences, and do so by spending more per pupil. For-profit schools, which sprang up like mushrooms in Chilean cities when vouchers were made available, are no better at producing high achievement scores for a child of a given socio-economic background than public schools. They *are* better at attracting higher-scoring students. They do that by locating, on average, in higher-income neighborhoods and tending to be selective (Parry, 1996). They are also better than public schools at reducing costs per pupil (public schools in Chile are more constrained in their hiring practices), and do that by paying their personnel less, mainly by hiring younger teachers. This implies that the path of least resistance for private, for-profit voucher schools in competition with public schools is to attract higher-scoring students by establishing themselves as somewhat higher socially and academically than the public schools in their area, then holding down costs. Not coincidently, Edison, the largest for-profit, private management company in the United States operating public and charter schools, uses precisely the same strategy. This can be interpreted as a positive effect of markets, but it hardly fulfills the promise of raising a community's academic performance.

Since for-profit, private voucher schools have, so far, cost less to operate in Chile, shifting resources to such schools from more expensive municipal schools may have released some public resources to improve the quality of low-scoring schools. The P-900 program, begun by the democratic government in 1990, is an example of efforts to improve public schools attended by low-income pupils. Evidence suggests that the P-900 program had statistically significant positive effects on Spanish and mathematics achievement. These findings are consistent with an extensive literature in developing countries that shows positive effects of basic resource investments in primary schools (Fuller & Clarke, 1994). In this sense, the voucher plan may have contributed to greater equity. However, the P-900 program was financed by external donors, such as the Swedish government and the World Bank, and we have no evidence that such externally financed Chilean government intervention would not have occurred anyway even without the voucher plan.

LESSONS FOR EQUITY FROM THE UNITED STATES AND CHILEAN VOUCHERS

We live in a world of residential segregation by race and social class. In addition, public education for low-income students in their neighborhoods is often of much lower quality than public education for the middle class and the wealthy (Benveniste et al., 2002). Even with school choice, the difficulty and cost of transporting children long distances induces most parents to choose a school close to home. Vouchers promise much greater school choice, namely, choice that includes higher-quality private providers locating in low-income neighborhoods.

Since low-income parents are most likely to be dissatisfied with their children's schools, voucher advocates argue that, with vouchers, low-income children will be at least as likely as higher-income children to get the substantial benefits of private education. Further, the competition of more private schools, particularly in low-income neighborhoods, would induce public schools to be more innovative and effective, or lose students. All this would increase satisfaction with schooling, help close the achievement gap between low- and high-income children, and increase educational and social equity (see Howell et al., 2000, for these claims).

Evaluations of U.S. voucher experiments suggest that a limited targeted voucher program that enables limited numbers of low-income students to attend *existing* private schools and is large enough to cover most, if not all, of the cost of attending these private schools probably could have a moderate positive effect on the achievement of African American students who currently attend the poorest-performing public schools. The number of students such a program could include depends on the number of places available in existing schools. If the voucher was large enough, a targeted program also could attract new high-quality private schools that would, by controlling students admitted, also create a positive peer effect.

That said, the research in the United States and Chile analyzing the effect of vouchers on educational quality suggests that claims by voucher advocates are exaggerated, for five main reasons.

1. In a targeted voucher plan, once spaces are filled in existing private schools, new private schools entering low-income markets are likely to be of lower quality than existing private schools in both lower- and higher-income markets. Thus, the small positive effects associated with voucher experiments are likely to dissipate as the number of private schools entering the market to take advantage of vouchers grows.
2. The more new private schools in low-income areas, the more parental education and motivation of students in those schools will resemble the average parental education and motivation in public schools, reducing any possible positive peer effect in private schools.
3. In a general voucher plan, in which all students, regardless of family income, are eligible and the voucher is the same amount for each student (as in Chile and New Zealand), low-income students are

least likely to have access to private education. Private providers are more likely to locate in higher-income areas, even when families cannot add on to the voucher by paying additional tuition.

4. Children from less-educated families cost more to educate to similar gains in achievement than children from better-educated families, mainly because better-educated families usually invest more in academic-type education for their children outside of school. So for the same level of voucher, any school, public *or* private, has difficulty matching suburban learning gains for inner-city children.

5. Vouchers are unlikely to improve public education by increased competition from private schools for the following reasons:

   • The negative impact on public schools when private schools "cream skim" the most motivated public school students tends to offset possible positive effects of increased competition on public education.

   • Governments—even those relatively hostile to public education, such as General Pinochet's—are reluctant to close neighborhood public schools or to reduce their funding.

   • In districts where the student population is growing rapidly— districts more likely to attract private schools—private education can expand with relatively little impact on the number of students in public schools. This was not the case in Chile because vouchers induced a very rapid expansion of private education. But in other countries, such as the United States, a moderate shift of public school students to private schools in the current period of rapid growth of the school-aged population might be a relief to public school districts hard-pressed for building space.

Vouchers are not likely to increase achievement gains for low-income (or high-income) students, but why not try them anyway? This is a question often posed by voucher advocates. If voucher plans were without cost, the answer would be clear: Let's try them. However, vouchers are not cost-less. As Henry Levin (1991, 1998) has pointed out, implementing voucher plans is a costly exercise. This is especially so if the public sector has to regulate private education.

Beyond the public costs of implementation and regulation, relying on voucher plans to solve the gap in achievement between low-income and high-income students, Blacks and Whites, or Latinos and Whites, would postpone even longer the finding of real solutions to the problem of educational inequity. Vouchers do little to address growing teacher shortages or the problem of recruiting higher-quality teachers. It is unlikely, for example, that private schools would find ways to recruit large numbers of math and science teachers at salaries even lower than those paid in public schools.

In the United States, vouchers also raise serious questions about the use of tax dollars to subsidize religious education. Since about 80% of American private school students attend religious schools, vouchers in most states would, in the first years of any kind of voucher plan, subsidize mostly religious schools. This is the case for all the current voucher experiments.

No doubt, greater choice is better than less choice. Vouchers provide more school choice. Equity is more likely to be promoted by a targeted voucher plan than a general one. We conclude, however, based on the empirical data available, that even targeted voucher plans are unlikely to promote much improvement in educational equity. Most likely, a relatively small group of low-income students would do somewhat better by shifting from public to well-established existing private schools. Some would argue that this is better than nothing, and perhaps that is so. Yet, other alternatives exist that also could benefit a few students without solving the much larger problems of education for low-income children. Magnet schools, schools within schools, and schools with smaller class sizes could all be offered to limited numbers of students at relatively low cost. However, any reform that claims to improve educational equity has to make gains available to most students, not just a few.

REFERENCES

Benveniste, L., Carnoy, M., & Rothstein, R. (2002). *All else equal: Are public and private schools different?* New York: Routledge.

Carnoy, M. (1998). National voucher plans in Chile and Sweden: Did privatization reforms make for better education? *Comparative Education Review, 42,* 309–337.

Carnoy, M. (2001). *Do school vouchers improve student performance?* Washington, DC: Economic Policy Institute.

Castaneda, T. (1992). *Combating poverty: Innovative social reforms in Chile during the 1980s.* San Francisco: ICS Press.

Chubb, J. E., & Moe, T. M. (1990). *Politics, markets, and America's schools.* Washington, DC: Brookings Institution.

Cookson, P., & Persell, C. H. (1985). *Preparing for power: America's elite boarding schools.* New York: Basic Books.

Coons, J., Clune, W. H., & Sugarman, S. (1970). *Private wealth and public education.* Cambridge, MA: Belknap Press.

Cox, C. (1997). *La reforma de la educacion Chilena: Contexto, contenidos, implementacion.* Santiago, Chile: Programa de Promocion de la Reforma Educativa en America Latina.

Espinola, V. (1993). _The educational reform of the military regime in Chile: The system's response to competition, choice, and market relations._ Unpublished Ph.D. dissertation, University of Wales, United Kingdom.

Fiske, E. B., & Ladd, H. (2000). _When schools compete: A cautionary tale._ Washington, DC: Brookings Institution Press.

Friedman, M. (1955). The role of government in education. In R. A. Solo (Ed.), _Economics and the public interest_ (pp. 123–144). New Brunswick, NJ: Rutgers University Press.

Friedman, M. (1962). _Capitalism and freedom._ Chicago: University of Chicago Press.

Fuller, B., & Clarke, P. (1994). Raising school effects while ignoring culture? Local conditions and the influence of classroom tools, rules, and pedagogy. _Review of Educational Research, 64,_ 119–157.

Garcia-Huidobro, J. E. (1994). Positive discrimination in education: Its justification and a Chilean example. _International Review of Education, 40_(3–5), 209–221.

Gauri, V. (1998). _School choice in Chile: Two decades of educational reform._ Pittsburgh: University of Pittsburgh Press.

González, P. (2001). _Estructura institucional, recursos, y gestión en el sistema escolar Chileno._ [Mimeo]. Santiago de Chile: Ministerio de Educación.

Greene, J., Howell, W., & Peterson, P. (1997, October). _Lessons from the Cleveland scholarship program._ Paper presented before the Association of Public Policy Management, Washington, DC.

Greene, J. P., Peterson, P., & Du, J. (1996, August). _The effectiveness of school choice in Milwaukee: A secondary analysis of data from the program's evaluation._ Paper prepared for presentation before the Panel on the Political Analysis of Urban School Systems, American Political Science Association, San Francisco.

Howell, W., & Peterson, P. (2002). _The education gap: Vouchers and urban schools._ Washington, DC: Brookings Institution.

Howell, W., Wolf, P., Peterson, P., & Campbell, D. (2000, September). _Test score effects of school vouchers in Dayton, Ohio, New York City, and Washington, D.C.: Evidence from randomized field trials._ Paper prepared for the American Political Science Association meeting.

Kemerer, F. (2002). After Zelman: Spotlight on state constitutional law. _Teachers College Record._ Available: www.tcrecord.org.

Jencks, C. (1966, Winter). Is the public school obsolete? _The Public Interest, 2,_ 18–27.

Jofre, G. (1988). El sistema de subvenciones en educación: La experiencia Chilena. _Estudios Publicos, 32,_ 193–237.

Larranga, O. (1995). Descentralización de la educación en Chile: Una evaluación económica. _Estudios Públicos, 60,_ 243–286.

Lauder, H., & Hughes, D. (1999). _Trading in futures: Why markets in education don't work._ Philadelphia: Open University Press.

Levin, H. M. (1991). The economics of educational choice. _Economics of Education Review, 10_(2), 137–158.

Levin, H. M. (1998). Educational vouchers: Effectiveness, choice, and costs. _Journal of Policy Analysis and Management, 17_(3), 373–391.

McEwan, P. J. (2001). _Peer effects on student achievement: Evidence from Chile._ Unpublished manuscript, University of Illinois at Urbana–Champaign.

McEwan, P. J., & Carnoy, M. (1998). *Choice between private and public schools in a voucher system: Evidence from Chile.* Unpublished manuscript, Stanford University.

McEwan, P. J., & Carnoy, M. (1999). *Competition, decentralization, and public school quality: Longitudinal evidence from Chile's voucher system.* Unpublished manuscript, Stanford University.

McEwan, P. J., & Carnoy, M. (2000, Fall). The effectiveness and efficiency of private schools in Chile's voucher system. *Educational Research and Policy Analysis, 22*(3), 213–239.

Metcalf, K. K., Boone, W. J., Stage, F. K., Chilton, T. L., Muller, P., & Tait, P. (1998). *A comparative evaluation of the Cleveland Scholarship and Tutoring Grant Program. Year One: 1996–1997.* Bloomington: Indiana University School of Education.

Neal, D. (1998). What have we learned about the benefits of private schooling? *Federal Reserve Bank of New York Economic Policy Review, 4*(1), 79–86.

Parry, T. R. (1996). Will pursuit of higher quality sacrifice equal opportunity in education? An analysis of the education voucher system in Santiago. *Social Science Quarterly, 77*(4), 821–841.

Parry, T. R. (1997a). Achieving balance in decentralization: A case study of education decentralization in Chile. *World Development, 25*(2), 211–225.

Parry, T. R. (1997b). Decentralization and privatization: Education policy in Chile. *Journal of Public Policy, 17*(1), 107–133.

Prawda, J. (1993). Educational decentralization in Latin America: Lessons learned. *International Journal of Educational Development, 13*(3), 253–264.

Rojas, P. (1998). Remuneraciones de los profesores en Chile. *Estudios Publicos, 71*, 121–175.

Rouse, C. (1998a). Private school vouchers and student achievement: Evidence from the Milwaukee choice program. *Quarterly Journal of Economics, 113*(2), 553–602.

Rouse, C. (1998b). Schools and student achievement: More evidence from the Milwaukee parental choice program. *Federal Reserve Bank of New York Economic Policy Review, 4*(1), 61–76.

Schiefelbein, E. (1991). Restructuring education through economic competition: The case of Chile. *Journal of Educational Administration, 29*(4), 17–29.

Somers, M.-A., McEwan, P. J., & Willms, J. D. (2001). How effective are private schools in Latin America? (Occasional Paper No. 37). New York: National Center for the Study of Privatization in Education, Teachers College.

Supreme Court of the United States. (2002). *Zelman v. Simmons-Harris.* 536 U.S. 2002.

Valdes, J. G. (1995). *Pinochet's economists: The Chicago School in Chile.* Cambridge: Cambridge University Press.

Wells, A. S., & Crain, R. L. (1992). Do parents choose school quality or school status? A sociological theory of free market education. In P. W. Cookson (Ed.), *The choice controversy* (pp. 65–81). Newbury Park, CA: Corwin Press.

Williams, J. (2000, May 16). Choice may draw 10,000 students in fall; 22 new schools will join voucher program for next school year, DPI announces. *Milwaukee Journal Sentinel,* p. 1A.

Winkler, D. R., & Rounds, T. (1996). Municipal and private sector response to decentralization and school choice. *Economics of Education Review, 15*(4), 365–376.

Witte, J. F. (1997). Reply to Greene, Peterson and Du: "The effectiveness of school choice in Milwaukee: A secondary analysis of data from the program's evaluation." Available: http://www.harvard.edu/pepg/op/evaluate.htm.

Witte, J. F., Sterr, T. D., & Thorn, C. A. (1995). *Fifth year report: Milwaukee parental choice program.* Madison: University of Wisconsin, Department of Political Science and the Robert M. La Follette Center for Public Affairs.

Zernike, K. (2000, September 15). New doubt is cast on study that backs voucher efforts. *New York Times,* p. A26.

12

Adequacy Litigations

A New Path to Equity?

MICHAEL A. REBELL

In its famous 1954 decision in *Brown* v. *Board of Education*, the U.S. Supreme Court held that each state, in providing the opportunity for education, must make it available "to all on equal terms." At the time, Thurgood Marshall, the lead attorney for the Black plaintiffs in this case, predicted that racial segregation in the schools would be eliminated within 5 years: "The basic postulate of our strategy and theory in *Brown* was that the elimination of enforced, segregated education would necessarily result in equal education" ("N.A.A.C.P. Sets Advanced Goals," 1954, p. 16; see also Carter, 1979).

Today, 50 years later, *Brown*'s vision of equal educational opportunity is far from being realized. More than 70% of African American and Latino public school students in the United States currently attend predominantly minority schools—a greater percentage than attended such segregated schools a decade ago (Orfield, 1999, 2001). Moreover, despite the greater educational needs of most poor and minority students, the inner-city schools that many of these students attend receive less funding and have fewer qualified teachers, larger classes, and inferior facilities compared with schools attended by more-affluent White students in the surrounding suburbs (*CFE* v. *State*, 2003; Council of the Great City Schools, 2001).

Earlier chapters in this volume have described the impact of the failure to fully implement *Brown*'s vision and the shift from "equity" to "excellence" in the education reform efforts of recent decades. These trends have led some skeptics to conclude that *Brown's* vision of equal educational opportunity is a chimera or, worse, an opiate to lull the disadvantaged into accepting the inherent inequalities of our capitalist society (see, for instance, Delgado & Stefanic, 1997). This chapter takes a more optimistic perspective. I focus on the spate of recent state court decisions that have invalidated state funding systems denying adequate education to poor and minority students. In fact, I argue that these "adequacy" litigations are a harbinger of a new wave of reform initiatives that may merge equity and excellence by procuring the major resource commitments necessary to ensure that at-risk minority students have a meaningful opportunity to meet challenging educational standards.

The success of these state court adequacy decisions reflects an underlying egalitarian dynamic in America's political and legal culture, which I previously have described in terms of a "democratic imperative" (Rebell, 1998). Drawing on Myrdal's (1962) notion of an unresolved "American dilemma"—or the conflict between American democratic ideals and ongoing prejudices against African Americans in particular—I define the "democratic imperative" as a periodic eruption of moral fervor that presses to eliminate the gap between the real and the ideal by implementing extensive political reforms that put into practice America's historical egalitarian ideals.

Viewed in historical perspective, therefore, what is significant about *Brown* is the way it has remade the political landscape[1] by activating a continuing progressive legal dynamic that—although it sometimes takes one step backward before taking two steps forward—over time chips away at the huge underlying problems of racism, unequal funding, and economic disadvantage that constitute the major barriers to equal educational opportunity. As Yale Law Professor Jack M. Balkin (2001) has noted, *Brown* exemplifies "the Constitution reflect[ing] America's deepest ideals, which are gradually realized through historical struggle and acts of great political courage" (p. 5). Thus, while the era of federal court desegregation mandates seems to be drawing to a close, a new era of state court education adequacy litigation is now advancing the equal educational opportunity vision—and thus the democratic imperative—in new ways and in new directions.

From this long-range historical perspective, I believe that our society is moving toward fulfilling *Brown's* vision of equal educational opportunity. Yet, the extent to which equity actually advances at any point in time or in any particular place will depend largely on the effectiveness of legal, political, and educational efforts to link these underlying egalitarian trends with immediate needs and possibilities. For example, during the desegregation era of the 1970s and 1980s, orders of the federal district courts resulted in stable racial integration and improved student achievement in some school districts, while in other places White flight and stagnant student scores were the courts' legacies (see, e.g., Stone, 1998). Similarly, although funding disparities among school districts have been reduced dramatically in some states where courts have invalidated state educational funding systems, elsewhere such court decrees actually have resulted in educational setbacks. In Kentucky, for example, issuance of a court order calling for fiscal equity and education adequacy resulted in a new funding system that narrowed the gap between per-pupil spending in high-wealth and low-wealth districts by 59% and in dramatic reforms of the entire education system (Hunter, 1999). On the other hand, following the California Supreme Court's 1996 decision in *Serrano* v. *Priest*, funding for education was equalized substantially, but at a relatively low level. Ranked fifth in the nation in per-pupil spending for education in 1964–65, California fell to 42nd in 1992–93 ("'Protecting' School Funding," 1993).

As is clear in the story of reform and top-down legal mandates discussed in Chapter 4 of this volume, active community involvement in reform efforts has been a major determinant of success in both the desegregation and education adequacy cases (Rebell & Hughes, 1996). Indeed, in the 1970s, the United States Commission on Civil Rights (1976, 1977a, 1977b, 1977c) found, based on a series of case studies and school superintendent surveys, that the support of a broad array of community participants substantially promoted public acceptance of desegregation plans. Similarly, the successful implementation in the early 1990s of the Kentucky Supreme Court's education adequacy order was facilitated in no small part by the extensive statewide dialogues that had been initiated in previous years by the Prichard Committee, a nonpartisan school reform group composed of political and business leaders, civic activists, parents, and professionals (Hunter, 1999). In this chapter, I present an overview of how similar constituency-building efforts hopefully are going to work in the implementation phase of a recent New York State court ruling in an important finance equity case.

Thus, I begin with a brief overview of finance equity litigation that emphasizes the remarkable pattern of plaintiff victories in recent education adequacy cases. This striking trend usually is explained in terms of plaintiff lawyers' strategic shift from "equity" to "adequacy" claims in their litigations—in other words, from a focus on equalizing all resources to a focus on providing the specific resources needed to provide all children the opportunity for a basic education. But that explanation does not go far enough. The significant questions to be addressed are:

1. Why do almost all state constitutions contain an education adequacy clause?
2. Why have lawyers invoked them for the first time in the past decade or so, even though they have been embedded in most constitutions for a century or more?
3. And, most important, why are judges upholding these adequacy claims in the vast majority of cases that come before them?

In the second section of this chapter I attempt to answer these questions by exploring the historical roots of the education adequacy clauses in the Revolutionary War and 19th-century common school eras, and in the framers' understanding that in a democratic society *all* citizens must be well educated. Although these clauses remained largely unenforced for a century or more, the continuing imperative of *Brown*'s vision of equal educational opportunity and the underlying premise of the modern standards-based reform movement—that all children can learn at cognitively demanding levels—together have revitalized the historical link between democracy and education in a manner that eventually may have profound egalitarian implications. Accordingly, the third section of this chapter argues that excellence and equity should be seen as complementary rather than competing concepts, and illustrates this argument by describing how courts in the adequacy litigations are beginning to articulate the specific high-level skills that *all* students actually need in order to be capable civic participants.

Yet, as I noted above, realization of the full potential of these legal advances requires sustained constituency building and effective political action. The courts cannot be the only venue of reform. Accordingly, the final section of this chapter will describe the extensive statewide public engagement process that the Campaign for Fiscal Equity (CFE)—of which I am the Executive Director and Counsel—has undertaken in conjunction with the major education adequacy litigation it has mounted in the State of New York over the past decade. CFE has fought for an adequate level of state funding for students in the New York City Public Schools, more than 80% of whom are poor and minority students, and for students in other high-need, underfunded school districts across the state. From the outset of the filing of the litigation, CFE has involved thousands of citizens throughout New York in an extensive deliberative process to help develop the positions that the plaintiffs presented to the court in the trial and to prepare the ground for successful implementation of a final court order. Now that the plaintiffs have prevailed in that case, the role of constituency building and public engagement has become even more critical, as the legal ruling can provide an important impetus for, but cannot in and of itself ensure, a fair and adequate education for the children of New York State.

EDUCATION ADEQUACY: A LITIGATION OVERVIEW

In the early 1990s, after overseeing almost 4 decades of implementation of school desegregation decrees by federal district courts, the U.S. Supreme Court began to focus on the question of when remedial decrees in long-standing desegregation cases should be terminated (Rebell & Block, 1985). In a series of such decisions, the Court determined that school boards that had "complied in good faith with the desegregation decree since it was entered" and had eliminated "the vestiges of past discrimination . . . to the extent practicable" (*Oklahoma City Public Schools* v. *Dowell*, 1991) would be freed from further judicial oversight, even if their schools remained substantially segregated and/or a significant achievement gap between students of different races remained (*Missouri* v. *Jenkins*, 1995). These developments led many civil rights advocates to conclude that the federal courts were abandoning any serious efforts to implement *Brown*'s vision of equal educational opportunity.

> Developments in federal school desegregation jurisprudence in the early 1990s . . . suggest that the litigation era reaching back to *Brown* v. *Board of Education* is now drawing to a close. . . . curtailing continuing federal court jurisdiction over a district that had once acted illegally opens the way for the district also to abandon some of the special efforts that had been imposed on it—both programs aimed explicitly at achieving racially balanced student bodies and those aimed more at improving the educational opportunities offered in the often heavily minority schools. (Minorini & Sugarman, 1999, p. 187)[2]

But at about the same time that the Supreme Court's insistence on effective remedies in desegregation was beginning to lag, civil rights advocates initiated new legal challenges to the systems that most states used to finance public education. Many of these suits resulted from a growing awareness among civil rights lawyers that substantial resources would be needed to overcome the accumulated vestiges of segregation and that most minority students attended school in poor urban or rural school districts that were substantially underfunded in comparison with schools in affluent, largely White suburban districts (see Reed, 2001).[3] The root cause of this inequity was that state education finance systems historically were based on local property taxes, a pattern that inherently disadvantages students who attend schools in areas with low property wealth.

The initial attempt to induce the courts to invalidate state education finance systems began in the federal courts. A case involving the impact of financial disparities on poor and minority students in Texas, *Rodriguez* v. *San Antonio Independent School District*, reached the U.S. Supreme Court in 1973. The *Rodriguez* plaintiffs lived in Edgewood, a district in the San Antonio metropolitan area whose students were approximately 90% Mexican American and 6% African American. The district's property values were so low that even though its residents taxed themselves at a substantially higher rate than did the residents of the neighboring, largely Anglo district, they were able to provide their schools only about half the funds, on a per-pupil basis, that were available to their more affluent neighbors. The Supreme Court agreed that Texas' school finance system was inequitable, but nevertheless it denied the plaintiffs' claim, primarily because it held that education is not a "fundamental interest" under the federal constitution (411 U.S. 1 at 32, 35–37, 49; for a detailed discussion of the Supreme Court's decision in *Rodriguez*, see Rebell, 2002).

The Supreme Court's ruling in *Rodriguez* precluded the possibility of obtaining fiscal equity relief from the federal courts. Surprisingly, however, the state courts, which historically had not been innovators in constitutional civil rights issues, picked up the baton. Shortly after the U.S. Supreme Court issued its decision in *Rodriguez*, the California Supreme Court held that even if education was not a fundamental right under the federal constitution, it clearly was so under the California constitution (*Serrano* v. *Priest*, 1976). Soon thereafter, courts in a number of other states also declared their state education finance systems unconstitutional.

The practical problems of untangling the complexities of local property tax systems and surmounting legislative machinations to preserve the status quo tended, however, to strain judicial capabilities. Difficulties in actually achieving equal educational opportunity in the initial fiscal equity cases, therefore, seemed to dissuade other state courts from venturing down this path (see Rebell, 2002). Despite an initial flurry of pro-plaintiff decisions in the mid-1970s, by the mid-1980s, the pendulum had swung decisively the other way: Plaintiffs won only two decisions in the early 1980s and, as of 1988, 15 years after *Rodriguez*, 15 of the state supreme courts had denied any relief to plaintiffs, compared with the seven states in which plaintiffs had prevailed.[4]

The U.S. Supreme Court's rejection of plaintiffs' claims in *Rodriguez*, together with the difficulties experienced by the state courts that issued remedial decrees in the early years, presumably should have sounded a death knell for the fiscal equity movement. Despite these setbacks, however, advocates and state court judges continued to seek new ways to ensure fair funding and meaningful educational opportunities for poor and minority students. Even more extraordinary is the fact that in the past decade or so there has been a strong reversal in the outcomes of state court litigations: Plaintiffs, in fact, prevailed in the vast majority (18 of 29) of the major decisions of the highest state courts since 1989.[5]

What is the explanation for the newfound willingness of state courts—which historically were reluctant to innovate in areas of constitutional adjudication—to uphold challenges to state education finance systems? And, further, how can it be that one-third of the recent pro-plaintiff decisions, that is, those in Montana (1989), Idaho (1993, 1998), Arizona (1994, 1998), New York (1995, 2003), Ohio (1997, 2000, 2002), and North Carolina (1997), have been written by the same courts that had ruled in favor of defendants only a few years earlier?[6]

The explanation for the marked increase in plaintiff victories since 1989 and the dramatic reconsiderations by an increasing number of state supreme courts undoubtedly are related to a new legal strategy many plaintiff attorneys adopted. This shift was from equal protection claims based on disparities in the level of educational funding among school districts to claims based on opportunities for an adequate education guaranteed by the applicable state constitution—so-called "adequacy considerations." Specifically, 16 of the 18 plaintiff victories in the past 14 years have involved substantial or partial adequacy considerations.[7]

The shift from equity to adequacy in legal pleadings, however, reflects more than a clever legal strategy by plaintiff attorneys. Judges have tended to uphold claims of denials of basic levels of adequate education to poor and minority children in recent years because concrete demonstrations of deprivation have highlighted dramatically, in a way that abstract discussions of property tax inequities never could, the extent to which children are being denied critical opportunities that are at the core of America's democratic promise. The adequacy cases, therefore, are the latest chapter in the continued unfolding of the democratic imperative in American history. They further illustrate how America's underlying egalitarian dynamic, after meeting resistance in one direction, will reassert itself with renewed vigor in another.

To understand precisely how the democratic imperative has emerged in the education adequacy cases and the full significance of this still-unfolding resurgence of the egalitarian ideal, we must reach back into history, beyond *Brown* and the modern civil rights era, to analyze the historical origins of the constitutional clauses on which most of the recent adequacy rulings are based.

THE HISTORICAL ROOTS OF EDUCATION ADEQUACY

Plaintiffs' success in the recent wave of education adequacy litigations reflects both a renewed attempt to implement *Brown's* vision of equal educational opportunity and also a flowering of egalitarian seeds that had been planted long ago in 18th- and 19th-century concepts of education reform. The founding fathers of the American Republic expected the schools to assist in building the new nation by "the deliberate fashioning of a new republican character, rooted in the American soil . . . and committed to the promise of an American culture" (Cremin, 1980, p. 3; see also Pangle & Pangle, 2000). This "new republican character" was to have two primary components. First was the implanting of "virtue," as defined by the classical notion that citizenship required a commitment to a shared public life of civic duty (Wood, 1969; see also Pocock, 1975; Willis, 1978). Second was a radical egalitarian notion that all citizens must obtain the knowledge and skills needed to make intelligent decisions. As John Adams put it:

> A memorable change must be made in the system of education and knowledge must become so general as to raise the lower ranks of society nearer to the higher. The education of a nation instead of being confined to a few schools and universities for the instruction of the few, must become the national care and expense for the formation of the many. (cited in McCullough, 2001, p. 364)

The civic republican and egalitarian ideals of the founding fathers were clearly spelled out in the education clauses of most of the New England state constitutions, which originally were written in the 18th century and have been largely unchanged since. Thus, the Constitution of the Commonwealth of Massachusetts proclaims:

> Wisdom and knowledge, as well as virtue, diffused generally among the body of the people, being necessary for the preservation of their rights and liberties; and as these depend on spreading the opportunities and advantages of education in the various parts of the country, and among the different orders of the people, it shall be the duty of legislators and magistrates, in all future periods of this commonwealth, to cherish the interests of literature and the sciences, and all seminaries of them; especially the . . . public schools and grammar schools in the towns. (1780, part II, ch. V, § 2)

A link between the development of "civic virtue" and education also appears in the constitutions of Vermont (1793, ch. II, § 68), New Hampshire (1784, part II, article 83), and Rhode Island (1842, Article XII, § 1). As Vermont's Supreme Court noted in interpreting the somewhat archaic "civic virtue" language, "The amalgamation was perfectly consistent with the commonly held view of the framers that virtue was essential to self-government, and that education was the primary source of virtue" (*Brigham v. State of Vermont*, 1997, p. 393).

The education clauses of state constitutions in most other parts of the country were written during the 19th century, and they generally were inspired by the common school movement that was the major education reform initiative of that era (Cremin, 1980). The common school movement, in essence, represented a delayed implementation of the egalitarian education ideals of the founding fathers, which had not been effectively implemented immediately after the Revolution largely because of the state legislatures' unwillingness to vote the taxes necessary to fund systemic schooling. As its name implies, the common school movement was an attempt to educate in one setting all the children, whatever their class or ethnic background, living in a particular geographic area. These schools would replace the prior patchwork pattern of town schools partially supported by parental contributions, church schools, "pauper schools," and private schools, with a new form of democratic schooling. The common school "would be open to all and supported by tax funds. It would be for rich and poor alike, the equal of any private institution" (Cremin, 1980, p. 138). This dynamic egalitarian ethic was driven by those who had faith in the power of education to "promote the well-being of the individual, the intelligent use of the franchise, and the welfare and stability of the state." At the same time, the common schools were strongly opposed by those who believed that "education gave rise, on the part of those born to inferior positions, to futile aspirations; that class distinctions made for social cohesion . . . [and] that no state could long withstand the financial strain involved in maintaining free schools" (Edwards & Richey, 1963, p. 299).

In the latter half of the 19th century, the fierce political battle to implement these common school reforms culminated in the incorporation in dozens of state constitutions of provisions that guaranteed the establishment of "a system of free common schools in which all the children in the state may be educated" (New York Constitution, 1894, Article XI, § 1).[8] Some states further emphasized the importance of fully educating all citizens by calling for a "*thorough and efficient* system of common schools throughout the state" (Ohio Constitution, 1851, Article VI, § 2; emphasis added).[9]

By the end of the 19th century, then, the vast majority of state constitutions included education clauses that reflected the strong democratic imperatives of the common school movement. Ironically, however, shortly after the common school movement had achieved this constitutional triumph, much of its dynamic egalitarian thrust seemed to have been spent.

As public school systems expanded at the end of the 19th century through compulsory education laws and the absorption of large numbers of immigrants in the urban centers, the original common school vision tended to atrophy, and the public schools increasingly became mechanisms for political acculturation and occupational sorting (see Katz, 1968/2001). Tyack (1974), for instance, describes bureaucratic structures for schooling created at the beginning of the 20th century to educate masses of students in urban areas as undermining common school ideals. This blunting of the original egalitarian ideal particularly affected the descendants of the African American slaves. African Americans, for the most part, had been excluded from the original common schools, and by the time they legally gained access to public school systems, those systems had become heavily stratified within and across district lines (see Glenn, 1988; Rippa, 1984; Tyack, 1974).

As the fervor of the original common school movement waned, the substantive guarantees to equal educational opportunity contained in the state constitution common school clauses tended to become rhetorical flourishes, often honored more in the breach than in actuality. The adequacy movement of recent years, has, in essence, focused judicial attention on this long-neglected language in state constitutional clauses, and in doing so it has revitalized their original underlying civic republican and common school ideals. Many of these cases have tied these historical ideals to contemporary educational and legal mandates that seek to implement in practical ways the original intent of the 18th- and 19th-century constitutional guarantees of an adequate education for all.

For example, the Supreme Court of Ohio, after closely studying the intent of the framers of its state constitution's education clause, emphasized its ideological origins in the common school movement and expressed an awareness of the far-reaching democratic implications of that ideology.

> The delegates to the 1850–1851 Constitutional Convention recognized that it was the state's duty to both present and future generations of Ohioans to establish a framework for a "full, complete and efficient system of public education." . . . Thus, throughout their discussions, the delegates stressed the importance of education and reaffirmed the policy that education shall be afforded to every child in the state regardless of race or economic standing. . . . Furthermore, the delegates were concerned that the education to be provided to our youth not be mediocre but be as perfect as could humanly be devised. . . . These debates reveal the delegates' strong belief that it is the state's obligation, through the General Assembly, to provide for the full education of all children within the state. (*DeRolph* v. *State of Ohio*, 1997, pp. 740–741)

Similarly, the Kentucky Supreme Court, in *Rose* v. *Council for Better Education, Inc.* (1989) stated that the intent of the delegates to the 1891 constitutional convention was to ensure that "the boys of the humble mountain home stand equally high with those from the mansions of the city. There are no distinctions in the common schools, *but all stand upon one level"* (p. 206; emphasis in original).

The courts in the recent adequacy cases also have emphasized that the democratic ethic reflected in the education clauses must be applied in a manner that relates directly to contemporary needs. As the Supreme Court of New Hampshire put it, "Given the complexities of our society today, the State's constitutional duty extends beyond mere reading, writing and arithmetic. It also includes broad educational opportunities needed in today's society to prepare citizens for their role as participants and as potential competitors in today's marketplace of ideas" (*Claremont School District* v. *State of New Hampshire*, 1993, p. 1381).

The committee that drafted New York State's education clause in 1894 seemed to be consciously communicating across the ages when it wrote:

> Whatever may have been their [i.e., the common schools'] value heretofore . . . their importance for the future cannot be overestimated. The public problems confronting the rising generation will demand accurate knowledge and the highest development of reasoning power more than ever before. (Constitutional Convention of 1894, 1906, p. 555)

In 2003, the New York Court of Appeals responded directly to this call from the past by specifically citing this 19th-century committee report and establishing a process to determine "what the 'rising generation' needs [today] in order to function productively as civic participants" (*CFE* v. *State*, 2003, p. 905). It concluded that although "a sound basic education back in 1894 . . . may well have consisted of an eighth or ninth grade education, . . . a high school level education is now all but indispensable" (p. 906). Similarly, the New Jersey Supreme Court held that although a high school education was not an attribute of a thorough and efficient education in 1895, it clearly was 80 years later (*Robinson* v. *Cahill*, 1973).

These state court interpretations, therefore, have created a direct link between contemporary school funding reform needs and the historical sources of this country's democratic traditions in the 18th and 19th centuries. These connections are reinvigorating the democratic imperative and providing a basis for accelerating progress toward realizing *Brown's* vision of equal educational opportunity. Especially significant in this regard is the contemporary courts' focus on the schools' responsibility to prepare students to be capable citizens in the modern world, a topic that will be explored in the next section.

LINKING EXCELLENCE AND EQUITY:
THE SKILLS NEEDED FOR CIVIC PARTICIPATION

In the mid-1980s a slew of commission reports warned of a "rising tide of mediocrity" in American education that was undermining the nation's ability to compete in the global economy (see Carnegie Forum on Education and the Economy, 1986; National Commission on Excellence in Education, 1983; Twentieth Century Fund, Task Force, 1983). Comparative international assessments revealed poor performance by American students, especially in science and mathematics (Linn & Dunbar, 1990; National Assessment of Educational Programs, 1990). These concerns culminated in the 1989 National Education Summit, convened by President George H. W. Bush and attended by all 50 of the nation's governors and a cadre of major corporate CEOs, where a new education reform movement was launched to articulate national educational goals and to establish explicit standards for educational achievement in each of the states (Ravitch, 1995; Tucker & Codding, 1998).

Standards-based reform, which is now being implemented in 49 of the 50 states, is built around substantive content standards in English, mathematics, social studies, and other major subject areas. These content standards usually are set at sufficiently high cognitive levels to meet the competitive standards of the global economy. In theory, once the content standards have been established, every other aspect of the education system—including teacher training, teacher certification, curriculum frameworks, textbooks and other instructional materials, and student assessments—must be revamped to conform to the standards. The aim is to create a seamless web of teacher preparation, curriculum implementation, and student testing, all coming together to create a coherent system that will result in significant improvements in achievement for all students (Fuhrman, 1993).

Standards-based reform emerged from concerns about America's ability to compete in the global economy, and its focus on outcomes and accountability seemingly has moved educational policy from an emphasis on equity to an emphasis on "excellence" (see Chapters 1 and 9, this volume). But inherent in the standards movement is also a powerful equity element, namely, its philosophical premise that *all* students can learn at high cognitive levels and that society has an obligation to provide them the opportunity to do so. As the New York State Board of Regents (1993) put it, "All children can learn; and we can change our system of public elementary, middle, and secondary education to ensure that all children do learn at world-class levels" (p. 1; see also Liebman & Sabel, 2003). This philosophical premise also has become the core of federal educational policy with the enactment in 2002 of the No Child Left Behind Act.

This law requires Title I schools to ensure that all students meet state standards within 12 years and that adequate yearly progress toward this goal—examined by racial, economic, and other groupings of student demographics—be demonstrated on an annual basis.

It is not a coincidence that the implementation of standards-based reforms and the accelerating plaintiff successes in the education adequacy litigations have occurred almost simultaneously since 1989. Standards-based reform has aided adequacy litigations in two major ways. First, the new state standards for defining and assessing educational achievement have provided courts with judicially manageable criteria for implementing workable remedies in cases where the courts have invalidated state education finance systems (Rebell, 2002). Second, the focus on standards has sparked intensive consideration of the basic goals of education in a democratic society and motivated contemporary courts to continue, update, and vastly expand the analysis, initiated more than 2 centuries ago by the founding fathers, of the specific skills citizens in a democratic society need in order to carry out their civic responsibilities. Thus, many of the state courts that have ruled on adequacy cases in recent years have expressly considered the purposes of public education in explicating the education clauses of their state constitutions. In doing so, they have agreed that "the original rationale for public schooling in the United States was the preparation of democratic citizens who could preserve individual freedom and engage in responsible self-government" (McDonnell, 2000, p. 1; see also *CFE* v. *State*, 2003; *Campbell School District* v. *State*, 1995; *Claremont School District* v. *State of New Hampshire*, 1993; *Robinson* v. *Cahill*, 1973). The U.S. Supreme Court's statement that our democracy "depends on an informed electorate: a voter cannot cast his ballot intelligently unless his reading skills and thought processes have been adequately developed," further supports this rationale for public school education (*Rodriguez* v. *San Antonio*, 1973).[10]

The focus of the contemporary standards-based reform movement on identifying and then actually developing in all children the specific skills that they will need to function productively as effective citizens in a democratic society has profound implications for education and for citizenship. The founding fathers and the leaders of the common school movement spoke eloquently of the need to equip all of the nation's future citizens with the intellectual skills they would need to be intelligent voters and civic participants, but the schools in their day did not seriously attempt to implement these ideals. Spurred by the standards-based reform movement and the adequacy litigations, schools today are attempting to put into practice this democratic ideal.

Benjamin Franklin epitomized the educational ideals of the nation's founders when he argued that a new republican curriculum must develop in students critical analytic skills in reading, writing, and oral rhetoric; "he urged that students be required to read newspapers and journals of opinion on a regular basis, and that they be incited to debate and argue over . . . the . . . major controversies of the day" (Pangle & Pangle, 2000, p. 30). Similarly, Thomas Jefferson thought each citizen would need "to know his rights; to exercise with order and justice those he retains; to choose with discretion the fiduciary of those he delegates; and to notice their conduct with diligence, with candor and with judgment" (Jefferson, 1818/1943, p. 1097). Horace Mann (1855), the founder of the common school movement, put it even more strongly.

> Education must be universal. . . . With us, the qualification of voters is as important as the qualification of governors, and even comes first, in the natural order. . . . The theory of our government is,—not that all men, however unfit, shall be voters,—but that every man, by the power of reason and the sense of duty, shall become fit to be a voter. Education must bring the practice as nearly as possible to the theory. As the children now are, so will the sovereigns soon be. (p. vii)

Ironically, of course, when Franklin and Mann recognized democracy's critical need for an educated electorate, both the franchise and access to education were greatly restricted. In their eras, and throughout much of America's history, Blacks and other minorities, as well as women and White men who did not own property, could not vote, serve on juries, or engage in other civic activities (Smith, 1997; *Taylor* v. *Louisiana*, 1975; *Thiel* v. *Southern Pacific County*, 1946). During the 19th century, the franchise was slowly extended to working-class men, then to the newly freed Black citizens, and early in the 20th century, to women (Keyssar, 2000). Yet stratagems like overly technical registration rules, poll taxes, and literacy tests effectively precluded many of the newly eligible citizens from actually voting (Keyssar, 2000). It has been only in the past few decades, since the enactment of the 24th Amendment to the federal Constitution in 1964, and the passage of the Voting Rights Act in 1965 (42 U.S.C.S. § 1971 et seq.), that substantial numbers of African American and Latino citizens actually have begun to vote.

Thus, the fact that throughout most of our history adequate education was not made available to all citizens was not of immediate political relevance because most of those who were uneducated also were not permitted to function fully in their civic roles. Today, however, as full access to the ballot and to other forms of political participation has been extended to virtually all citizens, the basic premise of democratic theory that all citizens in a democracy must be well educated has taken on urgent practical significance. This reality was illustrated dramatically during the 2000 Presidential election when it became clear that every vote really did count—

certainly in the state of Florida—and that the inability of certain voters to understand specific ballot instructions may have changed the outcome of the Presidential contest.

Furthermore, the need to actually provide an adequate education to all citizens has become even more urgent today when the information demands of the computer era have heightened the level of cognitive skills needed to be an "informed citizen." Civic participation now requires not only the ability to understand one's political interests and how various political issues relate to them, but also the capacity to sort and analyze the continuing stream of information that confronts all of us daily, in order to make sense of an ever-changing world.

In probing the purposes of education for a 21st-century society, the standards-based reform movement has begun to take seriously the need to provide all students the actual skills that they will need to function in a competitive economy and to carry out their civic responsibilities. The critical link between education and democracy, historically applicable only to an elite citizenship class in an age of limited information, is now seen as extending to all citizens. In this way, the concepts of "excellence" and "equity" increasingly are becoming merged, since the society requires all students to learn to function at high cognitive skill levels.

Recognizing this link, lawyers, activists, and plaintiffs in education adequacy cases have begun to articulate demanding concepts of "adequacy" in the educational opportunities they expect to be extended to historically disadvantaged minority populations. Although some people had anticipated that the concept of education adequacy that the courts would develop in this new wave of litigation would be defined in very minimal terms, in fact there has been a clear trend toward establishing a "high minimum," which

> focuses on what would be needed to assure that all children have access to those educational opportunities that are necessary to gain a level of learning and skills that are now required, say, to obtain a good job in our increasingly technologically complex society and to participate effectively in our ever more complicated political process. (Minorini & Sugarman, 1999, p. 188; also see Clune, 1994)

Brief Overview of the New York Adequacy Case

The most extensive judicial analysis of the specific skills students need to be effective citizens in our modern democratic society has been undertaken over the past decade by the New York State courts in the series of Campaign for Fiscal Equity litigations. In 1995, in the first phase of this case, the Court of Appeals, New York's highest court, issued a tentative definition of the constitutional concept of a "sound basic education," which emphasized that students need to "function productively as civic participants capable of voting and serving on a jury" (*CFE* v. *State*, 1995, p. 666), and then directed the trial court to gather evidence and further probe the meaning of these concepts. Responding to the Court of Appeals' directive, the trial judge, Leland DeGrasse, adopted an innovative, empirically grounded approach. He instructed the parties to have their expert witnesses analyze a charter referendum proposal that was on the actual ballot in New York City at the time the trial was in progress. The specific question posed was whether graduates of New York City high schools would have the skills needed to comprehend that document. The witnesses also were asked to conduct a similar analysis of the jury charges and of certain documents put into evidence in two complex civil cases that recently had been tried in the local, state, and federal courts.

Plaintiffs' experts identified the specific reading and analytic skills, as well as the historical and scientific knowledge, that students would need to comprehend these documents. In doing so, they related these specific skills to the standards for high school graduation set forth in the Regents' Learning Standards in English language arts, social studies, mathematics, and sciences. One of the defendants' experts undertook a computerized "readability analysis" of various newspaper articles dealing with electoral issues and of some of the jury documents that had been put into evidence. This computerized reading analysis focused on sentence length and other mechanical factors, rather than on the cognitive level of the materials being reviewed. He concluded that only a 7th- or 8th-grade level of reading skills was needed to comprehend these materials. Defendants' experts also introduced polling data, which showed that the vast majority of American voters obtain their information on electoral issues from radio and television news, implying that they do not require the analytic skills needed to comprehend complex documents.

The trial court first concluded, generally, that "productive citizenship means more than just being *qualified* to vote or serve as a juror, but to do so capably and knowledgeably" (*CFE* v. *State*, 2001). It then held that

> An engaged, capable voter needs the intellectual tools to evaluate complex issues, such as campaign finance reform, tax policy, and global warming, to name only a few. Ballot propositions in New York City, such as the charter reform proposal that was on the ballot in November 1999, can require a close reading and a familiarity with the structure of local government. . . . Similarly . . . jurors may be called on to decide complex matters that require the verbal, reasoning, math, science, and socialization skills that should be imparted in public schools. Jurors today must determine questions of fact con-

cerning DNA evidence, statistical analyses, and convoluted financial fraud, to name only three topics. (p. 485)

In June 2002, an intermediate appeals court reversed the trial court decision, holding that the constitutional mandate regarding sound basic education required only 8th- or 9th-grade level reading skills.[11] The Court of Appeals, however, soundly rejected the notion that middle school level skills suffice for the 21st century. As stated above, it decisively equated "sound basic education" with a "meaningful high school education" and upheld the trial court's ruling that "productive citizenship means more than just being *qualified* to vote or serve as a juror, but to do so capably and knowledgeably"(*CFE* v. *State*, 2003, p. 906).

The New York Court of Appeals' holding that students must be prepared to be *capable* citizens and the trial court's detailed analysis of the specific skills and the level of cognitive functioning that students need to function in that manner are likely to inspire similar analyses and analogous holdings by other courts. The CFE courts' concept of a capable voter or juror does not mean that such an individual would be expected to know the details of campaign finance laws or how to scientifically analyze DNA. It does mean, however, that voters should have the cognitive skills and the level of knowledge necessary to be able to identify their own political interests, to find information relevant to those interests, and to assess this information, as well as arguments made by candidates, in light of those interests (see Lupia & McCubbins, 1998; Nie, Junn, & Stehlik-Barry, 1996).

Although the schools' responsibility to provide all students with high-level cognitive skills has now become an integral aspect of the adequacy movement and will have wide-ranging egalitarian implications, the extent to which this piece of the democratic imperative will advance at a given time in any particular place will depend on the local political context and how each group of litigants and advocates responds to it. As I noted above, CFE has attempted to advance the democratic imperative in New York State by linking its litigation strategies and activities with an ongoing constituency-building and statewide public engagement process. A discussion of this still ongoing political and deliberative process is the subject of the next and concluding section of this chapter.

PUBLIC ENGAGEMENT AND LITIGATION: CFE'S NEW YORK EXPERIENCE

In 1993, responding to devastating cutbacks in education funding, a coalition of education advocacy organizations, parent groups, civic organizations, and community school boards formed a new not-for-profit organization, the Campaign for Fiscal Equity, Inc., in order to mount a legal challenge to New York State's arcane system for funding public education. The state's highest court had, a decade earlier, rejected an attempt by a group of property-poor Long Island school districts to invalidate the state's education aid formulas (*Levittown* v. *Nyquist*, 1982) on the basis of an "equity" claim, which argued that under the state and federal equal protection clauses, all school districts should receive essentially equal per capita funding. CFE advocates were hopeful that this time the combination of the legislature's continued failure to correct the gross underfunding of many high-need school districts and a new legal initiative based on the education adequacy approach described earlier in this chapter would allow a constitutional claim to succeed.[12]

Although over the previous 2 decades similar suits had been filed in many other states, CFE was the first plaintiff organization to make an explicit decision—even before drafting its first legal papers—to mount an extensive statewide public engagement campaign to complement the lawsuit. This early commitment to public engagement resulted from concerns about the unsatisfactory outcomes of the remedial stages in many of the early fiscal equity litigations, as well other education reform class action litigations. Too often, judicial intervention in cases in which plaintiffs had won dramatic legal victories did not result in effective, lasting solutions to deep-rooted education controversies. After considering this issue at length, CFE concluded that significant, long-lasting reform could best be achieved by involving the broad range of diverse stakeholders who are affected by educational policy reforms in both the development and the implementation of judicial remedies (see Rebell & Hughes, 1996). The initial analysis of the outcome of the first 2 decades of fiscal equity litigation supported this thesis, as it indicated that reforms appeared to be most successful in those states where a broad-based, grassroots movement had supported the reforms sought in the litigation (Campaign for Fiscal Equity, 1997–2001; Rebell, Hughes, & Grumet, 1995).

CFE's commitment to public engagement meant that principles for reforming the funding problems raised by the lawsuit would be developed early and would guide the legal strategies during the trial and appeals. It also meant that critical remedial concepts and legal strategies would be decided not just by lawyers and experts, but also by the broad group of stakeholders who would be drawn into the public engagement process— and that these stakeholders likely would then form a strong core of supporters who could help implement the remedies if the court ultimately adopted them.

Thus, since 1996, CFE has put into practice this commitment to public engagement as an integral aspect of its legal strategy. What follows is a description of how this has been done.

Defining a "Sound Basic Education"

The main goal of the CFE lawsuit has been to ensure that all of New York's students receive the "opportunity for a sound basic education" guaranteed by Article XI § 1 of the state constitution.[13] After the New York Court of Appeals distinguished the adequacy claims in this suit from its prior decision in the earlier "equity" case, *Levittown* v. *Nyquist*, 1982, and allowed the case to proceed to trial (*CFE* v. *State*, 1995), the key legal, political, and educational issue became precisely what constitutes "a sound basic education." The constitution does not define this term, nor did the New York State Court of Appeals definitively do so in its first decision. Instead, in its preliminary 1995 ruling, the court held that a final determination of this core constitutional issue should await an analysis of all the evidence developed at the trial. The state's high court did, however, set out a tentative definition as a "template" to guide the trial court in conducting the trial. The template described "a sound basic education" in terms of: "the basic literacy, calculating, and verbal skills necessary to enable children to eventually function productively as civic participants capable of voting and serving on a jury." The Court of Appeals also held that a sound basic education requires the following essential resources:

- Minimally adequate physical facilities
- Minimally adequate instrumentalities of learning such as desks, chairs, pencils and reasonably current textbooks
- Minimally adequate teaching of reasonably up-to-date basic curricula
- Sufficient personnel adequately trained to teach those subject areas (*CFE* v. *State*, 1995, p. 307, 317).

The Court of Appeals' innovative method of issuing a tentative definition, and then candidly committing itself to re-evaluate that definition when the case would later return to it on appeal, provided CFE an extraordinary opportunity for jump-starting the public engagement campaign it had been contemplating. Although the Court of Appeals probably intended that only the lawyers and expert witnesses would review its tentative definition, CFE decided to expand the dialogue to encompass the broad range of education stakeholders. Thus, the initial issue around which the statewide public engagement forums were organized was how to define a "sound basic education." The realization that their input might help determine the outcome of this major constitutional issue intrigued and excited many of the education advocates, parents, teachers, administrators, school board members, and other community members that CFE sought to engage in this public dialogue.

A critical "defining moment" for CFE's commitment to public engagement occurred in the early stage of this process. The Court of Appeals' template had stressed preparation for civic participation, but it did not, like courts in many other states, explicitly refer to preparing students for employment. The CFE legal team—which consisted of one other in-house lawyer and myself, as well as a dedicated complement of attorneys from the firm of Simpson Thacher & Bartlett that provided extensive pro bono assistance at the trial and with the appeals—were not inclined to second-guess the court's stance. Parents and advocates at the initial public engagement sessions agreed with our strategy of relying on the New York Regents' Learning Standards to develop evidence on the specific skills students need for civic engagement, but vociferously rejected our intent to soft-pedal the employment issue. They insisted that, whatever the legal niceties involved, a definition of sound basic education that did not provide explicit assurances that their children would be prepared to get a decent job was unacceptable. Given this overwhelming public response, we reconsidered our stance and decided to change our trial strategy and to press the employment issue in court. In order to do so, we needed to provide the Court of Appeals a strong evidentiary base that would establish the significance of this issue. Documenting the importance of preparing students to compete in the global economy of the 21st century and delineating the specific skills they would need to meet these challenges probably added at least a month to the length of the trial.

CFE's public engagement methodology sought to maximize consensus through ongoing discussion and refinement of initial positions. The emphasis was on finding positions that virtually all participants could support, or that, at the least, they could "live with." No actual votes are taken at public engagement forums, but active dissent is respected, and drafts are revised continually to respond to stated concerns of participants.

Thus, after 3 years of active statewide dialogue, a definition of "sound basic education" emerged that had widespread support throughout the state. The strongly supported public engagement position constituted the substance of the definition that CFE's attorneys asked the trial court to adopt when the trial began in Fall 1999. The proposed definition was formally presented by Tom Sobol, former State Commissioner of Education, who had agreed to be an expert witness for the plaintiffs; three other plaintiff witnesses also endorsed the definition. Dr. Sobol strongly supports public engagement, and he personally participated in a number of the forums.

The constitutional definition of a sound basic education that the trial court finally adopted contained almost all of the recommendations that had emerged from the public engagement process, including the key employment issue: "A sound basic education consists of the foundational skills that students need to become productive citizens capable of civic engagement and sustaining competitive employment" (*CFE* v. *State*, 2001).

The trial court also held that the template's original list of four essential resources should be expanded to the following sevenfold concept:

1. Sufficient numbers of qualified teachers, principals and other personnel.
2. Appropriate class sizes.
3. Adequate and accessible school buildings with sufficient space to ensure appropriate class size and implementation of a sound curriculum.
4. Sufficient and up-to-date books, supplies, libraries, educational technology and laboratories.
5. Suitable curricula, including an expanded platform of programs to help at-risk students by giving them more "time on task."
6. Adequate resources for students with extraordinary needs.
7. A safe orderly environment. (*CFE* v. *State*, 2001, p. 550)

Ultimately, the Court of Appeals upheld the strong emphasis on the development of employment skills on which the public engagement participants had insisted, specifically holding that students need to develop "a higher level of knowledge, skills in communication and the use of information, and the capacity to learn over a lifetime" in order to obtain self-sustaining employment (*CFE II*, 2003, p. 906). The court also upheld, explicitly or implicitly, the other aspects of the trial court's delineation of the foundational skills and essential resources, and, in order to emphatically reject the intermediate appeals court's conclusion that low-level skills would suffice for these purposes, it stressed that a sound basic education means a "meaningful high school education," not 8th- or 9th-grade level skills.[14]

Building a Statewide Coalition

The other major issue CFE included in its initial public engagement forums was the remedy question: How precisely should the education funding system be reformed? The first item that had to be addressed in this regard was whether the goal of the litigation should be strict dollar equity in spending, which could require substantial transfers of funds between rich and poor districts, or major resource infusions and educational improvements for students in New York City and other high-need, underfunded districts, without regard for the level of expenditure elsewhere. CFE put this question to its core New York City constituents in a series of all-day conferences attended by representatives of approximately 100 education advocacy, parent, and community groups during the first year of public engagement. These individuals were aware that the per-pupil expenditure for New York City public school students was $1,200 below the state average and $4,000 below average expenditures in the neighboring suburbs, even though New York City students often have far greater educational needs.

A strict equalization remedy had great appeal to many New York City parents and educators who resented the fact that thousands more dollars were being spent on the education of suburban students than on their children's education. "Don't my kids deserve as much as kids in the suburbs?" many parents asked. This view tended to predominate in the early discussions. But as the series of conferences progressed, there was a growing realization that taking money from the rich districts to provide more for the poor would likely spark a heavy political backlash from the suburbs and lead to an upstate/downstate confrontation that could threaten any possibilities for real reform. By the end of the third session, it was clear that sentiment in favor of the pragmatic course to increase the total education funding pie was overwhelming—in excess of 90%. Based on this strong sentiment, CFE has adopted a remedial position that seeks to "level up" the resources in New York City and other underfunded districts by expanding the pool of educational resources, rather than seeking a "Robin Hood" remedy that would take from rich districts to give to the poor.

This key strategic decision allowed the public engagement process to broaden into a full statewide dialogue the next year. Seeking to avoid the upstate/downstate splits that had stymied past efforts to reform the state funding formula, CFE worked to build coalitions with residents of urban, rural, and suburban districts throughout the state. This entailed promoting sustained conversations about directions for reform, not only with residents of poor urban and rural areas, who constituted CFE's natural allies, but also with residents of affluent communities whose political support (or at least attenuated opposition) was deemed an essential part of the political equation. By explicitly eschewing a Robin Hood remedy, CFE was able to appeal to the democratic ideals of the residents of affluent districts without threatening their immediate self-interests.[15]

The public engagement forums held in the suburbs fostered discussions that led residents of the affluent suburbs to identify with the plight of inhabitants of the inner cities. This allowed participants to focus on strategies for raising additional revenues and devising accountability mechanisms that would ensure that any such funds actually would result in demonstrable improvements in student learning. The significance of these discussions was described in an editorial published by the major newspaper of New York State's most affluent suburban county.

> This "public engagement process" is an exciting one. It includes hundreds of parents, teachers, administrators, advocates and representatives of civic, religious, business and labor groups from across the state exchanging ideas on critical issues, including how funding reform can dovetail with state Board of Regents' effort to raise academic standards. . . . The plan . . . is to offer participants an opportunity to directly influence reform positions [CFE] will present to the court. That in itself is refreshing. After years of watching state officials . . . avoid this admittedly difficult but vital area of reform, it's high time the fiscal inequities of the education system were addressed. And the fact that the public isn't being bypassed is heartening. ("A School Funding Remedy," 1998, p. A16)

CFE's forums have been co-sponsored by many other statewide organizations, such as the League of Women Voters, the New York State School Boards Association, the New York State PTA, the teachers' unions, the Urban Leagues of New York State, the New York State Business Council, as well as numerous local education advocacy, business, and civic organizations.[16] Not all of these groups support CFE's positions in the lawsuit, but they all agreed to participate in the public engagement process after it was made clear that the forums would promote candid, wide-ranging discussion of all issues and there would be no preconceived outcome for the deliberations.

The cooperative deliberations of the public engagement process also have evolved in many instances into more-direct advocacy partnerships. CFE has formed particularly strong ties with three groups that were formed specifically to advocate and lobby for education finance reform, namely, the Alliance for Quality Education (AQE), a statewide education advocacy coalition of about 200 member organizations; the Mid-State School Finance Consortium, a group that has grown to represent almost 300 of the school districts in central, western, and northern New York; and Reform Education Inequities Today (REFIT), a grouping of property-poor Long Island school districts.[17]

The fact that diverse constituencies from around the state participated in formulating many of the major positions that were adopted by the trial court meant that when the trial court's decision was issued in 2001, and the final Court of Appeals' decision was issued in 2003, they received broad statewide support from education stakeholders and newspapers and other media throughout the state (see, e.g., "Changing School Funding," 2001; "Fix the School-Aid Formula," 2003; "Judge Orders Reform," 2001; "Justice for Schools," 2003; "Schools Here May Gain," 2003). An Albany press conference held the day after the trial court issued its favorable decision dramatically illustrated the strength and significance of this support. The first reporter to pose a question asked, "Doesn't this victory for CFE mean that New York City schools will now receive more funding at the expense of the rest of the state?" I responded by turning the floor over to the spokesman for the Mid-State Consortium, who told the assembled press corps that he represented 275 upstate small city and rural school districts (more than a third of all the school districts in the state), and that they firmly supported the CFE decision because of their conviction that it would benefit *all* children in the state.

This level of statewide support continued even though the final Court of Appeals ruling technically applied only to New York City and not to the rest of the state. Immediately after that decision was issued, CFE put out a press release announcing that in practice the decision could be implemented successfully only on a statewide basis and that CFE was committed to continuing to press for statewide solutions. The statewide partners accepted those assurances, and another potential upstate/downstate confrontation was avoided.

In CFE II, the Court of Appeals issued a powerful three-part remedial order that requires the state to

1. Determine the actual cost of providing a sound basic education
2. Reform the current funding system to ensure that the resources necessary to provide a sound basic education are available in every school
3. Provide a system of accountability to ensure that the reforms actually do provide all students the opportunity for a sound basic education.

Since each of these mandates reflects reform initiatives that CFE has been advocating and requested the court to affirm, public engagement efforts are already underway in each of the areas to develop specific proposals that will be submitted to the governor and legislature for implementation within the 13-month time frame for compliance established by the court. In addition to promoting important public dialogues regarding these remedy issues, these conversations also will build an important political base—32 statewide organizations have joined CFE in sponsoring a costing-out study that will incorporate broad public input. This effort will help ensure that the proposals that result from these deliberations strongly influence the reforms that actually are put into effect.

The New York State public engagement process, therefore, illustrates how broad-based public dialogues can promote effective reform in controversial public policy areas by inspiring diverse groups of people both to understand the critical importance of equity-based reforms and to participate in devising feasible mechanisms for implementing them. The dialogues provide the courts and the media with detailed information about the complex range of factual and political issues that need to be considered in framing specific reforms, while also helping to develop the broad-based political constituencies necessary to convince the legislature and governor to enact them (Berry, Portney, & Thomson, 1993; Sturm, 1993).

CONCLUSION

Many political and legal commentators lament the apparent signs that the current era is one of retrenchment, not reform, in regard to realizing *Brown*'s vision of equal educational opportunity. Often overlooked in these assessments, though, is the significance of the stunning trend of plaintiff victories in an increasing number of state court education adequacy litigations. These cases are constitutionally grounded in the notion that for a democracy to flourish, all of its citizens must be well educated. The contemporary standards-based reform movement has given the courts effective tools for putting that theoretical ideal into actual practice. The overwhelming support, by Republican and Democratic lawmakers alike, for the core proposition of the No Child Left Behind Act—namely, that *all* children can and must meet state educational standards—is further evidence that the underlying democratic imperative in American's political culture is, despite periodic setbacks, continuing its steady progression (Liebman & Sabel, 2003).

The extent to which actual reforms will be implemented in particular states and particular school districts, and whether the positive potential of the federal law can be fully realized, will depend, however, on the effectiveness of advocacy efforts to engage the public at large and to build constituencies that can effectively press policymakers to fairly fund these initiatives and to strongly support public education. Equity and excellence are feasible joint goals—but their prompt attainment will require continued optimism, engagement, and investment.

NOTES

1. For discussions of how *Brown* has fueled momentous civil rights innovations in areas such as the rights of the disabled and gender equity, see, for example, Rebell (1986); Salomone (1986). Perhaps the most significant impact of *Brown* has been on public opinion. For instance, in 1942 only 2% of southern Whites (and 40% of northern Whites) believed Blacks and Whites should attend the same

schools. By the mid-1990s, 87% of Americans approved of the *Brown* decision (Kahlenberg, 2001).

2. See also Hansen (1993), who argues that courts, becoming increasingly frustrated by their inability to achieve success, simply are "giving up" in desegregation cases; and Shaw (1992), arguing that once a school district is relieved from court supervision, vestiges of segregation in areas like housing again become operative.

3. See also Smith (1993), arguing that access to a decent education is a more important remedial goal than racial integration; and Days (1997), describing ways that large numbers of Blacks turned away from the integrative ideal because of ineffective implementation of *Brown*.

4. The states in which defendants prevailed were Arizona (1973), Illinois (1973), Michigan (1973), Montana (1974), Idaho (1975), Oregon (1976), Pennsylvania (1979), Ohio (1979), Georgia (1981), New York (1982), Colorado (1982), Maryland (1983), Oklahoma (1987), North Carolina (1987), and South Carolina (1988). Plaintiff victories occurred during that period in California (1976), New Jersey (1973), Connecticut (1977), Washington (1978), West Virginia (1979), Wyoming (1980), and Arkansas (1983). For full legal citations to these cases and others cited in this chapter, see Rebell (2002).

5. Specifically, plaintiffs prevailed in major decisions of the highest state courts or final trial court actions in the following 18 states: Kentucky (1989), Montana (1989), Texas (1989), New Jersey (1990, 1994, 1998, 2000), Idaho (1993, 1998), Massachusetts (1993), Tennessee (1993, 2002), Arizona (1994, 1998), Kansas (1991, 2003), Missouri (1994), New York (1995, 2003), Wyoming (1995, 2001), Arkansas (1996, 2000, 2002), North Carolina (1997), Vermont (1997), New Hampshire (1997, 1999, 2002), Ohio (1997, 2000, 2002), and South Carolina (1999). During the same time period, defendants prevailed in the following 11 states: Wisconsin (1989, 2000), Minnesota (1993), Nebraska (1993), Virginia (1994), Maine (1995), Rhode Island (1995), Florida (1996), Illinois (1999), Louisiana (1998), Pennsylvania (1999), and Alabama (2002). The 1994 decision of the North Dakota Supreme Court in *Bismarck Public School District No. 1* v. *State* held that the state's education finance system was unconstitutional but not by the requisite "super majority" vote.

6. Reconsideration of pro-defendant court decisions also may come from sources other than the courts. In 1996, the Florida Supreme Court, in a close plurality decision, denied relief to the plaintiffs in a major education adequacy case, *Coalition for Adequacy and Fairness in School Funding, Inc.* v. *Chiles*. Two years later, however, the voters, through a 71% favorable referendum vote, amended the state constitution to include a guarantee for a "high quality system of free public education," which was even stronger than the adequacy standard the plaintiffs had sought in the litigation (see Mills & McLendon, 2000).

7. Adequacy concerns were major factors in the highest state court or final trial court decisions in Kentucky (1989), Idaho (1993), Massachusetts (1993), Tennessee (1993), Arizona (1994), New York (1995, 2003), Wyoming (1995), North Carolina (1997), Ohio (1997), New Hampshire (1997), Vermont (1997), and South Carolina (1999). Adequacy considerations were also significant in the remedies ordered by the state supreme courts in Missouri (1993), New Jersey (1990, 1994, 1998), and Texas (1995), and in the settlement entered into in Kansas in 1992.

8. See also, for example, Oklahoma's Constitution (Article XIII, § 1) ("establish and maintain a system of free public schools wherein all the children of the State may be educated"); Tennessee's Constitution (Article XI, § 12) ("The General Assembly shall provide for the maintenance [and] support . . . of a system of free public schools"). The Tennessee Constitution's original language paralleled the "civic virtue/cherish literature" phrases of the Massachusetts Constitution, but references to the funding of common schools were added in 1870 and strengthened in 1978 (*Tennessee Small School Systems* v. *McWherter*, 1993; Tennessee's Constitution, Article XI, § 12). The committee that drafted New York's constitutional clause in 1894 specifically rejected the Massachusetts language as being "archaic" (Constitutional Convention of 1894, 1906, p. 555).

9. Similar clauses calling for a "thorough and efficient" system of common schools or public schools are found in states such as New Jersey (Article VIII, § 4), Pennsylvania (Article III § 14), and West Virginia (Article XII, § 1). Language in other state constitutions requires the legislature to support a "thorough and uniform system of free public schools" (Colorado, Article IX § 2); or to "provide for an efficient system of common schools throughout the state" (Kentucky, § 183). The Arizona Enabling Act of June 20, 1910 tied federal land grants in the western territories to requirements that the lands or funds generated by them be used "for the support of common schools." The drafters of Arizona's Constitution "believed that an educated citizenry was extraordinarily important to the new state . . . [that] these were more than mere words . . . [and] that a free society could not exist without educated participants" (*Roosevelt Elementary School District* v. *Bishop*, 1994).

10. With industrialization, a focus on "instilling skills . . . useful in the workplace" also developed (McDonnell, 2000, p. 2); accordingly, the cases cited in the text, as well as many others, have included preparation for the competitive workplace as the second major purpose of public education.

11. Significantly, although the intermediate appeals court rejected the trial court finding that New York State's education finance system denies students the opportunity for a sound basic education, it upheld and endorsed its specific holding that students must be prepared to be *capable* voters and jurors, able to deal with complex issues like campaign finance reform, DNA evidence, and convoluted financial fraud (*CFE* v. *State*, 2002). At the same time, however, the intermediate appeals court inexplicably concluded that citizens could function at this high level with rudimentary (6th- to 8th-grade level) reading and math skills (*CFE* v. *State*, 2002).

12. The CFE litigation was initiated on behalf of students in the New York City public schools, but CFE's goal was later expanded to include appropriate remedies for all students throughout the state who were being denied the opportunity for a sound basic education. The Court of Appeals' ruling in *CFE* v. *State* (2003) technically applied only to New York City—because the evidence of education inadequacy presented at trial related only to the city—but the judges seemed to assume that in fact the mandated reforms would likely apply statewide, and CFE has explicitly called for statewide solutions.

13. Article XI § 1 requires the state legislature to "provide for the maintenance and support of a system of free common schools wherein all the children of

this state may be *educated*" (emphasis added). The Court of Appeals has held that the term *educated* means receive the opportunity for a "sound basic education" (*Levittown* v. *Nyquist*, 1982).

14. The intermediate appeals court's "8th grade is enough" ruling led to massive public outcry from educators, civic groups, and editorial boards throughout the state ("Blaming the Victim," 2002; "Court's Ruling Hurts Schools," 2002; "Shortchanging Schools," 2002). The ruling also became a major issue in the gubernatorial election, causing Governor George Pataki (2002), the prime defendant whose attorneys had argued for the 8th-grade standard in the courts, to publicly state: "I could not disagree more strongly with that logic and that decision."

15. When their immediate self-interests are not threatened, most Americans express strong support for egalitarian ideals. For example, in a nationwide poll commissioned by the Public Education Network and *Education Week* (2003) and conducted by Lake Snell Perry & Associates, Inc. in January 2003 (Sack, 2003), 67% of respondents said they would be willing to increase taxes if the increase were earmarked for public education, compared with 28% who were not willing; 64% expressed greater concern that education/healthcare would be cut than that their taxes might go up, compared with 31% who expressed greater concern about tax increases (Public Education Network and *Education Week*, 2003, pp. 7–8).

16. The typical format for the public engagement forums that have been held in dozens of urban, suburban, and rural settings over the past 7 years is a 3-hour evening event attended by 75–100 participants. The forums begin with an introductory background briefing that explains the significance of the CFE litigation but emphasizes that the public engagement forums have no preconceived outcomes and do not require any participants to support any party's position in the case. The bulk of the evening is then spent in small-group discussions, led by trained facilitators, followed by a final plenary session that explores areas of possible consensus.

17. CFE's lawsuit and public engagement activities have been important stimuli to the emergence and expansion of these organizations. AQE was formed in 1999 essentially to organize broad statewide support for funding reform in anticipation of a victory for plaintiffs in the CFE case; the Mid-State Consortium was established in 1991 as a small association of school superintendents in central New York, which expanded rapidly in response to publicity about the CFE suit and the growing prospect that the court actually might require funding reforms; REFIT's membership essentially consisted of the school districts that had brought the original *Levittown* litigation, which, after a second suit they had instituted in the 1990s had been dismissed, allied themselves with CFE.

REFERENCES

42 U.S.C.S./ § 1971 et seq. [Voting Rights Act].

Balkin, J. M. (2001). *What* Brown *v.* Board of Education *should have said*. New York: New York University Press.

Berry, J. M., Portney, K. E., & Thomson, K. (1993). *The rebirth of urban democracy*. Washington, DC: Brookings Institute.

Blaming the victim. (2002, June 26). *The New York Times*, p. A22.

Bismarck Public School District No. 1 v. State, 511 N.W.2d 247 (N.D. 1994).

Brigham v. State of Vermont, 692 A.2d 384, 393 (1997).

Brown v. Board of Education, 347 U.S. 483, 493 (1954).

Campaign for Fiscal Equity. (1997–2001). *Studies in judicial remedies and public engagement, 1&2*. New York: Author.

Campaign for Fiscal Equity, Inc. v. State of New York, 655 N.E.2d 661, 664–667 (N.Y. 1995).

Campaign for Fiscal Equity, Inc. v. State, 719 N.Y.S.2d 475, 487, 550 (2001).

Campaign for Fiscal Equity, Inc. v. State, 744 N.Y.S.2d 130, 137–139 (1st Dep't 2002).

Campaign for Fiscal Equity, Inc. v. State, 100 N.Y.2d 893 (N.Y. 2003).

Campbell School District v. State, 907 P.2d 1238, 1259 (Wyo. 1995).

Carnegie Forum on Education and the Economy, Task Force on Teaching as a Profession. (1986). *A nation prepared: Teachers for the twenty-first century*. Washington, DC: Carnegie.

Carter, R. L. (1979). Reexamining *Brown* twenty-five years later: Looking backward into the future. *Harvard Civil Rights–Civil Liberties Review, 14*(3), 615–624.

Changing school funding won't solve whole problem. (2001, January 11). *Binghamton Press and Sun-Bulletin*, p. 6.

Claremont School District v. State of New Hampshire, 635 A.2d 1375, 1381 (N.H. 1993).

Clune, W. H. (1994). The shift from equity to adequacy in school finance. *Education Policy, 8*(4), 376–394.

Coalition for Adequacy and Fairness in School Funding, Inc. v. Chiles, 680 So.2d 400, 407–408 (Fla. 1996).

Colo. Constitution/Article IX, § 2 [1876].

Constitutional Convention of 1894. (1906). Report submitted by the committee on education and funds pertaining thereto. In C. Z. Lincoln, *The constitutional history of New York from the beginning of the colonial period to the year 1905: Showing the origin, development, and judicial construction of the constitution* (Vol. 3, pp. 554–557). Rochester, NY: Lawyers Co-operative Publishing Company.

Council of the Great City Schools. (2001). *Beating the odds: A city by city analysis of student performance and achievement gaps on state assessments*. Washington, DC: Author.

Court's ruling hurts schools. (2002, June 28). *The Poughkeepsie Journal*, p. A10.

Cremin, L. (1980). *American education: The national experience 1783–1876*. New York: Harper & Row.

Days, D. E. (1997). Brown blues: Rethinking the integrative ideal. In N. Devins & D. M. Douglas (Eds.), *Redefining equality* (pp. 139–153). Oxford: Oxford University Press.

Delgado, R., & Stefanic, J. (1997). The social construction of *Brown v. Board of Education*: Law reform and the reconstructive paradox. In N. Devins & D. M. Douglas (Eds.), *Redefining equality* (pp. 154–171). Oxford: Oxford University Press.

DeRolph v. State of Ohio, 677 N.E.2d 733 (Ohio, 1997).

Edwards, N., & Richey, H. E. (1963). *The school in the American social order* (2nd ed.). Boston: Houghton Mifflin.

Fix the school-aid formula. (2003, July 14). *The Westchester Journal News*, p. 6b.

Fuhrman, S. H. (1993). *Design of coherent education policy: Improving the system*. San Francisco: Jossey-Bass.

Glenn, C. L., Jr. (1988). *The myth of the common school*. Amherst: University of Massachusetts Press.

Good enough? Hardly. (2002, June 27). *The Westchester Journal News*, p. 86.

Hansen, C. (1993, Summer). Are the courts giving up? Current issues in school desegregation. *Emory Law Journal, 42*, 863–875.

Hunter, M. (1999). All eyes forward: Public engagement and educational reform in Kentucky. *Journal of Law and Education, 28*(4), 485–516.

Jefferson, T. (1943). The University of Virginia. In S. Padover (Ed.), *The complete Jefferson* (pp. 1097–1115). New York: Tudor. (Original work published 1818)

Judge orders reform: Victory for school equity. (2001, January 11). *The Syracuse Post-Standard*, p. A8.

Justice for schools: New York's highest court says students are being shortchanged. (2003, June 27). *Times Union*, p. A14.

Kahlenberg, R. D. (2001, May 21). The fall and rise of school segregation. *The American Prospect, 12*(9), 41.

Katz, M. B. (2001). *The irony of early school reform: Educational innovation in mid-nineteenth century Massachusetts*. New York: Teachers College Press. (Original work published 1968)

Keyssar, A. (2000). *The right to vote: The contested history of democracy in the United States*. New York: Basic Books.

KY Constitution/ § 183 [1891].

Levittown v. *Nyquist*, 439 N.E.2d 359, 369 (N.Y. 1982).

Liebman, J. S., & Sabel, C. F. (2003). *A public laboratory Dewey barely imagined: The emerging model of school governance and legal reform*. Retrieved April 15, 2003 from http://www2.law.columbia.edu/sabel/papers/deweynextwavewebversion.doc.

Linn, R. L., & Dunbar, S. B. (1990). The nation's report card goes home: Good news and bad about trends in achievement. *Phi Delta Kappan, 72*(2), 127–133.

Lupia, A., & McCubbins, M. D. (1998). *The democratic dilemma: Can citizens learn what they really need to know?* Cambridge: Cambridge University Press.

Mann, H. (1855). *Lectures on education*. Boston: Ide & Dutton.

Mass. Constitution/part II, ch. V, § 2 [1780].

McCullough, D. (2001). *John Adams*. New York: Simon & Schuster.

McDonnell, L. M. (2000). Defining democratic purposes. In L. M. McDonnell, P. M. Timpane, & R. Benjamin (Eds.), *Rediscovering the democratic purposes of education* (pp. 1–18). Lawrence: University Press of Kansas.

Mills, J., & McLendon, T. (2000, April). Setting a new standard for public education: Revision 6 increases the duty of the state to make "adequate provision" for Florida schools. *Florida Law Review, 52*, 329–409.

Minorini, P. A., & Sugarman, S. D. (1999). Educational adequacy and the courts: The promise and problems of moving to a new paradigm. In H. F. Ladd, R. Chalk, & J. S. Hansen (Eds.), *Equity and adequacy in education finance: Issues and perspectives* (pp. 175–208). Washington, DC: National Academy Press.

Missouri v. *Jenkins*, 515 U.S. 70 (1995).

Myrdal, G. (1962). *An American dilemma: The Negro problem and American democracy.* New York: Harper & Row.

N.A.A.C.P. sets advanced goals. (1991). In G. N. Rosenberg, *The hollow hope: Can courts bring about social change?* (p. 43). Chicago: University of Chicago Press. (Reprinted from *The New York Times,* May 18, 1954, p. 16).

National Assessment of Educational Programs. (1990). *America's challenge: Accelerated academic achievement.* Washington, DC: Author.

National Commission on Excellence in Education. (1983). *A nation at risk: The imperative for educational reform.* Washington, DC: Author.

N.H. Constitution/pt. II, Article 83 [1784].

N.J. Constitution/Article VIII, § 4 [1947].

N.Y. Constitution/Article XI, § 1 [1894].

New York State Board of Regents. (1993). *All children can learn: A plan for reform of state aid to schools.* Albany: New York State Department of Education.

Nie, N. H., Junn, J., & Stehlik-Barry, K. (1996). *Education and democratic citizenship in America.* Chicago: University of Chicago Press.

No Child Left Behind Act (Pub. L. No. 107–110, 115 Stat. 1425, 2002).

Ohio Constitution/Article VI, § 2 [1851].

Okla. Constitution/Article XIII, § 1 [1907].

Oklahoma City Public Schools v. *Dowell*, 498 U.S. 237, 249–250 (1991).

Orfield, G. (1999). Conservative activists and the rush toward resegregation. In J. Heubert (Ed.), *Law and school reform: Six strategies for promoting educational equity* (pp. 39–87). New Haven, CT: Yale University Press.

Orfield, G. (2001). *Schools more separate: Consequences of a decade of resegregation.* Cambridge, MA: Harvard Civil Rights Project.

Pangle, L. S., & Pangle, T. L. (2000). What the American founders have to teach us about schooling for democratic citizenship. In L. M. McDonnell, P. M. Timpane, & R. Benjamin (Eds.), *Rediscovering the democratic purposes of education* (pp. 21–46). Lawrence: University Press of Kansas.

Pataki, G. (2002, September 12). [Remarks at Pace University].

Penn. Constitution/Article X, § 1 [1874] /Article III, § 14 [1968].

Pocock, J. G. A. (1975). *The Machiavellian moment.* Princeton, NJ: Princeton University Press.

"Protecting" school funding. (1993, June 28). *The Sacramento Bee,* p. B14.

Public Education Network and *Education Week*. (2003). *Demanding quality public education in tough economic times.* Washington, DC: Public Education Network.

Ravitch, D. (1995). *National standards in American education.* Washington, DC: Brookings Institute.

Rebell, M. A. (1986). Structural discrimination and the rights of the disabled. *Georgetown Law Journal, 74*(5), 1435–1489.

Rebell, M. A. (1998). Fiscal equity litigation and the democratic imperative. *Journal of Education Finance, 24*(1), 23–50.

Rebell, M. A. (2002). Education adequacy, democracy, and the courts. In T. Ready, C. Edley, & C. Snow (Eds.), *Achieving high educational standards for all* (pp. 218–267). Washington, DC: National Academy Press.

Rebell, M. A., & Block, A. R. (1985). *Equality and education: Federal civil rights enforcement in the New York City school system.* Princeton, NJ: Princeton University Press.

Rebell, M. A., & Hughes, R. L. (1996). Schools, communities, and the courts: A dialogic approach to education reform. *Yale Law and Policy Review, 14* (1), 99–168.

Rebell, M. A., Hughes, R. L., & Grumet, L. F. (1995). *Fiscal equity in education: A proposal for a dialogic remedy.* New York: Campaign for Fiscal Equity.

Reed, D. S. (2001). *On equal terms: The constitutional politics of educational opportunity.* Princeton, NJ: Princeton University Press.

R.I. Constitution/Article II, § 1 [1842].

Rippa, S. A. (1984). *Education in a free society: An American history* (5th ed.). New York: Longman.

Robinson v. *Cahill,* 303 A. 2d 273, 295 (N.J. 1973).

Rodriguez v. *San Antonio Independent School District,* 411 U.S. 1, 32, 35–37, 49 (1973).

Roosevelt Elementary School District v. *Bishop,* 877 P.2d 806, 812 (AZ. 1994).

Rose v. *Council for Better Education, Inc.,* 790 S.W.2d.186, 206 (KY. 1989).

Sack, J. L. (2003, February 26). Aid to schools gets support in voter poll. *Education Week,* p. 1, 10.

Salomone, R. C. (1986). *Equal education under law.* New York: St. Martin's Press.

A school funding remedy after all? (1998, January 11). *The Westchester Journal News,* p. A16.

Schools here may gain from N.Y. City ruling. (2003, June 27). *The Buffalo News,* pp. C1, C4.

Serrano v. *Priest,* 557 P.2d 929 (Cal. 1976).

Shaw, T. M. (1992, October). *Missouri* v. *Jenkins*: Are we really a desegregated society? *Fordham Law Review, 61,* 57–61.

Shortchanging schools. (2002, June 27). *The Albany Times Union,* p. A14.

Smith, R. M. (1993). Equal protection remedies: The errors of liberal ways and means. *Journal of Political Philosophy, 1*(3), 185–212.

Smith, R. M. (1997). *Civic ideals: Conflicting visions of citizenship in U.S. history.* New Haven, CT: Yale University Press.

Stone, C. N. (1998). *Changing urban education.* Lawrence: University Press of Kansas.

Sturm, S. P. (1993, July). The promise of participation. *Iowa Law Review, 78,* 981–1010.

Taylor v. *Louisiana,* 419 U.S. 522, 538 (1975).

Tenn. Constitution/Article XI, § 10 [1835]/Article XI, § 12 [1870, 1978].

Tennessee Small School Systems v. *McWherter,* 851 S.W.2d 139, 150 (TN. 1993).

Thiel v. *Southern Pacific County,* 328 U.S. 217, 222 (1946).

Tucker, M. S., & Codding, J. B. (1998). *Standards for our schools.* San Francisco: Jossey-Bass.

Twentieth Century Fund, Task Force on Federal Elementary and Secondary Education Policy. (1983). *Making the grade.* New York: Twentieth Century Fund.

Tyack, D. B. (1974). *The one best system: A history of American urban education.* Cambridge, MA: Harvard University Press.

U.S. Commission on Civil Rights. (1976). *Fulfilling the letter and the spirit of the law: Desegregation of the nation's public schools. A staff report of the United States Commission on Civil Rights.* Washington, DC: Author.

U.S. Commission on Civil Rights. (1977a). *School desegregation in Colorado Springs, Colorado. A staff report of the United States Commission on Civil Rights.* Washington, DC: Author.

U.S. Commission on Civil Rights. (1977b). *School desegregation in Greenville, Mississippi. A staff report of the United States Commission on Civil Rights.* Washington, DC: Author.

U.S. Commission on Civil Rights. (1977c). *School desegregation in Ossining, New York. A staff report of the United States Commission on Civil Rights.* Washington, DC: Author.

Vt. Constitution/ch. II, § 68 [1793].

Willis, G. S. (1978). *Inventing America: Jefferson's declaration of independence.* Garden City, NY: Doubleday.

Wood, G. S. (1969). *The creation of the American republic, 1776–1787.* Chapel Hill: University of North Carolina Press.

W.V. Constitution. Article XII, § 1.

Afterword

I am an advocate of quality public education for *all* children. The researchers in this volume provide the evidence for what so many advocates have known for a very long time: that the education reforms we have witnessed over the last two decades have resulted in neither an equitable nor excellent system of public education for America's poor and minority children.

I am grateful for the analysis the authors bring to the task of defining what transpires when excellence and equity are set up as opposing forces rather than as synergistic goals. Most notably, several of the authors use not only the lens of academic excellence to assess the effectiveness of the various improvement strategies of the 1980s and 1990s, but they also examine whether or not these education reform efforts result in increasing student achievement and strengthening public education systemically and as a public institution vital to the democratic goals of American society.

It is clear from the authors' arguments and research laid out herein, that equity is *the* necessary precondition for academic excellence, for systemic school improvement, and for the nation's democratic way of life. Were it not for the analyses set forth in this book, the American public would have no knowledge of the impact of the education reform policies of the 1980s and 1990s, most of which were exclusively focused on excellence and individual achievement. What will it take to move the authors' valuable analyses beyond academia and into the places where education policy is made—the statehouses, Congress, thousands of school districts and schoolhouses, and the minds of millions of Americans who are ultimately responsible for the quality of public education in America? How do we educate Americans to value the benefits of quality public education, and how do we inspire them to extend those benefits to every child in every community across the nation?

Our nation is at a crossroads. We can continue to tweak the public education system with "excellence only" reforms, all of which have limited merits and outcomes both for the children and for the system that serves them. Or we can educate the American public about the important issues in education and build the public's will to make the deep systemic changes that will result in both equity and excellence for *all* children in the public schools. The findings in this volume make it clear that the engagement and the mobilization of the American people to demand quality public education for *all* children is truly the next step—perhaps the only step—in reforming and preserving America's system of public education.

Although engaging Americans is both a necessary and a worthy task, it will not be easy to achieve. Public engagement and citizen mobilization are not benign activities. These are guided by a point of view influenced by the proponents' values. Various modes of public engagement are used with equal effectiveness by both ends of the political spectrum. Community activists, philanthropic entities, education reformers, the Christian Right, and neoconservatives all use the same engagement concepts and strategies, though their objectives vary dramatically. Therefore, the public engagement process and citizen mobilization effort that is needed now to address equity and excellence will need to have two goals: to ensure that *quality* public education is a civil right for every child, and to elevate public education to an unequivocal status as a fundamental institution of democracy.

Public engagement is a flexible concept covering a wide range of activities by which individuals can effect change. It involves individuals taking any action large or small to affect positive change. The activities of public engagement can be characterized in six categories: information dissemination; individual or group involvement and partnering; collaboration among organizations, institutions, and stakeholders; forming coalitions; constituency building; and citizen mobilization. These types of public engagement activities are the best strategies available for ensuring that everyone—voters, elected officials, educators, students, administrators, and parents and others—knows about the strategies for public school improvement. These various types of public engagement are capable of producing broad societal benefits, and numerous positive outcomes can occur when individuals take public action.

Citizen mobilization, a category of public engagement, is designed to delve deeper into the fabric of the nation's oldest social contract. This mobilization is activated when the constitutionally stated rights and benefits of democracy apply to some, but are not extended to all. The parties seek redress by using the already established and undisputed standards. When the threat is external, the mobilization is known as war. When the threat is internal, the mobilization is called a movement. There are several examples in American history of the impact of citizen mobilization and the building of a movement: the abolition of slavery, women's suffrage, and the voting rights acts of 1964 and 1965, whose 40th anniversary the nation celebrates this year.

Taken together, the authors' essays recommend bringing *equity* back as an equal partner with other education reform strategies to increase student achievement and advance systemic reform. The authors go so far to say that without the equal partnership of *equity*, increased student achievement is not possible for large numbers of children in the nation's public schools. And therefore, under the present policy conditions, too many of the nation's children are effectively denied access to the full benefits of American life.

Just as slavery threatened the existence of the Union in the 19th century, like the segregated public schools of the 20th century, so too does the inequity in the nation's public education systems in the 21st century threaten the survival of our democratic way of life. Citizen mobilization requires every citizen to question any policy or action as to how that policy can benefit all, and not just some, children in our schools. Citizen mobilization also requires that individuals acquire a certain level of knowledge and understanding of the results and consequences of every political and economic decision regarding our children's education.

Despite America's deeply held belief in the value of public education, parents and highly placed and influential politicians and policymakers have been the primary shapers of public education and of local public schools, while the general public's role has remained limited in time, scope, and breadth. This, then, is our challenge: to mobilize the public on behalf of public education, inform the public about the value and benefits of quality public education, and build a broad base of people who know what takes place in our public schools and know how to transform concern about public education into effective action. The time to bring the awesome force of citizen mobilization to advance the quality of public education for every child in America is now.

Wendy D. Puriefoy
President
Public Education Network
January 2005

About the Editors
and the Contributors

Janice Petrovich is Director of Education, Sexuality, and Religion in the Knowledge, Creativity, and Freedom Program at The Ford Foundation. She received her Doctoral degree from the University of Massachusetts in educational policy research, and her Masters and Bachelors Degree in chemistry from the University of Puerto Rico. Her publications include: "Hispanic Women Students in Higher Education: Meeting the Challenge of Diversity," with Sara E. Meléndez, in *Educating the Majority*, and "Enrollment in Higher Education: Where is the Decline?" *Educational Record*. She served at the request of President Bill Clinton on the President's Advisory Commission on Educational Excellence for Hispanic Americans and has also served on the boards of directors of various organizations, including the independent sector and Mount Holyoke College. Prior to her employment with The Ford Foundation, Dr. Petrovich was the National Executive Director of the ASPIRA Association, Director of Research Studies at the American Council on Education, and Director of the Research Institute of the Inter American University of Puerto Rico, where she founded the Center for Research and Documentation on Women.

Amy Stuart Wells is a Professor of Sociology and Education at Teachers College, Columbia University. Her research and writing have focused broadly on issues of race and education, and more specifically on educational policies, such as school desegregation, school choice, charter schools, and tracking, and how they shape and constrain opportunities for students of color. She is the principal investigator of a 5-year study of adults who attended racially mixed high schools and co-author of a report from that study, *How Desegregation Changed Us: The Effects of Racially Mixed Schools on Students and Society*. The forthcoming book from this study, *In Search of Brown*, will be published in 2005. Wells is the author and editor of numerous other books and articles, including editor of *Where Charter School Policy*

Fails: The Problems of Accountability and Equity (Teachers College Press, 2002); and co-author, with Robert L. Crain, of *Stepping over the Color Line: African American Students in White Suburban Schools* (1997).

Mark Berends is an Associate Professor of Public Policy and Education at Vanderbilt University. Prior to coming to Vanderbilt, Professor Berends was a senior social scientist at RAND for 10 years, where he led studies on New American Schools, the national evaluation of Title I, and the Comprehensive School Reform Demonstration program for the U.S. Department of Education. At Vanderbilt, Dr. Berends is conducting a study of the structure and effects of tracking in the United States—examining several cohorts of high school students between the early 1970s and 1990s. He continues to pursue this research with his collaborator, Sam Lucas of Berkeley. Over this same period, they are examining how family and school changes have contributed to mathematics achievement differences among various racial-ethnic groups. He is also involved in a new study using random assignment to examine the scaling-up of peer-assisted learning strategies for young readers in different elementary schools across the nation.

Susan Bodilly is a senior social scientist and Associate Director of RAND Education. Working at RAND for more than 20 years, her primary research interests and expertise lie in comprehensive school reform at the K–12 level, resource allocation and its impact on reforms, formative evaluation, and implementation analysis. For the past several years she played a leading role in RAND's evaluation of the New American Schools Initiative. In the past, she evaluated other K–12 improvement initiatives such as the General Electric College Bound program, attempts by high schools to integrate academic and vocational education, and attempts by the federal government to return Section Six schools on military bases to local control. She is currently: leading an effort to assess the Ford Foundation's Collaborating for Educational Reform Initiative; co-editing a book on scale-up issues in education; and analyzing the impact of Perkins legislation on vocational programs for the National Assessment of Vocational Education. At RAND, she has been the Group Manager for Health, Education and Welfare, and is responsible for the recruiting, hiring, and professional development of all Washington-based employees within this specialization.

Martin Carnoy is Professor of Education and Economics at Stanford University. He received his Ph.D. from the University of Chicago's Department of Economics. Before coming to Stanford in 1969, he was a Research Associate at the Brookings Institution. In 1984, he was the Democratic candidate for Congress in Silicon Valley. He has written on issues of economic policy, theories of political economy, the economics of education, and educational policy. He has also written extensively on educational financing issues, including the effect of vouchers on educational outcomes. Among his books are *The State and Political Theory* (1984), *Education and Work in the Democratic State* [with Henry Levin] (1985), *Faded Dreams: The Economics and Politics of Race in America* (1994), *Sustaining the New Economy: Work, Family and Community in the Information Age* (2000), and *All Else Equal: Are Private and Public Schools Different?* [with Luis Benveniste and Richard Rothstein] (2002). He is currently continuing his work on the privatization of education and on education accountability reforms in the United States.

Marguerite Clarke is an Advanced Studies Fellow at Brown University in Providence, Rhode Island. Formerly, she was an Assistant Research Professor in the Lynch School of Education, Boston College, and Associate Director of the National Board on Educational Testing and Public Policy. The recipient of a Fulbright fellowship, a Spencer/Hewlett postdoctoral fellowship, and other awards, Dr. Clarke is author or co-author of numerous articles, chapters, and technical reports on high-stakes testing. She has a Ph.D. in educational research, measurement, and evaluation, as well as degrees in bilingual/multicultural and elementary education.

Amanda Datnow is an Associate Professor of Education at the USC Rossier School of Education. She was formerly a faculty member at the Ontario Institute for Studies in Education at the University of Toronto and at Johns Hopkins University. Her research focuses on the politics and policies of school reform, particularly with regard to the professional lives of educators and issues of equity. Sociological perspectives inform her research on these topics, and her research methods are mostly qualitative. Recent books include *Extending Educational Reform: From One School to Many* [co-authored with Lea Hubbard and Hugh Mehan] (2002), *Gender in Policy and Practice: Perspectives on Single Sex and Coeducational Schooling* [co-authored with Lea Hubbard] (2002), and *Leadership Lessons for Comprehensive School Reform* [co-edited with Joseph Murphy] (2002).

Maya Federman is an Assistant Professor of Economics at Pitzer College and a Tomás Rivera Policy Institute Scholar. Her research is in the areas of education and immigration. Dr. Federman served as a staff economist with a focus on labor and education at the Council of Economic Advisors in the Office of the President.

Marilyn Gittell, the Director of the Howard Samuels State Management and Policy Center, also serves as a professor of Political Science at the

Graduate School and University Center of the City University of New York. She has written extensively about the politics of higher education, community development and community organizations, and state politics. Her publications include *Old and New Frontiers in Education Reform: Confronting Exclusion in the Democratic Tradition* (forthcoming), a study of efforts in five countries to extend access to education to marginalized populations; *Community Participation, Social Capital Building and the Urban Empowerment Zones* (forthcoming); *Social Capital and Social Citizenship* [edited with Sophie-Body Gendrot] (2003), a collection of articles from American, European, and African scholars about voluntary associations and the uses of social capital; *Politics of Community Development: CDCs and Social Capital* (1999); *Strategies for School Equity: Creating Productive Schools in a Just Society* (1998); and a chapter in *Regionalism in a Global Society* (2004) entitled "Regionalism and Federalism in the American System."

Lea Hubbard is an Associate Professor at the University of San Diego. Her work focuses on educational inequities as they exist across ethnicity, class, and gender. She has co-authored several books and written articles on the academic achievement of minority students and gender and education. Her latest book, *Extending Educational Reform: From One School to Many* [co-authored with Amanda Datnow and Hugh Mehan], explores what happens when school reform "goes to scale." Dr. Hubbard is currently writing a book on her study of San Diego school reform. She has taught courses on policy-making, multicultural foundations of education, gender and education, qualitative research methods, and sociology of education.

Jennifer Jellison Holme is a research associate on the UCLA–Teachers College, Columbia University "Understanding Race and Education Study." She received her Ed.M. at the Harvard Graduate School of Education and her Ph.D. in educational policy studies at UCLA, where she was the recipient of a Spencer Research Training Grant Fellowship and the Chancellor's Dissertation Year Fellowship. She has worked previously as a researcher on the UCLA Charter School Study and on the Harvard Project on School Desegregation. Her areas of expertise include school desegregation and the sociology of school choice.

Heather Beth Johnson is Assistant Professor of Sociology at Lehigh University. Her research focuses on understanding the perpetuation of race and class inequality in the contemporary United States. Her scholarship and teaching interests include the sociology of wealth, the sociology of children and childhood, and dominant ideology. Recent publications include "From the Chicago School to the New Sociology of Children: The Sociology of

Children and Childhood in the United States, 1920–1999," in *Children at the Millenium* (2001) and "Good Neighborhoods, Good Schools: 'Good' Choices and Race in the Minds of Whites," in *White Out: The Continuing Significance of Racism* (2003).

Sheila Nataraj Kirby is a senior economist and Associate Director of Quality Assurance for RAND Education. Her primary research interests are in the areas of economics of education and military manpower. She has conducted analyses of teacher supply and demand, nontraditional recruits to mathematics and science teaching, school choice, comprehensive school reform, Title I schools, and minority teachers. She is currently heading a large evaluation of Teachers for a New Era, an ambitious new reform initiative aimed at improving teacher education in several selected sites around the nation. She is also part of the management team overseeing the reform of K–12 education in a small country in the Middle East. She was an adjunct professor of economics and public policy at The George Washington University, where she has taught both economics and public policy courses for over 20 years.

Alejandra Lopez is a researcher in the Center for Education Policy at SRI International. She holds a B.A. in Psychology from Stanford University, and an M.A. and Ph.D. in Social Research Methodology from the UCLA Graduate School of Education. Her areas of expertise include: research design; racial, ethnic, cultural, and socioeconomic diversity in schools; educational access and equity; and methods for collecting and analyzing race/ethnicity data, particularly regarding mixed-heritage individuals.

George Madaus is currently the Boisi Professor of Education and Public Policy at Boston College. He was named as the recipient of the 2003 E.F. Lindquist award, presented by AERA and ACT to a distinguished research scientist for "significant contributions to the field of educational measurement." He is the former director of BC's Center for the Study of Testing, Evaluation and Educational Policy; and the former Executive Director of the National Commission on Testing and Public Policy. He has been the Vice President of AERA Division D, and a past President of NCME. He served on the 1974 and the 1985 Joint AERA, APA, and NCME Test Standards Committee, and on the 1981 Joint Committee on Standards for Educational Evaluation. He was Co-Chair of the APA, AERA, and NCME Joint Committee on Testing Practices, and served on the subcommittee that drafted the *Code of Fair Testing Practices in Education*. He has been a visiting Professor at the Harvard Graduate School of Education and at St. Patrick's College, Dublin, and is a member of the National Academy of Education.

In addition, he has been a Fellow at the Center for Advanced Studies in the Behavioral Sciences.

Patrick J. McEwan is an Assistant Professor in the Department of Economics at Wellesley College. He previously taught in the Departments of Educational Policy Studies and Economics at the University of Illinois at Urbana-Champaign. Professor McEwan's research focuses on the economics of education, applied econometrics, and education policy in Latin America. His research has been published in a wide range of economics and education journals, in addition to three books. He has consulted widely on education policy and evaluation at the Inter-American Development Bank, the RAND Corporation, UNESCO, the World Bank, and the ministries of education of several countries.

Roslyn Arlin Mickelson is Professor of Sociology and Adjunct Professor of Public Policy and Women's Studies at the University of North Carolina at Charlotte. She has published widely on ethnic minority student achievement issues, especially the educational equity implications of desegregation, resegregation, and the corporate agenda for school reform. Her book, *Children on the Streets of the Americas: Globalization, Homelessness, and Education in the United States, Brazil, and Cuba* was published in 2000. Mickelson received the 2004 Harshini de Silva Graduate Student Mentoring Award from UNC Charlotte.

Jeannie Oakes is Presidential Professor in Educational Equity and Director of UCLA's Institute for Democracy, Education & Access (IDEA) and UC's All Campus Consortium on Research for Diversity (ACCORD). Her research examines schooling inequalities and follows the progress of educators and activists seeking socially just schools. She is the author of 17 scholarly books and monographs and more than 100 published research reports, chapters, and articles. Oakes' 2001 book, *Becoming Good American Schools: The Struggle for Virtue in Education Reform*, won AERA's Outstanding Book Award. Oakes' most recent research investigates the issues raised in *Williams* v. *California*, a civil rights case arguing that California's education system is depriving more than a million California students of their right to educational equality.

Harry P. Pachón is president of the Tomás Rivera Policy Institute and Professor of Public Policy at the School of Policy, Planning, and Development at the University of Southern California. Dr. Pachón was executive director of the National Association of Latino Elected and Appointed Officials (NALEO) Educational Fund for 10 years, and also served as a policy analyst for the U.S. Department of Health, Education, and Welfare and as an associate staff member of the Appropriations Committee of the U.S. House of Representatives. He has authored over 20 articles in professional journals and co-authored three books.

Michael A. Rebell, Executive Director and Counsel, Campaign For Fiscal Equity, is an experienced litigator, administrator, researcher, and scholar in the field of education law. He is also co-counsel for plaintiffs in *Campaign for Fiscal Equity ("CFE")* v. *State of New York* (1995) and *Campaign for Fiscal Equity* v. *State of New York* (2003). In these cases, the Court of Appeals, New York State's highest court, has declared that all children are entitled under Article XI of the state Constitution to the "opportunity for a sound basic education." The Court upheld Plaintiffs' challenge to the constitutionality of the state's current system for financing public education and gave the state until July 30, 2004 to reform the system. Mr. Rebell has litigated numerous major class action lawsuits, including *Jose P.* v. *Mills*, which involved a plaintiff class of 160,000 students with disabilities. He has also served as a court-appointed special master in the Boston special education case, *Allen* v. *Parks*.

Janelle T. Scott is an Assistant Professor in The Steinhardt School of Education, New York University, where she teaches courses in education policy and politics. Prior to her appointment at New York University, Scott was an Assistant Director at the National Center for the Study of Privatization in Education at Teachers College, Columbia University. A former urban elementary school teacher, Scott earned a Ph.D. in Education Policy from UCLA's Graduate School of Education and Information Studies. Scott studies the politics of urban education, with an emphasis on issues of race, class, and equity. Research topics include charter schools, educational privatization, and the impact of school choice reforms on high poverty communities of color. Scott's recent research considers equity and empowerment within charter school communities partnered or contracted with educational management organizations as well as the role of churches and "faith-based" institutions in charter schools.

Thomas M. Shapiro is the Pokross Professor of Law and Social Policy at The Heller School for Social Policy and Management, Brandeis University. Professor Shapiro's primary interest is in racial inequality and public policy. He is the author of *The Hidden Cost of Being African American: How Wealth Perpetuates Inequality* (2004). With Dr. Melvin Oliver, he wrote the award-winning *Black Wealth/White Wealth*, which received the 1997 Distinguished Scholarly Publication Award from the American Sociological Association and the 1995 C. Wright Mills Award from the Society for the Study of Social Problems. His edited book, *Great Divides: Readings in Social Inequality in the United States* (3rd edition) was published in 2004.

Arnold R. Shore is Senior Advisor in the Office for Sponsored Programs at Boston College. He has served as Executive Director of the National Board on Educational Testing and Public Policy, and as Director of the Center for the Study of Testing, Evaluation, and Educational Policy. Dr. Shore's research interest is the application of social science to social policy. He is co-author (with Marguerite Clarke) of several National Board publications on the relationship of educational testing programs to teaching and learning.

Kevin G. Welner is an assistant professor at the University of Colorado, Boulder, School of Education, specializing in educational policy, law, and program evaluation. He is co-director of the CU-Boulder "Education in the Public Interest Center" (EPIC). His research examines the intersection between education rights litigation and educational opportunity scholarship. He has studied the change process associated with equity-minded reform efforts, such as detracking efforts driven by court mandates aimed at benefiting primarily Latinos, African Americans, and the poor. He authored *Legal Rights, Local Wrongs: When Community Control Collides with Educational Equity* (2001) and *Navigating the Politics of Detracking* [with Jeannie Oakes] (2000), and "Locking up the marketplace of ideas and locking out school reform: Courts' imprudent treatment of controversial teaching in America's public schools" (2003) in the *UCLA Law Review*, and "Rethinking expert testimony in education rights litigation" [with Haggai Kupermintz] (2004) in *Educational Evaluation and Policy Analysis*.

Index